T0246546

AT THE GATES OF
ROME

OSPREY
PUBLISHING

DEDICATION
For everyone who enjoyed *The Last Viking*

AT THE GATES OF
ROME

THE BATTLE FOR A DYING EMPIRE

DON HOLLWAY

OSPREY PUBLISHING
Bloomsbury Publishing Plc
Kemp House, Chawley Park, Cumnor Hill, Oxford OX2 9PH, UK
29 Earlsfort Terrace, Dublin 2, Ireland
1385 Broadway, 5th Floor, New York, NY 10018, USA
E-mail: info@ospreypublishing.com

www.ospreypublishing.com

OSPREY is a trademark of Osprey Publishing Ltd

First published in Great Britain in 2022

© Don Hollway, 2022

Don Hollway has asserted his right under the Copyright, Designs and Patents Act,
1988, to be identified as Author of this work.

For legal purposes the Acknowledgments on p. 368 constitute an extension of this
copyright page.

Artwork on page 2 of the plate section previously published in CAM 84: *Adrianople AD 378*.

This paperback edition was first published in Great Britain in 2024 by Osprey Publishing.

All rights reserved. No part of this publication may be reproduced or transmitted in any
form or by any means, electronic or mechanical, including photocopying, recording, or
any information storage or retrieval system, without prior permission in writing from
the publishers.

A catalog record for this book is available from the British Library.

ISBN: HB 978 1 4728 4998 4; PB 978 1 4728 4997 7; eBook 978 1 4728 4996 0;
ePDF 978 1 4728 5001 0; XML 978 1 4728 4999 1

24 25 26 27 28 10 9 8 7 6 5 4 3 2 1

Plate section image credits are given in full in the List of Illustrations (pp. 13–14).
Map by www.bounford.com
Index by Zoe Ross

Typeset by Deanta Global Publishing Services, Chennai, India
Printed and bound in Great Britain by CPI (Group) UK Ltd, Croydon CR0 4YY

Osprey Publishing supports the Woodland Trust, the UK's leading woodland
conservation charity.

MIX
Paper | Supporting
responsible forestry
FSC® C171272

To find out more about our authors and books visit www.ospreypublishing.com.
Here you will find extracts, author interviews, details of forthcoming events
and the option to sign up for our newsletter.

CONTENTS

DRAMATIS PERSONAE

Alaric I	*King of the Goths*
Ambrose of Milan (St. Ambrose)	*Roman politician and bishop*
Andragathius	*Gothic-born Roman general under Magnus Maximus*
Anthemius, Flavius	*Eastern Roman praetorian prefect, opponent of Stilicho*
Arbogastes, Flavius	*Roman general of Frankish birth*
Arcadius, Flavius	*Eastern Roman emperor, eldest son of Theodosius*
Athanaric	*Gothic chieftain*
Athaulf	*Goth, brother-in-law of Alaric*
Attalus, Priscus	*Western Roman senator, usurper, puppet emperor of the Goths*
Augustine of Hippo	*Theologian, philosopher, bishop, saint*
Bacurius Hiberus	*Georgian prince, Roman general*
Bathanarius	*Brother-in-law of Stilicho*
Bauto, Flavius	*Roman general of Frankish birth, father of Empress Eudoxia*
Brennus	*Gallic chieftain, 4th century BC*
Butheric	*Gothic chieftain in Eastern Roman service*
Camillus, Marcus Furius	*Early Roman soldier and dictator*
Chrysostom, John	*Archbishop of Constantinople*
Claudian (Claudius Claudianus)	*Western Roman court poet, propagandist for Stilicho*
Constans II	*Western Roman junior emperor, son of Constantine III*

Constantine III (Flavius Claudius Constantinus)	*Western Roman commander, usurper and co-emperor*
Constantius, Flavius	*Western Roman general, later Constantius III*
Didymus	*Spanish cousin of Arcadius and Honorius*
Edobichus	*Frank, general under Constantine III*
Eucherius	*Son of Stilicho and Serena*
Eudoxia, Aelia	*Eastern empress, daughter of Bauto, wife of Arcadius*
Eugenius	*Western Roman usurper and emperor*
Eutropius	*Eastern Roman consul, opponent of Stilicho*
Flaccilla, Aelia Flavia	*Empress, first wife of Theodosius*
Flavianus, Virius Nicomachus	*Western Roman prefect*
Fravitta	*Gothic chieftain, Eastern Roman general*
Fritigern	*Gothic chieftain*
Gainas	*Goth, Eastern Roman general*
Galla	*Daughter of Valentinian I, second wife of Theodosius I*
Galla Placidia	*Daughter of Theodosius I, adopted daughter of Stilicho, queen of the Goths, wife of Constantius III, mother of Valentinian III*
Gerontius	*Briton, general under Constantine III*
Gildo	*Berber commander of Roman North Africa*
Goar	*King of the Alans*
Godegisil	*King of the Vandals*
Gratian (Flavius Gratianus)	*Western Roman emperor*
Heraclianus	*Western Roman officer, governor of Africa, usurper*
Honorius, Flavius	*Western Roman emperor, younger son of Theodosius*
Innocent I	*Pope of Rome*
Ioannes	*Eastern Roman court official, lover of Eudoxia, possible father of Theodosius II*
Jovinus	*Gallo-Roman senator, emperor of Roman Gaul*

Jovius	*Western Roman court official*
Julius	*Eastern Roman commander after the Battle of Adrianople*
Justina	*Wife of Valentinian I, mother of Valentinian II and Galla*
Justinianus	*Briton, general under Constantine III*
Lagodius	*Spanish cousin of Arcadius and Honorius*
Marcomer	*Frankish chieftain*
Maria	*Western empress, daughter of Stilicho, wife of Honorius*
Mascezel	*Berber general, brother of Gildo, loyal to Rome*
Maximus of Hispania	*Usurper, puppet emperor of Gerontius*
Maximus, Magnus	*Roman usurper and Western emperor*
Nebiogastes	*Frank, general under Constantine III*
Olympius	*Court secretary and master of offices under Honorius, Western Empire*
Promotus, Flavius	*Eastern Roman consul and general*
Radagaisus	*King of the Goths in opposition to Alaric*
Respendial	*King of the Alans*
Richomeres, Flavius	*Roman general of Frankish birth*
Rufinus, Flavius	*Gaulish, Eastern Roman court official, opponent of Stilicho*
Rufinus, Tyrannius	*Monk, historian, and theologian*
Sarus	*Goth of the Amali clan, foe of Alaric, general under Stilicho*
Saulus	*Alan, Eastern Roman general*
Serena	*Niece and adopted daughter of Theodosius, wife of Stilicho*
Sigeric	*Goth, brother of Sarus, foe of Alaric*
Stilicho, Flavius	*Supreme military commander of Rome*
Sunno	*Frankish chieftain*
Symmachus, Quintus Aurelius	*Roman senator, pagan, supporter of Stilicho*
Theodoret	*5th-century Byzantine theologian and bishop*

9

Theodosiolus	*Spanish cousin of Arcadius and Honorius*
Theodosius I (Flavius Theodosius)	*Roman emperor*
Theodosius II	*Eastern Roman emperor, son of Arcadius and Aelia Eudoxia*
Thermantia, Aemilia Materna	*Western empress, daughter of Stilicho, wife of Honorius*
Timasius, Flavius	*Eastern Roman consul and general*
Tribigild	*Gothic general under Gainas*
Uldin	*Hunnish chieftain*
Valens, Flavius Julius	*Eastern Roman emperor*
Valentinian II (Flavius Valentinianus)	*Western Roman emperor*
Verenianus	*Spanish cousin of Arcadius and Honorius*
Victor, Flavius	*Son of Magnus Maximus, Western Roman Augustus*

CHRONOLOGY

Late 389 (?)	*Maria, daughter of Stilicho and Serena, born*
Late 390 (?)	*Thermantia, daughter of Stilicho and Serena, born*
391	*Assassination of Promotus*
	Stilicho defeats Alaric in Rhodope mountains
	Alaric named military tribune in Roman service
392	*Valentinian II assassinated*
394	*Claudian arrives in Rome*
	Battle of the Frigidus
395	*Theodosius dies*
	Arcadius weds Aelia Eudoxia
	Alaric dismissed from Roman service
	First Hunnic invasion of Eastern Empire
	Rufinus assassinated
398	*Gildonic War, Stilicho's Pictish War*
	Honorius marries Maria
399	*Eutropius named consul, later executed*
	Rise and fall of Gainas
401	*Barbarian uprising in Gaul*
402	*Alaric invades Italy. Battles of Pollentia and Verona*
404	*Empress Aelia Eudoxia dies*
	Claudian dies
405	*Fravitta executed*
405–406	*Radagaisus invades Italy. Battle of Faesulae*
407	*Vandals and Alans invade Gaul*
	Constantine III invades Gaul
	Empress Maria dies
408	*Emperor Arcadius dies. Theodosius II becomes Eastern emperor*
408 (Aug. 22)	*Stilicho executed*
409	*First siege of Rome*
409–410	*Second siege of Rome*
410	*Third siege, fall of Rome*
410	*Death of Alaric*

LIST OF ILLUSTRATIONS

On his numerous trips north over the Alps to put down barbarian
rebellions, Stilicho and his men almost certainly crossed this
Roman-era bridge in the 7,580-foot-high Septimer Pass,
Switzerland. (LOETSCHER CHLAUS / Alamy Stock Photo)

An 1894 depiction of Alaric's welcome in Athens, AD 395, by Ludwig
Thiersch. Victorian-era romanticists imagined the Gothic king
enjoying his new power like a Roman emperor. (pictore/Getty
Images)

The Rejection of Empress Eudoxia by John Chrysostom by Johann
Wolfgang Baumgartner, *c.* 1750. This event would be the spark
that set off the final split between the Roman empires. (Adam Ján
Figeľ / Alamy Stock Photo)

A high medieval depiction of the battle of Faesulae, AD 406, between
Stilicho and the Goth king Radagaisus. Giorio Vasari (1511–74).
(Photo by Fine Art Images/Heritage Images/Getty Images)

Sarcophagus of Stilicho. The encircled couple at the top-center are
thought to represent Stilicho and Serena. It now serves as the base
for the pulpit of the church of Sant'Ambrogio in Milan, Italy.
(Photo by: Leemage/Universal Images Group via Getty Images)

The Salarian Gate through which the Goths entered Rome was
demolished in 1921, but was built much like this San Paolo Gate,
with twin guard towers and a central arched gateway. (Heinz
Tschanz-Hofmann / Alamy Stock Photo)

"I am the Dark Barbarian / That towers over all" (Robert E. Howard).
Alaric's Entrance into Rome, 19th century, artist unknown.
(Bettmann/Getty Images)

It had been 800 years since barbarian conquerors last invaded Rome's
streets. Alaric's Goths made up for lost time. *The Invasion of the
Barbarians* by Ulpiano Checa, 1887. (HeritagePics / Alamy Stock
Photo)

Just as Nero supposedly played music while Rome burned in AD
64, Emperor Honorius was more concerned with his pet birds
than the city's fall in 410, as depicted in this cropped view of
The Favourites of the Emperor Honorius, by John William
Waterhouse, *c.* 1883. (Photo by Fine Art Images/Heritage Images/
Getty Images)

The monument to Stilicho, but with lines referring to him by name
chiseled off the marble, still stands in the Forum of Rome. (Photo:
Gabriel Dobersch)

AUTHOR'S NOTE

It has always been my preference when writing to enlist as many primary sources as I can and to quote them as much as possible. My intention is to let the people who were there tell the story, and step in only where necessary to summarize, update the language, correct them according to newer information, and keep everyone moving in the same direction. The resulting profusion of quotes always requires a book-consuming tonnage of citations, not to mention dozens of pages of endnotes and references. I always supply these in my first draft to my patient editors. However, it is my feeling that all those attributions are not necessary in a work of popular history meant for a non-academic audience, but further that the litter of citations actually distracts from the reader experience. Accordingly, though I will be careful to name speakers throughout, I am not citing every quote by specific source. (The exception is Edward Gibbon, who has been reprinted so many times I felt I should note from which edition and volume I pulled his quotes, those being the earliest ones I could find.) For those readers wishing to learn more about the sources, a full list and bibliography is provided at the back of the book.

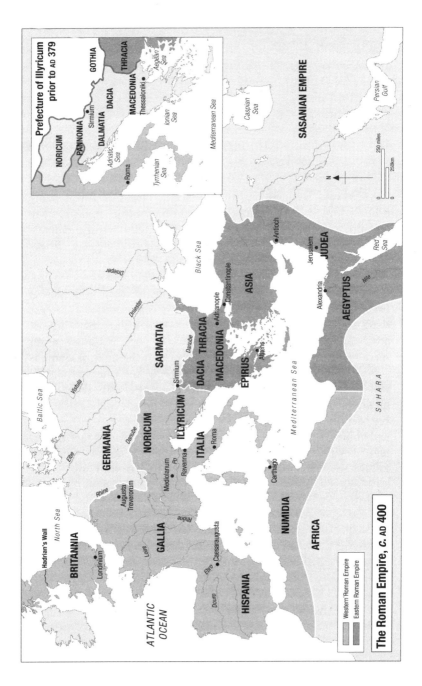

Prefecture of Illyricum prior to AD 379

NORICUM
PANNONIA
DALMATIA
DACIA
MACEDONIA
GOTHIA
THRACIA

Sirmium
Thessaloniki
Roma

Adriatic Sea
Ionian Sea
Aegean Sea
Tyrrhenian Sea
Mediterranean Sea
Caspian Sea

BRITANNIA
Hadrian's Wall
Londinium

GERMANIA
GALLIA
Augusta Treverorum
Caesaraugusta
HISPANIA

NORICUM
ILLYRICUM
ITALIA
Mediolanum
Ravenna
Roma

SARMATIA
DACIA
THRACIA
MACEDONIA
EPIRUS
Sirmium
Adrianople
Constantinople
Athens

ASIA
Antioch
Jerusalem
JUDEA
Alexandria
AEGYPTUS

NUMIDIA
Carthago
AFRICA

SASANIAN EMPIRE

ATLANTIC OCEAN
North Sea
Baltic Sea
Black Sea
Mediterranean Sea
Red Sea
Persian Gulf

SAHARA

Vistula
Elbe
Rhine
Loire
Douro
Ebro
Po
Danube
Dnieper
Dniester
Nile

Western Roman Empire
Eastern Roman Empire

The Roman Empire, c. AD 400

N

0   250 miles
0   250km

INTRODUCTION

MARCH, 1781

Over 1,300 years after the fall of the Western Roman Empire, and almost three centuries after that of the Eastern, Rome's former dominions had yet to improve on its imperial system of governance. Most of Europe was ruled by a handful of absolute monarchs, all shoving and elbowing each other for territory, power, and prestige. They may have fancied themselves as enlightened despots, looking out for the best interests of their subjects, but they were despots all the same.

In Scandinavia, Christian VII of Denmark-Norway, only half as insane and lecherous as the worst Roman emperors, ruled a North Atlantic empire stretching across the Faroe Islands and Iceland to Greenland, when he wasn't frequenting brothels or servicing his mistresses. In Vienna, Emperor Joseph II's efforts to preserve the Holy Roman Empire, which encompassed little of ancient Rome and much of modern Germany, came at the expense of the Germans, who had contributed greatly to the Roman Empire's downfall. Joseph's nemesis, Prussian King Frederick II, the Great, was laying the groundwork for the Germans to dominate the Roman Empire once again, employing his military genius, his father's brutal military discipline, and a long line of male favorites. In St. Petersburg, Empress Catherine the Great sought to expand Russia at the expense of the Poles and the Turks, while her own parade of lovers gave rise to rumors of extreme debauchery. King Louis XVI's France was going bankrupt, financing and fomenting military revolution abroad. And Charles III of Spain, whose empire still controlled half the New World from Alaska to the tip of South America, was backing that same revolution, intent on retrieving his recent losses to Great Britain, including Florida and Gibraltar.

The object of all that revolution, Britain's George III – also subject to bouts of insanity – was the least absolute ruler of them all. "I wish nothing but good," he insisted, "therefore, everyone who does not agree with me is a traitor and a scoundrel." Only his parliament and his subjects' treatment of his predecessors (variously overthrown, exiled, and beheaded) held his tyrannical inclinations in check.

London was abuzz that spring. Britain had set itself again at war, not only with its thirteen American colonies but with France, Spain, the Dutch Republic, and their colonies too – a veritable world conflict, in which Britain had no allies. News from across the Atlantic, always weeks out of date, was not good. The French had landed troops and were fighting alongside the rebels. The previous November a naval expedition against Spanish Nicaragua under dashing young Captain Horatio Nelson had withdrawn with 2,500 casualties to yellow fever and nothing to show for it, the costliest British loss of the war. In January the rebels had defeated a British army at Cowpens in South Carolina. And that very month, as yet unknown in the mother country, the rebel commander George Washington had set his French protégé Gilbert du Motier, the Marquis de Lafayette, in motion toward cornering British general Charles Cornwallis on the Yorktown peninsula, the campaign that would ultimately end the war.

Yet in their pubs and marketplaces the British middle class were largely ambivalent, even sympathetic toward the colonists, who sought only the same freedoms their domestic cousins already enjoyed. The loss of revenue and business partners in the Americas posed a greater threat to the British than some insult to King George's pride. Could their empire, itself only some 200 years old, survive the loss of two and a half million of its subjects, and all their trade with them?

At 7 Bentinck Street, in the Marylebone section of London, a 43-year-old Member of Parliament (M.P.) and part-time historian named Edward Gibbon was going some way toward answering that question. On the first of that very month, he had published the second and third volumes of *The History of the Decline and Fall of the Roman Empire*.

It was far from complete (the sixth and last volume would not come out until 1788), but in Volume III he had covered the fall of Rome itself in AD 410. Gibbon's British readers – and every British and American reader since – naturally perused his accounts of that earlier empire for any indicators of the fate of their own. Even Americans of the day appreciated the similarities. "Dr. [Benjamin] Franklin," Gibbon's fellow M.P. Horace Walpole wrote that April, possibly in jest, "…said he would furnish Mr. Gibbon with materials for writing *The History of the Decline of the British Empire*."

The idea for his masterpiece had come to Gibbon sixteen and a half years earlier, as a young man coming off a flirtation with religion, a broken romance, an uneventful stint in the military, and an escape from an overbearing father. As did many young upper-class Englishmen of the day, he had departed on a Grand Tour of the Continent, to become acquainted with foreign customs, art and culture, and along the way find meaning and perhaps himself.

It was in Rome, an obligatory stop on such a tour, that Gibbon found his answer. In the 18th century the city was becoming a mecca of art and culture to rival that of Florence and Venice a few centuries earlier, perhaps unseen since the days of the Empire itself. This renaissance had fired the excitement of Enlightenment artists and thinkers, in awe of a civilization which, despite the passage of thirteen centuries, in many ways still overshadowed their own. Steam power, machine tools, and mechanized factories were not yet widely adopted. Despite gunpowder, the printing press, and Christianity, Western man did not live a life much removed from that of his Roman forebears. In Gibbon's day, men still rode horses and carts and killed one another with edged and pointed steel. What could the past offer that still bore a lesson for the present? Of the once-glorious Forum of Rome – the Curia Julia where the Senate met for over 650 years, the Temple of Saturn, the Arch of Septimius Severus, the Temples of Vesta and of Castor and Pollux and more – nothing remained but crumbling ruins, overgrown with weeds.

To Gibbon, however, that was the point. "I can neither forget nor express the strong emotions which agitated my mind as I first approached and entered the eternal City," he wrote. "After a sleepless night, I trod with a lofty step the ruins of the Forum; each memorable spot where Romulus stood, or Tully spoke, or Caesar fell, was at once present to my eye; and several days of intoxication were lost or enjoyed before I could descend to a cool and minute investigation."[1]

It would be a turning point in the history of Rome. Not in the same manner as, say, Caesar crossing the Rubicon, Christ being crucified, or Diocletian dividing the Empire in two, but a literal change in the *history* of the "Eternal City," the manner in which it was written, and how future generations viewed it.

"It was at Rome, on the fifteenth of October 1764," recalled Gibbon, "as I sat musing amidst the ruins of the Capitol, while the barefooted fryars [*sic*] were singing Vespers in the temple of Jupiter, that the idea of writing the decline and fall of the City first started to my mind."[2]

In that year Britain was fresh off victory in the Seven Years' War (in the American colonies called the French and Indian War), taking as its prize most of France's North American territory. The British Empire had never seemed further from a fall, and Gibbon put the book, as perhaps irrelevant, in the back of his mind. Not until 1769, by which point Gibbon had already distinguished himself as a man of letters (though, in parliament, by never making a single speech), and the Americans were making noises about rebellion, did he first put pen to paper to attempt the task at which many earlier historians had failed. The work was made all the more daunting because Gibbon, unlike his predecessors, disdained secondary sources. "I have always endeavoured," he would write, "to draw from the fountain-head...my curiosity, as well as a sense of duty, has always urged me to study the originals."[3]

In what he called his "little palace" on Bentinck Street, Gibbon had amassed one of the great personal libraries of the age. (Late in life he undertook to catalog his books, using the backs of playing cards as his index. He left the task unfinished at his death, when the total was nearing 2,700.) He could take down and open any of these volumes and in his mind's eye see the pillars and temples of Rome rise from the pages and hear the ancients speak to him. In June of 1781 he wrote

[1] Gibbon, Edward. *The Autobiography and Correspondence of Edward Gibbon, the Historian*. London: Alex Murray & Son, 1869, p. 78

[2] Ibid., p. 79

[3] Gibbon, Edward. *The History of the Decline and Fall of the Roman Empire*. Vol. IV. London: W. Strahan, 1788, p. iii (hereafter *History*, with volume number)

to Lady Abigail Sheffield, wife of his good friend, constant patron, and frequent country-manor host John Baker Holroyd, 1st Earl of Sheffield: "I am surrounded with a thousand acquaintances of all ages and characters, who are ready to answer a thousand questions which I am impatient to ask." [1]

There was Aurelius Ambrosius, governor of Liguria and Emilia before becoming bishop of Milan and ultimately St. Ambrose, simultaneously one of Gibbon's least favorite sources and one of his most-quoted. Zosimus Historicus, Zosimus the Historian, whom Gibbon scorned as an ignorant, biased, even lying "Greek rhetorician," but with many of whose conclusions he agreed. Claudius Claudianus, called Claudian, titled *vir illustris*, Illustrious Man – vitriolic, satiric, a pagan derisive of Christianity, but who knew the players personally in the years leading up to the fall, and in Gibbon's opinion was "endowed with the rare and precious talent of raising the meanest, of adorning the most barren, and of diversifying the most similar topics."[2]

They were but a few among many. (For a full accounting of sources, see the listing at the back of this volume.) By combining and comparing their accounts, Gibbon was able to do what no historian had done before. The scope of his *History* is truly monumental, requiring some 1.6 *million* words, over 700,000 in the first three volumes alone. (For comparison, that's over twelve times the length of this little 130,000-word pamphlet.) It spans 1,500 years, from the death of Emperor Nerva and the succession of Emperor Trajan in AD 98 to 1590, when Rome was about to embark on a new Golden Age of baroque art and culture, the age of Caravaggio and Bernini. Gibbon's Empire included both West and East, the Holy, and the Catholic.

Our focus, however, will be much narrower: the few decades leading up to the critical year of AD 410, in the West, the Rome of his initial inspiration.

That Rome is not as epic sword-and-sandal films portray it, with hawk-nosed legionaries, sweaty gladiators, haughty patricians, and high-born ladies in clean, neatly draped stolas, a Rome still bending

[1] Gibbon, Edward. *The Autobiography and Correspondence of Edward Gibbon, the Historian.* London: Alex Murray & Son, 1869, p. 269
[2] *History*, Vol. III, p. 188

the world to its imperial will. Those days were gone. Our Rome was spiraling down into chaos.

Gibbon took the reign of the emperor Commodus, a dissolute would-be gladiator who ruled thirty years from AD 161 until his assassination in 192, as the beginning of the end. Over the ensuing 180 years the Empire nearly self-destructed in the "Crisis of the Third Century," decades of civil strife, economic upheavals, plague, invasions, and warfare. What came out at the far end in the mid-330s was an empire divided in two, East and West, each theoretically ruled by a senior emperor, the *Augustus*, and a junior emperor, the *Caesar*. The shining new capital of the East was Constantinople, where Europe and Asia met. In the West, it had long been Mediolanum, on the broad, flat valley of the Po River, closer to the geographic center of the Western Empire. In Rome, the Western Senate still gave the stamp of popular approval to imperial decrees, but the Eternal City had become a political backwater from which true power had long since passed.

And always, just beyond the Rhine and the Danube and pressing ever harder and more frequently across them, lurked the barbarians.

Much more is to be said of these in pages to come, but in short, these Nordic, Germanic peoples – among others, Alemanni, Vandals, and Goths – had migrated down out of Northern Europe, at first under pressure of their own population growth, then pushed from behind by an even more barbaric people, the Huns of the eastern steppes. The Iranian-born Alans had likewise been driven into this Central European pressure cooker. All had to decide who they could more easily push around, the ascendant Huns or declining Romans.

The story of this work is the resulting struggles between foreign invaders and native-born generals, senators, and bishops, under emperors who were anything but absolute. Any man with enough soldiers behind him might declare himself emperor and even make it so, but rising to position and power was less a way to avoid violent death than to invite it.

Post-Gibbon, historians have tallied over 200 reasons why the Western Empire fell, and are still counting. We will concern ourselves only peripherally with the millions of peasants, city dwellers, patricians, and plebeians who were sucked into that maelstrom, to focus more on those Romans and barbarians who aspired to mastery of the known world, most of whom never lived to see its end. Above all, there were two men – Flavius Stilicho, supreme military commander of Rome, and Alaric, king of the Goths – who had it in their power to halt the final collapse. The question, then, must be, *why didn't they?*

The tale of those two men, those fateful decades, and that irrevocable downfall, begins almost exactly 800 years earlier, well before even the Empire of Gibbon. Then, there was no Roman Empire at all.

There were, however, barbarians.

Rear mighty temples to your god –
I lurk where shadows sway,
Till, when your drowsy guards shall nod,
To leap and rend and slay.

For I would hurl your cities down
And I would break your shrines
And give the site of every town
To thistles and to vines...

For all the works of cultured man
Must fare and fade and fall
I am the Dark Barbarian
That towers over all.

Robert E. Howard
"A Word from the Outer Dark"

PROLOGUE

THE FALL OF ROME

387 BC

Barbari ad portam!
Barbarians at the gate!

That should have been the alarm call that July evening when foreign horsemen first came thundering down off the Pincian Hill north of Rome. It *would* have been the call, had there been any sentries on duty. These barbarians – Gauls, bearded and long-haired, half-naked in the summer heat, with fresh human heads dangling from the necks of their sweating horses – were astonished to find the Colline Gate, the city's northernmost, not only unguarded but wide open. A messenger was sent back to alert the bulk of the army, marching behind them. "The horsemen, who had ridden on ahead," recorded the Roman historian Titus Livius, known to posterity as Livy, "reported that the gates were open, there were no sentries on watch, no garrison on the walls."

This was too good to be true. The Gaulish chieftain Brennus, "Raven," was fresh off the greatest victory in the history of his people, and one of the greatest defeats of the Romans ever, certainly the greatest to that point. Now their proud city lay as helpless as a slave girl, to do with as the conquerors wished. Even "uncivilized" barbarians would have known better.

Over 360 years from the founding of the city as a cluster of mud and thatch huts huddling around a ford on the Tiber River, Rome was still a Mediterranean backwater. The center of the world was 2,500 miles to the east: the Persian Empire, then the world's greatest, stretching from the Balkans to India. What would come to be known as Classical Greece was still a collection of fractious city-states – Sparta, Athens, Corinth, Thebes, Argos – quarreling over the Aegean like cats in a bag. Alexander the Great would not be born for another three decades.

However, the Romans had already overthrown their Etruscan overlords and were asserting themselves over the Italian peninsula. Its northern third was still Celtic, what the Romans called Cisalpine Gaul, "Gaul this side of the Alps."

Writing some century and a half later, the Greek historian Polybius still had a low, probably stereotypical opinion of Gauls, who doubtless had changed little in the interim:

> They lived in open villages, without any unnecessary furnishing, for since they slept on beds of leaves and ate meat and were mainly occupied with war and farming, their lives were uncomplicated, and they had no understanding of art or science. Their only property was cattle and gold, because these were the only goods they could take with them anywhere they chose. They treated comrades as of the most importance, the most respected and powerful among them being those with the largest number of friends and followers.

About ten years earlier a Gaulish tribe, the Senones, had come over the Alps and descended into Italy, driving everyone before them. When finally they threatened the Etruscan town of Clusium in the borderland of Tuscany, the Romans sent brothers from the patrician family of Fabia as envoys. They found the Gauls to be crude statesmen.

"The Gauls look terrifying and their voices are deep and raucous," recorded the Greek historian Diodorus of Sicily, noting that they were men of few words, and those words mostly deceiving, boasting, or insulting. "And yet they are clever and are quick to learn."

They were unimpressed by the reputations of the Romans, but deigned to negotiate with them as protectors and representatives of the Clusines. The conditions for peace, as dictated by the Gauls, were simple: they demanded the Clusines' land, or war. "On any other terms there will be no peace," recorded Livy. "We will hear their answer in your presence, and if they refuse us territory we will fight while you are still here, so you may tell those at home how much braver than other men are the Gauls."

The Fabian brothers were not much better negotiators. They questioned by what right barbarians could demand territory from its proper owners.

"The entire tribe which is now called both 'Gallic' and 'Galatic' is mad for war, and both happy and eager for battle," wrote the 1st-century traveler and historian, Strabo, "...annoy them when, where, or with whatever excuse you please, and you find them ready to gamble their lives, with nothing to aid them in the fight but strength and audacity."

The Gauls' answer to the Fabians was that they took what they wanted by right of their swords. Fortune favored the brave.

"Blood ran hot on both sides," wrote Livy, "they took up arms and fell to battle." The Roman envoys not only took part in the fighting – a breach of neutrality – one of the Fabians ran a spear through a Gaulish chieftain and was even seen defiling the body.

This was murder. The barbarians forgot all about Clusium and withdrew to nurse a new hatred for Rome. Against such a vaunted state, though, tribal elders advised caution. Fresh envoys were sent to the city to demand the Fabians be handed over for justice. The senators made sympathetic noises but put the issue to the Roman people, who demonstrated their regard for Gallic ultimatums by voting the murderer and his brothers into high office, as tribunes.

This taste of civilization sent the barbarians home, vowing war. "Seething with anger – as a tribe they cannot control their emotions," wrote Livy, "they raised their flags and promptly set out on the march."

Recognizing that speeches and votes and popular opinion were ineffective and even detrimental in times of conflict, the Romans had often ceded their democratic rights in favor of a temporary dictator to carry the fight against fellow Italians. However, they had exiled their most recent, the extremely successful general Marcus Furius Camillus, under charges of embezzlement, and they did not recall him now. Against barbarians they evidently felt no dedicated war commander was necessary.

They were wrong.

The speed with which the Gauls came rumbling down through Italy took the Romans by complete surprise. "As they thundered past, the fearful cities gathered their weapons and the country folk fled," wrote Livy. "Horses and men, far and wide, covered a vast expanse of the land, and wherever they went they made it plain by shouting loudly that they were headed for Rome."

By the time the Romans had assembled something of an army, the barbarians were just eleven miles north of the city, where the Allia River, really no more than a brook, angled into the Tiber. On the little tongue of land between the waterways the Romans made their stand, their center stretched thin between their reserves, the left flank on the banks of the Tiber and the right on the far side of the stream, holding a small hillock.

Estimations of numbers in this battle vary widely. The ancients, as was their wont, cited epic throngs – 40,000 per side, according to 1st-century Greek historian Lucius Plutarchus, called Plutarch – but modern estimates run as low as 12,000 each. The Romans, used to raiding the neighboring city-states, still fought in the manner of the Greeks and Etruscans, bronze-armored hoplites. Unaccustomed to playing defense, they held ground with fixed hedges of spears – rigid, regimented, systematized, standardized. In a word, civilized.

The Gauls had no use for that, nor for elaborate stratagems and tactics. Combat, for them, was not about discipline and teamwork. It was about prowess as a man. Units organized not into spearmen, horsemen, and swordsmen, but around friends and relatives. Leaders. Chieftains strode out between the lines to bellow insults at the enemy and boast of their own valor. All roared at the top of their lungs, clashing swords on shields, pounding drums and blaring their tall bronze war horns overhead.

Barbarian or not, however, Brennus took one look at the Roman line and knew better than to launch his army at the enemy center and let those wings sweep around behind him. He preferred instead to drive the enemy flanks off the hill and into the river, thereby surrounding their center. According to Diodorus, "the enemy outflanking the Romans, their strongest and most capable troops (whether by design or by chance is unknown) faced those weaker and untrained soldiers on the heights."

On signal, the Gauls rushed upon the enemy.

The Romans had never been on the receiving end of a barbarian charge. The sight of these screaming half-naked savages waving their heavy Celtic broadswords unnerved them. Horsemen would have been warded off by the Romans' hedge of spears, but the Gauls simply batted the points aside and in the next instant began hacking away.

"The armies came together with a great shout," recorded Diodorus, "and the Gauls attacking those upon the hills soon cleared the heights of them, who retreated in great disorder into their own men down on the plain, so that by fleeing under the hot pursuit by the Gauls, they broke their own ranks, and set them to running as well."

The Roman left wing was likewise driven into the Tiber, where many drowned under the weight of their armor. The center, outflanked, was enclosed and swiftly, utterly destroyed. "The barbarians overran them," summed up Plutarch, "and after a confused and disgraceful struggle, routed them."

"None were slain in actual combat," sneered Livy, "but were cut down from behind while impeding one another's retreat in a tangled, struggling horde." For centuries July 18, the day of the Battle of the Allia, would be considered by Romans to be unlucky.

The Gauls themselves were surprised by the ease of victory. They suspected a ruse but, when no counterattack came, they piled the enemy weapons in heaps in an offering to their gods, as was their way. Then they set off for Rome.

Brennus, on arrival at dusk, was no less amazed to find the city wide open to attack.* Wary of a trap, hesitant to ride into a maze of unknown streets in the dark, the Gauls pitched camp outside, between the walls and the Aniene River, which today cuts through the north part of Rome before reaching the Tiber. Scout parties rode out to circle the city, whooping and yelling to terrorize everyone inside. "But all during that night and the next day," wrote Livy, "the citizens stood in stark contrast to those who had fled in such terror at the Allia."

---

*At this point the city walls, which Livy mistakenly attributed to the sixth Roman King, Servius Tullius (reigned 578–535 BC), had not yet been built. The actual "Servian Wall" was probably an earthen bank, fronted by a ditch and possibly topped with a stockade protecting the city's most vulnerable areas. An *agger*, a massive earth rampart, was added in the mid-5th century BC.

Now lacking the manpower to defend the entire city, the Romans had decided to pull back within and defend only the *Arx Capitolina*, the citadel on the northern crest of the Capitoline Hill. It was not much of a fortress, but was regarded as the symbolic heart of the city. As long as the Citadel remained Roman, Rome would live on.

The few survivors of the Allia and other men of military age, able-bodied senators, noble patricians and their families barricaded themselves inside with enough food and arms to last until help could arrive. The priests of the eighteen Roman gods and the priestesses of Vesta meanwhile buried those sacred relics they could not carry off, in clay jars next to the high priest's chapel.* They spirited the rest down across the Pons Sublicius bridge over the Tiber to the former Etruscan side. A column of common plebeians and their families filed across after them, weighed down with their worldly goods but relieved by their low station of the duty to die with their city.

After a good night's rest – not that they had been terribly exhausted by their victory at the Allia – in the morning the Gauls simply passed through the still-open Colline Gate into the city and spread out through the deserted streets, breaking into houses here and there, finding little of any worth left behind. Eventually they met in the Forum, the little valley between the Palatine and Capitoline Hills, there to stand dumbfounded by the already ancient splendors of Rome: the Regia, the residence of former kings; the Temple of Vesta and the House of the Vestal Virgins; the Shrine of Vulcan, where the city founder Romulus had made treaty with the neighboring Sabines; and the *Umbilicus Urbis*, the navel of the city, in which Romulus had sacrificed fruit from its first harvest, the point from which all distances in the Republic were measured, and which was furthermore said to be a gate to the underworld. Though made of timber and brick rather than the marble and granite of later years, everything was already centuries old, built when the Gauls still slew each other with weapons of bronze.

As of now, however, Rome was merely a frontier outpost of Gaul. While still getting over this new reality the barbarians were startled to see, on the porticoes of their mansions, some of the city patricians, in their finest clothing and wearing insignia of rank and awards,

*In his day, almost 400 years later, Livy noted that spitting on that spot was still forbidden.

seated like statues on ivory chairs, awaiting the conquerors' arrival. According to Livy, a warrior approached one of these aristocrats, and gave his beard a tug. (In those days the clean-shaven look, said to have been initiated by Alexander the Great, had not yet caught on, even among cultured Romans.) The nobleman promptly rapped the Gaul on the head with his ivory baton.

"He was slain first," wrote Livy, "the others were slaughtered. After this butchery of the nobles, not a living thing was spared. The homes were stripped, and then set afire."

Before long those garrisoned in the Citadel could look down from the Capitoline Hill and see flames rising from the rooftops, hear the crash of houses falling in, the cries of men and the screams of women and children as they were dragged from their hiding places. After a few days of this the city was destroyed, and the Gauls set their sights on the Arx.

Entreaties to surrender yielded nothing, so the Gauls gathered in the ruins of the Forum to make their typical all-out charge. This time, alerted by the Allia survivors, the Romans awaited patiently, knowing the steep going would slow the assault. And so it did. The barbarians were only halfway up the hill when the defenders plunged upon them, spearing and stabbing and sending them reeling back down.

This was a bit much for the barbarians' pride. They resolved to settle in for a siege. All the food in the city, however, had already been spirited away, eaten or burned, so raiding parties were sent out to scour the countryside and surrounding towns for provisions.

In the village of Ardea, twenty-some miles south of Rome, the former dictator Camillus learned of the barbarians' approach.

"When will I be of more use to you than in war?" he told the city fathers. "It was by never knowing defeat that I held my post in my native city; in peacetime my ungrateful countrymen exiled me. Now, men of Ardea, the choice is yours."

The Gauls, Camillus swore, were all brawn and bluster. If dealt a defeat they would run fleeing back to the Alps. Furthermore, he had a plan to do just that. The enemy foragers, fat on looted food and wine and thinking all resistance at an end, would pitch an ill-disciplined camp without defenses or sentries. "If you intend to defend your city and not allow this country to become a second Gaul," he told the

Ardeans, "take up arms, assemble the troops by the first watch and follow me not to battle, but a massacre. If I do not catch them asleep to be slaughtered like cattle, I will accept the same fate in Ardea that I met in Rome."

Sure enough, that night they found the barbarians encamped a short distance from the town, and took them by surprise. "They gave a loud shout and attacked," wrote Livy of the Ardeans. "There was no battle, only slaughter. The Gauls, defenseless and asleep, were butchered where they lay."

"Only a few escaped in the dark," added Plutarch, "and when day dawned, were spotted hiding in the fields, but horsemen rode them down and cut them apart."

Having thus demonstrated how to deal with barbarians, Camillus was soon begged by the Romans scattered in the nearby towns to resume his leadership. He made the most of the opportunity, refusing unless confirmed as dictator by the Senate. This presented a problem, since the Senate was still holed up in the Citadel in Rome. According to Plutarch, however, a young hero named Pontius Cominius agreed to sneak through the defenders to make contact.

Swimming the Tiber at night, he entered the city by the double-arched Carmental Gate on the riverbank, scaled the Capitoline Hill by a little-known path and hailed the Roman sentries on the summit. (The barbarians seem to have been chronically lax when it came to posting guards. According to Livy they permitted one of the Fabians to come down from the Capitoline Hill and cross through the lines, over to the Quirinal Hill to conduct an annual sacrifice, and when he was done even let him return again.) The Senate hastily convened an emergency session, granted Camillus his dictatorial powers, and sent Cominius back the way he had come. Camillus set about raising an army said to number more than 20,000 men.

Meanwhile, however, the Gauls discovered Cominius' route up the Capitoline. Brennus summoned his warriors. "It would be a shame, after the start we have made, to fail in the end, and to give this place up as unassailable, when the enemy themselves have shown us how to take it," he told them. "For where one man can easily climb it, there it will be just as easy for many to go one by one, even easier as they will help one another along. Every man will receive gifts and honors suitable to his valor."

So it was done. At midnight the Gauls scaled the cliff in such silence that they went unnoticed by the Roman sentries and even their dogs. A flock of geese, though, sacred to the goddess Juno – but, like the defenders, probably in a bad humor for lack of food – raised the alarm. Their honking and flapping woke the Romans, who grabbed up their weapons, rushed the cliff top and drove the Gauls tumbling back down the drop. In the morning, pinning blame for the surprise on a particular sentry, they threw him down after them.

With Gaulish foraging parties subject to ambushes in the countryside, neither side was able to replenish their stores of food. The barbarians were beginning to regret having laid waste the city. Their camp, in the airless valley between the hills, was subject to drifting ash and mosquitos. Malaria, an ever-present threat in Rome, soon broke out and the Gauls – northerners, with little resistance to the disease – began dying off in such numbers that they could not be buried. The dead were piled together and burned. The site was known afterward as the *Busta Gallica*, the Gaulish Crematory.

Brennus and his chieftains demanded the Romans be civilized and surrender the Citadel. They answered by tossing loaves of bread, which they could scarcely spare themselves, down the hill as a display of their provisions. Meanwhile they kept an eye out for the arrival of Camillus. He never came. It might be surmised that, as dictator, he was waiting for starvation to thin the ranks of his opponents in the Senate as much as the Gauls.

Finally, Brennus hinted that the barbarians might be willing to abandon the siege in exchange for financial remuneration. "The Gauls, it is true, butchered every senator they found in the city except the Capitol, which was the only place defended," recorded the North African theologian, philosopher, and bishop Augustine of Hippo, in the 5th century AD, "but they at least allowed those who were in the Capitol to buy their lives, even though they could easily have starved them to death if not storming it."

The tribune Quintus Sulpicius came down to strike a bargain. To the Gauls, it turned out, Rome was worth half a ton of gold, or a little more, since the Romans accused them of cheating with heavier weights on the scales. Brennus just laughed and threw his broadsword, belt and all, on top. Sulpicius demanded, "What do you mean by this?"

"*Vae victis*," Brennus told him.

Woe to the vanquished.

But he spoke too soon. Likely having gotten word that the Senate was handing away the city gold, Camillus finally put in his appearance. Both Livy and Plutarch have him, with his new army backing him, striding right into the middle of the peace conference and clearing the gold off the scales. Now it was Brennus protesting that the deal was already made, to which Camillus replied that the Senate had no authority to bargain anything without his approval as dictator: "*Non auro, sed ferro, recuperanda est patria.*"

Not with gold, but iron, is the country to be saved.

There followed what Livy described as something of a battle, but Plutarch as more of a shoving match, there being no room amid the ruins for either side to assume any kind of fighting formation. In this contest the disease-weakened Gauls came off second best, and Brennus took his people away, to camp about ten miles east at the village of Gabii, on the shore of an extinct volcano's crater lake. The next morning Camillus fell on them there. "Here the slaughter was complete," proclaimed Livy, "the camp was taken, and not a single man survived to carry word of the catastrophe."

"Of those who escaped," says Plutarch, "some were immediately chased and cut down, but most of them scattered, only to be set upon and killed by the people of the local villages and towns."

Nothing more is heard of Brennus. It's presumed he was killed with the rest. The Senones would battle Rome on and off for another century, even making common cause with the Etruscans, until finally defeated at Lake Vadimo in 283 BC. The memory of them, however, left its mark on the Roman psyche. Almost 800 years after the sack, the Roman priest, theologian, and historian Jerome of Stridon wrote:

> In the old days the Roman Empire was tainted with shame forever because after laying waste the country and defeating the Romans at the Allia, Brennus and his Gauls entered Rome itself. Nor could this ancient blemish be wiped clean until Gaul, the birthplace of the Gauls, and Gaulish Greece, where they settled after vanquishing East and West, were mastered.

That was all in the future. For the time being Marcus Furius Camillus was the hero of the day. On his return to the city he was hailed as another Romulus, another founder of Rome, and like him titled by senatorial edict *pater patriae*, the father of the country. Though many plebeians argued to abandon the ruins of the city, Camillus ordered it rebuilt. He saw to the reinforcing of the original Servian Wall, almost seven miles around, with blocks of volcanic stone, in places thirty feet high and twelve feet thick. Revising Roman arms, armor, and tactics to better deal with the barbarians' heavy swords, it was Camillus who did away with the Greek-style phalanx and shield wall for the *legio*, the levy of cohorts and centuries, with cavalry, light infantry, and heavy infantry. He went on to defend Rome against the Etruscans, southern Latins, and more Gauls. He held the office of consular tribune and served as dictator five times until his death of plague in 365 BC, the longest effective one-man rule of Rome for some 280 years.

The lesson was clear. In times of war, a military strongman was necessary to face down threats from outside. Placating foreign interlopers was the road to ruin.

But over the ensuing centuries the Romans forgot the admonition of Brennus.

Vae victis.
Woe to the vanquished.

PART ONE

AD 378–395

*In this manner, through the tumultuous passion of savage people,
the fall of the Roman Empire was brought to pass.*

Ammianus

I

ADRIANOPLE

AD 378

*When through persistence and honor the republic
achieved power, when great princes had been conquered by war,
when barbaric tribes and peoples had been subjugated, when
Carthage, Rome's rival for dominion, had been totally destroyed,
and every sea and land was part of her domain,
then fate turned against her.*

Sallust

Nearly eight centuries passed.

From 390 BC to AD 378, Rome changed drastically. From a struggling little republic in the backwater of history it became an empire. The Romans conquered the Gauls in France and sealed off Britannia below Hadrian's Wall. From the Atlantic to the Euphrates, the Rhine to the Sahara, the Western world yielded to Rome's will. According to the late 4th-century writer Publius Flavius Vegetius Renatus, "The Romans owed their world conquest to nothing more than continuous military training, strict discipline in camp, and unceasing development of the art of war."

Yet in the 1st century BC the Romans came up against a people, barbarians though they were, whom they could not defeat. According to the conqueror of the Gauls himself, Julius Caesar, these barbarians had been crossing the Rhine River out of Germania, their homeland beyond, and like him had driven the Gauls before them. In civilized fashion, Caesar met with envoys of these barbarians. They offered to become willing allies of Rome, if Caesar would allot them land in Gaul or cede to them that which they had already taken. If not, they warned, they could become implacable foes. Caesar declined their offer. Rome did not negotiate with barbarians. But Rome soon learned these Germanics – Vandals, Alemanni, Franks, Goths – were a breed apart from the Celts of Britannia and Gaul.

They are thought to have numbered some fifty different tribes, and if they had ever united their empire would have covered a territory rivaling even the Roman. It was a united Germanic army under the leader Hermann, called Arminius by the Romans, who dealt the legions a disastrous defeat in the Teutoburg Forest in the year AD 9, in which as many as 20,000 Romans were slaughtered. (That Arminius had lived among Romans and been given Roman military training was, like Brennus's warning, another lesson the Romans forgot.) A string of similarly catastrophic defeats over the ensuing centuries dissuaded the Romans from expanding their empire into Germania. The Rhine, emptying into the North Sea, had its headwaters near those of the Danube, which emptied into the Black Sea, and together they formed a natural, though not insurmountable, border between civilization and barbarity. After their many setbacks, the Romans settled for Romanizing Germans on their side of the rivers.

This policy of *assimilatio* – whether forced or not – had greatly benefitted both Rome and barbarians. "This, more than anything else, is why Rome flourished," declared Plutarch, "she always united and assimilated within herself those whom she conquered."

In the centuries after Brennus's sack, the Republic extended citizenship to the surrounding peoples of Italy as they were conquered. Snooty patricians and equestrian classes may have looked down their noses at these new "Romans," but no more than they did at the city's plebeians and slaves. Then, in the wildly expansive first centuries of empire, emperors realized that to control such a huge domain was beyond even Rome's manpower. They solved the problem by making nominal Romans of the barbarians in Gaul, Britannia, Hispania, and other conquered territories. Even Rome's emperors came from wide-flung provinces: Spain, North Africa, Croatia, Serbia, Syria. And in AD 212 Emperor Caracalla went all the way, declaring every free man in the Empire a Roman.

For a people, citizenship and assimilation meant dispersal throughout the Empire, losing their own culture, obeying Roman law, and adopting Roman ways, when necessary enforced at the point of a sword. It required a conquered people to submit to Roman will.

But as Caesar had found, some people refused to submit.

In AD 376 a Goth army crossed over the Danube River. Over the course of two years, they defeated a Roman army at the provincial capital of Marcianople, fought another to a draw and annihilated a third at the coastal city of Dibaltum, killing one Roman general and taking another prisoner. They ran rampant over Thrace, and wherever they went, woe and misery followed.

"Without regard for age or sex they came, destroying everything in one vast massacre and burning," wrote the contemporary historian Ammianus Marcellinus, "tearing babies from their mothers' breasts and killing them, raping their mothers, butchering women's husbands in front of them and making them widows, even as boys and young men were dragged over their parents' dead bodies."

Greek-born Ammianus, himself a former imperial officer, was living in Rome at the time, but he had served in the East and followed events there. "Numerous old men," he wrote, "wailing that they had lived long enough as they had lost everything, and together with beautiful women, had their hands tied behind their backs, and were driven from their land, mourning the ashes of their homes."

On the evening of August 8, AD 378, the Roman Army of the East lay encamped beneath the walls of Andrianople, modern Edirne in European Turkey, about 130 miles northwest of Constantinople. Preparations were being made for battle against the Goths when one of their priests arrived from their wagon fort, ten miles or so distant. He bore messages of import from their king, Fritigern, for the Eastern Roman emperor, Valens.

Flavius Julius Valens – *Imperator Caesar Dominus Noster* Flavius Valens, *Augustus* – was fifty years old. "He was indolent and slow, of a swarthy complexion," remembered Ammianus, "with a cast [*strabismus*] in one eye, a flaw, however, which was not noticeable from a distance; his limbs were well formed, he was neither tall nor short, knock-kneed and a bit pot-bellied."

Over the fourteen years of his reign Valens had become all too familiar with these Goths. For a century and a half, they had alternated between begging the Empire for sustenance and invading to take it. Barely a year and a half into Valens's rule, in 368, he had run them back over the Danube and returned to Constantinople thinking he was done with them.

That, however, was before the coming of the Huns.

The Romans had as yet only rumors of this horse-borne scourge of the far eastern steppes, but the Goths had bitter firsthand experience. Caught between hammer and anvil, the barbarians felt the Romans were the lesser of evils. As their priest reported, their king only sought sanctuary for his people in Thrace, imperial territory. If Valens would agree to that, Fritigern would call off the war.

Land for peace. This was the same bargain Germanic peoples had sought from Caesar over four centuries past, and they were still seeking it. It must have annoyed Valens no end that he had already agreed to it, two years earlier, while away in Anatolia battling the Persian Empire. The influx of tax revenue and fresh recruits would have been welcome in his campaign against the Persians, and as a people the Goths would have served as a buffer against these Huns, whoever they were, if they became more than a threat lurking beyond the river.

His administrators and officers on the frontier allowed the Goths over the Danube, but penned them on the Roman bank. Rations consisted of spoiled meat and moldy bread, the price of which soon reached untenable levels. The Goths traded away their slaves for food, and when the slaves were gone, they sold their children, including those of noble families. "The parents agreed even to this, in order to secure their children's safety," wrote the 6th-century Byzantine bureaucrat and historian Jordanes, thought to be of Goth blood himself, "reasoning that it was better to lose freedom than life; and certainly better to be fed as a slave, than starve in freedom."

This, however, may have been the Romans' goal all along. Zosimus, the Byzantine court treasurer who would make his name instead as a historian, and who never spared the ancient Romans of any guilt, interpreted it less as slavery, or even as hostage-taking, than as compelling the Goths to hand over their future generation of leaders for assimilation. Valens had ordered them scattered into nearby cities to be raised as Romans. "The sons of the Goths had been judiciously distributed through the cities of the East," wrote Gibbon, "and the arts of education were employed to polish, and subdue, the native fierceness of their temper."[1]

Assimilation would have certainly benefitted the Goths as well as it had the Gauls, Britons, Franks, and all the other barbarian peoples before them. To be accepted as Roman citizens was all they wanted. To serve as mercenaries in Rome's legions against the hated Huns would not have been too costly a price to pay.

Alas, citizenship was not offered to them. And conditions along the Danube did not improve. The local Romans were making too much money from sales of cut-rate food and barbarian slaves. To the Goths it seemed that the Romans treated them little better than had the Huns. Accordingly, Fritigern simply led them off the reservation, into open Thrace.

"That day was the end of the poverty of the Goths and the safety of the Romans," concluded Jordanes, "for the Goths, no longer outsiders and refugees, but united as overlords, now ruled the locals and all the northern territory up to the Danube."

The subsequent victories had equipped the Goth warriors with captured Roman arms and armor, and swelled their numbers, including even Adrianople's garrison of Goth mercenaries, who – beset by a hostile populace – deserted to join their barbarian brothers. So recently refugees in a foreign land, the Goths had become a mobile nation of perhaps a hundred thousand, moving over Thrace in a wagon train miles long. Even renegade Alans and Huns flocked to Fritigern, for barbarians rarely owed allegiance to any lord, but followed whoever might profit them most through victory. Fritigern himself was barely in control of them, as his priestly messenger revealed to Valens.

"He had no other way to cool the anger of his countrymen," according to Ammianus, "or to encourage them to accept Roman peace terms, unless when the time came he could show them an army close by and ready to fight, and by striking fear into them in the emperor's name, allay their stubborn love of fighting."

[1] *History*, Vol. II, p. 621

The Goths had crossed the border seeking refuge, not war. They felt the recent battles had been forced upon them, and their victories had led only to more battles. As the Empire had proven again and again, it could always raise fresh armies, not least from among other barbarians. On the other hand, a defeat would cost the Goths everything.

So, parade your army, Valens, but expect the Goths to flee at your approach, despite the fact that they had not dodged, nor lost, a fight against Rome so far.

To the Romans, it had to be either some kind of trick or a colossal bluff. What civilized man could know the mind of a barbarian?

There's no way to prove it, but a civilized barbarian was very likely attending that audience with the Goth priest in the imperial tent. In 378 Flavius Stilicho was in his late teens or a little older, but already a member of the *protectores domestici*, the imperial bodyguard, which also served as a cadet corps to train future commanders. As such, he would have witnessed his emperor's dealings with the Goths and, if we flatter him a bit, may even have been consulted for his opinion, since he was half-barbarian by birth.

Stilicho's heritage comes down to us from only a few sources. In later years his veritable press secretary, the Egyptian court poet Claudian, never failed to extol his patron's virtues, yet had little to say about his parentage. "I will not tell of your father's warlike deeds," he wrote to Stilicho. "Had he never done anything important, had he never led those red-haired companies in battle out of loyalty to Valens, simply being the father of Stilicho would have spread his fame far and wide."

In that period the "red-haired companies" in question, *rutilantes crinibus alas* in the original Latin, were mounted auxiliaries, barbarian cavalry. For all their innovations in infantry tactics and equipment, the Romans never developed much in the way of their own cavalry. They got their *alae* from the "allies" who supplied the old Republic with most of its horsemen, and the Empire by tradition still employed mercenaries in that role. In giving a job description for Stilicho's father, Claudian renders it all but certain that he too was in the Roman camp at Adrianople.

Stilicho's contemporaries certainly considered him a half-breed. Jerome of Stridon, in a letter written a year after Stilicho's death, called him *semibarbarus*, a half-barbarian. Whether he meant semi-barbaric by blood or by deed, Jerome had a low opinion of both. And fellow Roman priest, historian, and theologian Paulus Orosius would later claim outright that Stilicho "was born of the Vandals, that cowardly, avaricious, faithless, sly race."

Orosius was from Galicia, modern Portugal, where he wrote his *Historiae Adversus Paganos*, History Against the Pagans, some ten years after Stilicho's death, when the Vandals were battling the Goths for control of Hispania and it was politically fashionable to blame Stilicho for the acts of both. In 378, though, the Vandals had so far been to the Goths what the Goths were to the Huns: victims. As the Huns had pushed the Goths into confrontation with the Empire, so the Goths had done to the Vandals, some half-century earlier. Some of the tribe had retreated west, into Germania, and others south, into Dacia, where Emperor Constantine, striking the eternal bargain with Germanics, assimilated them, granting them land and citizenship. Jordanes wrote of them, "Here they made their home for about sixty years and obeyed the emperors' commands as subjects."

Stilicho's father was probably born in this era, as a Roman citizen, and evidently rose through the ranks of the cavalry auxiliaries. All this vague ambiguity has led some historians to posit that Stilicho was in fact a full-blooded Roman who was simply derided for perceived barbarian sympathies, but that view is not widely held. The greatest evidence of Stilicho's barbarian blood is simply his surname. *Stilicho* is not Latin, not Roman. It comes down from the proto-Germanic *stillijaz*, meaning still or quiet. No self-respecting 4th-century Roman would take such a barbarian name without good reason. As Romans typically named eldest sons after their fathers, we might also assume Stilicho's father's first name was Flavius, but then a full-blooded Vandal would perhaps not have adopted a Roman name except as an alias or *nom de guerre*. On the other hand, Flavius was a very popular and common Roman name, the equivalent of today's English "John," perfect to Romanize a little half-barbarian boy. That it originally meant golden or golden-brown may indicate that Stilicho had the fair hair of his Germanic ancestors.

But what of his Roman ancestors?

How Stilicho's father, the barbarian cavalryman, met his Roman mother, and furthermore how that very unusual match turned to matrimony, will forever remain a romantic mystery, for she is otherwise a complete unknown. Judging by later female names in the family – Stilicho had a sister, of whom almost as little is known, including her name – historians guess his mother's first name was Maria, and judging by her son's high position at a young age, she may have been a daughter of a noble family, possibly even related to the imperial bloodline. Marriage between Romans and barbarians was frowned upon and actually made illegal in the early 370s, thereafter requiring *conubium*, imperial dispensation.

By that time Stilicho was ten years old, and this is all speculation, of course, but sons of Roman servicemen were expected to serve in their turn, Stilicho was of military age, the military was beneath the walls of Adrianople with the emperor, and he was a member of the imperial bodyguard, training for the highest levels of command. Put all that together, and it's conceivable, even probable, that he was there in the imperial tent as Valens and his generals decided how to deal with the Goths. He would not have been the only barbarian officer present.

Bacurius Hiberus, "the Iberian," was a prince of that country (modern Georgia), which had of late fallen under Persian sway, and he now served Valens as a tribune of cavalry. Zosimus called him "an expert in military matters, and not disposed to evil," so circumspect about his religion that even his friends had no idea if he was Christian or pagan. Flavius Richomeres, a full-blooded Frank (another Germanic tribe, which had superseded the Gauls on the Roman side of the Rhine and, as an ally of Rome, supplied its armies with mercenaries), was a *comes domesticorum*, count of domestic troops, a general in the Western army. He had been sent ahead as a liaison by Valens's twenty-year-old nephew, the Western emperor Flavius Gratianus. Richomeres had fought Fritigern and the Goths to a bloody draw, and from that experience advised Valens to await his nephew's arrival before engaging them at Adrianople. And according to Ammianus, as Valens's *magister equitum*, master of cavalry, Victor, "a man of measured and wary disposition, urged him to wait for his imperial ally, and in this was supported by a number of other officers, who thought the reinforcements by the Gallic [Western] army would likely cow the angry pride of the barbarians."

Though Valens's barbarian commanders were united in their advice to wait, his Roman generals were eager to fight. Profuturus and Traianus, "ranking, ambitious officers, but with no great aptitude for war," as Ammianus put it, had supported Richomeres in fighting the Goths to a draw, but won themselves no glory and wanted another crack at them. Traianus' successor as *magister peditum*, master of infantry, was Sebastianus, a former governor of Egypt and a Western general who had bragged to Valens of his recent successes at hunting down random Goth foraging parties.

These foragers were key to imperial strategy. Valens's *speculatores* and *exploratores*, his spies and scouts, had reported the Goths numbered only about 10,000 warriors in camp – surprisingly few to protect such a large band of women and children – leading the Romans to think most of the enemy warriors were ranging over Thrace, scavenging provisions. Valens's army was at least half again as large. (The exact head count isn't known. Ammianus, whose chronicle of events is otherwise most complete, inexplicably neglects to tally manpower.) His nephew Gratian had been delayed putting down another German uprising along the Rhine, but was coming down the Danube to share the upcoming victory with his uncle.

This was not necessarily good news from Valens's viewpoint. For a minimal contribution in manpower, Gratian would claim an equal share of the glory. There was already sedition in the streets of Constantinople due to Goths pillaging practically in the suburbs. Valens needed to appear as the defender of empire. If the scouts' reports and Fritigern's offer were to be believed, on the appearance of the imperial army the Goths would simply flee or submit.

"The fatal intransigence of the emperor prevailed," wrote Ammianus, "fortified by the flattery of some of the commanders, who advised him to hasten with all speed, so that Gratian might have no share in a victory which, as they fancied, was already almost gained."

When the priest and his retinue arrived back in the Gothic camp that night, word must have spread like wildfire that battle was certain on the morrow. The wagon train's exact location is to this day uncertain, but most historians place it on a ridge line to one side or the other of the Tundzha River, north of Adrianople, where it had access to fresh water but was still defensible against attack. The Goths, who had been on the move for three days in search of sustenance, typically circled their wagons for the night, but Fritigern's wagon train was a mobile city with a population in the order of 30,000 and probably 2,000 to 5,000 wagons. Nose to tail they would have made a circle a mile or more around, too thinly spread and vulnerable for easy defense, and they probably formed several tighter, concentric or spiraled circles. News of the impending fight would have run through this improvised fort almost as quickly as a bugle call. Men set aside their more mundane chores to sharpen notched sword blades and ponder whether donning their hard-won Roman helmets and armor would be wise the next day, considering the stifling August heat. Horsemen groomed their mounts and picked hooves clean of stones, for with Vandal auxiliaries in the imperial ranks (as the priest and his attendants would have observed) there was sure to be a cavalry fight. Women lingered over the evening meal, knowing it might be the last they shared with their men. Germanic warriors looked forward to battle as a chance to prove their mettle; being morose or fatalistic served no purpose. Therefore drink flowed, musicians played, there was dancing and singing in the firelight and children and dogs ran and chased among the wagons. It was an exciting time to be a boy among barbarians.

In the year 378 Alaric of the Goths was just eight or nine years old, a good ten years or more younger than his future counterpart Stilicho and not yet old enough to be considered a man. That may be the reason he was still alive and free, being too young to have made much of a slave, as so many other Goth youths had been sold to their Roman masters. Alaric may have been high-born, but all that is known of his ancestry is that he was a son of the Balti, the "Bold" clan, whose name may reflect the Goths' semi-mythic origins on the island of Gotland in the Baltic Sea. Alaric was said to have been born on an island himself: Peuce (anglicized as Pine) Island, in the very mouth of the Danube, today part of its silted-up delta but then a true island of some 540 square miles.

At his age, having known little else, he might have taken Fritigern's traveling nation to be the natural way of things, but it had not always been so for the Goths, arguably not since their Scandinavian days. The Romans saw the Goths as two peoples, the *Tervingi*, the "forest-dwellers," and *Greuthungi*, the "steppe-dwellers." In the 6th century the Roman senator Magnus Aurelius Cassiodorus would make them better known as *Visi* (Western) Goths and *Ostro* (Eastern) Goths, when the former ruled Spain and the latter ruled Italy. In the 4th century, however, the Goths themselves made no such distinction. Families and clans mixed and mingled freely, coming together and parting as necessary, going their own way any time the pickings looked better elsewhere. Add in Hunnish mercenaries and their Alan compatriots and the mix became even more volatile. For any leader to have held them all together for such a length of time was something of an anomaly. In Fritigern's tent that night there must have been some consternation that his cavalry commanders Alatheus, a king in his own right, and Saphrax, leader of the Alans, were somewhere farther up the river valley, foraging for supplies. They may not have yet learned of the Roman approach, and if they had, it would not have been inconceivable for them to tarry a bit, leaving Fritigern and the Goths to face the enemy alone. Yet in name at least the Goths were united as one against Rome. Young Alaric, if he didn't on that night before battle, would soon enough take a life-lesson from Fritigern's example of leadership.

For now, though, as a boy too young to join battle himself, it sufficed to admire warriors cheerfully facing what might be their last night on earth, perhaps to borrow one of their swords to swing and imagine the great deeds that might be done with it, and almost certainly to take a moment to join them in prayer. To the majority of Goths, the Christian god and the Germanic god Odin were of small distinction. One had hung on a cross, and the other on a tree, both for the sake of their people. The difference was of little import. Barbarians worshiped whichever god their lord decreed.

At dawn the Romans formed up for the march according to the age-old order set down centuries earlier by the Greek historian Polybius and the former Jewish rebel (later defector and scholar) Josephus. To ward off ambush, *sagittarii* and *equites sagittarii*, foot archers and light cavalry with bows or javelins, and the skirmishers, slingers, and crossbowmen of the light infantry ranged out ahead, with more cavalry fanning out to either side to screen the army's flanks. Behind them came the vanguard, heavy infantry armored in *lorica hamata*, ring mail – a Celtic (barbarian) invention

– and here in the East many in *lorica squamata*, scale mail. At the head of the main army rode the emperor, Valens, resplendent in his best armor. With him rode standard bearers to mark him for all to see, bodyguards to shield him, commanders and officers to carry out his will, and trumpeters and buglers to relay his commands.

Then came the Army of the East. Two of the emperor's personal armies, and probably three regional armies, those of the Orient (Syria), Thrace, and Illyricum (western Balkans). Heavy cavalry, mailed, bearing lances and broadswords with long reach. The awe-inspiring *cataphracti*, heavy shock cavalry, men and horses alike draped in mail from the head to the knees, faceless, terrifying. Five thousand legionaries, marching six abreast, bristling with spears, helmeted and armored, bearing heavy round shields (instead of the curved, rectangular *scuta* of bygone days). Six thousand auxiliaries – archers from Crete, Africa, and the Middle East, slingers from the Balearic Islands and Aegean, even a contingent of Arab cavalry and mercenaries. Border troops, scraped from the frontier forts, survivors of previous engagements with the Goths and probably not eager to face them again.

Unusually, no baggage train followed this army. Wagons and carts, pack animals and slaves laboring along under heavy loads, ballistas and onagers (field crossbows and small catapults) for an army this size would probably have trailed behind for over two miles, but they make no appearance in accounts of the battle. Likewise, the usual parade of camp followers – women and children, sutlers, prostitutes, personal servants and slaves – that shadowed every army of the age appear to have stayed home this time. Valens seems to have anticipated a quick victory, or a show of strength followed by no battle at all, and a triumphant return to the city that evening. According to Ammianus, "the Roman banners were advanced with alacrity, the baggage having been left at the foot of the walls of Adrianople, with an adequate guard of legionaries. The emperor's treasure and imperial regalia were inside the walls, with the prefect and the leading members of the council."

Where Stilicho was in all this went unrecorded. An as-yet-unknown youth, even among the *protectores*, he warranted no special mention in the annals. He may have been part of the "adequate guard of legionaries" who remained behind to guard the imperial freight, the treasury and officials. That he was a member of the imperial guard would seem to imply he rode out as part of the emperor's retinue.

That he survived the battle implies he did not.

Over level ground Roman legions would normally have covered the distance to the Goth camp by mid-morning. The ground north of Adrianople, however, is not level, but rolls in successively higher foothills and deeper ravines, today's Derventski Heights, severe enough to form a natural border between Bulgaria and European Turkey. The legions made only about a third of their usual speed, laboring up and down in the August heat. "Then," records Ammianus, "having crossed the broken ground between the two armies, as the sweltering day was proceeding toward noon, finally, after marching eight miles, our men sighted the enemy's wagons, which as the scouts said were all arranged in a circle."

What eight-year-old boy in the Goth camp would not have viewed the day's events from under one of those wagons on the outer rim of the circle, peering through wheel spokes (or more likely between the wheels, if they were solid discs) to miss nothing? King versus emperor, surely a battle for the ages! Fritigern, at the head of his chieftains, leading the Gothic army out beyond the wagons onto the slope between them and the Romans, ready to face the enemy of his people in the open, his men waving their shields, spears, and swords in greeting the foe. "Following their tradition," wrote Ammianus, "the barbarian army raised a ferocious, unnerving racket, while the Roman generals ordered their battle line."

The sight and sound of this barbarian horde, numbering many more than the 10,000 men his scouts had reported, must have given Valens pause, but he was committed now. In the hazy, dusty distance helmets and spearpoints glittered in the shimmering heat as the Romans arrayed their legions and cohorts in battle formation. "The right wing of the cavalry was in the vanguard," Ammianus tells us, "most of the infantry was kept in reserve. But the cavalry's left wing, of which a large number were still marching on the road, were coming as quickly as possible, though with much difficulty."

The perfect time to attack Roman legions was while they were still in the midst of their very civilized ordering, organizing, and positioning, yet Fritigern did not. He stalled, sending emissaries across the field under truce to talk. Valens, without the numerical advantage of which he'd been assured and now expecting the battle to be a much closer, riskier contest, nevertheless ran a bluff of his own, finding reason to turn the envoys away until his legions could form up. "The emperor, offended at their lack of rank," reported Ammianus, "answered that if they wanted a lasting treaty, they must send him noblemen of adequate dignity."

The messengers returned to the Goths with the imperial demand. Fritigern gave it some thought, and sent them back with yet another offer: to negotiate himself, in person, in the Roman camp, if Valens would in turn send hostages of sufficient rank and value to guarantee his safety. Richomeres volunteered. Back and forth the envoys went, while the legionaries, warriors, and horsemen stood sweating it out under the summer sun. Fritigern was running out of time. By now it had to be common knowledge in the Goth camp that Alatheus, with the Goth cavalry, and Saphrax and his Alans were still nowhere to be found. If rumors of betrayal were not circulating among the women and children in the circled wagons, they might already be rife among the Roman high command.

As the sun passed overhead and sank into the hot afternoon the imperial troops ran out of patience. Anyone watching from the Goth wagon fort might have noticed, even as the delegation with Richomeres was setting out to cross the field toward the barbarian lines, a ruckus over on the right. Some Roman auxiliary horsemen – probably Vandals, with Stilicho's father perhaps among them, barbarians eager for glory against their ancestral foes – had taken it upon themselves to win the battle of Adrianople all on their own.

Ammianus claims these cavalrymen were under the command of Bacurius, the outcast Iberian prince, whom contemporary sources all regarded as skilled and courageous in battle. His attack, though impetuous and probably unplanned, was likely to succeed. The best way to defeat a wall of barbarian shields was not to tackle it head-on, but to turn its flank. Attacking one end of the line would turn the battlefield ninety degrees, leaving what had been the far end of the line suddenly in the distant rear. Most of the Goths had just been put out of the fight. And their wagon fort was wide open to attack.

According to Ammianus, the imperial cavalry thundered right up to the enemy wagons. Barbarian women were no shrinking damsels when it came to a fight, and nor were their children. Everyone in the Goth camp who could grab a weapon, would have – bows and arrows, javelins, swords; among barbarians, even eight-year-old boys could handle a knife – and all steeled themselves for a fight to the death.

Night had fallen before the first survivors found their way back to Adrianople, arriving before the torchlit gate in ones and twos. The battlefield had been so large and the action so disjointed that no one man could yet know the entirety of the shocking, disastrous turn of events. By piecing together the stories, however, the sentries, the garrison, the city officials, and later Ammianus, could relate the tale of Rome's worst defeat in at least a hundred years.

Just as the imperial auxiliaries were about to assault the wagon train, they ran into a second troop of barbarian riders – Alatheus and Saphrax, with the Goth cavalry and Alans. "These, coming down out of the mountains like a thunderbolt," wrote Ammianus, "dazed and slaughtered everyone who got in the way of their lightning charge."

The timing was so fortuitous that it seems obvious that Fritigern's allies, as would Wellington at Waterloo, Meade at Gettysburg, and Sitting Bull and Crazy Horse at Little Bighorn, had taken advantage of the terrain to conceal themselves, awaiting the moment to strike. And now the moment was upon them.

The Roman auxiliaries, having ridden so far forward, found themselves all alone, trapped between the oncoming horsemen, the wagon circle, and the main Goth battle line. Ammianus admits, "They were abandoned by the rest of the cavalry and, hard-pressed and outnumbered by the enemy, overwhelmed and crushed, like the ruin of a walled fortress."

A cloud of sun-dried dust, churned up by the milling horses, obscured the glitter of swords, the flicker of arrows, and men tumbling from the saddle. "And while weapons and missiles of all sorts were clashing in vicious battle, and Bellona [goddess of war], blowing her trumpet of woe, was raging more wildly than usual to inflict catastrophe on the Romans," concluded Ammianus, "our men began to retreat."

Orosius, writing nearly four decades after the battle, was harsher in his judgment. "As soon as the Roman cavalry squadrons were thrown into disarray by the Goths' sudden charge, they left the infantry companies totally exposed."

The auxiliaries – those who survived – wheeled their horses as best they could and made for the safety of the Roman lines. The Goth and Alan cavalry pursued, all the way around the right end of the barbarian shield wall and the Roman left as well, effectively turning the tables on the imperial line. Now it was the legionaries who were outflanked. Unlike the Romans, however, the barbarians made this no half-hearted attack. Richomeres' gambit be damned, Fritigern saw his chance and took it. Roaring, the entire Goth line surged forward, an unruly mob, but with edged weapons. That concerted effort was their only attempt at tactics.

The Roman legionaries, though – Gauls, Franks, Sarmatians, even Goth mercenaries – were hardly less Germanic than Fritigern's Goths. They had been raised in a tradition of all-out barbarian warfare, but honed by Roman training and discipline to a fine edge. A Goth charge did not intimidate them. They stood firm and held their ground.

"Then the two lines of battle smashed into each other, like the rams of ships," recorded Ammianus, "and shoving with all their strength, were tossed back and forth like ocean waves." The melee was a confused, pushing, shoving scrum full of deadly points and edges. Arrows, javelins, and lead-weighted darts, *plumbatae*, arched overhead to drop onto unsuspecting targets among the close-packed throng, and to raise a shield against them left a man exposed to a killing blow. The legions had long since given up the *gladius*, the short stabbing sword of the Republican days, in favor of the longer barbarian-style broadsword, and the Goths were armed much the same, but in that tight-packed brawl there was hardly room to swing or thrust. According to Ammianus the combatants were "so crowded together that a soldier could scarcely draw his sword, or pull back his hand after reaching out." Even so, the legionaries in their armor might have withstood the assault by half-dressed barbarians.

It was that impulsive initial charge, and subsequent repulse, of the imperial auxiliary on the left that was Rome's undoing. The Goth and Alan cavalry, having driven the imperial auxiliaries from the field, found themselves unopposed, with the enemy battle line stretching away before them and the Roman flank, already engaged with the Goth infantry to their front, laid utterly bare. The Romans who had sought to turn the battlefield ninety degrees suddenly found it turned back upon them. The barbarian cavalry swept in behind them.

The Battle of Adrianople in AD 378 (there were at least seven others, in 324, 813, 1205, 1254, 1365, 1829, and 1913, leading to the city's claim to be some of the most fought-over ground in history) has often been characterized as a victory of cavalry over infantry, a signal change in warfare marking the rise of the armored knight who would dominate the Middle Ages. But in truth most of the fighting took place on foot, with sword, spear, and shield, where men cursed and stabbed, hacked and clawed, no longer for the Empire nor for some imagined Gothic nation, but simply for their lives. Most of them, on the imperial side at least, did not succeed. Not even a Roman legionary could stand against barbarian warriors to his front while barbarian riders closed in from behind him.

The Goths enveloped the imperial left flank, crushed it as in a vise, and began rolling up the enemy line. As a former officer, Ammianus well knew the horrors of ancient man-to-man combat:

> When the barbarians, pouring forward in immense numbers, overthrew horse and man alike, and in the press of battle no direction to retreat could be found anywhere, and the crushing crowd left no chance of escape, our soldiers too, showing extreme contempt of death, received fatal blows even as they struck down their foes, and on both sides the stroke of blades split helmet and breastplate.

In vain. Courage and valor matter little when tactics have failed, and at Adrianople civilized warfare proved insufficient against sheer barbarity. In the end the Goths simply swarmed over the Romans. Ammianus, with access to survivor testimony, recorded, "Finally our ranks were broken by the oncoming mass of the barbarians, and since that was their last chance, they took to their heels and fled as best they could."

Those, according to Orosius, were the lucky ones: "Then the infantry legions, surrounded on all sides by enemy cavalry, first overcome by showers of arrows and then crazed with terror, scattered and completely cut to pieces by the swords and spears of the pursuers, were slaughtered."

Curiously enough, most of Valens's barbarian commanders escaped. Richomeres got away, as did Bacurius and Victor. But Traianus, Sebastianus, and no fewer than thirty-five Roman tribunes were left among the dead. Only the fall of darkness prevented total annihilation. Adrianople was the worst defeat for the Romans since their loss to the Sassanid Persians at Edessa, a little over a century earlier. Ammianus, claiming that two-thirds of the imperial army died on the field, deemed it worse than that: Rome's greatest defeat since the loss to the Carthaginian, Hannibal, at Cannae, 600 years in the past.

As little mention there is of Stilicho's father before the battle, there is none after. If he lived to see the defeat at Adrianople, he most certainly did not live through it. As for Stilicho himself, if he took part in the campaign, his survival is more proof that he never left the city, because the citizens of Adrianople shut the gates to the survivors. The city fathers anticipated a siege, in which case the fewer mouths they had to feed the better, and a bunch of worthless losers and cowards weren't going to contribute much to the defense.

And the one man who would certainly have been admitted into the city, Emperor Valens, never returned.

There was no moon that night. The battlefield lay blanketed in darkness, footing on the slope of the ridge made tricky with congealing blood, spilled entrails, and the tangled limbs and bodies of men and horses. The families in the Goth circle welcomed the survivors back to their fires. All turned their backs on the dead and dying outside the wagon wall, for barbarian or not, those were Romans. The moans and cries of the suffering were drowned out with a victory celebration.

Before dawn the Goths were out looting the battlefield. For a barbarian boy it would have been a treasure trove more valuable than gold: helmets and shields, swords and spears and daggers. Smoke probably still rose from the farmhouse to the Roman rear where, a prisoner had told the Goths, Emperor Valens had fled after being hit by an arrow. He was still being treated when Goth warriors, not knowing who was within, came to ravage the house. "While the pursuers were attempting to break down the bolted doors," Ammianus reported, "they were showered with arrows from a balcony above, and fearing the delay would cost them the chance for pillage, they piled bundles of straw and firewood against the house, set them on fire and burned it down, men and all."

The prisoner, who had survived the blaze by jumping out a window into captivity, informed the Goths they had burned Valens inside (and, doubly lucky, the same prisoner later escaped to tell the tale for posterity). They were very sorry. Not for having killed an emperor, of course, but for having lost the glory of taking him alive.

And when the battlefield was picked clean and there was no longer any such thing as an ill-equipped Goth, the warriors all regrouped and set out on the march for Adrianople. Looting a battlefield was one thing. Looting a city was another. The barbarians had no knowledge of sophisticated catapults and siege towers, and unlike Brennus's Gauls before the walls of Rome, Fritigern's Goths were not accommodated with city gates left wide agape. Imagine their surprise on finding the remaining third of the Roman army penned outside the walls, much as the Goths had been penned on the banks of the Danube. Truly there was no pity in the Empire, and in their dealings with it the barbarians had lost theirs as well. Ammianus is unclear on the details of the brief siege. There seems to have been a bit of a struggle, before some 300 of the Roman troops, mostly barbarians themselves, ventured out with a plea for mercy and an offer to switch sides.

The Goths put them all to death in sight of the walls.

As though the gods disapproved, a summer thunderstorm dampened the barbarians' sense of urgency. They retreated back to their wagons and contented themselves with sending a priest to implore the city to surrender, and Roman deserters to trick their way inside and open the gates. These ruses failing – the deserters were beheaded – the barbarians tried an all-out assault on the bastions, which also failed.

Unable to take a small city, Fritigern then convinced his people to follow him in taking a great city, no less than Constantinople, capital of the Eastern Empire. The results were predictable, though not for the reasons that might be expected. Stymied by its great wall (built by Emperor Constantine thirty to forty years earlier; the city, though already imposing, was not yet anywhere near the impregnable fortress it would become through the Middle Ages), and battling imperial troops outside the city, the barbarians were ultimately put off by a single man, an Arab mercenary. Naked, he slew one of the Goths, cut his throat and, in plain sight of all, sucked out his blood. It was enough to put off even Fritigern's warriors. Even barbarians weren't that uncivilized.

So the Goths marched off, little Alaric among them, leaving Constantinople in peace. The lesson was clear to all. Barbarians could destroy entire armies in the field, even Roman armies. But great cities – the very highest achievement of civilization – were beyond their ability to conquer.

But a more accurate interpretation of events was: the barbarians simply weren't yet civilized enough to take down a civilization.

II

AD 379

*After our terrible Iliad by the Danube, fire and sword were
borne over Thrace and Illyricum. Our armies disappeared
like a phantasm. No emperor ruled over the State, and no
mountains appeared high enough, nor rivers deep enough
to keep the barbarians from swarming across them to
our destruction.*

Themistius

In the chaotic aftermath of Adrianople, with wild Goths ranging over
the mountains of Thrace and tame ones living in every city of the
East, the Romans came up with a very systematic, civilized method
of crisis management. Julius, the former commander of Thrace and
now by default *magister militum per Orientum*, military commander
in chief of the East and practically its acting emperor, was empowered
by the Senate in Constantinople to deal with the barbarians as he saw
fit. He started with those youths who had been taken hostage from
Fritigern's refugee camp along the Danube and scattered among the
cities of the east. They were to have been raised as Romans. Now they
would get a taste of Roman justice.

According to Ammianus, "He sent secret messages to the governors
of the various cities and fortresses, all Romans – at this time, unusual
in itself – ordering them, all on the same day as though by planned

signal, to kill all the Goths who had earlier been brought in to the vicinities they controlled."

As Zosimus put it, "They told the barbarians of each town that the emperor [Gratian] intended to present them numerous gifts of both money and property, in order to bind them in thanks to him and to the Roman people. To that end they were ordered to gather on a given day in the major cities."*

On the appointed date the garrison of each city escorted its barbarian wards to the local forum or marketplace to receive their just rewards. "When they arrived," wrote Zosimus, "the soldiers, on signal, climbed upon the roofs of the buildings in the various marketplaces where they were stationed, and threw such numbers of darts and stones at the barbarians that they killed every man."

Ammianus approved: "This clever plan was carried out without any hitch or hindrance, and by such manner the Eastern provinces were saved from great dangers."

More good reason why young Alaric was not among those children abducted from Fritigern's camp – few, if any, of them survived. Word of the concerted atrocities, though, would certainly have spread from every city across Thrace. Such "civilized" treatment would not soon be forgotten.

Stilicho, the half-Vandal with no love for Goths, may well have been among the soldiers who carried out this atrocity, for he was semi-unemployed, an imperial bodyguard without an emperor.

It was a problem facing the entire Eastern Empire.

Besides getting himself killed by vastly underestimating his barbarian foes, Valens's other great fault as an Eastern emperor was in never having named a *Caesar*, a junior or co-emperor, much less a successor. His widow, the *Augusta* Albia Dominica, ruled as regent. Their only son, Valentinianus Galates, had died young, and little is remembered of their daughters Anastasia and Carosa; whether they were of age, or married, their husbands were evidently not imperial material.

Gratian, just nineteen years old, had never faced such a decision. He had been named *Caesar* by his father, the Western emperor

---

*Gratian was already emperor of the West and became de facto overall emperor on the death of his uncle Valens.

Valentinian I. His own junior emperor, his four-year-old half-brother Valentinian II, had been foisted on him by his stepmother, the widowed empress Justina, or more precisely the generals and legions loyal to her and her boy. Rather than commit to civil war, the elder brother had ceded title of Italy, Illyricum, and Africa to the younger, reserving Gaul and Britannia for himself, though retaining de facto control over all. Still under threat from Germanic barbarians across the Rhine, Gratian could not take time to handle the affairs of the East. Designating a man who could, however, presented an opportunity for him to create himself an ally.

The prospects were slim. By his massacre of Romanized Goths Julius had made himself the least likely candidate to achieve peace with the rest. Many of Valens's surviving generals, Richomeres and Victor and Bacurius, were barbarians themselves, automatically out of the running. Most Roman applicants for the job had died with Valens at Adrianople and the rest, having fled for their lives, were not likely to inspire followers, for most of their legions still lay rotting on the battlefield. None had the power or authority to rule over the East as Gratian's equal.

"The emperor, undecided as to what measures to take," wrote Theodoret, "now that the barbarians, encouraged by their victory, both were and appeared nearly invincible, decided that the way out of his troubles was to appoint Theodosius to the supreme command."

On the bank of the Sava River in Sirmium (modern Sremska Mitrovica, Serbia), capital of Illyricum, Flavius Theodosius was no doubt expecting Gratian's summons, probably in the imperial palace itself. He was no novice at handling barbarians. His father, Flavius Theodosius the Elder, had been *comes rei militaris Britanniarum* (imperial commander of the Army of Britannia) under Valentinian I. In 368 the younger Theodosius had served under the older in successfully putting down the "Great Conspiracy" of Picts, Scots, and Saxons who had risen up in Britannia against Roman rule. In the 370s, he helped his father to put down a revolt in Africa as well, and then went to Illyricum, where the Sarmatians had destroyed two Roman legions. He had dealt them such a defeat that, as Ammianus put it, "he sated the very birds and beasts with the blood of the multitudes deservedly slain."

Experienced barbarian fighters, with legions at their beck and call, father and son were a power to be reckoned with. So much so that in 375, when Valentinian died, the elder Flavius was recalled, arrested, and executed for mysterious reasons – possibly as a threat to the ascension of young Gratian and Valentinian II – on which young Theodosius, then about thirty, bowed out and retired to his ancestral estate in Spain.

During the Adrianople campaign, with Valens operating in the East and Gratian in the West, Illyricum had been something of a middle ground and a military backwater, which is probably why Theodosius, recalled to duty, had been cooling his heels there. But there is a theory that, operating out of his self-imposed exile, and with the backing of Gratian's own generals, he took advantage of the young emperor's weakness and was prepared to mount a usurpation if not granted half the Empire. With much of the East in near anarchy, Gratian gladly put the whole mess into Theodosius' hands. In January of 379, at Sirmium, he invested Theodosius as *Augustus* of the Eastern Empire. And, crucially, a chunk of the West as well.

"The provinces of Thrace, Asia, and Egypt, over which Valens had reigned," wrote Gibbon, "were resigned to the administration of the new emperor; but, as he was specially entrusted with the conduct of the Gothic war, the Illyrian prefecture was dismembered; and the two great dioceses of Dacia and Macedonia were added to the dominions of the Eastern empire."[1]

As Illyricum – basically the Balkans from the eastern coast of the Adriatic, just across from Italy, to Macedonia and Dacia – had traditionally been considered part of the West, this new division of empire was to have major implications in years to come. And that was only the first change Theodosius forced on the East. Before risking passage through hostile Thrace, he moved his capital from Sirmium to Thessaloniki, on the Aegean coast. As though being punished by the gods, he was almost immediately struck with an illness so severe that, facing death, he underwent baptism by the city's bishop, Ascholius.

In the history of the Empire it's an event analogous to Constantine the Great, in AD 312, seeing a vision of a cross in the sky predicting his victory in battle, upon which he converted to Christianity and

[1] *History*, Vol. II, p. 624

legalized the religion. Theodosius took it a step further. His subsequent miraculous recovery and newfound faith (and the Orthodox, Catholic bishop Ascholius) inspired him, in conjunction with Gratian and Valentinian II, to issue the Edict of Thessaloniki, making Christianity the state religion of the Roman Empire.

But only one creed of Christianity.

Only 400 years old, the religion was still young, still in the process of resolving the various implications, inconsistencies, and objections raised by a myriad of religious thinkers: Nicenes, Arians, Donatists, Docetists, Marcionists, and Montanists. The main struggle was between the Nicene Catholics and the Arians. The latter, put simply, denied the Holy Trinity and believed that Jesus, though the representative of God on Earth, was not eternal but had existed only from birth, and was therefore not divine. This creed, reviled by the Nicene church as heretical, nevertheless had many adherents. Emperor Valens had been an Arian. So were many of the members of his former court. So were the Goths.

That mattered not to Theodosius, nor to his co-signers Gratian and Valentinian. As the Edict put it:

> We order the followers of this law to embrace the name of Catholic Christians; but as for the others, since, in our judgment they are foolish madmen, we decree that they shall be branded with the ignominious name of heretics, and shall not presume to give to their conventicles the name of churches. They will suffer in the first place the chastisement of the divine condemnation and in the second the punishment of our authority, which in accordance with the will of Heaven we shall decide to inflict.

Predictably, outlawing the Goths' religion was insufficient to cause them to repent. That was going to require money and manpower. Both were in short supply. With the barbarians ranging over the countryside and holding entire towns for ransom under threat of a sack, commerce and trade had ground to a halt. To raise funds, Theodosius increased the number of government positions and auctioned them off. "So he sold the governing of provinces to anyone who would buy them," wrote Zosimus, "without concerning himself with the reputation or aptitude of the buyers, regarding whoever offered the most in gold or silver as best qualified. Goldsmiths, bankers, and even the lowest professions, were thus seen wearing the insignia of government."

To raise troops, Theodosius resorted to conscription. Potential draftees had no financial incentive to enlist and every reason to avoid fighting Goths. Many cut off their own thumbs to make it impossible for them to wield a sword. Valentinian I would have burned them alive for that, but Theodosius was so desperate for soldiers that he simply demanded that towns conscript two thumbless draftees for every able-bodied recruit. Desertion was rife, and heavily punished, but Theodosius reassembled something of an army. "Military discipline was soon returned to a high competency," wrote Jordanes, "and the Goths, seeing that the timidity and apathy of former princes was at an end, became fearful, for the Emperor was famous for both his sharpness and judgment. With grim commands and kind generosity he inspired a dispirited army to deeds of valor."

The Romans weren't quite yet mounting a comeback. In Macedonia, at the head of his new legions, Theodosius suffered a defeat by the barbarians, possibly still led by Fritigern. But his general Modares, himself a renegade Goth, fought a guerrilla war in the barbarian manner, managing to surprise an enemy encampment, slaughter the menfolk, and take the women and children as slaves. Clearly the best way to fight barbarians was with other barbarians.

Somehow Alaric, now about nine or ten, again escaped Roman servitude – possibly his family were wealthy enough not to sell him – but life among the Goths was anything but easy. They were still nomadic, calling no city their own except while they paused outside its walls to demand tribute. Fritigern, knowing a dead cow couldn't be milked, was careful to leave submissive towns intact. So the Goth wagon train trundled around and around Thrace, a kind of rapacious, rolling monster. Young Alaric and his family, like all the tribe, would have lived out of the back of a wagon, surviving on the contributions of city dwellers.

As he acquired troops, however, Theodosius moved them into these towns as garrisons, so that when the Goths came back around they found their sources of supply cut off. Their fragile alliance began to unravel. "Splitting up the Gothic army," wrote Jordanes, "Fritigern set out to pillage Thessaly, Epirus and Achaea [Greece], while Alatheus and Saphrax with the remainder of the troops made for Pannonia [northwest Balkans]."

"This was the situation in Macedonia and Thessaly," recorded Zosimus, "when the emperor Theodosius made his grand entrance into Constantinople as if in triumph for some great victory." Partly because he had been sick and bedridden in Thessaloniki for much of the period, it wasn't until November of 380, almost two years after being named *Augustus*, that Theodosius dared cross over to Constantinople.

At that point, only half a century after its re-foundation as the City of Constantine, the former *Nova Roma* was as yet nowhere near its ultimate glory as the Eastern capital. Out of those fifty years, emperors had resided within its walls fewer than ten. Valens had detested the city, and of his entire fourteen-year reign only lived there one year. Stilicho was almost certainly residing in the capital when the new emperor and his family arrived. There had been Spanish-born emperors before, and very good ones – Trajan and Hadrian – but none for many years. This family from the far end of the Western Empire very likely had the blood of conquered Celts and Phoenicians in their veins, but Theodosius also claimed the blood of the Julii, the family of Caesars. He must have presented a novelty, and something of a threat, to the Greek bureaucracy, barbarian military, and Arian priesthood entrenched in the East.

As portrayed on coins and statues, Theodosius was short-haired and clean-shaven in the Roman fashion, about thirty-three years old when he arrived in the capital. The *Augusta*, Aelia Flavia Flaccilla, also Spanish, was about twenty-four, only a few years older than Stilicho. With her hair up in an elaborate bun or wig she appears older on her coins and statues, and her husband's travails may have worn her. By this time she had born Theodosius a son, Flavius Arcadius. He was only three, and it was as yet impossible to tell what kind of man he would become, yet the assumption at court had to be that he would himself one day be emperor.

Of more interest to Stilicho, however, were Theodosius' adopted daughters, Serena and Thermantia. They were actually the emperor's nieces, daughters of his late elder brother Flavius Honorius and his wife, believed to be named Maria. (Their fates are unknown.) "Upon your father's death," the poet Claudian would later wax lyrical to

Serena, "your eminent uncle adopted you, and to comfort you after that bitter loss, gave you, his niece, more love than he could have given any child of his own."

She and Thermantia were both much older than little Arcadius, though younger than Stilicho. (Roman girls were considered marriage material from the age of twelve, though fourteen was more usual.) Serena, though of Spanish blood, was blond, and though there seems to have been a natural attraction, the daughter of an emperor was above a young officer's dreams. "Now that you are of marriageable age," declared Claudian of her, "the aspirations of the young men of the court run high, but the prince hesitates to choose the happy man who is to share your seat and regal privilege."

More than a father, more than an emperor, Theodosius was ardently religious, an Orthodox Christian in a land of Arians, though he seems to have enforced his anti-Arian edict only at his personal whim. Stilicho's barbarian blood was Vandal, not Goth, and he may not have been Arian either, which would have immediately set him apart from, and given him a leg up on, the ex-Arians of the late emperor's court in the new emperor's estimation. This religious bickering among the Christians had weakened them against the wholly Arian Goths. That was about to change.

Life was becoming harder and harder for the Goths, including Alaric. They were now not so much nomads as fugitives, barred from safe harbor in any but the meanest Thracian village. Divided and scattered as they were, they no longer posed much of a threat to anyone, and what threat they did present was summarily crushed by the two Roman emperors.

Zosimus tells us Gratian "sent a sufficient force under the command of Bauto, accompanied by Arbogastes. Both of these were Franks, but strongly attached to the Romans, free from corruption or avarice, and prudent as well as brave soldiers."* When they advanced with the imperial army into Macedonia and Thessaly, the Goths who had been plundering there immediately retreated into Thrace.

"Yet he put no faith in arms," added Jordanes of Gratian, "but sought to win them over with kindness and gifts. So he offered them a truce, made peace, and gave them provisions." Thrace, already picked

---

*Arbogastes was Richomeres' nephew. The contemporary Greek historian Eunapius further claimed he was Bauto's son, but this is not widely accepted by modern historians.

clean, could no longer support a nation of barbarians. Alatheus and Saphrax accepted Gratian's offer.

Fritigern may have preferred war, but appears to have lost the confidence of his own people and was deposed, or perhaps even assassinated. The victor of Adrianople makes no further appearances in history. An old rival, Athanaric, whom Fritigern had once overthrown, reappeared in his absence. In the old days he had made peace with Valens, and now sought it with Theodosius. Unlike most of his people, Athanaric was not an Arian; as did Theodosius, he considered it heresy. They quickly reached an accord. In 381 Athanaric journeyed to Constantinople as Theodosius' guest.

"I see now what I have often heard but never believed," marveled the king at the sight of its massive walls, the great harbor filled with ships, and citizens from as far away as England, Africa, and India. "Truly the Emperor is a god on earth, and he who raises a hand against him is guilty of treason."

Athanaric died that same year, but not before striking a deal with Theodosius similar to the one he'd struck with Valens. In 382 the Goths were welcomed into the Empire as *foederati*, federates, an independent nation. They would not receive the benefits of citizenship (*civitas*), but would be subsidized by the state with food, cattle, and money, and permitted to trade with the Roman towns of Thrace. In return, they would supply men for the imperial legions and serve as a buffer if the Huns undertook to attack the Empire. In effect Theodosius was buying off his enemies, and buying himself an army at the same time.

The philosopher and statesman Themistius, called *Euphrades*, the Eloquent, who would serve as tutor to Theodosius' son Arcadius, lauded the emperor's wisdom:

> You have not exterminated those who wronged us, but assimilated them. You did not chastise them by taking their land, but have created more farmers for us. You did not slaughter them like untamed beasts but charmed away their barbarity just like someone who, having netted a lion or a leopard, does not kill it but tames it to become a beast of burden.

Treating barbarians as *foederati* was not unprecedented. Rome had struck similar bargains with outsiders, going all the way back to the days of the Republic. Around the year 330, Constantine the Great granted the Vandals, Stilicho's father's people, lands along the Danube, and in 358 the emperor Julian had made *foederati* of the Franks, who had then settled in northern Gaul and helped defend it. The difference was that those were conquered peoples, who were admitted into the Empire as citizens. They were *assimilated*. They pledged loyalty to the Empire over their own leaders, and contributed a percentage of their warriors to the legions. More importantly, they were scattered to underpopulated regions of the Empire, losing their cohesion as separate nations, forcing them to blend in with Roman citizenry and become valued allies.

The Goths, however, had not been conquered. They came into the Empire on their own terms. Despite Themistius' view, they were not assimilated, not scattered. They remained a unique entity, a barbarian nation within the borders of the Empire. For them it amounted to a successful invasion. Not only had they defeated a Roman army and claimed a swath of imperial territory for their women and children, but now Roman legions would help them defend it.

Themistius helped sell the deal to the critics of the emperor, of which there were many. "Do you protest that they have not been exterminated as a race?" he demanded. "...I say, which is better, that Thrace should be populated with corpses or with farmers in the fields, that we should travel through horrid desolation or well-tended farmlands?"

The Goths themselves were not entirely sold on the deal. Zosimus wrote, "Some of them said that it was better to break the oaths they had sworn when entering into Roman service, while others maintained that they ought not for any reason break their agreements."

Theodosius did his best to render them powerless. He was wary enough of his new barbarian recruits that he immediately sent great numbers of them to Egypt, in exchange for an equal number of African troops of proven loyalty. If things went bad and the Goth warriors rebelled, they could do it far from home, where they could do little damage to the vitals of the Empire. And if things went well and their training took effect they might even turn Roman, a kind of stealth assimilation.

At least, that was the plan.

At this point in time Alaric was still young, probably not yet a teenager. When the Goth warriors marched off to join the Roman legions, he was left behind. Instead of swords, shields, and armor, there were plows, hoes, and scythes; instead of war horses, there were mules and oxen; instead of excitement and glory, there was hard work and drudgery. The nomadic barbarians settled down into a semblance of civilized life. They were a free people, but they were not Romans, and they were not allowed to forget it. Memories of the war were too fresh. Towns and markets that had been closed to them during the fighting might officially be open during the peace, but resentment still simmered between citizen and non-citizen. "That which is Roman and that which is barbarian," maintained the contemporary lawyer and politician Aurelius Prudentius Clemens, "differ from each other as the four-footed beast differs from the two-footed, or the mute from the talkative."

Each side believed itself superior to the other. Each side believed a final reckoning still waited. "It was generally believed," Gibbon tells us, "that the Goths had signed the treaty of peace with a hostile and insidious spirit; and that their chiefs had previously bound themselves, by a solemn and secret oath, never to keep faith with the Romans; to maintain the fairest show of loyalty and friendship, and to watch the favorable moment of rapine, of conquest, and of revenge."[1]

[1] *History*, Vol. II, pp. 638–639

III

A WORLD DIVIDED

AD 383

*When Theodosius first became emperor, he made friends and
allies of some barbarians, to whom he gave both promises and
large presents, nor did he neglect to gain through friendship the
admiration of each tribe's chieftains, but welcomed them
even to his own table.*

Zosimus

In 383 unruly Goths were just another item on Theodosius' list of
concerns. By this time Persia and Rome had been at war, off and on,
for over 400 years. In the beginning the Parthians and the Republic had
fought over the remains of the Seleucid Empire left over by Alexander
the Great. In the east, the Parthian Empire gave way to the Sassanid
Empire, and in the west the Republic became the Roman Empire, but
like massive icebergs the two leviathans ground away at each other
without causing major damage. Victories were won and defeats suffered,
on both sides – over the centuries the Persian capital of Ctesiphon was
sacked five times by the Romans – but every time the pendulum soon
swung back. Both sides fostered a buffer zone of Middle Eastern client
states and protectorates, which suffered most of the warfare on their
territory, and which changed sides according to the balance of power.

Now, however, the superpowers had their own worries. Theodosius
had the Goths. The young Iranian King of Kings, Shapur III, had his

own rebellious nobles, bold enough to have killed his predecessor. To subdue them, he needed to be able to turn his back on Rome for a while.

Some historians think Stilicho went to Persia on the occasion of Shapur's accession in 383. He was still in his mid-twenties and not in command of the delegation, let alone empowered to make treaties, as his later chronicler Claudian claimed: "You had barely reached legal age when you were dispatched as peace envoy to Assyria, your youth entrusted to make a treaty with so great a people."

Still, it must have been a marvelous adventure for a young man to visit such a faraway land, so non-Roman. "Crossing the Tigris and the deep Euphrates, you came to Babylon," continued Claudian, who wrote eloquently of the fire rituals of the Persians' Zoroastrian faith.* He speaks of Stilicho taking part in the royal hunts, of killing tigers with the bow and lions with the sword. (Since the days of ancient Assyria the Persians considered lion hunting a royal ritual.) And he tells of the throngs crowding the streets to catch sight of the Roman procession and Arab girls swooning with admiration for Stilicho.

However little the young officer actually had to do with it, peace was declared between the empires. "A treaty was made between the Romans and the Persians," recorded the Syrian chronicler Joshua the Stylite, "that, if they had need of one another when at war with any nation, they would help one another by sending 300 able-bodied men, armed and mounted, or 300 staters [Greek coins, whether of gold or silver] in place of each man, according to the desire of the party in need."

But while Theodosius was reaching an accord with the Persians, at the other end of the Empire Gratian was losing control.

On the very western edge of the Empire, in the old Roman fort at Segontium (modern Caernarfon) on the rainy, windy coast of Wales, a contingent of Roman legionaries had put an ultimatum to their commander, the *comes Britanniae* Magnus Maximus. They proposed

*Though Claudian was an avowed pagan, he was a monotheist, if not Zoroastrian then perhaps a follower of its offshoot, Manichaeism, then flourishing in the Middle East.

to rise up against the Western emperor Gratian – mutiny, rebellion, treason – and they wanted him to lead them.

In the fifteen years of his reign Gratian had managed to antagonize almost every one of his subjects, from his Christian bishops – he was unable or unwilling to settle the conflicts between the various sects – to the pagan senators of Rome, who were offended when he removed the gold statue of Victoria, goddess of victory, from the Forum and withdrew government support of pagan activities. But most critically, even more than Theodosius, Gratian antagonized his legions because of his predilection for barbarians. He had taken a contingent of Alemanni into his service and soon adopted their ways. "Gratian admired the talents and customs of these favorite guards, to whom alone he entrusted the defense of his person," wrote Gibbon, "and, as if he meant to insult the public opinion, he frequently showed himself to the soldiers and people, with the dress and arms, the long bow, the sounding quiver, and the fur garments of a Scythian warrior."[1]

But Gratian's troops, from different tribes that had often warred with the Alemanni, aspired to be Roman and wished to follow a Roman emperor, not an aspiring German. "The unworthy spectacle of a Roman prince, who had renounced the dress and manners of his country," concluded Gibbon, "filled the minds of the legions with grief and indignation."[2]

In Britannia, Maximus' soldiers were themselves barbarian, Belgians and Gauls – his cavalry commander, the *magister equitum* Andragathius, was a Goth – but they didn't see themselves as such. They were legionaries, Romans, posted far from home in Wales to defend the Empire against Irish pirates and raiders. Maximus had served under old Count Theodosius and may even have been his nephew, a cousin of Emperor Theodosius. He had helped them put down the "Great Conspiracy," and had gone on to serve the elder Theodosius in Africa and Thrace. On his execution Magnus had not gone into safe seclusion like the younger Theodosius, but became overall commander of Britannia, where he was beloved by his troops and subjects alike. (To this day he is held up as the founding father of several Welsh royal dynasties.) In 379, when as senior emperor

[1] *History*, Vol. III, pp. 4–5
[2] Ibid., p. 5

Gratian cast about for a new emperor of the East, Maximus was passed over for Theodosius. In 381, when Theodosius was mollifying the Goths, Maximus put down yet another invasion of Britannia by the Picts. But in 383, when Gratian playacted a barbarian, Maximus' legions called upon their commander to lead them against him. Orosius admitted, "The army in Britain decreed Maximus emperor against his wishes."

Perhaps. Mutiny, rebellion, treason, it was all those things – but only if Maximus failed to win.

By August 383 Gratian was camped at Lugdunum (modern Lyon, France), an old Gallic fortress on the heights above the confluence of the Rhone and Saone Rivers. This was perhaps symbolic on his part. Lugdunum had been the site of a battle in February of AD 197 between the emperor Septimius Severus and another usurper, Clodius Albinus, which resulted in Severus' victory and sole rulership over the Empire. But Lugdunum was also a junction of the Via Agrippa, the Roman road network built by Gauls on the authority of that emperor, offering Gratian escape in any of several directions. And he needed escape. After only a few skirmishes against Maximus, his troops had deserted him. Gratian's only hope was to seek sanctuary in the court of his twelve-year-old brother Valentinian II in Italia. Many of the boy's generals and officials, however, favored Maximus as well, and Gratian might have to flee to the East, with Theodosius.

Imagine his relief when a mule-borne litter appeared on the opposite riverbank and word arrived that it bore his wife. (Not his first wife, Empress Flavia Maxima Constantia, who had died of unknown causes earlier that year, but his second wife, Laeta, whom Gratian evidently married within a few months or weeks of being widowed.) His affection for his new bride, of whom little else is known, is evidenced by how eagerly Gratian crossed the river to greet her, and, "not suspecting any trickery," according to the 5th-century Christian church historian Socrates Scholasticus, "walked into the hands of his enemy as a blind man falls into as ditch; for [Maximus' cavalry commander] Andragathius, suddenly jumping out of the litter, slew him."

With Gratian lying dead on the riverbank, Maximus would have continued on into Italy to unseat Valentinian II. The boy dispatched a suitable middleman, Bishop Ambrose of Milan, to talk him out of it. Threatened with excommunication, Maximus proved amenable. Gratian's general Bauto, still loyal to the family, had enough men to block the Alpine passes, and by his death Gratian had made Theodosius senior emperor. Maximus knew from their days in Britannia that Theodosius was an eminently more capable military commander than the sons of Valentinian I. "Maximus, who now thought himself a permanent fixture in the empire, sent an envoy to the emperor Theodosius," recorded Zosimus, "...to propose to him a treaty of friendship and alliance, against all enemies who might make war against Romans, and if refused, to declare against him in open warfare."

Theodosius was not so secure in the East that he needed a war in the West. "The assassin of Gratian had usurped, but he actually possessed, the most warlike provinces of the empire," wrote Gibbon. "[T]he East was exhausted by the misfortunes, and even by the success, of the Gothic war; and it was seriously to be apprehended, that, after the vital strength of the republic had been wasted in a doubtful and destructive contest, the feeble conqueror would remain an easy prey to the Barbarians of the North."[1]

With the provision that Valentinian would remain on his junior throne, Theodosius gave in to Maximus' demands. The usurper retained Britain and Gaul, and received Spain and western North Africa as well. The three emperors settled into a precarious balance of power, but it must have been obvious to Theodosius how tenuously he held the throne. In January 383 he had secured his own succession by naming his son Flavius Arcadius, a mere six years old, as his junior emperor. In September the empress Aelia Flaccilla delivered his second son, Flavius Honorius.

And Theodosius took a further step to secure his dynasty, by seeing to the marriage of his adopted daughters. The choice of husbands was of literally historic import. Theodosius' younger son Honorius was newborn; the elder, Arcadius, still a boy. Marriages would introduce adult males into the line of succession. The emperor would be putting his entire dynasty – the future of the Empire – into each man's hands.

[1]*History*, Vol. III, p. 10

His eldest daughter Thermantia was wed to an unnamed general. Though no primary source says so, since his Frankish general Bauto was repaid with a consulship (the highest elected office in the Empire, though in practical terms appointed) and also married at this time, it's possible, and given future events even likely, that he married Thermantia. Serena, the younger daughter, was probably around the same age as Alaric, fourteen or so, not quite in direct line to the throne, but long overdue to be wed. "A maiden ripened to marriageable age burdened a father's heart, and the emperor pondered whom to choose to be her husband and future ruler of the world," wrote Claudian. "Quite anxiously he searched east and west for a son-in-law worthy of marriage to Serena. Only merit could be considered; through camps, cities and nations roamed his careful and hesitant thoughts."

Yet the answer was before him all along.

"All the while," wrote Claudian, "beneath a foreign sky grew the young Stilicho, living unsuspecting of his fortune, of the destined bride that awaited him far away, and in a distant world was the joining of such destinies made ready."

On his return to the imperial court Stilicho was in his early twenties, a worldly traveler and aspiring diplomat, with that dash of barbarian blood adding to his allure. Not long afterward the young officer was informed that Theodosius was entrusting him not only with his daughter, but with the Empire. "You were chosen," lauded Claudian (writing in later hindsight, as at this point he and Stilicho had still not met), "by the opinion and judgment of him who chose you as worthiest of all the suitors of the entire world, and of becoming son-in-law to the imperial family."

It says something of Theodosius that he was willing not only to welcome a half-barbarian into the imperium, but to elevate him nearly to the throne itself. To make him a match deserving of Serena, Stilicho was ennobled with the title of *comes stabuli*, count of the stables. It sounds like Imperial Stable Boy, but in reality it made Stilicho responsible for the acquisition and training of horses and mules for the entire Eastern Empire. This was no small or unimportant task when cavalry was establishing itself over the infantry as the main arm of the Roman military – Emperor Valens had once held the post – and the fact that most of those riders were barbarian-born shows the wisdom of Theodosius' choice.

Presumably Stilicho and Serena were both in favor of the match. Whatever faults Theodosius had as an emperor, this choice as a father was not one of them. The marriage of Serena to Stilicho would be one of the steadfast constants during the hard decades in store. "Our emperor is happy in his choice; he assesses and the world concurs," proclaimed Claudian, "he is the first to recognize what we all see. Aye, for he has joined with his children and with his palace one who never chose comfort over war, nor the contentedness of peace over danger, nor even his life over his honor."

As befitted a state occasion, the ceremony was lavish, carefully planned, and choreographed. Claudian recorded, "The maiden appears, accompanied by her parents wearing red. To one side stands her father, famous for his victories, on the other was the queen [the *Augusta* Aelia Flaccilla], fulfilling a mother's loving duty and arranging the bridal veil beneath its weight of jewels."

The bride was handed by her adoptive father directly to her husband. As a matter of tradition if not religion, they shared a cake of spelt wheat, a hybrid of common bread wheat and emmer wheat, said to have been a gift to the Greeks by Demeter, mother-goddess of agriculture and law. As pagans had done in honor of Ceres, her Roman incarnation, they possibly lit a sacred flame. A pig was probably slaughtered, not as a sacrifice like in the old days, but in preparation for a feast thrown by the young husband in celebration of his new life together with his bride.

"The marriage bed," acclaimed Claudian with his usual enthusiasm, "was ablaze with glittering gold and imperial purple."

While Stilicho was becoming a man among the Roman aristocracy, Alaric was becoming a man among the Goths. Life under the aegis of the Empire was everything the barbarians had wanted – peaceful – and yet this peace was entirely destructive to their way of life. This was confirmed by the 1st-century Roman senator and historian Publius Cornelius Tacitus in his *De origins et situ Germanorum* (On the Origin and Situation of the Germans). He wrote it some 280 years before Alaric's day, but in the ancient world time passed more slowly and change was much more gradual, particularly among rural barbarians. Life in Thrace differed only in detail from that in Germania three centuries past. The Goths may have become somewhat more civilized, but it had done them little good.

"They pass much of their time in the hunt," scoffed Tacitus, "and still more in sloth, given to sleeping and feasting, the most courageous and warlike doing nothing, and handing off management of the house, the farm and the land, to the women, old men, and weakest members of the family. They themselves lie buried in idleness; it is a strange feature of their natures that men so fond of doing nothing, are so averse to peace."

A young man growing up in that environment, seeing the heroes and champions of his boyhood shackled to a life of toil, drudgery, and drunkenness, might wonder if the old Germanic rituals still offered meaning. "Before the village council a chieftain, or the young man's father kinsman, bestows on him a shield and a spear," recorded Tacitus. "These are what the toga is with us, the first honor a youth is awarded. To this time he was a member of a household. Now he is a member of the tribe."

In the old days, such weapons had been of real value. In peaceful Thrace they would have been more symbolic, but symbolic of something gained, or lost? "To surrender your shield is the worst of crimes," wrote Tacitus, "and no man so disgraced is allowed at sacred rites, or among their council. Indeed, many who escape battle, instead end their shame with the noose."

Alaric might have wondered when, or if, he would ever have need of his shield and spear, and if so against whom, barbarian or Roman. Across the Danube, the Huns still ranged up and down the steppe. In 386 a band of Goths under their king Odothaeus arrived on the far bank of the river, demanding sanctuary in Roman territory. That this was a veritable repeat of the situation ten years earlier, when Fritigern had come pleading for a homeland, and that a Gothic horde needed delicate handling, was a lesson seemingly lost on the Romans. Theodosius' commanders on the scene handled it even worse than had Valens's.

Flavius Promotus, the *magister peditum per Thracias*, master of infantry in Thrace, lined the Roman side of the river with troops to prevent a crossing. Meanwhile he sent a picked number of his own barbarian mercenaries across the river to infiltrate Odothaeus' people by pretending to make an offer to betray the Romans, but actually to learn their plans. They intended to cross the river in force, by night, and take the Romans by surprise in their camp. On the appointed evening, a moonless night, the barbarians set out across the water in boats, with their best warriors in the lead.

Out of the darkness came Roman galleys. Oars threshing, they ran down the barbarian boats. Men, women, children, and animals alike were spilled into the river. "The fish of that northern river never fed so well on the corpses of men," enthused Claudian. "The island of Peuce was heaped high with bodies. Even with five mouths [of its delta] the river could hardly rid itself of barbarian blood."

Any warriors who managed to reach the other side were cut down piecemeal by legionaries ready to receive them. "The battle being ended," recorded Zosimus, "the soldiers began to loot. They carried off all the women and children, and confiscated all of their provisions. Promotus then sent for Theodosius, who was not far off, to come behold his brave feat."

The emperor was appalled. Like Valens, he had anticipated strengthening his army with Goth recruits for the inevitable struggle ahead with Maximus. He immediately gave the survivors their freedom and presented them with gifts to regain their good will. But Promotus went unpunished, and now there were more Goths within the Empire harboring a grudge against it.

Theodosius did his best to make amends. A contingent camped outside the walls of Tomis (modern Constanta, Romania, on the shore of the Black Sea), unsatisfied with the emperor's beneficence, threatened to sack the town. When his Roman garrison proved reluctant to sally out against them, the local commander, Gerontius, took it on himself to go out alone, shaming his men into driving off the barbarians. Rather than acclaim him, Theodosius had Gerontius arrested, accused of stealing the Goths' treasure. Gerontius beggared himself making reparations to the court.

Theodosius was appearing to go down the same road as Gratian, siding with his barbarian subjects over the Romans, as well he might given the makeup of his army. If catastrophe befell the emperor and his sons – plagues and disease often swept the land, coups and assassinations were never out of the question – the loyalties of his Frankish general (and possible son-in-law) Bauto and his half-Vandal son-in-law Stilicho, and that of their troops, were an open question. The imperial family's ties to Rome became even more tenuous that year when newborn daughter Pulcheria died and Empress Flaccilla, weakened by the shock, soon passed away as well. As with many royal deaths, the event would lead to war.

In his new capital at Augusta Treverorum (modern Trier) in Belgic Gaul, Maximus was ready to complete his conquest of the West. He had named his young son Flavius Victor as his junior emperor, and no longer had need of the young emperor Valentinian II. The boy had proven to be little more than a tool wielded in turn by his Arian mother, the ex-*Augusta* Justina, Ambrose the Nicene bishop of the Western imperial capital Mediolanum, and even Rome's pagan contingent, headed up by the city prefect, Quintus Aurelius Symmachus. In March of 386 the Arian faction, headed by Justina, demanded that Ambrose hand over two churches in Mediolanum for Arian services. He refused, on pain of death: "I will die at the foot of this altar rather than abandon it."

Maximus, an ardent Nicene and the first Christian emperor to execute Christian heretics, used this religious quarrel as a pretext to invade Italia. According to Rufinus of Aquileia, "Maximus, eager to cleanse himself of the taint of usurpation and to show himself as a rightful emperor, wrote Valentinian that what Justina was attempting was sinful, that Christianity was under attack and the decrees of the Catholic church were being ignored. At the same time he set out toward Italy."

He was supported in this by Symmachus, who had unsuccessfully petitioned the late Gratian, and now Valentinian, to restore pagan customs and particularly the gold statue of Victoria to the Curia Julia, the house of the senate in Rome: "Who is such a friend to the barbarians that they have no need of an Altar of Victory?"

Symmachus was a distant relation of Ambrose's, but in this three-way tug of war the bishop rebutted, "If the ancient rites pleased the gods, why did Rome then take up foreign ones?"

The senators, many of them still pagan, had less to fear from Maximus than from Valentinian and his Arian Christian mother. (Christians of the time were actually more tolerant of pagans, whose souls could be redeemed, than of Christians with differing beliefs, who were simply heretics.) They threatened the boy with the loss of their support, and that of their pagan followers. "This took Valentinian by surprise," recorded Zosimus, "putting him in such desperate straits, that his attendants feared he would be taken by Maximus and executed."

The young emperor, his mother and his sisters Galla, Grata, and Justa immediately fled their capital at Mediolanum, taking a boat east to seek asylum with Theodosius. In case the Eastern emperor showed little sympathy for the house of Valentinian, which had put his own father to death, Justina instructed Galla, a renowned beauty, to tearfully throw herself on the widower's mercy.

"Becoming more inflamed with passion for Galla every day," scoffed Zosimus of Theodosius, "he asked Justina to grant him her daughter, since his former wife Flaccilla had died. Her answer was that she would never agree, unless he would declare war on Maximus and avenge the murder of Gratian."

It would be wrong to say the war commenced because of a woman. Theodosius had to have known the issue of Maximus would need addressing eventually. His former compatriot (and possible cousin) had now usurped two emperors and was unlikely to be satisfied before he usurped a third and united both the Eastern and Western Empires. But Theodosius was in a stronger position than Gratian and Valentinian. By his marriage to Galla in 387, he not only netted himself a pretty young wife, but allied himself with the Valentinian dynasty and allayed fears that he was turning his own dynasty over to barbarians. Within a year or so Galla bore him a daughter, Galla Placidia, strengthening the Roman side of his family and his ties to the Valentinians. Stilicho in the East, and probably Bauto in the West, far from feeling threatened, could rest assured that they had married into not one but two imperial clans.

But in Italy, Maximus knew he needed allies of his own, and knew where to find them. They were already living in the East, and serving in Theodosius' legions. In the ranks of the army, and in the huts and hovels of their villages, word soon spread among the Goths that the emperor of the West was willing to pay to have trouble made for the emperor of the East.

For Alaric, this was very likely his first intimation that the Romans were no more united than the various barbarian tribes, and that the two empires, East and West, could be played against each other.

In 388 he was eighteen or so, about the same age Stilicho had been at Adrianople, already of fighting age among his fellow tribesmen, and eligible to join the legions.

"If their lives sink into the complacency of lengthy peace and indolence," Tacitus had written of the Germanics, "many of their noble young men join those tribes who are waging some war, both because peace is repellent to their race, and because they win fame more easily in the midst of danger, and cannot gain a large following except through violence and war."

Being shipped off to Egypt, though, was surely not Alaric's intention. By now it was plain that everything the Goths received from Theodosius and the East came at a cost. With a choice of two emperors, some of the *foederati* were surely willing to give the usurper Maximus a hearing.

"When all was readied for his journey," recorded Zosimus of Theodosius, "he was notified that the barbarians mixed in with the Roman units had been offered great reward by Maximus if they would betray the army. Upon learning their scheme was uncovered, they fled to the swamps and marshes of Macedonia, where they hid themselves in the woods. Being chased and hunted with great tenacity, most of them were killed."

It can't explicitly be proven, but judging by ensuing events historians believe one of these would-be traitors to the Empire, and now fugitives from its justice, to be none other than Alaric. If he had enlisted as a legionary, he served only long enough to receive rudimentary training. Now he was embarking on a new career: that of a *latro*, a brigand.

IV

LEADERS

AD 388

*See how, under Christian rulers in Christian days, civil wars
are resolved when they cannot be avoided. The victory was
secured, the city conquered, and the usurper seized.*

Orosius

In many respects Theodosius' entire reign as emperor – and in
fairness, the reign of most emperors in the later imperial period –
can be seen as a series of fires needing to be put out. No sooner
was one crisis resolved than another flared up in its place. After the
mutineers among his Gothic mercenaries had been rooted out and
put to flight, Theodosius was still left with 40,000 barbarian troops,
including Alan and Hunnish cavalry and his son-in-law Stilicho,
now elevated to the rank of *comes domesticorum*, commander
of the imperial guard. But still the problem of Magnus Maximus
needed to be resolved.

It would have to be done without the faithful general Bauto, who
died in 388. Theodosius had his young daughter Aelia Eudoxia
brought east to be raised in the house of Flavius Promotus and
his wife Marsa. This high regard for the daughter of his barbarian
consul gives credence to the otherwise unsubstantiated marriage
of Bauto to Theodosius' daughter Thermantia, sister-in-law of
Stilicho. Nothing more was heard of her, and she is also presumed

dead, but the fostering of her daughter by Promotus would set a precedent for Stilicho.

Theodosius sent his Frankish general Arbogastes along the Danube in a flanking maneuver to threaten Gaul, and meanwhile prepared a fleet to land Justina and Valentinian in Italy where they might quickly march to occupy Rome. Then, with Richomeres, consuls Flavius Timasius and Promotus, and guard commander Stilicho, Theodosius led his army across Illyricum for his final confrontation with Magnus Maximus.

The usurper came to meet him on the bank of the Sava River at Siscia (modern Sisak, Croatia). The fighting itself was one-sided and of little mention. On arrival Theodosius sent his barbarian horsemen plunging across the river to drive Maximus' barbarian infantrymen off the high ground on the opposite bank. A counterattack was interrupted by the fall of night, and then, at Poetovio (modern Ptuj along the Drava River), by the wholesale desertion of Maximus' troops. The suddenly powerless would-be emperor fled for Aquileia, at the northeast reach of the Adriatic, with Theodosius giving chase. His Goth henchman Andragathius drowned himself to avoid capture. According to the 5th-century Palestinian historian Salminius Hermias Sozomenus, called Sozomen, Maximus was killed by his own men to avoid Theodosius' wrath, but Zosimus reported he was taken prisoner sitting on his throne and delivered to the imperial camp, where Theodosius expounded at some length on his crimes before having him executed. In his role as *comes domesticorum*, Stilicho was doubtless present at the execution, a lesson in good intentions gone wrong. "Maximus was a spirited, capable man, worthy of the throne," admitted Orosius, "if he had not raised himself to it by usurpation, breaking his oath of loyalty."

But Theodosius didn't stop there. For good measure, he sent Arbogastes to Trier to eliminate Maximus' young son and co-emperor, the *Caesar* Flavius Victor. The Frank duly carried out his orders. This execution – the state-sanctioned murder of an acknowledged Roman ruler by a barbarian – also set a new precedent.

For now, though, Theodosius, just nine years earlier a disgraced general in exile, was for all intents and purposes sole ruler of the Roman Empire, East and West. He dutifully made the trip down Italia to Rome itself. Stilicho sent for Serena to join him on what was almost certainly their first visit to the Eternal City. Compared to Constantinople, or even Mediolanum, it must have been an eye-opening experience.

At this point Rome was about 1,100 years old. Some fifty generations of citizens had trod its narrow cobbled streets, pushed and shoved among its squalid tenements, scratched vulgar graffiti on its walls, and tossed their garbage and sewage from its windows. When Stilicho and Serena visited, there were perhaps 750,000 of them, down from probably over a million in the early days of the Empire. (Evidence of decline, if anyone noticed.) The city air was tainted with a stench of wood smoke, rancid flesh from the fish stands and meat markets, urine from the leather tanners and cloth dyers, and excrement from the public toilets. Its streets and plazas and forums were a congested, colorful mix of clothing, hair color, and skin tones, and cacophonous with a jabber of languages from as far away as Britain in the north and Carthage in the south, the shore of the *Mare Atlanticum* and the banks of the Euphrates.* The difference between rich and poor was as great as it had ever been. The countryside was being swallowed up by the estates of the rich, who used every excuse to keep their laborers from being drafted into the army, every chance to use slaves to replace the laborers, and every opportunity to avoid paying taxes, thereby pushing the unemployed rural folk off the land. Perhaps a quarter of the urban population were perpetually out of work and simply lived off the *cura annonae*, the public dole of bread, olive oil, wine, and pork, because the politicians had learned the hard way that if the supply was ever cut they would have a mob uprising on their hands. The tax base was drying up, the debased currency was worth less every day, and the imperial treasury was running low. The Empire could barely afford an army of Romans, let alone pay *foederati* mercenaries. Theodosius had quite a job ahead of him.

We know Stilicho and Serena accompanied the imperial procession because it is the most likely occasion for the birth of their son, Theodosius' grandson Eucherius, named after the emperor's uncle. Rome evidently had symbolic value for Stilicho as well, if he had his heavily pregnant wife travel there, either from Mediolanum or

---

*In Constantinople the dominant tongue was Greek, but in Rome it was Latin.

Ravenna by road or from Constantinople by ship, in order for her to give birth in the fabled city. Their son would be born a literal Roman. The happy event was later documented by Claudian, who wrote of Rome, "Here Eucherius first saw the light, here his mother the queen [in the sense of being an emperor's daughter] showed the infant to his imperial grandfather, who rejoiced to hold a grandson on his knee and let him crawl on his purple robes."

The birth of his grandson may have put Theodosius in a generous mood. Augustine of Hippo recorded his benevolence: "He did not allow private feelings to affect his treatment of anyone after the war." He spared Symmachus, the treacherous senate leader, who had sought sanctuary in a church in fear for his life. And to prevent young Valentinian from dropping the reins of empire again, Theodosius called once more on his general Arbogastes.

"Arbogastes was a barbarian," wrote Orosius, "who excelled in initiative, wisdom, courage, daring, and strength." Socrates Scholasticus called him "a man rough in manners and exceedingly bloodthirsty," but Zosimus, ever favoring pagans over Christians, claimed he was "exceedingly loyal to the Romans, free of dishonesty or greed, and sensible as well as courageous." This time he was to serve not as assassin but as babysitter. Theodosius appointed him to the unique rank of *magister militum praesentalis*, military commander in chief representing the emperor. In title he would be subservient to the junior (though rightfully senior Western) emperor but in practice superior to him, answerable only to Theodosius and in effect ruling in his name.

Theodosius obviously had no issue with Franks and Gauls and Goths and Vandals doing his bidding, and may even have preferred them when it came time for dirty work. But allowing semi-tame barbarians to act in the name of the Empire was to have severe repercussions.

Evidence of the confused relations between the Goths and the Empire is the fact that, a dozen years after they slew upward of 10,000 Romans and an emperor at Adrianople, they slaughtered 7,000 Romans on an emperor's behalf, at Thessaloniki.

Almost 700 years old, older than the Empire, Thessaloniki, modern Thessalonica, was the second-largest city in the East. It had surpassed Sirmium as the capital of Illyricum, and even served as the Eastern imperial capital during the first years of Theodosius' reign. Its people had been civilized, as defined by city living, since the days of Alexander the Great (founder Cassander of Macedon named it for his wife Thessalonike, Alexander's half-sister) and were not fond of having Goths billeted upon them. Barbarian ways were not civilized ways.

Exactly what triggered the massacre is open to interpretation. Several original sources make mention of the incident, but they and their translators vary in details. The consensus is that in early 390 Butheric, Theodosius' *magister militum per Illyricum* (military commander in chief in Illyricum), was a Goth – perhaps the closest thing to a Gothic leader at the time. (Note the *-ric* suffix of his name, which corresponds to the title *reiks*, judge, and denotes something like a regnal name.) He took offense when a Thessalonian charioteer raped a cup-bearer, a servant in a local tavern. Some say the victim was male. Gibbon claims the victim was the Goth's lover, and by some translations of Sozomen it was Butheric himself, when the charioteer "saw him shamelessly bared at a tavern, and attempted an indecency."

The Roman view of sex crimes depended very much on who committed them, and against whom. Romans cared less about the gender of sex partners than who took the receiving role, seen as feminine and submissive, unmanly. The *Lex Scantinia*, a law dating from Republic days, held it a crime to debauch a freeborn male. The penalty appears to have been a hefty fine, 10,000 *sesterces* – silver coins weighing about 2½ grams each – roughly $15,000 in today's money.

Barbarians, as might be expected, took a less tolerant view. The *Lex Visigothorum*, Law of the Visigoths, a legal code compiled in the mid-600s, was derived from the *Codex Euricianus*, the Code of Euric, King of the Visigoths in the mid-400s, which itself was a combination of Roman law and pre-existing barbaric justice. To judge by these, a rapist was to receive 200 lashes, and be given to the victim or her family as a slave, along with all his property. Furthermore, "in cases of pederasty, where guilt has been proven after thorough enquiry by the judge, both parties shall be emasculated at once," with the proviso that unwilling victims were to be spared.

In light of that, though the exact charges and eventual penalty are unknown, Butheric showed mercy – or covered up his own indiscretion

– by merely throwing the charioteer into prison. The Thessalonians, however, didn't see it his way. Back then charioteers were even more popular than celebrity athletes are today. Immense sums of money changed hands with each race.* To keep a champion driver from the reins was tantamount to fixing the match. "Some great races were to be held at the hippodrome," recorded Sozomen, "and the people of Thessaloniki demanded the prisoner's release, considering him essential to the proper conduct of the match. When their request was ignored, they rose up in rebellion and in the end killed Buthericus."

Thessaloniki was a Nicene city, and the Goths were still Arians, so there may have been religious animosity involved. Theodosius was ardently orthodox, but also resolutely sympathetic to barbarians, their manpower being essential to his reign. He was residing in Mediolanum when he received news of the uprising, and reportedly flew into a rage. The death of a Roman general, even one barbarian-born – *especially* one barbarian-born – could not be tolerated. Modern historians differ on whether Theodosius ordered punishment out of anger, or cold calculation, or even found out about it after the fact; it's said that on reflection he sent word rescinding his initial order, too late.

It may be put down to yet another of his barbarian officials, his *magister officiorum*, master of offices, Flavius Rufinus. The innocuous title sounds like that of a harmless administrative paper-pusher, but actually entailed command of the *agentes in rebus*, the imperial courier service, who also acted as agents, spies, and secret police, and was in actuality one of the most powerful postings in the government. "Of his appointed magistrates, Rufinus was considered the chief," reported Zosimus, "who was born a Celtic Gaul, and commanded the imperial guards. Upon him the emperor rested his entire confidence of all his business, holding no one in greater regard."

Claudian took a somewhat more jaundiced view of Rufinus. "Everything was for sale. He gave away secrets, tricked supplicants,

---

*Over a few years in the mid-2nd century the Spanish charioteer Gaius Appuleius Diocles earned an estimated 35.8 million *sesterces* – about $15 *billion* today – enough to pay all the imperial legions for several months or feed Rome for a year. He still ranks as the highest-paid athlete ever.

and sold honors that had been awarded by the emperor. He engaged in one crime after another."

Rufinus is accused of having encouraged maximum retribution for the murder of Butheric, but he had, or would have, many enemies at court who may have laid blame on him. What matters is the result. According to the contemporary historian and theologian Tyrannius Rufinus, also called Rufinus of Aquileia (not the same Rufinus as Flavius), "The Emperor ordered the people of Thessaloniki invited to public games in the circus, in order to suddenly surround them with soldiers and kill them without mercy."

Wedged against the outer walls in the southeast corner of the city, Thessaloniki's hippodrome – the circus, the chariot racetrack – was lost long ago, but is thought to have been similar in size to Constantinople's, with seating for perhaps 100,000. With most of the city populace inside, happy to accept the emperor's peace offering of games and thrilling to the exploits of their freed hero, it would have been simple enough for the *foederati* to block most of the exits and avenge their leader.

"As soon as the assembly was complete, the soldiers, who had secretly been posted round the Circus, received the signal, not of the races, but of a general massacre," wrote Gibbon. "The promiscuous carnage continued three hours, without discrimination of strangers or natives, of age or sex, of innocence or guilt."[1]

It's unknown how many Romans were put to the sword, and how many were simply trampled or crushed in the panic. We only have an estimate of the total dead. "Scores were cut down like ears of grain being reaped," reported Theodoret. "It is claimed seven thousand died."

Gibbon puts the number at 15,000: "The apology of the assassins, that they were obliged to produce the prescribed number of heads, serves only to increase, by an appearance of order and design, the horrors of the massacre, which was executed by the commands of Theodosius."[2]

According to Theodoret, Bishop Ambrose had no illusions as to who was the real culprit: "Rufinus, you are a bold dog. It was you who

[1] *History*, Vol. III, pp. 50–51
[2] Ibid., p. 51

perpetrated this horrible massacre. You have shrugged off the shame, and though you are guilty of this mad affront to God you stand here fearless and unblushing." Still, Ambrose famously refused Theodosius communion until he showed sufficient regret for the massacre. The face-off between bishop and emperor turned into something of a power struggle between church and state that lasted several months, until Theodosius finally gave in and begged forgiveness.

God forgave Theodosius, but the Romans would not soon forgive, or forget, the Goths.

About 160 miles due east of Thessaloniki across the Melas Gulf, and some hundred miles downstream from Adrianople, the Hebros River (Maritsa in modern Bulgaria) widened into a broad, marshy delta before emptying into the Aegean Sea. The only town of note, Ainos (modern Enez in European Turkey), stood on a tongue of coastal rock in the middle of this delta. In those trackless marshes and fens the Goth mutineers and bandits found sanctuary, and soon made a nuisance of themselves.

Today the river is unnavigable due to numerous dams and low bridges, but in those days shallow-draft galleys ranged far upstream to deliver typical Mediterranean cargoes of salt, spices, fruit and nuts, olive oil, and fish sauce in exchange for Thracian cereals, charcoal, livestock, wine, leather, honey and wax, timber, and metalwork. (Thrace was a rich source of iron, gold, and silver.) The Via Egnatia, the main Roman road from Constantinople across the northern Aegean coast to Thessaloniki, the Adriatic, and Italy, passed near Ainos, making it a crossroads of trade and ripe picking grounds for brigands, apparently including Alaric.

Banditry had always been rife in the Roman Empire, and worsened in recent years. There was no such thing as a police force except for hire. Attacks by marauders were a leading cause of death. Entire parties of travelers might simply vanish a few miles outside the protection of city walls. Tombs were commonly inscribed *interfectus a latronibus*, Was Killed by Robbers. On the other hand, a bandit's life was almost as dangerous as his victims'. Prison sentences were considered a waste of time and resources. Punishment was swift and severe, usually immediate execution. To pursue a living, bandits needed a good hideout.

Zosimus wrote, "The barbarians, who had hidden themselves in the swamps and woods near the lakes after escaping the punishment of the Romans, and having found a respite while Theodosius was preoccupied with the civil war, plundered Macedonia and Thessaly meeting no resistance."

But a year after the massacre in Thessaloniki, the civil war with Maxiumus was over and affairs in the West were settled. It had been too long since the Eastern emperor had ruled from the East. His neglect had led to family trouble. His junior emperor Arcadius, barely a teenager, was flexing his imperial muscles to the detriment of his stepmother Galla, whom he had banished from the palace. It was time for the *pater familias*, the head of the household, to take charge again.

Late in the summer of 391 Theodosius made his way from Mediolanum through Thessaloniki toward Constantinople. Alaric and his bandits, prowling the Via Egnatia, must have been astounded to learn of the procession's approach. Besides the imperial guard there would have been droves of rich bureaucrats and administrators, noblemen including the consuls Timasius and Promotus, all their servants and slaves, ordinary workmen, and innumerable carts and wagons to transport all the tentage, gear, food, and supplies for everyone. It was undoubtedly the richest caravan in the world, and the bandit army showed military expertise in picking away at it. "Hearing news of the recent victory, and that the emperor was approaching," wrote Zosimus, "they again hid themselves in the marshes, and coming out stealthily at daybreak, carried off everything they could lay hands on before retreating to their hideout. So successfully did they carry out these robberies that the emperor soon thought them not men but demons."

Claudian, who admittedly often waxes hyperbolic, does credit that, "When he [Theodosius] returned from Thrace, Alaric blocked the Hebros waters to him."

According to Zosimus, the emperor, feeling invincible after the victories in the west and eager to trap these bandits, went off in disguise with a few men and horses to deal with them himself, personally beating their whereabouts out of a local informer. "Then, joining his army which was camped nearby, he led his forces to the barbarians' hideaway. He attacked and slew without regard for age, dragging some out of the swamp in which they were hidden, and butchering others in the water, thereby achieving a great massacre of the barbarians."

The consul Timasius was of no outstanding ability, his main attribute being that he was a relative of Theodosius' first wife, Empress Aelia Flaccilla, but he was not without experience with barbarians. He was a survivor of Adrianople, and judging by her name his wife Pentadia, by whom he had a young son, was Gaulish. He advised the emperor to let the surviving bandits scuttle back to their swamps, and give his troops time to rest and eat.

But Alaric and the bandits had not gone. They waited for the legionaries to relax their guard, then fell on them and came near to trapping Theodosius himself in his tent. "The emperor and his closest attendants," wrote Zosimus, "were utterly surprised and attempted to escape the incipient danger by a quick retreat."

They ran into Promotus coming the other way. He conducted the emperor, fellow consul, and their retinues to safety, then counterattacked and drove off the bandits yet again. Zosimus tells of repeated slaughter among Alaric's men, but the close call was enough for Theodosius. Considering his point made, and that warring with robber bands was beneath imperial concern, he declared victory and resumed his travels. The renegade Goths could take a certain pride in seeing him on his way, and some historians assert that Alaric's first appearance on the world stage was to boast of running off an emperor.

"When he returned to Constantinople," recorded Zosimus of Theodosius, "he was full of pride because of his success over Maximus, but was so depressed over what he and his army had been through with the barbarians in the marshes, that he resolved to be done with wars for all time."

He left the problem of Gothic bandits to his underling Rufinus. This didn't sit well with Timasius and Promotus, who felt the Master of Offices too often stirred up trouble and left others to deal with it. In return Rufinus badmouthed Promotus to the extent that the consul slapped him in public. Rufinus went running to the emperor. "Rufinus, who for numerous reasons was an enemy to many people, through his obsessive ambition to be superior to everyone," wrote Zosimus, "…persuaded the emperor to dispatch Promotus away from the court to conduct military exercises."

But while the consul organized his legions for the campaign, Rufinus sent word ahead. "He paid some barbarians to lie in ambush as Promotus was entering Thrace," accused Zosimus. The ex-*foederati* among the bandits still harbored a grudge against the consul for the slaughter on the Danube and the fight in the marshes, and the ex-legionaries among them had military training. There was more than one way to earn Roman gold, and some involved killing Romans – for instance, taking money from Rufinus to kill Promotus. "These, as they had been ordered, took him by surprise and slew him."

Promotus had served the Empire in Africa, presumably under Theodosius the Elder. His two sons were playmates of the emperor's boys, Arcadius and Honorius, and probably Stilicho's son Eucherius as well. Promotus had taken Bauto's daughter, Aelia Eudoxia, into his own home to raise as a daughter. Of him Zosimus wrote, "He was above the desire for wealth, and had acted with sincerity toward both the empire and the emperors, but received his just reward for foolishly serving those who conducted the public business so negligently and impiously."

A good man was dead, and the robbers were still at large. An example needed to be made of Alaric and his men, but who to administer it?

Over the intervening years Stilicho had only risen in Theodosius' estimation. He was now a father of three, his son Eucherius and two small daughters, Maria and Aemilia Materna Thermantia. (Their birth dates are unknown. Eucherius was born in Rome soon after the defeat of Maximus in late 388 or early 389. So Maria, likely named after her grandmother on one side or the other, could have been born no earlier than late 389, and Thermantia, probably named for Serena's grandmother, the wife of Theodosius the Elder, no earlier than late 390.) By 393 the former *comes domesticorum* was *comes et magister utriusque militiae*, count and commander in chief, though probably only *per Thracias*, of Thrace. That had been Promotus' last rank and command, and now it was time to avenge him.

This would not be a matter of cornering a handful of robbers; by this time they amounted to a small rebel army, who had the sympathies even of some of Theodosius' Goth mercenaries. Two of their generals, Fravitta and Eriulf, drank too much at dinner in the palace. Fravitta, a pagan, favored the treaty with the Romans. Eriulf, an Arian, did not. They fell to quarreling, to the point that Theodosius called a halt to festivities. As they went out, however, Fravitta's anger got the better of him. He drew his sword and killed Eriulf. Before their men went at each other, Theodosius' imperial guards – perhaps at Stilicho's command – separated them. Pagan or not, Fravitta's loyalties were confirmed, and his standing at court assured.

That of the Goths as a whole was not. The bandits and rebels out in the marshes were setting a bad example. Alaric, now in his early twenties, had proven himself a leader capable not only of holding such a mixed band together, and leading it, but of cornering and killing a Roman general. Perhaps to catch a barbarian required another barbarian.

Maybe it was Stilicho's barbarian blood that led him to not underestimate Alaric the way Promotus had. Assigned the task of handling the renegade Goths, in short order his forces drove them out of the swamps of the Hebros delta. Alaric and his band sought the next-best refuge: the narrow passes and deep gorges of the Rhodope Mountains, just to the northwest. The twisted maze of ravines cloaked in oak and pine forests could hide an entire army. But it could hide a pursuing army as well, and Stilicho soon proved he was more than a match for Alaric, particularly in maneuvers. According to Claudian, Stilicho used the local geography against the Goths: "You alone succeeded in penning the vast army of barbarians, who had long been ravaging the land of Thrace, within the narrow confines of a single valley."

The choice was between driving in on the trapped enemy, or letting them starve. According to Claudian, Stilicho was game for either. Now, however, came fresh orders from Constantinople. The rebels were to be spared.

Theodosius, as he had with Athanaric after Adrianople, had decided that it was better to have such capable troops as Alaric and his men fighting for the Empire than against it. Promotus' death was to be swept under the carpet. The imperial henchman Rufinus, newly promoted to *praefectus praetorio Orientis*, a post originating as commander of the Praetorian Guard, the imperial bodyguards, but now amounting to prime minister of the East, arrived to deliver the news, conduct the negotiations, and possibly cover up his own involvement in the consul's killing. For Claudian, who would have heard the story years later from Stilicho, the fault lay entirely with the Master of Offices: "These tribes would have been totally destroyed had not a traitor whispered a devious trick in the emperor's ear, causing him to stay his hand, resulting in swords sheathed, the siege raised, and the prisoners granted amnesty."

The rebels were not only to be spared, they were to be admitted into the Roman army. More than that, Alaric was to be given rank – named tribune, in command.*

Theodosius had set the precedent, after Adrianople, by making over the barbarians into an imperial army. Now the technique was proven to be no fluke, but standard policy. The Empire would make a habit of placating the Goths.

Stilicho would not. Possibly – probably – because of his Vandal blood, he was one of the few Roman generals who could, and would, defeat the Goths on the battlefield. He was to find, however, that they rarely stayed beaten. For his part, Alaric could plainly see that the Empire was not a monolithic, united entity. It was a conglomeration of factions, often at odds, detesting each other more than they did the Goths, who therefore could be played against each other.

For now, though, Stilicho owed it to Emperor Theodosius to stand by and let the Master of Offices fritter away his victory. By imperial decree, Alaric and Stilicho, instead of enemies, were declared comrades in arms.

Tribunus militum, military tribune, as opposed to *tribunus plebis*, people's tribune, a political posting.

V

The Battle of the Frigidus

AD 394

Since the Emperor knew they [the Goths] were loyal to him and his people, he took more than twenty thousand of their warriors to war against the tyrant Eugenius.

Jordanes

By grooming barbarians like Alaric and Rufinus for high office, Theodosius might have convinced himself that he had become adept at domesticating them for Roman service. Yet they were dangerous pets, needing a strong master lest they run wild again. In Vienne, in Gaul, his tame Frank, Arbogastes, was taking his stewardship of the young junior emperor Valentinian II to extremes.

"The Frankish allies held command of the military, and even the civilian offices were controlled by Arbogastes' faction," recorded the 5th-century historian Renatus Profuturus Frigeridus, "and despite their oaths of loyalty none of the soldiery listened to the emperor or obeyed his commands."

As Theodosius' appointed representative in the West, given the authority to run the Western Empire, Arbogastes ran it as though he was himself emperor. He filled the ranks of his army and replaced Valentinian's courtiers with his fellow Franks, more loyal to him than the emperor. Quickly the Western government became less Roman than barbarian. Valentinian, now about twenty-one, felt he should be the one giving the orders. Instead he was a prisoner in his own palace. Appeals to Theodosius coming to nothing, he finally, unwisely, summoned Arbogastes to the throne room and literally handed him his dismissal in writing. According to Gibbon, the barbarian merely tossed the papers on the ground: "My authority does not depend on the smile, or the frown, of a monarch."[1]

As might be expected upon such insult to his young manhood, Valentinian felt himself obliged to kill the barbarian personally, and tried to draw a sword from a guard's scabbard. He was restrained, no doubt to the amusement, or disappointment, of Arbogastes. The barbarian settled the matter by a more civilized method. A few days later Valentinian was found dead, rope marks about his neck. The story was put out that he had hanged himself in despair, but it was widely assumed that Arbogastes, who after all had already assassinated one junior emperor, Maximus' son Flavius Victor, had ordered this other one strangled.

As a barbarian, the Senate would have denied Arbogastes the imperial crown. Apparently still desiring the legitimacy of Roman approval – because without it, he would sooner or later have to face Theodosius as had Maximus, a usurper – Arbogastes made himself Western emperor in all but name. He raised up one Flavius Eugenius, then nothing more than a lowly secretary of the court, and proclaimed him *Imperator Caesar* Flavius Eugenius *Augustus*, Emperor of the Western Roman Empire.

A portrait of Eugenius on a silver *siliqua* coin dating from his reign shows him in profile, with a pearl diadem, a short beard, and a very Roman hawk nose. He was not a born ruler, but that is the exact reason why Arbogastes had chosen him. "Eugenius," wrote Sozomen, "who was hardly sincere in claiming he was Christian, was ambitious to reign, and assumed the regalia of imperial power."

Since his conversion Theodosius had championed Christianity. He had outlawed paganism, forbidden pagan holidays, sacked pagan temples, and even banned the Olympic Games as a pagan festival. (They would not be revived as the modern games until 1896.) But with his new title and Arbogastes' backing, it was within Eugenius'

[1] *History*, Vol. III, p. 58

power to reassert the pagan Rome of old. They reappointed sixty-year-old Virius Nicomachus Flavianus as praetorian prefect (prime minister, an appointment Theodosius had rescinded), and made him consul of the West, nominally the second most powerful man behind the emperor. Flavianus renewed public, pagan religious ceremonies, restored shrines to the old gods, and generally revived paganism across the Western Empire. Matters reached the point that Bishop Ambrose of Mediolanum bolted to Florence, from where he scolded "Christian" Eugenius for his leniency toward pagans, and wrote to Theodosius in Constantinople, imploring him to intervene.

So the question Eugenius, Arbogastes, and Flavianus had to put to the gods was, of course, not only whether Theodosius in the East would challenge their supremacy in the West, but whether paganism would ultimately triumph over the rising tide of Christianity. Conveniently for their purposes, Flavianus was also *haruspex*, a seer.

Sozomen tells us, "Flavianus, then a praetorian prefect, an educated man, and one appearing to have a talent for politics, was noted for being skilled with all means of predicting the future." He had a calf's throat cut and its liver excised. By comparing the organ's color and texture to that of the heavens, a seer could answer simple yes/no questions about the future. According to Sozomen, "He encouraged Eugenius to declare war by assuring him that the throne was his destiny, that his military endeavors would result in victory, and that Christianity would be abolished."

Arbogastes, for one, would have put much stock in such predictions. In those days Germanic religion (the Franks, like the Vandals and Goths, were a Germanic people) was an admixture of the old gods – the *Allfadir*, All Father Woden (Odin), Donar (Thor), and the rest – with their counterparts among Roman deities. Unlike the Romans, prior to becoming civilized the Franks had not drawn the line at human sacrifice. Their wild-eyed, white-gowned, knife-wielding priestesses had slashed men's throats to bleed them into magic cauldrons and spilled their guts on the ground to divine the future. If Arbogastes had his way – and if the gods were with him, and Eugenius and Flavianus – they might very soon have a surplus of live prisoners to do with as they willed. Rufinus tells us these three "tainted Rome with the blood of their cursed victims, analyzing the organs of cattle, and, from their foresight based on these entrails, announced that Eugenius was certain of victory."

Theodosius' response to yet another usurpation was to place his trust in yet another outlander of dubious loyalty, and in his own preferred form of prophecy.

This outlander is described to us mainly by people who hated him, most of them with good reason. Claudian probably never met him, but by the decade's end would know him by reputation, and famously spared him no vitriol. "His skin had grown slack with age; his face, more wrinkly than a raisin, had sunken in due to the lines in his cheeks," he would claim. "…His gray skin and skeletal frame revolted his masters' hearts, and his horrible complexion and rail-thin body offended everyone who saw him, frightening children, disgusting people at dinner, disgracing other slaves, terrifying those who met him like an evil omen."

In his defense, it was a hard life that had twisted the features of Eutropius, emissary of the court of Theodosius. If Claudian is to be believed, as a youth in Syria or Armenia he had been castrated and sold as a gelding into the sex-slave markets of Anatolia. Even as his boyish beauty and usefulness wore out, however, he had learned to survive by his wits, becoming a procurer and pimp to the greatest men of the Empire. In the service of the barbarian general Flavius Abundantius, the *magister utriusque militiae*, master of cavalry and infantry, supreme military commander of the Empire, he had found his way to the imperial court in Constantinople. Even as Abundantius became consul, his creature Eutropius made himself useful to the emperor Theodosius. This talent for serving great men – and Theodosius' personal superstition – was why Eutropius was dispatched across the Mediterranean to Egypt and over 350 miles up the Nile to the riverside town of Lycopolis, the City of Wolves.

So far upriver that its citizens spoke their own dialect of Coptic, Lycopolis, modern Asyut, lay in the Nitrian Desert between a pair of 2,000-foot mountain ranges that shielded it from rain and made it the driest city in Egypt. Once sacred to Wepwawet and Anubis, Egyptian gods of the wolf and jackal – gods of the dead – in more recent times it had become better known for monasticism, asceticism, and devotees to the Christian God, most notably the hermit John of Lycopolis. As Gibbon told it, "In the neighborhood of that city, and on the summit of a lofty mountain, the holy John had constructed with his own hands an humble cell, in which he had dwelt above fifty years, without opening his door, without seeing the face of a woman, and without tasting any food that had been prepared by fire or any human art."[1]

"John the Egyptian monk," recorded the *Gallic Chronicle*, a contemporary set of annals documenting the years from Theodosius' accession, "…on account of the purity of his life earned the grace of prophecy from the Lord."

As he had with Maximus, the Eastern emperor hesitated to march on the pagans Arbogastes and Eugenius. After all, it was he who had ordered the massacre in Thessaloniki, sent the Frank to assassinate Maximus' Christian son, Victor, and assigned him as guardian over ill-fated Christian Valentinian II as well. An onlooker might have concluded that the greatest threat to Christianity in the Empire was the emperor himself.

"Theodosius was undecided as to whether he should go to war," wrote Sozomen, "or whether he should attack Eugenius…. So he sent Eutropius, a palace eunuch of tested loyalty, to Egypt with orders to fetch John to the court if possible, but if he refused to come, to learn what course to take."

By this time John was apparently some ninety years old. His body had withered to the point that his beard no longer grew. He granted audiences only through a small window in the door to his mountaintop cell. If he saw into the soul of Eutropius, he made no mention of it. By now, however, he was accustomed to advising high officials, and to the eunuch's question carefully couched his answer.

"The monk could not be prevailed upon to visit the emperor, but he sent word through Eutropius that the war would end in Theodosius' favor, and that the tyrant would be put to death," recounted Sozomen, "but that, after the victory, Theodosius would himself lose his life in Italy."

The emperor may have felt he had little to lose. In May of 394 his beautiful young wife Galla died of a miscarriage, and their unborn son John with her. "Theodosius grieved for the dead Empress for about a single day," wrote Eunapius, "for the preparations for the ensuing war overshadowed his sorrow for his wife." Their first son, Gratian, had died as an infant, and their daughter Galla Placidia was at most four years old. Theodosius' elder son, the *Augustus* Arcadius, being

[1] *History*, Vol. III, pp. 60–61

about seventeen, he named his younger son Honorius as *Augustus* beside him and put his *praefectus praetorio Orientis*, Rufinus, in charge of both as *epitropos*, guardian.* The emperor then called upon his son-in-law Stilicho, now *magister utriusque militiae per Thracias*, master of Thracian troops, and summoned up his Gothic auxiliaries, including their new tribune, Alaric. And in the same month his wife died, Emperor Theodosius led the Eastern Roman army out of the capital of the East, to conquer the capital of the West.

Mediolanum had been a walled city since the days of the Republic, and its walls had been expanded by Emperor Maximian in the late 200s, but its outermost wall was that of the Alps. Over the centuries those lofty snow-covered peaks had forced armies, including Hannibal's and Caesar's, through a few well-known passes. To the east, the Julian Alps have their own set of choke points. Two thousand feet up, the wide Illyro-Italic Gate, today called the Postojna Gate, connects the Great Hungarian Plain to northern Italy. In prehistory this was part of the Amber Road from the Baltic, and was said to have been taken by Jason and the Argonauts in their search for the Golden Fleece. In recognition of its importance, in AD 14 the Legio XIII *Gemina*, the Twin Legion, laid a road the length of the valley, which by AD 270 had developed into part of a strategic, fortified network, the *Claustra Alpium Iuliarum*, the Barrier of the Julian Alps. As Sozomen wrote, "Raising an army, Eugenius took control of the gates of Italy, which the Romans so call the Julian Alps, a high and steep mountain range. These he seized prior to battle and fortified, for there was only one path through the narrows, each side blocked by cliffs and the tallest mountains."

In September of 394 Theodosius led his imperial army, 50,000 strong, down out of the Julians toward the coastal plain. Above the winding column, among its holy crosses, rose the standards and banners of the East: Armenia, Iberia, and Isauria (southern Turkey), Parthia and Media (Iran), Arabia and Egypt. Bacurius Hiberus, the tribune of impetuous cavalry at Adrianople, had not been blamed

---

*Theodosius seems to have eschewed the title of *Caesar*, junior emperor, for his sons, even in their minority. This was not so much a diminishment of the title *Augustus* but perhaps, as future events would show, a demonstration of his intent to create an even higher rank for himself.

for their failure, but had risen to the post of *comes domesticorum*, count of military staff, and *dux Palaestinae*, military commander in Palestine, commanding the troops from Asia Minor and the Middle East. Saulus, a pagan despite his biblical name, led the contingent of Alans. Old Richomeres had passed away before having to face his nephew Arbogastes; in his place was the former consul Flavius Timasius, now *magister equitum et peditum*, master of horse and foot, overall military commander.

"When he marched against Eugenius," reported Socrates of Theodosius, "a very large number of the barbarians from beyond the Danube volunteered to fight, and followed him on his campaign." These barbarian auxiliaries marched at the front: no fewer than 20,000 Goths. Their chieftain, Gainas, had risen from foot soldier to become *comes rei militaris*, imperial commander of the army. And Alaric, just a few years earlier nothing more than a bandit chief, was now a Roman tribune. If luck was with him, he might even someday succeed to Gainas's title, but for one who stood in his way.

"He also named Stilicho general," wrote Eunapius of Theodosius, "a man of barbarian descent, who enjoyed imperial authority because he was married to Serena." Third in command, as *magister utriusque militiae per Thracias*, master of Thracian troops, Stilicho had enlisted the warriors of that province in the emperor's service. He and Alaric, so recently opponents on the battlefield, must have found themselves uneasy allies on this march.

Theodosius was doubtless surprised that the rebels had not already come through the valley the other way to intercept him out on the inland plain. Arbogastes was evidently wary of the imperial cavalry and not inclined to give them room to maneuver. Lest Theodosius pin them under siege, the rebels did not even man the old Roman fortifications nearer the coast. Arbogastes had chosen rather to bet everything on a decisive battle, and to make the most of the mountainous terrain. He chose as his site the "Door to Roman Italia."

"It is there," wrote Claudian, "where the farthest reaches of the Alps narrow down into sinuous valleys and cover large areas with unbreakable barriers of tumbled rock."

Just east of the city of Ajdovscina in modern Slovenia, which grew up around a Roman fortress there, the narrow valley of Bela (White) Creek threads out onto the broad plain of the Vipava River. In Roman times this was the Fluvius Frigidus, Cold River, and then, as now, it sprang full-force from under the Nanos Plateau and ran down through a fertile land of fruit orchards and grape arbors leading to the Adriatic coast. Any invaders out of the east would traverse this valley on their way to Mediolanum.

Orosius wrote, "Eugenius and Arbogastes had arrayed their army in battle formation on the plain and, having very shrewdly sent parties ahead in ambush, had occupied the alpine slopes and the necessary passes in order to achieve a strategic victory, despite being fewer in number."

"On coming down from the heights of these peaks," Sozomen reported, "Theodosius saw the plain before him covered with foot soldiers and horsemen, and at the same time learned that enemy troops were behind him, setting ambushes on the mountain crags." That a pagan army opposed him, there could be no doubt. Flavianus had raised a statue of Jupiter on the field, and Arbogastes' troops – Franks, Alemanni, Gallo-Romans, and his own Gothic mercenaries – lined up under banners of the pagan demigod Hercules.

Theodosius called his generals to a council of war. It's easy to imagine young Alaric and Stilicho among the veteran commanders at this meeting, eyeing each other and swallowing their mutual dislike. In Alaric's view Stilicho, the half-breed barbarian, had attained rank largely by privilege of birth, marrying up, and pretending to be a full-blooded Roman. As far as Stilicho was concerned, Alaric had achieved position by making himself less troublesome to the Empire as an officer than as a robber chief, and in his Roman arms and armor was engaged in no less a masquerade. Yet both were here in service of the same, greater cause.

Theodosius had bigger worries than animosity among his officers. Arbogastes and Eugenius had let him file his army, unopposed, into a trap. The pass they were in was too narrow, and the hills to either side too steep, for the mass of imperial forces to move up from the rear and engage. Effectively outnumbered across their front, the emperor's generals recommended pulling back to try again in the spring, but Theodosius refused. It would be wrong, he told them, to show such weakness before the Holy Cross for which they fought, and to the image of Hercules on the standards of the enemy. "He said this in true faith," declared Theodoret, "though the available troops were few and disheartened."

The decision having been made to fight, Theodosius put the brunt of it on the Goths. "He thought it best to put the barbarian troops in the vanguard and to send them first," wrote Zosimus. "He ordered Gainas with his troops to make the initial attack, and the other barbarian commanders to follow him with cavalry, horse archers, or infantry."

Gainas, Alaric, and the Goths must have taken these orders with some doubt. To hurl themselves, outnumbered and lightly supported, at a prepared position made no sense. Alaric in particular, being so recently a foe of the Romans, might be excused for wondering why he and his men had been selected for such a task. Even Gibbon suspected that Theodosius, having nothing to lose, "cherished a secret wish that the bloody conflict might diminish the pride and numbers of the conquerors [Goths]."[1]

But Gainas had not risen so far in Roman service by disobeying orders or showing fear. Over 200 years later the Byzantine emperor Maurice, author of the war manual *The Strategikon*, wrote of the Germanics, "Bold and reckless as they are, they consider any lack of bravery and any slightest retreat as a disgrace." Twenty thousand Goth tribesmen answered their emperor's call and prepared to die.

Standard Roman military practice was for cavalry to form on the flanks of the infantry line and attack from there, but there was no room for that in the confines of the valley, and it's unclear from the chronicles whether the Goths' initial charge was made on foot or horseback. Cavalry or infantry, at the Frigidus, made little difference. Sozomen recounted, "The vanguard of Theodosius' army attacked the infantry waiting on the plain, and a savage and very uncertain battle began."

Details of the Battle of the Frigidus are sparse. We know the two sides tore at each other all day, to no result. Few of the combatants were actual Romans. Syrian fought Frank who fought Goth who fought Alemann, or other Goth, in a tangle of weaponry and armor and curses from across 2,800 miles of empire, all splashed with sweat and blood, while the air overhead whistled with arrows, javelins,

---

[1]*History*, Vol. III, p. 62

plumbatae, and *franciscae*.* Theodosius' Goths – Alaric's Goths – made two charges and their eastern allies backed them up, to no avail. "In that area of the field where the Romans fought their own countrymen the outcome was in doubt," recorded Socrates Scholasticus, possibly a bit biased against *foederati*, "but where the Emperor Theodosius' barbarian auxiliaries were engaged, Eugenius' troops proved much superior."

According to Orosius, half the Goths in the imperial army – 10,000 men – were slain that day, and their incipient retreat was nearly fatal when some of the Western Romans gave chase. "When the emperor saw the barbarians being struck down, he threw himself in great despair on the ground, and begged God's help in his hour of need," wrote Socrates, "nor was his request unheard; for his commander Bacurius, filled with sudden, unexpected courage, rushed with his men to where the barbarians were in direst straits, broke through the enemy ranks, and routed those who only a moment before were on the verge of victory."

According to most accounts, the Battle of the Frigidus lasted two days. Eunapius, however, maintained a different darkness fell over the battle: "In the middle of the day the sun went dark and the stars came out, so that the soldiers, in sudden confusion, perished in darkness, with great loss of life on both sides." And Zosimus, relying heavily on Eunapius, concurs: "When the two armies were engaged, so great an eclipse of the sun occurred, that for more than half the battle it was night instead of day."

Turning back the astronomical clock, it can be seen that a total eclipse did occur in that part of the world, visible in both Rome and Constantinople, but on November 20, 393, almost a year prior to the Battle of the Frigidus. No other sources besides Eunapius and Zosimus mention an eclipse in connection with the battle. To match it to that date requires moving the date of Theodosius' invasion, the succession of his sons, and even the date of the last ancient Olympic Games. It seems more likely that Eunapius got his dates wrong and his "nights" mixed up (perhaps on purpose, to invoke the hand of God), and Zosimus repeated the error. He took note of at least one effect: "Since they fought a kind of night battle, so great a slaughter occurred that at

---

*Frankish throwing axes, which by the next century would be their characteristic weapon.

the time the greater number of Theodosius' allies were slain along with their commander Bacurius, who fought very bravely leading them, while the other commanders barely escaped with the rest."

Upon the fall of darkness Theodosius' forces fell back, surrendering the field. Yet with Arbogastes' reserves in the hills around and behind them, the Eastern forces could not withdraw. Trapped in the narrow valley, having lost half their number, the Goths could well imagine that on the morrow the Western army, and their own inept emperor, would see the rest of them slain as well.

"When night fell and the armies had retired," Zosimus recounted, "Eugenius was so pleased with his triumph, that he awarded money to those who had acted with the greatest valor in the battle, and permitted them to celebrate, as though after such a defeat there was no likelihood of more fighting." Flavianus' divination was bearing out. The old gods had asserted themselves over the upstart Judean deity. The Western triumvirate were already envisioning the revival of pagan Rome. According to Paulinus, deacon of Mediolanum, "Arbogastes and the prefect Flavianus had sworn as they were leaving Mediolanum, that on their return, they would make the basilica of the church at Mediolanum into a stable and would draft the clerics into military service."

For his part Theodosius had to consider that in this contest of the gods, his had come out second best. His former commander Arbogastes had out-fought him, and his Gothic allies had failed him. To retreat and fight again might be their way, but it was not the Roman way. According to Maurice, "If a battle ends in a defeat, we think it unwise and pointless to send those same defeated troops back into combat immediately, or within the next several days. We strongly advise any general to not even think of doing this."

But for Theodosius even retreat meant coming under the arrows and bolts of the enemy on the heights above the valley behind him, possibly even being surrounded and annihilated. To achieve victory would require a miracle from the God of Abraham. The emperor retreated alone to his tent on a rise above the camp to ask for it.

Where Alaric and Stilicho were in all this went, still, unremarked in the chronicles. The pair were as yet only minor characters in history, and neither distinguished himself much at the Frigidus. As a chieftain among the Goths, Alaric surely took part in the initial fighting, in which half his brethren were slaughtered to no purpose. That evening he had to be wondering whether he would soon join them. The shock of such killing must have stunned the survivors like a punishment by the Christian God, but Germanic warriors wasted no time in mourning. "They soon cease with tears and sorrow, grief and regret," Tacitus had written. "They think it womanish to cry over their friends, but manly to remember them."

For his part Stilicho had most likely spent the day at the side of his superiors, Theodosius and Timasius, watching the bitter defeat play out. It would have been difficult, however, for him not to take note of the Goths' utter bravery in the face of death, even as he took a lesson in imperial gamesmanship. In retrospect, and in light of future events, Theodosius may have been testing his underlings. It would be only natural for him to have the ex-bandit chief Alaric and his men prove their loyalty to the Empire. And it was Stilicho's duty to obey orders as well, whether or not he agreed with them.

Imagine these two crossing paths in the imperial camp that night. As a commander it would have been essential for Stilicho to gauge the Goths' willingness to continue the fight in the morning. Whether or not he found Gainas and Alaric at all enthusiastic about the prospect can only be conjectured, as can their opinion of a Roman who led from the rear. Then again, come dawn they would all very likely be facing death together, which tends to render all of men's differences petty in comparison.

As for the emperor, Theodoret recounted, "Before dawn sleep overcame him, and as he lay there he dreamed of two men in white garments riding white horses, who bade him be cheerful, control his fear, and in the morning arm and assemble his men for battle. 'For we have been sent to fight for you,' they told him, and one said, 'I am John the Evangelist,' and the other, 'I am Philip the Apostle.'"

The emperor was not alone in this vision. A tribune brought him a common soldier who reported having the same dream, which Theodosius took as vindication: "The empire's protector has given the message to this man as well, that he may bear witness that I speak the truth."

Modern skeptics might assume the soldier alone had the dream, which Theodosius claimed for his advantage. It was not a vision of the saints, however, which proved to be the emperor's deliverance. "The first way to salvation," reported Orosius, "was in the arrival of Arbitio, a count of the opposing side."

This *comes* had been among those assigned by Arbogastes to occupy the slopes of the valley and cut off Theodosius' retreat. It is uncertain, and doubtful, whether he was the same Arbitio who, some 40 years earlier, had served as general and consul under the emperors Constantius III, Julian, and Valens, who would have by this time been an old man, more likely dead. This Arbitio may well have been his son, though, for he was, as Ammianus described his namesake, "a man of sharp wit and always willing to betray anyone."

"When he had found the unwitting emperor in his trap," continued Orosius, "he went over to the side of the *Augustus*, not only relieving him of danger, but suggesting a defense for him." Seeing these traitors as God's answer to his prayers, Theodosius immediately struck a bargain with them. With his rear secure and his manpower replenished by the turncoat troops, the emperor still had a choice to make. Retreat or attack?

"Let us put aside our fear," Theodosius told his men. "Let us follow our vanguard [i.e., the Goths] and our commander [i.e., God]. Let none weigh the odds of victory by the number of the men involved, but let every man depend on the generalship of our leaders."

Zosimus, having already expended one miracle in his retelling, claims the emperor and his troops caught the enemy at dawn, still amid, or recovering from, their victory celebrations: "While they were resting themselves, the emperor Theodosius about daybreak surprised them with his whole army, while they were still lying on the ground, and slew them before they knew he was coming."

Theodoret, however, credited another miracle: "A violent wind blew right in the enemy's faces, turning aside their arrows and javelins and lances, so that their missiles were of no use, and neither foot soldier nor archer nor spearman could inflict any damage upon the imperial troops."

"Some soldiers who took part in the battle told me that the missiles they threw were snatched out of their hands by a powerful wind, which blew from the direction of Theodosius' army upon them," concurred Augustine, "nor did it only speed along the darts which were hurled against them, but also blew back upon them the darts they were throwing."

This miracle, at least, is not out of the question. Even today the Vipava Valley is notorious for the severity of its *bora*: cold, high-density air pouring down out of the alpine hilltops with hurricane force, in excess of 125 miles per hour, so common that trees in the valley grow with their branches permanently swept downhill. Socrates calls the bora that blew that day at the Frigidus a "violent wind," and Orosius "a great and extraordinary whirlwind." Theodoret claims vast clouds of dust were blown into the defenders' faces, and though the bora is usually noted more for stinging rain the effect was the same. All agree it was enough to turn back the defenders' darts and arrows and javelins to fall among them.

Meanwhile Theodosius' troops, with the wind at their backs, launched their missiles ahead of them and fell upon the foe like avenging angels. Few if any other battles of the ancient world were ever fought in hurricane-force winds, where freezing rain washed away the warm splash of blood. We can be assured Stilicho and Alaric were both in the thick of it now, cutting and slashing and stabbing at their emperor's command. "The Alpine snows were stained red," proclaimed Claudian (the battle taking place in late summer notwithstanding), "the cold Frigidus, its waters filled with blood, ran steaming hot, and would have been clogged with heaps of the dead had not their own streaming gore helped it along."

Hyperbole aside, as proof of the Christian God's intervention, this blast of icy wind unnerved Arbogastes' pagans. Theodoret declared, "The defeated then realized the divine help given to the victors, dropped their weapons, and pleaded with the emperor for quarter."

Theodosius' warriors swarmed over the enemy lines. If the wind didn't topple Flavianus' statue of Jupiter, the Christians did. So quick was the turnaround, what with the wind and noise and confusion, Eugenius wasn't even sure what was happening. Seeing troops running up the hill toward his position, he asked them if they were bringing Theodosius in chains, per his orders. "No," they told him, "we are not bringing him, we are here to deliver you to him, as our great ruler has ordered." They dragged him off his chariot and locked him in irons. In less than an hour Emperor Eugenius went from celebrating his triumph to being a prisoner of war.

"The victory being so turned," recorded Socrates, "the usurper fell before the emperor's feet, and begged for his life." Blaming Eugenius for the death of Valentinian (which in fairness was Arbogastes' doing), for his usurpation (which he may have undertaken at the point of the Frank's sword), and for the war waged against his rightful overlord (in which Theodosius was the aggressor), the emperor also made a point of ridiculing the pagans' confidence in their banners of Hercules and statue of Jupiter, before at last pronouncing judgment. As Gibbon recounted it, "The rhetorician Eugenius, who had almost acquired the dominion of the world, was reduced to implore the mercy of the conqueror, and the unrelenting soldiers separated his head from his body as he lay prostrate at the feet of Theodosius."[1]

As for the rest of the pagan triumvirate, Arbogastes and Flavianus escaped captivity, but had nowhere to go. Hunted, on the run, within a few days of the battle both killed themselves.

"Butchered men are piled up on a heap and fill the lowest valley as high as the hills," trumpeted Claudian, "corpses tangled in their own blood; the netherworld is shaken with the influx of dead."

"So here a civil war was resolved by the blood of two men," wrote Orosius, "as well as those ten thousand Goths whom Theodosius ordered to attack first, and whom Arbogastes is said to have completely slaughtered." In a rather sinister aside, he confided, "To have lost those was certainly a gain, and their loss a victory."

For the Eastern Empire the triumph at the Frigidus, and for the West the defeat, was total. The remains of the rebel army offered no resistance to Theodosius as he continued his march to Aquileia and from there to Mediolanum, with his commanders Stilicho and Alaric at the head of the conquerors, and the head of Eugenius raised aloft on a spear. Most of the enemy survivors promptly went over to the imperial side, and why not? Only one Empire remained, and one true religion. Paganism had been decisively and demonstrably defeated. The soldiers, the common people of the Empire, even the senators in Rome could see the Christian god was all-powerful, and had made his

---

[1] *History*, Vol. III, p. 64

earthly minions so as well.* Eugenius was the last Roman emperor to support polytheism. With the religious issue resolved, only the political structure needed revisiting. The civil wars were over. The Empire was united under one emperor. Theodosius I would be known to history as Theodosius the Great.

There remained the question of the Goths, of course. Gainas and Alaric had done their duty, and paid for it in blood. They and their people were due their reward. As was Stilicho, who had stood his ground when fortune boded ill, and stood now with his emperor in victory. Their futures were as bright as that of the Empire.

After the battle, around the year's end, seven priests headed up by the monk Petronius (who would one day become bishop of Bologna and ultimately the patron saint of that city) made the pilgrimage from Jerusalem to visit the hermit John on his mountaintop at Lycopolis. They spent three days learning at his door, and on their departure, according to the 18th-century English Roman Catholic priest and hagiographer Alban Butler, John gave his blessing: "Go in peace, my children, and know that the news of the victory which the religious prince Theodosius has gained over the tyrant Eugenius, is this day come to Alexandria: but this excellent emperor will soon end his life by a natural death."

On their return downriver the priests indeed received news of Theodosius' victory at the Frigidus. How John could possibly know this will ever be a mystery. He passed away, by all accounts in his cell, on his knees in prayer, at the end of the year or early in 395.

Right about that same time, the second part of his prophecy played itself out.

<hr>

* It should be noted that some modern, secular historians scoff at the "Christian vs. Pagan" aspect of the Battle of the Frigidus, claiming the original writers had such a religious bent that they exaggerated their depictions. Still, Claudian and Zosimus were avowed pagans and didn't dispute the outcome. The West was led by pagans, and the East by a zealous Christian, and in those religious times most people would have seen the hand of God in events.

VI

*After Theodosius, the champion of peace and of the
Gothic people, had passed from human concerns, his sons
brought on the ruin of both empires by their opulent living
and by depriving their allies, the Goths,
of the customary rewards.*

Jordanes

Those waning months of 394 after the Battle of the Frigidus were perhaps the last golden age of Rome. With Arcadius, seconded by Rufinus, firmly on the throne in Constantinople, Theodosius summoned little Honorius and Galla Placidia to meet him in Mediolanum, where the younger son would henceforth rule as emperor of the West. There was to be an *Augustus* for the Eastern throne and another for the Western, with Stilicho, now elevated to *comes et magister utriusque militiae praesentalis*, count of the military and imperial commander in chief, looking after Honorius in the West, and Rufinus guiding Arcadius in the East. And – this is the most important part – Theodosius would rule over them all.

Not since the days of Constantine the Great, and arguably not since Emperor Diocletian a hundred years in the past, had one man ruled supreme from the Atlantic to the Euphrates. Theodosius would reign from a new, overall position, more than a *Caesar*, more than an *Augustus*. He would be a kind of *pater patriae*, the father of the country, in the manner of Romulus, Camillus, and the supreme emperors in the glory days of Rome.

That title of *pater patriae*, however, was officially conferred only by Senate approval, and they had not bestowed it on Theodosius, who journeyed to Rome to browbeat the pagan senators into accepting Christ. Zosimus reported, "In a speech he called on them to repent of their past mistakes, as he called them, and to join the Christian faith, which promises forgiveness of all sins and sacrileges..."

> But not a single one of them would agree, nor give up the ancient rituals which had been handed down to them from the founding of their city, but continued in unreasonable belief. Having observed them almost twelve hundred years, in which time their city was never conquered, if they changed faiths for others they could not predict what might ensue.

So Theodosius informed them the state would no longer subsidize pagan worship. "He ordered the pagan idols to be overthrown everywhere," approved Augustine of Hippo, "knowing well temporal rewards are not given by the power of demons, but by that of the true God."

Furthermore, according to Zosimus, "the priests of both sexes were defrocked and exiled, and the temples were forbidden to sacrifice."

The emperor's children were of like mind. "Serena, derisively insulting the gods, decided to visit the temple dedicated to them," continued Zosimus, who was himself pagan. "There, seeing some jewelry around the neck of the statue of Vesta befitting the worship that was paid to the goddess, she plucked them off the statue, and strung them around her own neck."

At the sight, an old crone came out to upbraid the princess for her affront. Serena not only cursed her out, she had her attendants drive the old woman off. Before she was gone, though, the crone – in fact, one of the last of the Vestal Virgins – prophesied that retribution for such sacrilege would fall on Serena, her husband, and her children.

"Serena took no notice of what she had said," confides Zosimus, "but left the temple happy with her new jewelry."

None of the Christians at the time seem to have recalled the story of Eve and the forbidden fruit.

The wrath of God, or the gods, descended on the emperor soon after his visit to Rome. "After defeating Eugenius, Theodosius the emperor lingered for some time at Mediolanum, and here he came down with a serious sickness," recorded Sozomen. "He recalled the prediction of the monk, John, and believed that his illness would be fatal."

It seems Theodosius was afflicted with edema, swelling due to fluid retention, possibly related to a heart condition. Such a death is neither quick nor painless. There are several forms of the disease, which is usually a symptom of a deeper malady, varying by the location of fluid accumulation. That Theodosius did not reportedly display swelling of the arms or legs, due to failure of the right side of the heart to pump blood to the lungs, might indicate that it was the left side of his heart failing to pump out his lungs. The emperor basically drowned, slowly, in his own blood.

"The Emperor Theodosius was, because of the worries and weariness caused by this war, thrown into physical sickness," wrote Socrates Scholasticus, "and concluding his disease would be the death of him, he became more worried about the affairs of state than his own life, considering how terrible disasters often befell the people after an emperor's death."

With his last rattling breaths, according to Claudian, he called his son-in-law Stilicho to his side: "Triumphant Stilicho, whose bravery in war and whose loyalty in peace I have proved – what military feat have I achieved without your aid? What victory have I won that you did not help me win?"

Having made his name as a poet in his native Egypt, Claudian had only arrived in Rome from Alexandria in 394, possibly even before the battle of the Frigidus, but as a court poet knew his job depended on glorifying and vindicating whoever was in power: Arbogastes, Theodosius, Stilicho. He dutifully set down the emperor's dying wish as Stilicho told it, very likely embellishing it for public consumption: "So come, since heaven claims me, and take up my work. Be sole guardian of my children, be the protector of my two sons."

The history of Roman boy emperors was not promising. Elagabalus, Severus Alexander, Gordian III, and Philip II had ruled in name, but always as puppets with powerful adults manipulating their strings, and they had paid the fatal price for their inexperience, usually assassinated by their own men. Theodosius did not wish the same fate for his sons, who took more after their gentle mother than him. And if he could not be there to guide and protect them, he needed someone worthy of taking his place, someone to become *pater patriae*.

How long Theodosius and Stilicho were alone together is not recorded. What was said is not known with any certainty. The entire scene must be regarded as apocryphal because, as has perplexed and bewildered historians to this day, neither Theodosius nor Stilicho saw to it that there were any witnesses, and as Ambrose attested, the emperor left behind no written will. But Stilicho went into that room as *comes et magister utriusque militiae praesentalis* and – according to him, at least – came out with the additional title of *parens principum*, official parent, not only of Honorius and Galla Placidia, but of Arcadius as well – head of the Theodosian dynasty and regent of the entire, united Roman Empire.

"When Theodosius had fought and killed the tyrant [Eugenius]," Claudian wrote to Stilicho, "he rose up into heaven, leaving the governance of the world to you. With a strength equal to his you bear up the unsteady structure of the empire that threatens each moment to fall."

Not everyone agreed.

"The whole empire being entrusted to Arcadius and Honorius, they indeed appeared entitled to the imperial authority," wrote Zosimus, "although the actual control of business was under Rufinus in the east, and Stilicho in the west." No one disputed that Theodosius had meant for Stilicho to serve as guardian of Galla, Honorius, and the West. His claim to also oversee the reign of Arcadius and the East, however, would be nothing but trouble. Even Stilicho must have been well aware of that. Arcadius was of legal age and required no regent. More than that, in Constantinople Rufinus, architect of the massacre in Thessaloniki and the death of Promotus in Thrace, and now consul and *praefectus praetorio Orientis*, chief minister of the East, had the elder *Augustus* wrapped around his finger and would not willingly relinquish his grip.

A contest between Rufinus and Stilicho meant yet more civil war, with no assurance who would come out on top, though Stilicho had the armies of both East and West under his command. Historians still argue whether he was honestly carrying out the will of his father-in-law, or seizing the moment to make a naked power grab. It's a dispute that will never be resolved. The written accounts, originally set down by those already for or against Stilicho, have all been chronicled and analyzed by historians of similar sympathies. The best way to judge Stilicho's intentions, therefore, is by his subsequent actions.

Right up to the moment of his death.

For the moment, as had been true for years and would continue to be true for years, the balance of power between East and West would be determined by which side was taken by the Goths. In the taverns and brothels of Mediolanum, that topic was surely the topic of heated discussion. There were two kinds of Goths in the Roman camp, two sides to the issue: loyalists like Fravitta and Gainas, enlisted in the legions and casting their lot with Rome, and *foederati* like Alaric – auxiliaries, part of the army yet separate from it, wanting to be Roman but still seen by the Romans as mere barbarians. Like any Roman legion, the *foederati* included women, children, slaves, and animals among their number, but the population of adult males was dwindling more rapidly in the service of Rome than ever at the hands of the Huns. Theodosius had sent half their warriors away to the Middle East. Of the half that remained, half had been slain at the Frigidus. To serve much longer as the sword hand of the Empire would render the Goth nation extinct.

It was apparent, however, that with the West pacified, the next war would be in the East. Across the Danube and the Caucasus Mountains, the distant thunder of Hunnish horses was getting louder, closer. With its army in the West and its Gothic buffer state diminished, the East itself for the first time lay wide open to the nomadic hordes. The Goths, however, had come in under the banner of Rome to escape Hunnish predation. Were they now expected to go east and fight Huns for Rome?

Imagine Gainas, Alaric, and the other Goth commanders, doubtless in their best new Roman togas and haircuts, summoned to the imperial palace in Mediolanum to receive the decision of Stilicho regarding their futures. Gainas probably had, but Alaric almost certainly had not, to this point experienced the full splendor and magnificence of Roman civilization. Polybius describes the plains of the Po Valley as rich in wine, grain, and fine-wooled sheep, with forests full of swine for both public and private consumption, and people famous for their hospitality. Mediolanum itself had started out in 600 BC as little more than a barbarian village on the banks of the Po, but in the 4th century the poet Decimius Ausonius, himself a Gallo-Roman from Aquitaine in modern France, acclaimed it among the ten most beautiful cities in the Empire. He cited its population of 100,000 cultivated and cheerful people, their elegant homes, chariot track, theater, plentiful temples, a mint, and the Baths of Hercules, for which a whole quarter of the city was named, all adorned with porticoes and marble statuary. Mediolanum, he declared, suffered nothing by comparison with Rome.

It was a homeland of which the Goths had only dreamed, and here they were in its very capital, looking forward to receiving their slice of it. Alaric in particular must have expected to be granted high rank and honor for his role in the victory at the Frigidus.

The ruins of the palace still stand in the western end of Milan, of which it was once the greater part. Within its walls was a self-contained city, complete with its own baths, chapels, military and civilian offices, and of course the imperial residence. It would have been a somber place, so soon after the death of the emperor. Perhaps Gainas and Alaric encountered little Honorius and his sister Galla, deprived of their playmates (for Serena and her children still resided in Constantinople at this time), little royals being schooled in the ways of government as they had been so cruelly schooled by life, or wandering the marbled halls and chambers in lonely grief. For a hundred years emperors had issued world-changing decrees and rendered life-and-death decisions from within these walls, as Arbogastes and Eugenius had made theirs. Today's missive by the de facto emperor, Stilicho, would be no less fateful.

Alaric and his Gothic troop were dismissed. They were being sent home.

This reeked of the same Roman thinking that had sent them first against the rebel army of Arbogastes and Eugenius at the Frigidus. Joining the Empire had cost the Goths much and gained them nothing. They still faced two impediments to their prosperity, both Rome and the Huns. They had expected to have the support of one against the other. And if they no longer had that, who instead was to lead them?

By his murder of Eriulf, Fravitta had chosen to be Roman instead of a Goth, making himself anathema to his own people, among whom he might more reasonably expect assassination than acclaim. And Gainas, though a Goth, was not of noble blood, having risen to mercenary command on the strength of his sword arm. Everything these two had, they owed to Rome. They were Roman officers, not Gothic. Both would remain in service to Rome. Neither of them had a say in the future of the Goths.

Then there was Alaric.

Alaric had shown both willingness and ability to fight Romans, and had made himself a Roman tribune by making himself a threat. He had every reason to try that ploy again, but if he and his dwindling contingent rose up now, they could expect to be crushed by Stilicho's combined armies, Gainas and Fravitta and the loyal Goths among them. In the West, Alaric and his people were disposable, to be used and thrown away, subject to the whim of Stilicho.

But in the East there was Rufinus, who had found the Goths, even rebellious ones, useful in the past, and might have use for them again.

Rufinus might seem an unlikely source of charity. After the assassination of Promotus, he had stepped over innumerable more dead bodies on the rise to his current post, and haunted the imperial palace in Constantinople like a specter hovering over the shoulder of Arcadius. Unlike Claudian, Philostorgius, a church historian who lived in Constantinople at the time, had met both the consul and the emperor personally. He described Arcadius as short and physically unimposing, dark-complexioned by his Spanish blood, slow to speak and dull of eye.* Rufinus, on the other hand, Philostorgius described as tall and manly, with a sharp eye and quick tongue. It would have

---

*In 1949, during excavations for Istanbul University in what had once been the Forum of Theodosius in Constantinople, workers uncovered a bust of Arcadius carved of marble from Mount Pentelicus in Greece. It was intended to be mounted on a torso, which was not found. The emperor wears a diadem edged with rows of pearls and rectangular stone on his forehead. Done in the angular, figurative, post-classical style of the late 4th century, it gives the emperor a goggle-eyed, incredulous expression.

been easy enough for such an imposing counselor to rule through the boy, eliminating personal enemies while he was at it.

In 391 the consul and praetorian prefect of the East, Flavius Eutolmius Tatianus – wealthy and flamboyant, fond of erecting statues of himself across the Empire – had stood in Rufinus' way. Rufinus had accused him of corruption, for which Theodosius dismissed Tatianus in disgrace, and his son Proculus, the prefect of Constantinople, with him. Rufinus succeeded to Tatianus' consulship and prefecture. Tatianus had accepted his fate, but Proculus fled for the hinterlands, possibly to stir up trouble.

Lucianus, the *comes Orientis* of Antioch, had been a minion of Rufinus until he spoke ill of the minister to Arcadius. The exact accusation is unspecified, but must have been serious. Zosimus relates, "Rufinus, as if in resentment for the blame laid to his charge by the emperor, without communicating his design to any person, proceeded with a very small retinue to Antioch. Having entered that city at midnight, he seized Lucianus, and brought him to trial without any accusation. He afterwards commanded him to be beaten on the neck with leaden balls until he expired." This act was so reviled by the Antiochenes that in atonement Rufinus, for all his sins a zealous Christian, paid for a beauteous portico to be erected to replace the city's Temple of Mercury.

On his return to the capital, however, Rufinus reverted to form. With a promise of leniency he convinced Tatianus to summon Proculus back to the capital, but on his arrival had the son beheaded in front of the father. Tatianus was also condemned to death, but in a cynical show of mercy reprieved and exiled. There was only one final step in Rufinus' master plan.

"Rufinus began to plan his way to becoming emperor," wrote Zosimus, "by marrying his own daughter, who was now of age, to the emperor [Arcadius], for by doing so he would be well positioned to run the government." By such marriage, Rufinus would make himself an imperial father-in-law, akin and equal to Stilicho. However, while he was away in Antioch another scheming climber had made a move behind his back.

The eunuch Eutropius, having lost his patron Theodosius, had been working overtime to ingratiate himself with Arcadius at Rufinus' expense. In their race to provide the young emperor with an empress, the eunuch proved himself the more experienced procurer. "He was devoted to his work," admitted Claudian, "he knew his business and had mastered every strategy to undo one's chastity. No amount of security could guard the marriage bed from his assault, no bars could hold him at bay."

He recommended to Arcadius none other than Aelia Eudoxia, the daughter of the late Frankish general Bauto, raised in the house of Rufinus' victim Promotus. "Seeing that the emperor was open to suggestion, he showed him her picture," wrote Zosimus, "by which he aroused Arcadius with so ardent a passion for her, that he soon persuaded him to resolve to marry her."

So blindsided was Rufinus that when, in April 395, imperial messengers set out with gifts to fetch the bride for her wedding, he supposed they were coming to his house instead of Promotus'. Eutropius, in arranging the imperial marriage, inserted himself as one of Arcadius' new favorites and was promoted to *praepositus sacri cubiculi*, provost of the sacred bedchamber, grand chamberlain of the palace.

Adding insult to injury, word came from the West that, although they were both as yet too young for marriage, Stilicho had betrothed his eldest daughter Maria to Arcadius' little brother Honorius. Some sources assert the match was made aside Theodosius' deathbed, to the dying emperor's satisfaction. It could not be long before Stilicho's son Eucherius was paired to the emperors' half-sister Galla Placidia.

Outmaneuvered on two fronts, Rufinus realized the game had changed. And in any three-way match, the way to beat two opponents is to set them against each other.

Before the end of January 395, the *foederati* packed their belongings, took up their weapons and followed their new leader home. Much as Fritigern had led his people from the banks of the Danube, Alaric led his on the road back to Thrace. Stilicho probably did not pause in his new duties to see them off. It must be wondered how much his dismissal of Alaric was based on, and how much it affected, his personal feelings toward his former adversary. If he and Alaric had struck up any kind of friendship after the Frigidus, this certainly dealt it a setback. Zosimus minced no words about it: "Stilicho, overall commander of the army, selected the strongest and bravest warriors for himself, and sent the weakest dregs of it back east."

119

There was no room for friendship at this level. Stilicho had acted in cold blood. The fact was that Alaric's Goths were not only redundant, but an impediment. The signatories to the agreement of 382, Athanaric and Theodosius, were dead. Honorius – meaning, Stilicho – was not obligated to it, and had even less reason to grant favor to the weakened Gothic nation. Those Goths already mingled among the legions were more than enough. The West was not capable of supporting both its own army and that of the East. The former, bled by repeated defeats at the hands of the latter, rumbled with dissent. The very presence of the Goths may have been an incitement to both Romans and western barbarians who had so recently been their enemies. The residents of Mediolanum surely objected to having barbarians billeted on them even more than had those of more eastern Thessaloniki. Even the looming threat of the Huns worked in Stilicho's favor. With the Goths' Thracian homeland at risk, he could expect Alaric to hurry home to defend it, thereby putting his people between Constantinople and the Huns by their own choice. Had Stilicho kept the ex-bandits in service, when the Huns attacked he might well have expected them to rebel and desert, likely at the most inopportune time. Now, if they wished to make trouble, they could make it for Rufinus.

It had been Roman gamesmanship of the highest order, a demonstration of civilized calculation over simpler barbarian motivations. In the history of commandments dealt from the palace of Mediolanum, this one must have been viewed at the time as among the least momentous. It's very possible that Stilicho did not even bother to invite Alaric to the palace to inform him of the decision face to face, but simply dispatched a messenger as an afterthought to the *foederati* camp to deliver his orders. It was fateful only in hindsight. Yet what might have become of Rome, if Stilicho had retained Alaric and the Goths in imperial service?

And at some point, out on the valley plain in the January cold, Alaric must have looked back over the procession of his people, trudging along beside their wagons, making their way up into the wintry Julian Alps. They were a sorry lot, on the road to nowhere. The Romans were not their friends. They were surrounded by enemies. Yet they trusted Alaric to find a way forward for them.

Alaric was not prescient. He could not know what lay ahead. He knew, though, he could rely on no one. In Constantinople, Rufinus was nothing if not treacherous, but he at least could be depended upon for his treachery. Stilicho, even with his Vandal blood, was no better than the rest, and because of his Vandal blood perhaps the worst of all.

"The shepherd must not mingle wolves with his dogs," Bishop Synesius of Cyrene would warn Emperor Arcadius in Constantinople, "even if caught as pups and they seem tame, or in a moment's lapse trust them with his flock; for the instant that they perceive any weakness or laxity in the dogs, they will attack them, and the flock, and the shepherds likewise."

In his imperial trappings, his comfortable palace life, Stilicho was a wolf who aspired to be a dog. The Romans thought themselves so civilized, so superior to outlanders. Masters of the world. In truth, though, they had gone soft. For generations now, they had done nothing but try desperately to hold on to the empire their forefathers had bequeathed them, until they were left fighting among themselves over the scraps. They had forgotten how to be conquerors.

The Goths had not forgotten. In fact they were just starting to learn.

If Alaric could not be the dog, he would be the wolf.

PART TWO

AD 395-408

The Goths, leaving the rest behind, departed from there
and initially allied themselves with the Emperor Arcadius,
but later on, for barbarians cannot abide loyalty to the Romans,
under Alaric's leadership, they became enemies of both emperors,
and, starting with Thrace, regarded all Europe as enemy territory.

Procopius

VII

*Europe is left to be the sport and prey of Gothic hordes even
to the borders of fertile Dalmatia. All that tract of land lying
between the stormy Black Sea and the Adriatic is laid waste
and plundered, no inhabitants dwell there.*

Claudian

Alaric and his ex-*foederati* had marched west across the Balkans
under the flag of Theodosius as part of a Roman army, equipped
and supplied at imperial expense. They marched back east as
vagabonds, entitled to no military rations or supplies, an army
of the hungry and homeless. "Alaric became rebellious and a
lawbreaker," wrote Zosimus, "for he was angered that he was not
given command of some military forces other than the barbarians,
which Theodosius had promised to him when he helped to defeat
the usurper Eugenius."

Plundering Roman territory may not have been their original
intent, but one man's living off the land is another man's looting and
pillaging. The Goths spent ten weeks crossing Illyricum. First Pannonia
(today eastern Austria and western Hungary), then Dalmatia (the
Balkan states, Albania/Croatia/Bosnia and Herzegovina/Serbia), and
upper Moesia (northern Macedonia) were made to share in Alaric's
pain and feel his wrath. The Goths appear to have made wide circles,

though, around the former capitals at Sirmium and Thessaloniki and the lesser cities in between, Naissus and Philippopolis. The science of siege was still beyond them, and there was no point in out-waiting walled cities when there were plenty of defenseless towns and villages in their path to serve as sources of loot.

By the time Alaric's column came down out of the mountains, his followers had been transformed, no longer a band of robbers, but once again a nation on the move. And in consideration of their shoddy treatment at Roman hands, they now chose a ruler of their own. "The contempt of the Goths for the Romans soon intensified," wrote Jordanes, "and anticipating their valor would be eroded by long peace, they raised up Alaric as their king."

Though he is not known by any other, this might even be the first time Alaric went by that name. His prior exploits became known and remarked upon only in hindsight, when he was already famous, or infamous, as Alaric I. Also, historians dispute whether he was actually a king at this point in his career – *reiks*, as noted, translates more precisely as judge – but the difference was in title only.

"They choose their kings by blood, but their generals for worth," wrote Tacitus of the Germanic tribes. "These kings do not have limitless or arbitrary power, and the generals lead more by example than by rank. If they are spirited, if they are notable, if they fight at the head of their men, they lead because they are respected." Alaric may or may not have been royal by birth, but he became king because of his charisma and leadership. Men followed Stilicho because he was in command. Alaric commanded because men followed him.

That winter of 394–395, the depredations of a ragtag band of outcast barbarians in Illyricum mattered less in Constantinople than events beyond the eastern frontier.

"Suddenly messengers flew back and forth and the whole East was struck with fear," recalled Jerome. "For news came that the Huns had poured forth in hordes…and that, racing here and there on their fleet horses, they were terrorizing the world with dread and blood."

Until that winter the Roman world had known the wrath of the Huns only secondhand, from terrified barbarian tribes begging for shelter and protection from them. A century later Zosimus had more than enough familiarity with Huns. His is the view, handed down through the centuries, which has come to stereotype them – as worse than barbarian, nearly animal. "They were incapable of fighting on foot, nor even knew how to walk, since they never set foot on the ground, but lived always, even in sleep, on horseback, yet the speed with which they wheeled their mounts, the suddenness of their appearance and retreat, shooting as they rode, caused great slaughter…"

"Though they take the form of men, they have the savagery of wild beasts," agreed Jordanes, calling them "more fierce than ferocity itself." And Claudian called them "the most notorious of all the children of the north."

The Roman Warm Period that had parched Valens's soldiers at Adrianople was well and truly drawing to a close. That winter, it was said, the broad Danube froze over completely. The Huns, who hailed originally from beyond the Volga River, in successive decades had crossed it, the Don, the Dnieper, the Southern Bug, and the Dniester on their way around the north shore of the Black Sea. And now the Danube was to be their highway to Thrace.

No one knows how many Huns crossed the river that winter. Though their invasion of 395 is widely attested as their first major contact with Rome, the church historian Socrates Scholasticus, living at the time, makes no specific mention of it. According to his contemporary Philostorgius, "The Huns, who had taken that part of Scythia across the Danube and laid waste to it, afterwards crossed the river when it froze over, and launched an invasion of Roman territory." Philostorgius' original text, however, is lost. All we have is a summary of it by Photius, the ecumenical patriarch of Constantinople four centuries later, which compresses decades into that one sentence, and continues, "then spreading over all of Thrace, they ravaged all Europe."

If the Hunnic invasion across the Danube is debatable, their invasion that spring to the east of the Black Sea, over the Caucasus Mountains into Anatolia and Persia, is not. Claudian, at least, accounts for both: "Some pour across the frozen surface of the surging Danube and break with the chariot wheel what previously knew nothing but the oar," he recorded, "others invade the wealthy East, led through the Caspian Gates and over the Armenian snows by a newly-discovered pass."

This phase of the invasion is better attested. The 7th-century Syriac Orthodox priest Thomas the Presbyter, in compiling his *Book of Caliphs*, recorded of AD 395, "And in this year the accursed Huns invaded the lands of the Romans." The *Chronicle of Edessa*, compiled by an anonymous Syrian historian in the mid-6th century, states, "In the year 706, the month Tammuz [on the Babylonian calendar, dating from the founding of the Seleucid Empire; July 395 on the Gregorian], the Huns arrived at Osroene in Mesopotamia."

Edessa, in modern Turkey, was then the capital of the kingdom of Osroene, one of those buffer states between the Eastern Roman Empire and the by-then Sassanian (Persian) Empire. It was Roman territory. The distance to Edessa from the key Darial Pass through the Caucasus is over 700 miles. The Huns not only covered it in six months, they conquered it.

They ranged down the Tigris–Euphrates plain as far as the Persian capital at Ctesiphon, a city which, like the Goths, they were unable to take, but, according to Thomas, they "plundered many villages by the Euphrates and Tigris, and killed and took a great many prisoners," said to be around 18,000.

Jerome was living in Bethlehem at the time, supposedly working in the very cavern where Jesus was born, where among other projects he was transcribing the Old Testament from Hebrew into Latin. He heard of the death and destruction from waves of refugees fleeing ahead of the storm.

In the past year the wolves (not just of Arabia but of the entire North) were unleashed upon us from the farthest reaches of the Caucasus and quickly overran these great territories. So many monasteries they captured! So many rivers they made run red with blood! They laid siege to Antioch and captured other towns on the Halys [modern Kizilirmak or Red River], the Cydnus [Berdan], the Orontes, and the Euphrates. They carried off droves of prisoners. Arabia, Phoenicia, Palestine and Egypt in panic imagined themselves already enslaved.

How an army of nomadic barbarians managed to conquer such a swath of territory from two of the world's most advanced civilizations might appear to be a bit of a mystery, but people of the time had their suspicions. There is a source of some relevance by an unknown Syrian author, written just a few decades after the invasion. *Euphemia and the Goth* is a work of romantic fiction, complete with a love triangle, betrayals, murders, courtroom drama, and a climactic beheading, but for our purposes what matters is the setting. The author, in a bit of an info dump, puts the story in Edessa at the time of the Hunnic invasion: "In the year 707 by the reckoning of the Greeks [395/6; the various calendars don't overlap exactly], the Huns invaded, taking many prisoners and advancing all the way to Edessa."

The unnamed Goth in question plays the villain, getting his comeuppance at the end. It's evident that Syrian readers of the day were familiar with the Hunnic invasion, and with Goths garrisoned in Edessa, who were probably part of the contingent Theodosius had sent to the Middle East, easily believed to be an untrustworthy lot: "And Addai, then the military governor, did not permit the *foederati* to go out against them because of treachery in their ranks."

This goes some way to supporting the idea that Addai, also given as Addaeus, feared the Goths might rebel in support of Alaric, who was even then menacing the East. In fact, the two concurrent invasions might be connected, and perfidy wasn't limited to the Goths. Addai might have been acting under the orders of Rufinus himself to facilitate the Hunnic invasion. According to Joshua the Stylite, "All Syria was handed over to them by the prefect Rufinus' treachery and the general Addai's sloth."

"Armenia and the Eastern territories were now overrun by the barbarian Huns," concurred Sozomen. "Rufinus, prefect of the East, was suspected of having secretly invited them to pillage the Roman provinces in order to advance his own ambitions, for he was said to aspire to rule."

Socrates Scholasticus agreed: "He was thought to desire the throne for himself, and was said to have invited into the Roman lands the barbarous Huns, who had already plundered Armenia and were then invading other eastern provinces."

According to Claudian, ever ready to accuse the enemies of Stilicho, the idea had come to Rufinus soon after the assassination of Promotus, four years earlier: "...that vile traitor, that colluder with the Goths, tricked the emperor [Theodosius] and delayed the incipient battle, intending to make an alliance with the Huns, who he knew full well would fight and readily ally with Rome's enemies."

That, as with much of Claudian's invective, is a bit over the top, but Rufinus' connivance with the Huns was apparently common knowledge. Why he would make such a deal with the devil remains open to question. It seems the prefect's enemies left only their opinions, and no proof, to posterity. None of them, however, had to defend the Empire without an army to do the fighting.

As *praefectus praetorio* and consul of the East, Rufinus held a civilian position, with no soldiers under his direct command. Except for a few handfuls of garrison troops, Theodosius had taken the Army of the East with him, and it was still in the West, under Stilicho's control. Having invited the Huns onto his doorstep, Rufinus could legitimately demand that Stilicho return it to Constantinople.

On the other hand, without an army to supply and pay, the East was rich. The wealthy old cities of Greece, Egypt, and the Middle East had always been cash cows for the Romans. As paymaster general for the government and the military, Rufinus had access to his own treasury. When the Huns began their invasion in 395, all he had to fight them with was money. Money, fortunately, was all he needed.

Hunnish mercenaries had served in both the Goth and Roman armies going as far back as Adrianople. They were not yet the monolithic horde under unified command that they would become under Attila, but numerous small troops moving in generally common purpose, that purpose being to enrich themselves. As praetorian prefect Rufinus was in charge of troop conscription. He even employed a number of Huns, who owed no loyalty to any Roman except those who purchased it, as his personal bodyguard.* It wouldn't have been hard for him to contact one of the outlier raider bands in Thrace or the Armenian frontier, make them an offer, and invite their friends in on the deal.

It was doubtless seen as treachery by many, but it simply was easier and cheaper – just good business – for Rufinus to pay the Huns to make trouble for the old traditional enemy, Persia. If a few Roman

---

*In this increasingly lawless time such a personal escort was becoming popular among the rich and powerful. These mercenaries were called *bucellari*, biscuit-eaters; Rufinus and men like him literally provided their bread.

frontier provinces were ravaged as well, it wouldn't be the first time; better them than Constantinople. And just to be sure, he had the Gothic *foederati* in the East stand down. Further proof of the theory is in Rufinus' dealings with the barbarians then advancing on the capital, under Alaric.

The Huns may have ravaged Thrace and Anatolia, but they had not threatened Constantinople. On the approach of Alaric, though, Claudian declared, the city was "stricken with panic at the oncoming war; outside the walls it sees the flicker of torches, the trumpet's call, and its own roofs become target for the enemy's artillery."

The Goths laid waste the outlying farms and suburbs and made captives of any inhabitants who had not sought shelter within the city walls, notably sparing properties belonging to Rufinus. Claudian has the consul looking down on all this from the battlements: "He sees the entire countryside, excepting his own lands, afire, and takes joy in his great evil, making no secret of the fact that the city's enemies are his allies."

That's typical Claudian overstatement; the relationship between Rufinus and Alaric more resembled the proverb dating from the 4th century BC: *the enemy of my enemy is my friend.* To remind Alaric of their mutual antagonism for Stilicho, Rufinus went out through the gates alone to negotiate, in his best imitation of barbarian fashion: furs and a Gothic-style sword belt, bow and quiver. Claudian sneered, "One who rides a consul's chariot and wields a consul's powers shamelessly adopts the customs and costume of barbarians."

Rufinus knew that to take down the likes of Eutropius and Stilicho, he would need a powerful ally, a man with troops behind him who was willing to disobey imperial decree. A man like Alaric. Besides, Rufinus was dealing from a position of strength. Even with a minimal garrison Constantinople, supplied by sea, could hold off a siege indefinitely. The Goths could remain camped on the city's doorstep, filthy, starving, and disease-ridden, until winter set in, or until Stilicho returned with the Army of the East. Long before that, instead of Rufinus it would be Alaric with an uprising on his hands.

Then again, destroying Constantinople wasn't Alaric's goal. All the farms and hamlets burned along the way were simply a show of force, for purposes of demonstration. Just as Fritigern had bullied tribute out of the towns and villages of Thrace, Alaric simply wanted concessions from Constantinople. A new deal, like the one Athanaric had made with Theodosius. Subsidies, like Theodosius had paid. A homeland, as Theodosius had promised. Like Theodosius, Rufinus was well known for dealing with barbarians. He and Alaric simply had to agree on a price.

With the Huns now threatening it from across the Danube, Thrace was no longer an enticing homeland. But Theodosius and Rufinus had proven not averse to having barbarians molest faraway Roman provinces. In the end, it seems, Rufinus made Alaric the same kind of offer he was accused of having made to the Huns: just enough money to make the Goths go away and plunder elsewhere. As Zosimus put it, "So Rufinus made a secret agreement with him, persuading him to lead his barbarians, plus auxiliaries of any other tribe, in order to easily make himself master of an entire province."

Alaric knew just the place.

"Alaric marched out of Thrace," continued Zosimus, "into Macedonia and Thessaly, devastating everything in his way."

Again, probably exaggeration. Macedonia, homeland of Alexander the Great, had been a Roman province for almost five and a half centuries, and prospered under imperial peace. There were rich iron, copper, and gold deposits in the mountains, wide fields of crops and pastures full of livestock on the Thessalian plain, and plentiful estates of the wealthy. It was enough for the Goths to requisition supplies along the way, demand tribute from the reluctant, and take whatever they wanted from the unwilling. Devastation was uncalled for, unless the Goths let their barbarian blood get the best of them and wrought destruction for the sake of it.

They rounded the western coast of the Aegean, the route of invasions going back as far as 480 BC, when the Persians under Xerxes had driven the Greeks ahead of them, and 169 BC, when the Romans did likewise. The locals doubtless saw the Gothic incursion as no less than an invasion. Alaric encountered little resistance from peace-loving Macedonians. "On his approach, however," recorded Socrates Scholasticus, "the Thessalians rose against him at the mouths of the river Peneus, where a pass leads over Mount Pindus to Nicopolis in Epirus."

This was the Vale of Tempe, on the border of Macedonia and Thessaly, where the modern Pineios River runs down out of the Pindus range to the Aegean, a narrow pass farther north but no less strategic than Thermopylae. It's where the Romans broke through Macedonian defenses on their way to conquering the entire peninsula by 146 BC. Running between 1,500-foot cliffs, the gorge in places is less than a hundred feet wide and, as Leonidas' Spartans had at Thermopylae, easily blocked by a small force. Evidently there were enough hostile Thessalians to make a stand. Goths who had fought at the Frigidus must have thought they were reliving that nightmare, channeled by the terrain so that only the foremost part of their manpower could be brought to bear. Alaric suffered an unexpected defeat. Little is known of the fight, but Socrates wrote, "When it came to an engagement, the Thessalians slew about 3,000 of his men."

That, as is often the case with ancient sources discussing ancient battles, is probably an exaggeration. Still, considering that fewer than 10,000 Goth warriors had survived the Frigidus, and that not all the survivors had joined his exodus, this was not a loss Alaric could well afford. Yet there was no going back, and the Vale isn't the only gateway into southern Greece. The Goths retreated only far enough to circle around the north of Mount Olympus, taking the longer, more difficult pass of the Sarantoporos River. Like the Vale, this lets out into the fertile interior plain of Larissa, where Achilles was born and Hippocrates died, farmland lush with olives and grapes, orchards and grain fields, rife with cattle and horses. The Goths might well have thought they had finally reached the promised land. Before they could unload their wagons, however, word came that another fight was in the offing.

Stilicho was on his way.

The commander in chief had been preoccupied. As Claudian pointed out, "Stilicho and only Stilicho was in charge of all the nations between the rising and setting suns." It stands to reason that he had more on his mind than a small band of barbarians making trouble. The Empire was veritably surrounded by troublemaking barbarians.

The tribes across the frontiers had been watching to see how much the bloodshed at the Frigidus had weakened the Roman West. For years the Frankish chieftains Marcomer and his brother Sunno had conducted an on-and-off skirmish with Maximus and their fellow Frank, Arbogastes, with both sides launching raids and reprisals across the Rhine. Saxon pirates menaced the shores of Gaul, and up in Caledonia the Picts threatened to overrun Hadrian's Wall and invade Britannia.

This invasion of Greece by Alaric, however, was much closer to home, and it soon became apparent that Rufinus had a hand in it. All this time Stilicho had been receiving correspondence from Serena, in Constantinople. She had been keeping an ear tuned to the palace gossip and caught wind of Rufinus' dealings with Alaric. Claudian would later compliment her, "You showed your vigilance when Rufinus, hatching his plots, sought to destroy his master by treacherously stirring up the Goths against Rome, for you uncovered his evil conspiracy and, in fear for your husband's safety, warned him with letters and messages."

If Stilicho had released Alaric from service in order for him to go bother Rufinus, it had backfired. Stilicho and Rufinus were each willing to exploit Alaric in order to make trouble for the other, but now the Goths were threatening one of the richest provinces of the Empire. Technically Greece was part of the East, a problem of Rufinus' making for Rufinus to resolve. But Stilicho had Rufinus' army, and had laid claim to the guardianship of Arcadius. Part of that meant defending him – defending the East – against any threat, external or internal. To return home to Constantinople having defeated the Goths and saved Greece would earn Stilicho the gratitude of Arcadius, and give him the authority to depose Rufinus.

"As soon as winter winds gave way to those of spring and the hills lost their coat of snow," wrote Claudian, "Stilicho, leaving Italy's meadows peaceful and safe, assembled his two armies and marched to the lands of the rising sun."

Leaving garrisons in the outposts of Noricum and Pannonia to watch their backs, Stilicho and Gainas marched east, and then south, down the eastern Adriatic coast into Greece.

So Alaric liked invasions. Time now to see how he liked being on the receiving end.

VIII

*Now when this Alaric became king, he called a council
of his people and convinced them to find a kingdom of their own
rather than serve others out of indolence.*

Jordanes

"Stilicho had hardly crossed the Alps," recorded Claudian, "when the barbarian hordes began to cut back on their raiding and, fearing his approach, assembled on the plain and enclosed their pastures in a defensive ring. They then built an unassailable fortification, with a double moat, stakes planted two deep at intervals around its summit, and wagons covered in oxhides all around, like a wall."

Alaric excelled not only at mounting an invasion, but also at mounting a defense. Stilicho, Gainas, and their armies arrived on the plain of Larissa to find the Goths holed up in a wagon circle, doubtless smaller than the one Fritigern had drawn at Adrianople, but ready for a fight to the death.

This in itself presented no problem to the Romans. Though it's unknown just how many followers Alaric counted among his barbarian troops, after his losses in the Vale of Tempe they could not have numbered much more than four or five thousand, including women and children. In the old days that amounted to less than one Roman legion. In the late Empire, legions were composed of fewer men, and it might have required anywhere from one to five to match the Goths man per man. But, excepting garrison troops along the frontiers, Stilicho had legions of both the Western and Eastern armies with him – infantry, cavalry, even artillery like ballistas and onagers. The Goths had not mastered the making or operation of siege machinery, and had they come out from behind their defenses to destroy Stilicho's, they would have been overwhelmed on the open ground and massacred. They could only have sat there in their wagon fort and taken it while Roman catapults pounded their tents flat and their wagons into splinters. Even without that, Stilicho needed no more than a small fraction of his manpower to overrun the wagon train and utterly wipe the Goths off the map of Greece to the last man, woman and child.

He did not.

Historians have questioned why Stilicho hesitated to destroy his former comrade. Comradeship probably had nothing to do with it. The fact was, Stilicho had no reason to rush into battle. Half the fight might be against his own troops.

In the summer of 395 a sizable part of Stilicho's army was the Western contingent, repeatedly and badly beaten by its Eastern counterparts, still stinging from the most recent defeat within the past year. Those men had to be wondering why they had been marched to Greece under an Eastern commander to fight the East's battle. If they rebelled, or even held back a little in the fight, it would have thrown any attack into turmoil, which Alaric's Goths could have exploited the way Fritigern's had at Adrianople. On top of that, many of Stilicho's Eastern contingent, like Gainas, were themselves Goths, and many of them kinsmen of those inside Alaric's wagon circle. They may have shown little enthusiasm for attacking their brethren. The upshot was that Stilicho's actual fighting force was much smaller than it seemed, and he could barely trust the rest.

The point here was not just to defeat the barbarians, but to make it look easy. If Stilicho returned to Constantinople having lost half his forces in a poorly fought, bloody, Pyrrhic victory, he would not be hailed a hero, but vilified and possibly cashiered, exiled, or worse. He doubtless remembered Adrianople, where Valens attempted to assault a Goth wagon fort, only to be destroyed by hidden, unsuspected barbarian forces.

Compared to Stilicho, on the other hand, Alaric was arguably the more experienced battle commander, but he was vastly outnumbered. So, like Valens and Fritigern, both leaders set about delaying actual combat as long as possible.

Communication lag in those days being what it was, in Constantinople Rufinus received word of Stilicho's advance into Greece after the fact.

"Rufinus was seized with panic and fear as soon as he saw this in the distance," wrote Claudian. By allowing Alaric to plunder, the consul had probably hoped to entice Stilicho to send Arcadius the Eastern army to use against the Goths, which would at last have given Rufinus some actual military power. For Stilicho himself to come, leading the combined armies of East and West, was more than expected. The armies would arrive not long after word of their approach. Rufinus could literally number his remaining days by the date of their arrival.

According to Claudian, Rufinus hurried to throw himself on Arcadius' mercy. "I beg you, protect me from the sword's edge; let me evade Stilicho's cruel threat," he pleaded, and in case that didn't work, reminded Arcadius that the Eastern army was rightfully his. "...Let him leave Illyricum, deliver us his Eastern troops, and divide the soldiers fairly between the two brothers. You are not just heir to the scepter, but to your army."

But Rufinus also fell back on the ploy that had served him well the last time Alaric and Stilicho had come up against each other, in the Rhodope Mountains when Alaric was just a bandit leader.

No matter how powerful he was, Stilicho still had to bow to the wishes of an emperor.

"Meanwhile Stilicho, eager to advance upon the enemy across the narrow stretch of land between him and the fortifications, arouses with speeches the courage of his troops, already yearning for battle," claimed Claudian. "...Neither hilltop nor deep moat could stop their attack; their sheer speed would have overwhelmed any barrier."

He ignores the fact that the legions had been in such a state of readiness for days or weeks, and that Stilicho missed a perfect chance to annihilate the threat of Alaric and his renegade Goths. The two sides were still in position when a missive arrived from Constantinople.

It was signed by Arcadius, but clearly had been written by Rufinus. On reading it, according to Claudian, Stilicho addressed his troops: "Cities chosen for burning, walls ordered for demolition, I call you as witnesses. I withdraw. I leave this sad world to its fate. Furl your banners, officers. Go home, soldiers of the east. We must obey orders. Silence, you war horns; archers, lower your bows. The enemy is in our grasp, but spare him. It is Rufinus' command."

Arcadius had ordered the army to stand down. Furthermore, Stilicho was to send the Eastern contingent on to Constantinople, and himself return with the defeated, depleted Westerners to Italy. Rufinus had betrayed them.

Claudian would have it that the legions, Romans and barbarians alike, wailed and wept in bitter disappointment, begging to carry on the battle and swearing their allegiance to Stilicho even as the heroic leader regretfully turned into his tent. An emperor's order was to be obeyed, even if written by a traitor. The reality is that Stilicho, even if he had destroyed Alaric, could hardly march on Constantinople against the wishes of Arcadius, for that would make him the traitor. And even if he had schemed after the throne, as many a Roman general like Maximus and Arbogastes had schemed before him, that he did not march is further proof that Stilicho did not have what they had – the unwavering loyalty of his legions. Stilicho was half-barbarian. His Roman troops distrusted his barbarian blood, and his barbarian troops distrusted the Roman.

But Stilicho had men whom he did trust. Gainas, the Goth in command of the Eastern army, was given special orders before he led his legions off toward Constantinople.

Yet before sending him on his way, and starting his own return to Italia, Stilicho must surely have hesitated. The die had been well and truly cast. Theodosius had trusted Stilicho to hold the Empire together, and already East and West were at odds. There was no turning back. Stilicho was risking all, for Serena, little Eucherius, Maria, and Thermantia still resided in Constantinople, within the reach of Rufinus. Stilicho was betting their lives as well as his own.

And more than that. Rufinus had been thwarted by Eutropius in his aim of marrying his offspring into the imperial family. Stilicho had already married into the imperial family, and was but one step away from the imperial throne. His son Eucherius was more than half-Roman, and a likely match for his cousin Galla Placidia, the emperors' half-sister. What might his future bring? Co-emperor? Or more even than that – supreme emperor?

This was nothing more than a reasonable line of thought. Stilicho would have been foolish not to consider it, not least because others like Rufinus were certainly considering it. Even for some ancient historians, though, such motivation cast Stilicho in a bad light, and was perhaps his reason for allowing Alaric's escape: to continue making trouble for Rufinus. "What each man did and what he tried to do, their fates made plain," wrote Orosius. "Rufinus, aspiring to become royalty, brought in the barbarians. Stilicho, wishing it for his son, supported them [i.e. let the Goths go], so that in the crisis the requirements of the state might obscure his evil goal."

Easily said, but Orosius risked nothing in the telling. By sending Gainas and the Eastern army to Constantinople, Stilicho was betting not only the lives of his family, but the future of his dynasty.

That autumn, the better part of a year after his death, the body of Theodosius I, the Great, finally reached Constantinople.* Since the death of Constantine I in 337, Eastern Roman emperors had been interred at the Church of the Holy Apostles on the *Mese*, Constantinople's broad central thoroughfare. (With exceptions: after Adrianople Valens's body was never found; Gratian and Valentinian II were Western emperors, murdered in Gaul.) Next to the Hagia Sophia, the city's largest and busiest church, it was destroyed in 1461 by invading Muslims and replaced with a mosque, but six imperial sarcophagi, called *larnakes* by the Greeks, survived. Two now stand in the atrium of the city's oldest church, the Hagia Eirene, and four outside Istanbul's Archaeological Museum, all empty. Each is carved

---

*Romans and early Christians did not normally embalm the dead, but in the case of such a long delay some method of preservation must have been employed. In 2008 the body of a woman who died in northern Greece around AD 300 was found to have been embalmed with resins, fats, oils, and spices such as myrrh. She is thought to have been merely wealthy. In the case of a deceased emperor even greater efforts would have been made.

from a single block of porphyry, rare red-purple granite quarried from a single mountain on Egypt's Red Sea coast and reserved for imperial use.

Though the original church is gone, according to the 12th-century Byzantine priest Nicholas Mesarites, who doubtless served there himself, on November 8 Theodosius was interred in its eastern apse, near the sarcophagus of Constantine the Great. After the service his body, wrapped in a shroud of purple silk with gold trim, was placed in a lead-lined coffin, which was then lowered into the sarcophagus. The massive porphyry lid was slid over the opening. The tomb was decorated with candles and gilt and silver icons. The mourners quieted and the procession filed out, with Arcadius attended by his new wife Aelia Eudoxia and his two top ministers, Rufinus and Eutropius.

The gloom of the occasion, however, could hardly cloud the dark heart of Rufinus. By this time he would have received word that Stilicho had obeyed the imperial order, repaired toward Italia and sent the Eastern army home as commanded. Rufinus would have considered the game won. If Stilicho would not dare to attack when Rufinus was helpless, he would certainly not dare when Rufinus had an army – the superior Eastern army – at his beck and call. "Plan my destruction from afar, friend Stilicho," he gloated (at least, according to Claudian). "…Pierce me from there with your arrows, if you can. Seek in your fury a sword that from Italy can reach my city's walls."

Over the course of the month the army under Gainas crossed Thessaly and Macedonia to Thessaloniki, and then the Hebrus (Maritsa) River, the Rhodope Mountains, and the Thracian highlands until it reached Heraclea, also called Neapolis, on the coast of the Sea of Marmara. "When these troops appeared outside Constantinople," records Zosimus, "Gainas came forward, and informed Emperor Arcadius of their arrival, and that they had come to assist him in his hour of need."

That must have been a tense scene in the throne room. Gainas the Goth, a general of Rome, who was expected to just hand the army over to Rome's adversaries; Rufinus, for whom getting control of the army meant ultimate triumph; Eutropius, the eunuch and palace chamberlain, for whom Rufinus' triumph and power meant almost certain death; and Arcadius, probably oblivious to all this, for he was not known for quick wit, and what eighteen-year-old boy would not be thrilled to have an army of his very own? Let the Huns try to invade, let Alaric do his worst. Arcadius would ride to meet them like a Roman hero of old!

First, however, there were niceties of military ritual and tradition to be observed. "The emperor showing pleasure at their arrival," wrote Zosimus, "Gainas advised him to observe them on their grand entrance into the city, this being an honor usually given soldiers on such occasions."

Arcadius agreed to review the troops outside the city in the morning. With that, Gainas took his leave to prepare for the ceremony. When the emperor retired for the evening, Rufinus invited his closest underlings and minions and co-conspirators in the court – it would probably be wrong to call them friends, since according to Claudian all they had in common was covering up their mutual guilt – to his home for a feast of celebration. Arcadius might dream of leading the army, but everyone knew he would be nothing but a figurehead. What rewards Rufinus and his minions would reap, though, with legions to do the stealing and imperial sanction for it all!

In one of Claudian's most masterful scenes, considering that he spent the entire time in Italy and never met Rufinus personally, he has the consul sleeping fitfully, troubled by the ghosts of his many victims, one of whom nevertheless renders a comforting prophecy: "Up from your couch! Why does your anxious mind still scheme? The coming day shall bring you rest and an end to your toil. You will be raised high above the people, and happy crowds will carry you in their arms."

In the morning, Gainas assembled the army on the Campus Martius, the plain west of the city, a glittering sea of steel beneath a forest of upraised spears and the streaming dragon banners of the East. Infantry in plumed helmets and gleaming scale mail, rank upon rank of shields making walls sturdier than the one that circled the city. Cavalry – blond, lightly armored Germans on wiry northern steeds and Armenian cataphracts in all-over mail, their impatient, stamping mounts likewise draped to the knees in steel. All awaited the emperor's pleasure.

The city gate opened and Arcadius appeared, accompanied by the empress Aelia Eudoxia, the consul Rufinus, Eutropius, and the rest of his entourage, all dressed in their finest. In this period the Eastern Romans had not yet adopted the heavier, colorful Greek fashions that would typify the later Byzantine Empire, but still dressed as members of the *gens togata*, the "toga-wearing race."* Arcadius and Rufinus, as emperor and consul, wore *togae pictae*, painted togas, purple with gold trim, but only the emperor wore a diadem, in gold studded with pearls. Rufinus is said to have worn a superhumeral, the heavy collar of embroidered cloth of gold, studded with pearls and gemstones, which was a badge of imperial office, but also favored by wealthy matrons; Claudian sneered that, putting on imperial airs, the consul looked like a woman. Further demonstrating his undisguised ambition, he had minted gold medallions to be handed out to the troops, adorned not with Arcadius' image, but with his own. He personally conducted the review on the emperor's behalf, or in the emperor's place, recognizing and calling out each unit by name. It was the high point of his life. He was imperial ruler in all but title, and given the army and but a little time, he might rule in fact.

Gainas and some of his legionaries – presumably high-ranking officers, not obliged to march in formation – gathered in a circle around him and Arcadius. This was not unexpected. Many of them had never seen Arcadius in the garb of emperor, or Rufinus as consul, and they rarely got the opportunity to be this close to what amounted to a god on earth. According to Zosimus, Arcadius enjoyed the attention: "The soldiers paid him the traditional marks of respect, which he accepted with thanks."

Rufinus, on the other hand, got carried away by it all. In his excitement and pride he is said to have actually grabbed the emperor's robe and urged Arcadius to bring him up on the dais and declare him co-emperor on the spot.

Rufinus didn't notice the soldiers closing around him until they reached for their swords. One of them gave him a message from their commander: "Most foul of the foul, did you hope to bind us in the

*The impractical toga was falling out of favor among commoners, particularly under the influence of trouser-wearing barbarians, but in 382 Gratian, Valentinian II, and Theodosius had issued a sumptuary law that senators might don the poncho-like *paenula* as everyday wear, but were required to wear the traditional toga for official functions. In 395, bowing to the growing anti-barbarian sentiment in the imperial court, Honorius forbade Roman citizens to wear Gothic boots or trousers, on pain of banishment.

yoke of slavery? Did you not know that I would return? Should I allow myself to be called another man's servant, I who administer the law and restored freedom to reign? I have won two civil wars and twice forced my way over the Alps. All these struggles have taught me never to serve a tyrant."

The betrayer was betrayed. To avoid defiling the ceremony Rufinus had left his Hunnish bodyguard at home. Claudian has him standing, stunned and transfixed, like a once-mighty lion beset by gladiators in the arena, as one of the soldiers – according to Zosimus, Gainas himself – steps forward with blade drawn. "It is the hand of Stilicho, whom you bragged of expelling, that strikes you," he tells the consul, "his sword, which you thought far from reach, that stills your heart."

Stilicho had found a sword after all, that could reach from Italy to Constantinople. Gainas stabbed Rufinus with it.

"On Gainas's signal," recorded Zosimus, "they all attacked Rufinus, closing in and hacking at him with their swords." They murdered him, just as senators had assassinated Julius Caesar almost 450 years earlier. And then for good measure, and at the very feet of the shocked and horrified imperial couple, they literally cut Rufinus to pieces, tore his limbs from his body and spilled his entrails over the parade ground.

Eutropius can easily be imagined watching all this with a smile of satisfaction. "Eutropius," confided Zosimus, "who acted as Stilicho's tool in all his designs against Rufinus, had overseen and controlled everything done in the court."

Rufinus' remains, Claudian asserts, were trampled into the earth by a vengeful mob, while the consul's head was mounted on a spear and borne into the city in triumph.

Raised above the joyful people, carried in their arms. Rufinus' dream, according to Claudian, had come true.

IX

Triumvirate

AD 396

*The world had nearly become one single empire under the
rule of the two brothers (for who, with the terrible
punishment so fresh in mind, would dare try a similar
usurpation?) when suddenly – it is a monstrous story which
scarcely can be told – a eunuch came forward
to become Rufinus' heir.*

Claudian

Four hundred years after Stilicho and Alaric had passed from the
scene, Italy was still a battleground. In 774, the Carolingian kings
of the Franks had conquered the Lombards – two Germanic tribes
vying to resurrect Roman glory. In 800, in Rome, Pope Leo III
crowned the Frankish king Charlemagne as Holy Roman Emperor,
a title grudgingly conceded by the Byzantines, who still considered
themselves the legitimate Roman Empire. Like the Western Roman
Empire, by 888 the Carolingian was torn apart by petty kings and
warlords, with Italian "emperors" ruling little more than northern
Italy. Over a forty-year span the last of them, Berengar I, managed
to rise from Margrave of Friuli on the north coast of the Adriatic,
to King of Italy and then Holy Roman Emperor, despite losing
every battle he ever fought against pagan Magyar raiders and seven
other claimants to the throne. Rather than as a warrior, he is better

remembered for his strategic gift-giving. Among these donations, bequeathed to the Cathedral of Milan which still displays them in its treasury, was the Cross of the Kingdom, a gold cross-reliquary studded with precious stones and pearls and worn by the emperors during their coronations, and a carved ivory diptych of Stilicho, Serena, and Eucherius.

These diptychs – artworks made of two panels, in ancient times hinged together to close like a book to protect the carvings inside – were fashionably distributed to commemorate social events like weddings or promotions, particularly to the rank of consul. In 393 the consul Quintus Aurelius Symmachus, he of the plots with the usurper Maximus against Valentinian II, had ivory diptychs made and distributed at games to commemorate his son's promotion to *quaestor* (judge), and again in 401 for his promotion to *praetor* (higher court judge).

The Diptych of Stilicho on display at the Milan cathedral is of ivory, thought to be one of the few portraits of him done from life.[*] Stilicho's panel shows a middle-aged man with an oval face, neatly trimmed beard, and late-Roman bowl-style haircut. He is well dressed in a long Greek-style cloak, a *chlamys*, with a rosette pattern, fastened at the right shoulder with a *fibula*, a brooch. His long-sleeved tunic is cinched at the waist with a *cingulum* or belt, supporting a short sword and scabbard, of possibly Hunnish design. He appears to be bare-legged and wearing pointed-toe, buckle-on shoes. His upraised right hand holds a spear taller than he, and his left rests on a round shield with a scaled decoration and pointed boss.

The left-hand panel portrays a tall, aristocratic woman, taken to be Serena. She wears her hair upswept in a heavy top bun, with pendant earrings and a matching double necklace of round stones or possibly pearls. Her long-sleeved, floor-length *stola*, the garb of a married woman, is held tight under the bust by an ornamented, possibly jeweled belt. Rather than a spear, her upraised right hand holds a flower, delicately, by the stem; her left supports the draping of her *palla*, her mantle. At her side, waist-high to her, stands a boy,

---

[*]There is a case to be made, though not very convincingly, that the diptych actually portrays the *magister militum* Flavius Aetius, the Roman general who played Stilicho's role in the mid-400s, using a combined Roman/*foederati* army to halt an invasion by Attila's Huns in 451.

presumed to be Eucherius, dressed like a miniature version of his father, in a chiton covered with a long *chlamys* and shoulder clasp. He holds a rectangular box, believed to depict a closed diptych – a diptych within a diptych.

In fact, the Stilicho Diptych is thought to actually commemorate the occasion of Eucherius' appointment, at age seven or eight, as *tribunus et notarius*, tribune and notary, an entry-level posting to the imperial bureaucracy. As this took place in 395 or 396, it captures Stilicho, *comes et magister utriusque militiae praesentalis*, and his family at the height of his powers. On his shield hangs a small medallion with two tiny faces, very indistinct – the entire piece is only about a foot tall and six inches across – assumed to represent his very young daughters, Maria, aged six or seven, and Thermantia, five or six. However, they might equally well represent the imperial brothers, Honorius and Arcadius, whom Stilicho was pledged to protect.

In the East, Arcadius and Eutropius doubtless saw things differently. Still, East–West relations got off to a good start. In a gesture of good will, and probably to rid himself of a spy even he couldn't afford to kill, Eutropius had allowed Serena and her children to leave Constantinople and join Stilicho in Mediolanum, as evidenced on the diptych.

Stilicho had removed his adversary in the East, but his own position was still precarious. With only the weakened, demoralized Western legions under his command, and not yet powerful enough to risk the ire of the wealthy, pagan senators and patricians by drafting manpower from their country estates, Stilicho sorely needed fresh recruits. They might do little to invigorate the army's spirit, but nothing revives a soldier like the prospect of conquest. The depleted legions were still more than a match for, and an enticing opportunity for employment to, the barbarians to the north. Therefore, in the summer of 396, Stilicho undertook a campaign of combined intimidation and recruitment, in Gaul.

He marched his troops over the Alps to the headwaters of the Rhine, and followed its valley down into the barbarian heartland. "Coming down from the river's source to where it splits in two," extolled Claudian, "and to the marshes at its mouths he sped like lightning. The general's pace outran the swift river, and his army grew like the Rhine's stream."

Faced with a choice of fighting or joining, the Germanic tribes along the river quickly remembered their place, and their obligations. The ranks of the legions swelled with new recruits. The farther north the army marched, the stronger it grew.

Those tribes on the far side of the frontier took note. The Frankish chieftain Marcomer was either captured or gave himself up; his punishment, such as it was, was banishment to a villa in Etruria, modern Tuscany. His brother Sunno attempted to take his place as the head of the tribe, for which they killed him.

"Then, mightiest," Claudian addressed Honorius, "you have seen from headwaters to shore Rhine's princes come, bowing their heads in fearful capitulation… Germany pledges loyalty to the faraway Honorius and raises suppliant prayers to him."

Downstream, for decades the Saxons had been migrating from their homeland east of the Elbe into what is now the Low Countries, the Netherlands and Belgium. Their seaborne raids menaced both sides of the English Channel, to the point that the Romans had established a separate military command, the *litus Saxonicum*, the Saxon Coast, a chain of fortresses around Caletum (modern Calais) in Gaul and Portus Dubris (Dover) in Britannia. These were strengthened and better manned. The Saxon threat subsided, but a power vacuum remained across the Channel.

"Britannia was deprived of all her warriors and armed bands, of her adamant commanders, and of the bloom of her manhood, who went with Maximus and never returned," recorded the 6th-century British monk and historian Gildas the Wise, "and being utterly ignorant of the art of war, she groaned in agony for many years under the cruel mastery of two foreign tribes – the Scots out of the northwest [in those days, meaning the Gaelic Irish], and the Picts out of the north."

Stilicho was now so flush with troops in Gaul that he dispatched some across the Channel – according to Gildas, perhaps even the very same legionaries who had marched with Maximus. "Forgiving their previous rebellion, a legion was immediately supplied with weapons and sent," he wrote. "When they had crossed the Channel and landed, they quickly sought battle with many of their savage enemies, and killed them in great numbers. All were driven beyond the borders, and the humiliated Britons saved from the cruel slavery which threatened them."

147

The army replenished, the Germanics tamed, the Scots and Picts repelled; Stilicho accomplished all this in the course of one summer, and returned over the Alps to Mediolanum stronger than ever. That he had followed Theodosius' example and filled the legions to an even greater extent with Germanic barbarians was just one more step in their gradual transformation. They were no longer so much Rome's legions, as Stilicho's.

The important thing was that now, from a position of strength, Stilicho could once again look to the East and the task of reuniting the Empire.

Like his predecessor Rufinus, Eutropius, the eunuch and ex-slave turned palace grand chamberlain, was likewise consolidating his new power and ridding himself of enemies. Arcadius, still just a teenage boy, was preoccupied with his new plaything and bedmate, the beautiful Eudoxia, for whom he had Eutropius to thank. She, on the other hand, could thank the eunuch for her elevation to imperial consort, though she had so far been denied the title of *Augusta*, which would have bestowed imperial power on her. If the youngsters had any pretensions to power beyond that of figureheads, the memory of Rufinus being hacked to pieces at their feet relieved them of it. It was said that after the assassination, Gainas's killers had paraded the prefect's severed hands through the city, tugging on the sinews to make the fingers curl as though still demanding contributions from everyone.

Eutropius, on the other hand, had achieved his life's goal. As a eunuch he had no family to promote to the throne. He was a slave no more, but in a position to make all the world's people his slaves. Claudian captured his apparent attitude:

When this part-man, old and worn out, had been raised to such a zenith of power that he never would have thought possible, of which he never dared to dream – when he had held the law in his hands, the heads of the nobility bowed before him, and Fortune heaped such wealth upon him, whose only fervent prayer had been freedom – he immediately forgot his former masters, and his slavish mind dreamed of even further advantage.

Firstly, he appropriated all of Rufinus' ill-gotten properties, distributing some to his followers and supporters and keeping the rest for himself. Rufinus' wife and daughter sought refuge for their lives in a church, until Eutropius magnanimously granted them safe passage – meaning, banished them – to Jerusalem. The eunuch's former master Abundantius, who presumably knew too many of his secrets, was exiled to the Middle East. Then Timasius, the relative of Arcadius' late mother, the *Augusta* Aelia Flaccilla, and former commander of the Army of the East, had to go; now that he had Gainas and the Eastern army on his side, Eutropius had too many generals with Theodosian loyalties. Timasius was banished to the Kharga Oasis, deep in Egypt's Western Desert, 125 miles from the nearest port on the Nile, effectively the end of the earth. He never returned and is presumed to have died there.

If the rest of old aristocracy of the East held the loss of their rightful offices against the eunuch, they did best to keep it to themselves. Zosimus wrote, "Eutropius, being drunk on riches and imagining himself raised above the clouds, planted his spies in almost every country, to pry into everyone's business and affairs. There was nothing from which he did not gain some profit."

Claudian concurred. "Mounted above the door of his office is a list of the provinces and their prices: so much for Galatia, for Pontus so much, so much will purchase Lydia. Would you govern Lycia? Then pay this many thousands. Phrygia? A bit more." As evidenced by both Rufinus and even Theodosius, the sale of offices was no particular evil, but each of these three seems to have taken the practice to a further extreme than his predecessor. Claudian, even in the midst of excoriating Eutropius (on behalf of Stilicho), at least understood his motive: "He wants everything to have its price to console him for his own ill fortune, and himself so often sold, he desires to sell everything."

There was, however, one man, one people in the Eastern Empire still owing nothing to Eutropius: Alaric and the Goths.

Since squeaking out the clutches of Stilicho on the plain of Larissa, Alaric had not been lingering in place waiting for Romans in Mediolanum and Constantinople to decide his fate. He was a king now, and acted like one. Macedonia and Thessaly were only stepping stones on the way to the real prize: classical Greece.

The Goths resumed their southward march along the coast, approaching the ancient gateway to Greece at Thermopylae just as the

Persians had in 480 BC. The Greeks might have stopped them there, the way the Spartans had Xerxes, the way the Thracians had stopped the Goths there in the mid-3rd century, the way they had stopped Alaric at the Vale of Tempe, but they were betrayed. Before his death, Rufinus had appointed one Antiochus, described by Zosimus as "used to doing nothing but evil," as proconsul of Greece. And Gerontius – perhaps the same Gerontius who had been punished by Theodosius for his treatment of barbarians back in 386 – now commanded the garrison at Thermopylae. According to Zosimus both had been ordered to stand down and let the Goths through, but then according to Zosimus anything untoward is always the result of treachery. It's more likely they simply didn't have enough troops to resist Alaric. Zosimus recorded, "Arriving at Thermopylae, he sent messengers to the proconsul Antiochus and Gerontius commanding the garrison, to inform them of his coming. As soon as Gerontius received this missive, he and his garrison withdrew and gave the barbarians free passage into Greece."

Being conquered by Rome in AD 146 was the best thing that could have happened to Greece. After some minor rebellions and scuffling during the Roman Civil War, the Empire forced the ancient city-states to cease their squabbling and unite as the province of Achaea. It was a senatorial province, meaning it was under civilian rule, with no legions garrisoning its cities. The Achaeans lived in an idyllic paradise they had rarely known when they were ruled by the Mycenaeans or Macedonians. The province was so wealthy, so civilized, that even some of its slaves were highly educated as doctors and teachers.

According to Zosimus, Boeotia (central Greece) was first to feel the wrath of the Goths.

> On arrival, they immediately started laying waste the countryside and pillaging all the towns, slaying all the men, young and old, and bearing off the women and children, along with their money. In this invasion, all Boeotia, and wherever in Greece the barbarians went after Thermopylae, were so devastated that the traces are still visible today.

He exaggerates only slightly. Alaric's purpose here, like any upstart Roman general set on establishing a power base from which to further his ambitions, was not to plunder Greece, but to subdue and rule it. Cities and villages that resisted were certainly put to the sword but, like Fritigern, Alaric was happy to accept tribute and be on his way. Thebes – that 2,000-year-old city destroyed by Alexander and restored by his heirs – was left intact, though possibly because it was fortified with walls. And when the Goths reached Athens – even older, even grander, leveled by Sulla in the First Mithridatic War, then elevated and revered again as a seat of learning where the Roman elite sent their youth for education – Alaric laid waste the suburbs, but proposed peace in exchange for tribute. "He was given a warm reception and entertained with all possible cordiality," admits Zosimus, "afterward receiving gifts and leaving the city and all Attica [the peninsula on which Athens stands] unharmed."

Not all the Greeks were as submissive. The Goths stormed over Megaris, the entryway to the isthmus that connects upper Greece to the Peloponnesus. Corinth and Argos were plundered and even Sparta, once home of proud Leonidas and the 300 Immortals, but long since fallen into decline, was sacked and the inhabitants sold into slavery.

The Goths' conquest of Greece signaled to some the end of the classical world, a new Dark Age like that after the fall of Bronze Age Mycenae. They lamented that lives of peace and plenty had turned them soft, and that the future would require fewer men of philosophy and idle thought in the manner of Aristotle, Plato, and Socrates, and more men of action like Achilles and Leonidas. "The Roman world is crumbling," declared Jerome, "but still we hold our heads high rather than bowing them. How brave, do you think, are Corinthians now, or the Athenians or the Lacedaemonians or the Arcadians, or any of the Greeks over whom the barbarians run roughshod? I speak of only a few cities, but at one time these were the capitals of great lands."

What seemed most shocking to the cultured Greeks was that their fabled polities, so old they had arisen out of the mists of prehistory – and so civilized that they had inspired the Romans, by following and perfecting and expanding their example, to subjugate the world – should fall to mere barbarians, even if led by a prince. "These men were formerly good only for slavery, who have never owned any property," warned the Greek bishop Synesius, who lived in Athens when the Goths arrived. "...So mastery is necessary with them, and they will either plow farms as they are ordered...or they will flee again, and tell those beyond the river that they need no longer obey Romans, for a young nobleman is their leader."

This was not some upstart general declaring his far-flung corner of the world as his imperial domain, as had Maximus. Nor was it a barbarian ruling through a puppet Roman, as Arbogastes had through Eugenius. This was a threat to the balance of power between East and West, potentially a new Triumvirate like that of Pompey, Crassus, and Caesar, or even that of Maximus, Eugenius, and Theodosius. There was no longer only a Roman East and West, but something of a Central as well. Alaric had done what few men before him had managed. He had cut himself a kingdom out of the very heart of the Empire, and if he was not yet a third emperor in title, he had made himself one in fact.

And if he declared himself an emperor, who was to stop him?

X

ENEMIES ON ALL SIDES

AD 397

For us there is nothing that Stilicho will not suffer, no personal
danger he will not risk, whether hardships on land
or hazards at sea.

Claudian

The port of Ravenna, on a swampy delta island where the Montone and Ronco Rivers converged, was in this period a city of 50,000 souls and the preeminent naval base on the Adriatic. It had been founded over 400 years earlier by the emperor Octavian, who realized the importance of naval power after his victory over Antony and Cleopatra at Actium, farther down in the Ionian Sea, in 31 BC. He ordered Ravenna's port, the Classis (modern Classe, from the Latin for "fleet"), to be dug out of an extant natural lagoon, with piles driven into the bottom to support oaken docks and piers. Like Portia and Ostia for Rome or Piraeus for Athens, Classis had become a city in itself, both a commercial port and a military installation. There was a *pharos*, a lighthouse inspired by that of Alexandria, and the Fossa Augusta, a thirteen-mile canal lined with docks, warehouses, and military facilities, linking the rivers to the lagoon and the sea. In its day, according to the Roman historian Lucius Cassius Dio, the Classis was capable of supporting 250 ships of the *Classis Ravennas*, the Ravenna Fleet.

In the mid-3rd century, however, when the Empire was going through its crisis of invasions, rebellions, and civil wars, Ravenna had been sacked twice. The harbor was neglected, deteriorated, and began to fill with silt. As with the harbor, so with the fleet. Constantine the Great had conscripted many of its ships into the Eastern navy. The last imperial sea battle had been between him and his co-emperor Licinius, in 324. Since then the Ravenna Fleet had atrophied at the dock. The technology for building the heavy capital ships of the past, the quadriremes and quinqueremes that had dominated at Actium, had been discarded or lost. Light duties of patrol and escort could be amply conducted by triremes and bireme *liburnae*. To do the heavy lifting there were transport ships, the *corbitae* and *onerariae*, some capable of packing 2,000 tons of cargo or 400 passengers, but only slowly, under sail. Even in its glory days, the Roman navy served as an adjunct to the army, delivering the legions to where the fighting was, even if it was aboard enemy galleys.

In the spring of 397, the fighting was to be in Greece. Again.

As Gibbon put it, "The last hope of a people who could no longer depend on their arms, their gods, or their sovereign, was placed in the powerful assistance of the general of the West; and Stilicho, who had not been permitted to repulse, advanced to chastise the invaders of Greece."[1]

With Alaric and his Goths still squatting on the Peloponnesus, and Arcadius – meaning Eutropius – doing nothing about it, Stilicho saw it as his responsibility once more to run the barbarians out of Achaea in order to defend the Empire at large. It was his doing, after all, that had unleashed them on the East. This time, rather than march around and down the far side of the Adriatic – a hike of over two months that would once again tip off Alaric to his approach and allow the Goths to wall themselves up inside one of their newly subjugated cities – he proposed to get there by sea, a voyage of just eight or nine days.

"Stilicho," wrote Zosimus, "having embarked a considerable number of troops, hurried to assist the Achaeans in their hour of need." Part of his decision for taking the short route that spring was that the fleet did not launch until after April, due to the death of Bishop Ambrose on Easter Saturday. The old prelate had given

[1] *History*, Vol. III, p. 140

Stilicho's regency an imprimatur of legitimacy, though they had not always gotten along. The previous year, when he sent men to drag a criminal out of Ambrose's church where he had claimed sanctuary, Stilicho had eventually been forced, like Theodosius after the massacre at Thessaloniki, to show contrition and make amends. Such being the power of the church over the state, it behooved a political and military leader to secure God's blessing, even if it delayed the proceedings. Even a fleet the size of Stilicho's could use the Lord's assistance.

Probably nobody in living memory could recall the last time Ravenna had launched such an armada. To load an entire army aboard ships required disassembled siege machinery, wagons, bundles of spears and arrows, swords and shields and armor, horses and mules and oxen, tons of wine amphorae and sacks of grain, all marched up the gangplank or swung aboard by crane. The docks and piers lining the canal and port bustled with sailors, harbor pilots, oarsmen, cargo masters, signalmen, woodworkers and sailmakers, armorers, and, of course, thousands upon thousands of legionaries. If most of the troops were German, most of the sailors were from across the Adriatic in Illyricum – Liburnians, Pannonians, Dalmatians. If not for the fact that, out of necessity, most all spoke Latin, nothing would ever have been accomplished.

"The wind can barely fill so many sails," marveled Claudian, possibly as a comment on the time required of the voyage; convoy speeds are always constrained by the slowest ships, in this case the oarless, wind-driven *corbitae* and *onerariae*. Dodging storms, for the Italian coast of the Adriatic is bereft of the islands and inlets that shelter the Balkan side, the Roman fleet made its way down the back of the Italian boot, skirting its spur, the Gargano Promontory, and probably overnighting in the harbors of Barium and Brindisium before cutting across the narrowest stretch of open water, the Strait of Otranto, to the Illyrian side. There, Aulum in Illyricum (modern Vlore in Albania) and Corcyra (Corfu in Greece) offered huge natural harbors. South of that, the fleet bore to port, into the narrowing Gulf of Patras, through the Strait of Rio – less than two miles wide, with ridges on each side, a natural wind tunnel that could either speed the sailing ships along or bring them to a standstill – into the Gulf of Corinth. Claudian reported, "Neptune delivers favorable currents for the fleet that will save Corinth."

At the far end, the Isthmus of Corinth was the only land bridge between the Peloponnesus and the mainland. By landing there and holding it, Stilicho could cut the Goths off from half of Greece, and perhaps even trap them on the Peloponnesus. The flaw in this strategy was that the Gulf is less than twenty miles across at its widest, and in some places only a quarter of that. The fleet might easily be seen from either the north or south banks. Alaric would have been smart to have sentries posted on the highest points to give him advance warning.

On the mainland side, the spies would have been reporting back to Constantinople. Affairs in Greece were to be none of Stilicho's concern; his intervention was neither requested nor wanted. His landing in Corinth amounted to an invasion. He doubtless assumed that his young brother-in-law Arcadius and at least temporary ally Eutropius would understand he was doing them a favor, and permit him a free hand in dealing with renegade barbarians.

If so, he assumed wrong.

Corinth was no longer the great *polis* it had been in ancient times, when it had rivaled Thebes and Athens as one of the richest city-states in Greece. Only part of that was due to Alaric's invasion. In AD 365 the city had been almost totally leveled by an earthquake, rebuilt, and then shaken down again ten years later. Yet it was still a crossroads of commerce, from the mainland to the Peloponnesus and from the Aegean to the Ionian. By the time the Goths got there, it had been rebuilt yet again, on a smaller layout but to a grander scale. There is no record that the Romans had to retake the city by storm or siege, even though the Acrocorinth, a stronghold perched atop a jagged, 1,800-foot rock peak overlooking the town, had been an impregnable fortress going back to Macedonian times. The Goths apparently abandoned it all prior to the Roman landing. Alaric would come to regret that decision.

The two armies conducted a running fight across the northern part of the Peloponnesus. As Gibbon put it, "The woody and mountainous country of Arcadia, the fabulous residence of Pan and the Dryads, became the scene of a long and doubtful conflict between two generals not unworthy of each other."[1] The battles are not well recorded, but Claudian, who may have taken part in the campaign to document it

[1] *History*, Vol. III, p. 140

on behalf of his patron Stilicho, wrote, "The barbarian wagons are spattered with blood. Droves of fur-clad warriors are cut down by disease and the sword." And Zosimus concurs that Stilicho "forced the barbarians to flee to Pholoe."

From Corinth to Mount Pholoe, modern Foloi in the northwest Peloponnesus, is about seventy miles as the crow flies, but by land, in mountainous Greece, over a hundred, all up and down. Pholoe was, and still is, situated atop a 2,250-foot plateau covered in 9,000 acres of lofty Hungarian oak. It was famous among the ancient Greeks as the place where Hercules, on his way to capture the troublesome boar on nearby Mount Erymanthos, stopped to dine with his friend, the centaur Pholus, and, when they were attacked by other centaurs, accidentally killed him. Even today the forest, a protected ecological zone, is nearly trackless, villages are few and scattered, and visitors easily become lost. Alaric must have hoped to hide his army amid the endless trees, the way he had hoped to hide it in the marshes of the Hebros delta or the gorges of the Rhodope Mountains four years earlier. Stilicho, however, having the advantage of numbers, not only didn't lose his enemy, but surrounded him. Death by siegeworks would be a triumph of civilized technology over barbarian simple-mindedness.

"A tribe who at one time the entire world could hardly contain, are now trapped on one hill," proclaimed Claudian. At Foloi, under the ceiling of towering oaks, little light reaches the forest floor, not much grows except ferns and asphodels, and until the acorns come down only small game – rabbit and squirrel – is available, few of which would have reached the innards of a encircled barbarian camp. The Goths quickly ran low on food. To speed the process along, Stilicho set his engineers on the source of their water, the Peneus River (modern Pineios) which flowed down from Mount Erymanthos. They cut it off. "Thirsty and penned inside their palisade," continued Claudian of the Goths, "they searched in vain for the vanished waters, once within reach, but Stilicho had diverted into another channel."

Too late, Alaric must now have realized he would have been better off under siege in the Acrocorinth, which had its own freshwater spring. Yet once again Stilicho, when he had his enemy pinned and ready for destruction, hesitated to deliver the death blow.

Tacticians and strategists might argue that waiting for the Goths to surrender or starve was the militarily expedient way to accomplish victory without risking battle but, with hindsight, historians and armchair generals have faulted Stilicho. Zosimus sneered, "He might have easily exterminated them all, through the lack of supplies, had he not given himself over to lavishness and decadence."

It's hard to see with what lavishness and decadence Stilicho could have distracted himself around Pholoe, an area which even today is sparsely populated. There are other more likely reasons for Stilicho's hesitancy.

Stilicho's army, though larger than the last time he faced Alaric in 395, now had an even higher ratio of barbarians to Romans. His new German recruits had been only too glad to sign up for Roman training, equipment, and pay when all they had to do was march behind Stilicho's standards and intimidate other tribesmen into doing likewise. Facing battle against experienced, veteran, fellow barbarians with nothing to lose was a different matter. If Stilicho's *foederati* found more common cause with a proven, full-blooded barbarian leader like Alaric than a half-Roman like Stilicho, they might well switch sides and turn on him. In sailing to Greece to face Alaric, Stilicho was practically running a huge bluff, even among his own troops.

Then there is the theory that Stilicho spent the time attempting to bargain with Alaric. Perhaps he had made a mistake in not giving the Goths citizenship and their leader command. They had proven themselves formidable fighters when they had to – that is, when they had their backs to the wall, and were denied what they wanted by their imperial overlords. If Alaric really only wanted official recognition and a homeland, what if he was granted it by the West instead of the East? The Goths might not only serve as a buffer between the two domains. If Stilicho found it necessary to march on Constantinople in order to reunite the Empire, he might not still be able to depend on Gainas's loyalty, and would need all the troops he could get.

Stilicho may well have been biding his time while he talked his former comrade back over to his side. Alaric, though, had no reason to trust the West, and every reason to hope Stilicho's presence would pressure the East into making him a better offer.

To reach the ear of the emperor, word of the doings in the Peloponnesus had to bypass Constantinople and cross the Bosporus to Ancyra in Phrygia (today Ankara, Turkey), where the imperial family fled every summer to escape the heat and stench of the capital. While the empress Aelia kept the emperor Arcadius occupied – that June their first child, daughter Flacilla, was born – it was left to his chamberlain Eutropius to manage imperial affairs. The wily eunuch's goals were not always the same as the emperor's.

For Eutropius, as for Rufinus, having Stilicho in the East was a much greater menace than the one presented by Alaric. For all his depredations in Greece, the Goth had no pretensions to the Eastern throne. "Eutropius knew well that Stilicho was master of the West," wrote Zosimus, "and so contrived means to prevent his coming to Constantinople."

Though they had, at least for appearances, worked together to remove Rufinus, Stilicho still maintained a claim to Eutropius' position as power behind the throne. Furthermore, if Stilicho was to defeat Alaric, there was nothing to stop him from marching on the capital, probably with his ranks bolstered with Alaric's mercenaries. Eutropius had at his command only the army under Gainas, Stilicho's former and, Eutropius had to assume, still-loyal lieutenant. He might well simply hand it back over to his former commander, presumably after assassinating Eutropius as he had Rufinus.

Barbarian commanders were the wild cards on both sides. Neither Eutropius nor Stilicho could fully trust his own army. Both could use an ally. The situation called not for force, but guile. *The enemy of my enemy is my friend*. As Rufinus had been, Eutropius was clearly familiar with the concept.

This ongoing tussle between East and West had led both sides to neglect the South. Trouble was afoot in North Africa, a province of the West and a crucial one, today subsumed by the Sahara Desert but in those days the fertile breadbasket of Rome. Practically from the day Carthage was razed to the ground by Scipio Africanus in 146 BC, the Romans had remade the land between the desert and the sea into an agricultural paradise: eventually, a rich source of figs, grapes, fruit, and beans, more olive oil than Italy, and a million tons of grain every year.

Given all this, the wonder is that the Romans did not install a more reliable system of government there. Besides Carthage, what is now northern Tunisia alone was host to some 200 Roman cities, supplying fifteen percent of Rome's senators, several popes, and even an emperor. Lucius Septimius Severus (r. AD 193–211) had been born in Leptis Magna, modern Khoms on the Libyan coast, next to Carthage and Alexandria the most important city in the province.

Yet Roman Africa's population was only minority Roman. The majority were Punic – descendants of the Carthaginians – and Berber tribespeople. These Berbers (the word has the same Greek root as "barbarian") differed ethnically from the Germanics, but politically they were the same, having an on-again, off-again relationship with Rome. The current Berber governor, Gildo, ruled his domain as a tyrant. "He gives in to the most varied vices," accused Claudian, although later, when he needed to justify a war. "...He never quiets. When greed is satisfied lust is unbridled. By day he is a menace to the rich, and by night to the married. Any man who is rich or has a beautiful wife is arrested on some trumped-up charge. If no charge is brought against him, he is invited to a feast and there murdered."

As long as the grain still flowed to Rome, Theodosius could overlook such transgressions by Africans against Africans. He even arranged the marriage of Nebridius, nephew of his first wife Aelia Flaccilla, to Salvina, the daughter of Gildo, though according to Jerome with ulterior motives: "Theodosius, indeed, procured for him an African wife of the highest rank, who, since her country was then rent by civil wars, became something of a hostage for its allegiance."

With his family married into the imperial dynasty, and given his title – he is the only man known as *comes et magister utriusque militiae per Africam*, a position which may even have been created for him – Gildo was, in theory if not physically, as near an imperial throne as Stilicho, and closer than Eutropius. Therein lay the problem.

"Some said that, driven by some kind of envy, he determined to add Africa to the provinces of the Eastern Empire," claimed Orosius, "but according to another view, he believed that there was little hope for the young emperors, since before them hardly any boy who inherited the throne had ever lived to manhood."

If Gildo expected, as was reasonable, both young emperors to be usurped and assassinated before their time, he would have to pick sides between their successors. Given his family ties, it's hardly surprising he chose the East. It would be easier to bump an unrelated eunuch out of the picture than an imperial father-in-law. However, even Gildo's family were divided on this. His brother Mascezel, for one, sided with Rome. Gildo did not take kindly to such disloyalty. As Orosius recorded, "Mascezel, thoroughly disagreeing with Gildo's rebellious designs, left his two sons with the soldiers in Africa and returned to Italia. Gildo, becoming suspicious of both his brother's absence and his nephews' attendance, treacherously took the youths captive and had them killed."

With a schism opening between Africa and Italia, Eutropius took advantage of the opportunity. Emissaries plied the Mediterranean waters between Constantinople and Carthage. Meanwhile, to blunt the advances of Stilicho, Eutropius had Emperor Arcadius convene the Eastern Senate in Constantinople. Decisions were reached and decrees issued. More messengers departed the capital, this time bound for Greece.

Imagine Alaric's surprise when, counting down the days to his inevitable surrender to his Roman master, he learned Stilicho's forces were breaking camp, abandoning their earthworks and trenches, packing up their gear and readying to march. His curiosity was soon enough abated. Probably the same emissaries who had brought word from Constantinople to Stilicho were able to pass through the abandoned siege works to bring it to Alaric as well.

The Goths were free to go.

The contemporary scribes sought reason for Stilicho to once again turn loose his quarry – licentiousness, duplicity, bribery, sheer inattention – but there was no need. Stilicho relented because, once again, he was ordered to relent, by Constantinople.

The similarities between the events in Greece of 395 and 397 are so great that by some interpretations of Zosimus, who neglects to give dates, they are one and the same, a single confrontation between Stilicho and Alaric that ends in the death of Rufinus. Zosimus, however, based his account on the *Universal History* of the Greek sophist and historian Eunapius, much of which is lost now and may have been lost then. Modern historians largely agree there were two confrontations with similar outcomes. Orosius, looking back on events from only twenty years later, fumed that Alaric and the Goths were "often vanquished, often cornered, but always allowed to get away."

The difference is, this time, Stilicho was not only ordered to cease warring with the Goths, but ordered to leave the East, and never come back. The Eastern Senate had declared him *hostis publicus*. Public enemy. An enemy of the state.

Alaric, on the other hand, was to be granted what he had wanted all along. He was to be named *magister militum per Illyricum*, with all the power and wealth that came with the position. The lesson was reinforced that, much as the West opposed Alaric, when pushed the East would appease him. The Goths were both pawns and players in the power struggle between the Roman empires, each of which sought to use the barbarians against the other.

What mattered now was that, lacking official approval from Constantinople, Stilicho was no longer entitled to support from the Greek cities around him. Alaric, on the other hand, could now demand such support, in the name of the state. Suddenly Stilicho was the invader, and Alaric the imperial defender.

Just in case Stilicho decided to disobey the imperial decree, Alaric abandoned Pholoe as well and put space between him and Stilicho's army. Some historians believe the Goths marched thirty miles north to the Strait of Rio, the narrows that Stilicho's fleet had passed through weeks before, where they hired boats and ships to ferry them across. Others claim they retraced their steps to cross the Isthmus of Corinth. Either way, they made good their escape into Epirus, the western, upper Greek mainland.

Again following orders, Stilicho let them go. His concern now was keeping his army intact and supplied in what was suddenly hostile territory. "He instructed his soldiers to plunder whatever the barbarians had left behind, thus giving the foe a chance to escape from Peloponnese and carry their booty with them to Epirus," recorded Zosimus, who shows his own disdain for the Goths by adding, "and to plunder all the towns in that land."

Stilicho summoned his fleet, re-embarked his army, and sailed back to Italy. There he received still more bad news. In North Africa, Gildo had renounced his allegiance to Honorius and the West, declaring instead for Arcadius, Eutropius, and the East. Claudian lamented, "From Nile to the Atlas Mountains, from scorched Barca to Cadiz in the west, from Tangier to the Egyptian coast, Gildo has taken the land as his own. A third of the world belongs to one bandit chief."

Gildo almost certainly thought of himself as Roman. His father had been a Berber prince, but also a Roman officer, and the son did not think of himself as a usurper. He had not actually staged an insurrection, and never threatened to lead troops against Rome to take the throne of Honorius.

He didn't have to. All he had to do was cut off grain shipments to Rome.

The city's population at this time is thought to have been at least 500,000 and as many as 750,000. Assuming a consumption of about 450 pounds of bread per person per year, they required from about 110,000 to 170,000 tons of grain per year – 300 to 450 tons *per day*. The *cura annonae*, the free bread, olive oil, wine, and pork subsidized by the government to feed the city's poor, was much more than just a social safety net. The *Collegium Pistorum*, the College of Bakers established in 168 BC to regulate the supply and price of bread, had its own seat in the Senate. The importance of keeping the mob fed was well known to its rulers. As early as AD 22, Emperor Tiberius had written his Senate that "if neglected, it will result in the utter ruin of the state."

Give credit to Eutropius. The tables had been instantaneously and completely turned. With Arcadius as his dupe, Alaric and the Goths as his allies, and Gildo on his side, a eunuch and former slave had made himself the most powerful man in the Roman world. Stilicho had been reduced to scrambling just to keep the tottering Western Empire on its feet. No one could blame him if he began to see Eutropius, and the Eastern Empire itself, not just as a rival, but as an actual impediment to unification – a challenger to the rightful seat of empire, Rome.

XI

BARRING THE GATES

AD 397

What has happened to the strength of Latium and the vigor of Rome? To what a wisp of our past glory are we gradually reduced!

Claudian

In the autumn of 397 the Roman West was at crisis point. The Scots and Picts were threatening Britannia again. Goths in Illyricum, opposition in Constantinople, revolt in Africa, Rome threatened with starvation, and little money with which to do anything about it. On top of that, was Honorius.

Now a teenager, anxious about his manhood, the young emperor was impatient to prove himself, even if that meant a dangerous mid-winter sea crossing with a battle at the end of it. "My vessels should have already been crewed without regard for rough seas. I myself am ready to sail in the lead ship. Let every foreign country that is loyal to me come to our assistance," he told Stilicho (at least, according to Claudian). "…Or should I sit here and take such dishonor? Shall I give up as a man what I led and reigned over as a boy? Twice my father hastened to the Alps to defend the realm. Am I to be an easy victim, an object of derision?"

Honorius was a teen, yes, but a teen whose whims were backed with imperial powers. He required handling as carefully as any of

Stilicho's other pressing problems. When it came to Gildo, at least, Stilicho assured him, "It's enough for you to order his downfall. Your name will strike more terror into him than your sword."

Stilicho had requisitioned grain from Spain and Gaul, enough to get Rome through the winter, but there was no getting around that the city required African grain to survive. Somebody was going to have to go get it.

Stilicho did not intend to set foot in Africa himself. It was now part of the East, from which he was banned. For him to lead an invasion there would be to incite civil war. The first thing he did was put the onus for such a war on the Western senators. Their incentive was that he would restore to them the power of *senatus consultum*, the right to pass laws, which had been lost to them since the early days of the Empire. Symmachus, as leader of the pagan party in the Senate, was more than amenable to the bargain. Stilicho was Christian, but tolerant of pagans like Symmachus and Claudian, and it behooved the aristocrats to do whatever they could to resolve the problem with Gildo. Many of them owned vast estates in Africa that would be lost to them if the land went over to the East. So among the first laws they passed was to declare Gildo, like many a Carthaginian before him and as Stilicho himself had been declared, *hostis publicus*, an enemy of the state.

That done, to keep this fourth little Punic War, the Gildonic War, contained and finished quickly, Stilicho would fight it by proxy. So to command the African expedition he called upon Mascezel, Gildo's brother, who had come to Rome to declare his loyalty and lost his sons for it. Through him, Stilicho could claim that Rome was not invading Africa, but simply supporting a loyal minion in a family squabble. Mascezel was Berber royalty, who could lay legitimate claim to his brother's title and power, and had the motivation of blood vengeance to spur him on. Stilicho told Honorius, "Let Gildo be driven before the man he drove away, and fear the man whose children he murdered. As he is being dragged away to execution let him see his brother's hand in it."

They furnished Mascezel with 5,000 troops, good troops, including Gauls and the Illyrians of the Jovian and Herculian legions of the imperial guard. In November, as the fleet readied to depart, Honorius delivered a rousing speech, worthy of an emperor – at least, according to Claudian:

> My men, so soon to defeat Gildo, now is the time to do as you promised and carry out your threats... If, in addition losing Illyria, Africa is to be lost to native kings, what land is still ours? The empire of Italia, which once reached to the Nile and the Red Sea, today reaches no farther than the Adriatic. Will Sicily now be the most distant province of Rome, when in the old days neither Egypt nor India were farthest? Go, take back that southern kingdom a rebel has stolen from me. It depends on you whether Rome, the invincible mistress of the world, stands or falls. You owe me a multitude of peoples, nations and cities lost. Fight just one battle in defense of Africa. Let the restoration of the empire depend on your oars and sails. Give back to Africa the laws of Rome she has cast aside.

Having ensured Stilicho was too busy elsewhere to threaten him in Constantinople, Eutropius had only one more possible avenue of resistance to his rule: the church. The opportunity to change that had presented itself on September 27 when Nectarius, the bishop of Constantinople, died. Eutropius used his influence with Arcadius to choose his replacement, a priest and former hermit called John Chrysostom, the "Golden Tongued."

Short, skinny, and in perpetual bad health due to his ascetic ways, John was nevertheless popular for his championing of the poor, plain speaking, and lack of hypocrisy. Back in 388, when the Antiochenes rose up in protest over tax increases and desecrated statues of Theodosius and his family, John scolded, "Sincerely improve yourselves now, not like during one of the many earthquakes, famines, droughts or similar calamities in which you quit sinning for three or four days and then resume your old ways again." He made himself a favorite of both the citizenry and the imperial government.

Eutropius felt the proper place for Christianity's best orator was in the capital, speaking on his behalf. John was so beloved in Antioch that riots were feared on his departure, so Eutropius basically had him secretly smuggled to Constantinople, where the archbishopric was thrust upon him. John accepted the post as God's will. He was invested on February 26.

If Eutropius thought he had God in his pocket, however, he was in for a surprise. John Chrysostom was no man's puppet.

February of 398 was a critical month on both sides of the Empire. In North Africa, Mascezel's fleet had landed, and his army disembarked. In Mediolanum, Stilicho was attending to higher priorities, closer to home: his duties as a father. Not only as *pater patriae*, father of the state, but as *pater sponsae*, father of the bride.

Maria was then only about nine or ten, young even for Roman girls to marry and probably younger than Serena had been when she wed Stilicho. Serena, according to Zosimus, thought her daughter still too young for marriage, "and that to give such a young and innocent girl to a man's embrace was an offense to nature."

Maria may have been too young to concern herself with the opposite sex, but Honorius was not. To this point he had been interested primarily in his pet fowl and in hunting, but lately he found himself more and more preoccupied with his young cousin once removed. "A blush often colored his cheeks, betraying his thoughts. Often his hand, unbidden, scribbled the loved one's name," noted Claudian. "...The eager lover is annoyed by waiting."

Stilicho had denied Honorius the opportunity to prove himself on campaign. If he and Serena denied him the chance to prove himself as a man, they risked much more than a teenage tantrum. Honorius was the Western emperor, if not a god on earth as in the old pagan days, then God's chosen representative on earth. Stilicho and Serena would forget that at their peril. If Honorius began to resent them, Stilicho's enemies at court might fan the flame. And Stilicho had enemies, particularly among the aristocrats who were used to swaying, if not dominating, boy emperors like Valentinian II and Gratian, and who furthermore held Stilicho's barbarian blood against him. A teenage boy's sexual frustration might easily turn to anger, and an emperor's anger could be murderous.

So in February 398 little Maria was made ready to do her duty. "Go, join with the man who is worthy of you, and share with him a world-spanning empire," Claudian has Venus encouraging her. "...The whole world will be your dowry."

On this occasion the poet, having been at court a few years now, was hitting his stride. He composed a lengthy *epithalamium*, meant to be sung to a bride on her way to the bedchamber, and four shorter *fescennines*, odes traditionally sung at harvest and religious festivals, but by the time of the late Empire often sung so bawdily at weddings that they were proscribed by law. Claudian, mindful that his readership would include not only the imperial family in Mediolanum but the senators in Rome and aristocrats throughout the Empire, kept his verses relatively clean. He casts Honorius as the great hunter, whose prey falls willingly before him and whose spear-thrust the lion is thankful and proud to accept. Maria, on the other hand, is portrayed as the shy, even unwilling, object of affection: "A maiden's shame now overwhelms the nervous bride, her veil is wetted with innocent tears."

Claudian has the wedding, attended by Venus and the Nereids, presided over by the *pater familias* Stilicho: "Let regal blood unite again with regal blood. Perform a father's duty and unite these children with your illustrious hand. You married an emperor's daughter, and now in turn your daughter will marry an emperor. Is there reason for jealousy? An excuse for envy? Stilicho is father of both the bride and bridegroom."

Stilicho's soldiers, wearing white, their weapons set aside for the day, cluster round to sing the praises of their chieftain: "May your son Eucherius exceed his father's virtues. May the lovely Thermantia, your daughter, live to see a marriage like this. May Maria's womb swell and a little Honorius, born to the purple, rest in his grandfather's lap."

The emperor presents his bride with the Roman jewels of state, worn by empresses down through the generations. In the climactic verse, Claudian encourages Honorius (who, it must be remembered, was still an untried teen) to prove himself, both as a man and as a Roman leader, by conquering his bride as he might conquer a foe. Modern readers would not be wrong to call it rape: "Do not hesitate to attack, young lover, even though she claws you savagely with cruel fingernails…. Thorns defend the rose and bees defend their honey. Coy refusals only increase the pleasure. The desire for what is denied is the most passionate. The sweetest kiss is flavored with tears."

Whether Honorius ever carried through with this advice, however, is open to question. Zosimus noted that Serena, reluctant to surrender Maria to such treatment, still looked out for her daughter: "She knew a woman familiar with managing such business, and through her contrived that Maria would live with the emperor and share his bed, but that he would not be able to take her virginity."

Rome at its height. A reconstruction of the Forum, 1911. (Getty Images)

Emperor Flavius
Julius Valens.(Alamy)

Roman solidus (gold coin) depicting
Emperor Valens. (Alamy)

At Adrianople, the Goth cavalry enveloped and annihilated the Roman infantry. (Artwork by Howard Gerrard, © Osprey Publishing Ltd)

Solidus of Emperor Theodosius I. (Alamy)

Marble bust of a woman, *c.* 380–90, thought to be of Augusta Aelia Flacilla, wife of Theodosius I. (The Metropolitan Museum of Art, New York)

Emperor Theodosius bends the knee to
Bishop Ambrose in Mediolanum after the
massacre at Thessaloniki in AD 390.
(Getty Images)

Eastern Roman Emperor
Flavius Arcadius. (Alamy)

Western Roman Emperor
Flavius Honorius. (Alamy)

Emperor Honorius depicted on a
Roman *solidus*. (Alamy)

Gilded glass medallion depicting
Galla Placidia (right) and her children.
(Getty images)

The Diptych of Stilicho, *c.* AD 395.
(Getty Images)

On his numerous trips north over the Alps to put down barbarian rebellions,
Stilicho and his men almost certainly crossed this Roman-era bridge in the
7,580-foot-high Septimer Pass, Switzerland. (Alamy)

An 1894 depiction of Alaric's welcome in Athens, AD 395. (Getty Images)

The rejection of Empress Eudoxia by John Chrysostom would be the spark that set off the final split between the Roman empires. (Alamy)

Above A high medieval depiction of the battle of Faesulae, AD 406, between Stilicho and the Goth king Radagaisus. (Getty Images)

Below Sarcophagus of Stilicho. The encircled couple at the top-center are thought to represent Stilicho and Serena. (Getty Images)

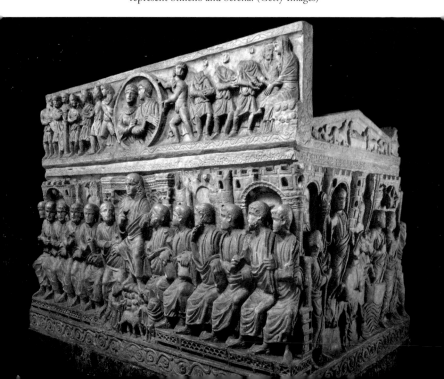

The Salarian Gate through which the Goths entered Rome was demolished in 1921, but was built much like this San Paolo Gate, with twin guard towers and a central arched gateway. (Alamy)

"I am the Dark Barbarian / That towers over all" (Robert E. Howard). *Alaric's Entrance into Rome*, 19th century, artist unknown. (Getty Images)

It had been 800 years since barbarian conquerors last invaded Rome's streets. Alaric's Goths made up for lost time. (Alamy)

Just as Nero supposedly played music while Rome burned in AD 64, Emperor Honorius was more concerned with his pet birds than the city's fall in 410. (Getty Images)

The monument to Stilicho still stands in the Forum of Rome. (Photo: Gabriel Dobersch)

Philostorgius claimed Stilicho saw to it that Honorius was given a potion to cause impotency.* If all this was an excuse for the lack of imperial children, there's another. Little Maria, even if she was raped, was simply not yet old enough to become pregnant.

In North Africa, Mascezel marched his men south to meet Gildo's forces near Kasserine.† According to Orosius, Gildo's army numbered some 70,000 men (though historians believe he exaggerated by a factor of ten, and that his troops were mostly unreliable tribal mercenaries), but on the eve of battle Mascezel was comforted by a dream in which the late St. Ambrose appeared to him, prophesying victory. The deacon Paulinus of Milan, who heard the story from Mascezel himself, reported that the bishop's spirit held a staff, which he struck on the ground, saying "Here, here, here," which the Berber took as a sign that he would triumph on the third day.

On the appointed date, as the two sides parleyed before battle, one of Gildo's standard bearers evidently broke the truce. "Thereupon Mascezel cut his arm with a sword," reported Orosius, "crippling his hand and by the force of the blow causing him to drop the banner to the ground. At the sight, the other troops, thinking that the vanguard was already giving up, reversed their standards and immediately surrendered to Mascezel."

Zosimus claims there was some sort of battle, in which Gildo's forces turned on him. He made for the coast and attempted to escape by sea, but contrary winds forced him back to shore. He was captured at Thabraka (modern Tabarka on the Tunisian coast), and on July 31, 398, he either was strangled or hanged himself.

The whole campaign was over so quickly that civil war between East and West was averted. Gibbon, perhaps in a hurry to get on with his monumental tale, omits the episode entirely. Africa was made part of the West again before Eutropius could do anything about it. In any case he had more immediate concerns. The Western Empire was not the only one with threats on its frontiers. The Huns, whom Rufinus had

---

*The 1st-century Greek physician, surgeon, and philosopher Aelius (or Claudius) Galenus, called Galen of Pergamon, claimed a concoction of skink (lizard) kidneys and lettuce seed mixed in water would prevent or lower an erection. The 2nd-century Alexandrian medical writer Aelius Promotus recommended a rub of mountain mint crushed in a mix of wine and milk.

†The same pass where, in February 1943, Axis armies under German Generalfeldmarschall Erwin Rommel would deal Americans a sharp defeat.

bribed to fight elsewhere, were raiding into Asia Minor again. Claudian wrote of burning towns and farmland, women and cattle driven north into captivity and men into slavery: "The spoils are too much for the fierce barbarians. With their fill of booty they turn to killing."

On top of the slaves and loot taken, the Huns were doubtless hoping to extort more money from Constantinople, particularly from spineless Romans who would consent to be led by a eunuch. As Claudian put it, "Our enemies laughed at the sight, feeling that at last we had run out of men."

They were in for a surprise. Eutropius had what Rufinus had not: an army. In the spring of 398, while Mascezel was leading his invasion of Africa, Eutropius rode out at the head of the Army of the East. Since Romans were little more inclined than barbarians to take orders from a eunuch, it's probably more true that Gainas led the army, with Eutropius riding along as the representative of Arcadius. Either way, they drove the Huns before them, out of Anatolia. It's unclear if there was a battle of any kind – this was decades before the Huns united under Attila, and they were still a disorganized rabble, as yet incapable of facing a real army – but the effect was the same. The Huns retreated back over the Caucasus, from which they would not return for a generation. When the army returned to Constantinople, Eutropius claimed credit for the victory.

"Eutropius returns triumphant," conceded Claudian from Mediolanum, nevertheless holding a low opinion of men who would follow such a leader. "There follow companies of infantry, cavalry like their general – maniples of eunuchs, an army worthy of Priapus.* On his return his minions meet him and embrace their champion."

Stilicho could afford to let Eutropius have his day in the sun. It was to his advantage to have the East defended and kept intact. Stilicho would have ordered no less himself, had he been in control in Constantinople.

But he wasn't. He was barely in control of the West. Even in triumph, Stilicho and Eutropius had added nothing to the wealth and glory of the Empire. But then, they weren't conquerors. They were fighting not to win, but not to lose, against an inexorable pressure being exerted on all sides.

---

*The Greek god of fertility and male genitalia, notable for his permanent erection.

XII

Barbarians Ascendant

AD 398

*A barbarian named Gainas, who had joined the Romans, and
risen from the lowest ranks to command of the army, formed a
plan to usurp the throne of the Roman Empire.*

Sozomen

Poor Gainas. It was his army that Eutropius had led against the
Huns in Asia Minor, or more precisely it was Gainas, as *magister
equitum et peditum*, who had led the army against the Huns, but
Eutropius who took the credit. All those years of doing Rome's dirty
work – coming up through the ranks only to lose half his men at
the Frigidus, remaining loyal when Alaric went his own way, killing
Rufinus on Stilicho's orders as though nothing more than a common
street thug – and now Gainas, even as supreme commander, had to
bend the knee to a eunuch. It was an insult to any right-thinking
Roman, let alone one of barbarian heritage.

More than that, there was nowhere else for Gainas to go except
down. Eutropius had a record of dealing harshly with those who
became powerful enough to present a threat, like Timasius – a relative
of Emperor Arcadius – and even his own former patron Abundantius.
Perhaps Gainas had been lucky so far. Men only rose so far under
Eutropius before he had them removed.

But perhaps not, if they struck first.

"With this in mind," wrote Sozomen, "Gainas summoned his countrymen, the Goths, from their lands to the Roman provinces, and named his relatives as tribunes."

One of these kinsmen was Tribigild. (Modern historians question any blood relationship between him and Gainas, except that they were both Goths.) Zosimus called him "a man unusually bold, ready for any risky undertaking. He commanded no Romans, but barbarians, stationed in Phrygia, whose care was entrusted to him by the emperor."

The Goths who had come after Alaric's people and crossed the Danube back in 386 – those who had survived slaughter under the galleys of Promotus – had been resettled in west-central Anatolia, probably to serve as a buffer against Hunnish or Persian invasion. It was their menfolk under Tribigild's command. Tribigild owed his command, and his loyalty, to Gainas. And now there were two Goth armies within easy march of Constantinople.

Let Eutropius try to do away with Gainas now, and they would find out who really held the power.

In Mediolanum there was a similar question as to who gave the orders. Mascezel, the conqueror of Africa, was basking in his triumph and more than a little overbearing about it. "This Mascezel, it is true, became full of himself with an arrogance born of success," admitted Orosius, "and declined to associate with the holy men who had given him the victory, as a champion of God."

As a prince of the Berbers Mascezel could, after all, look forward to assuming his dead brother's rank as *magister utriusque militiae per Africam*, which would in theory put him nearly on a par with Stilicho. Then there were Gildo's extensive assets and estates. They had become the property of Emperor Honorius, but it was obvious that the boy could not administer them in person. A new post, *comes Gildoniaci patrimonii*, count of Gildo's property, was created specifically to take charge of it all in the emperor's name. Mascezel might reasonably expect to receive that title as well, along with Rome's gratitude.

Having just done away with one Berber chieftain, however, Stilicho had no desire to put another in his place. Notably, even Claudian's account of the war with Gildo abruptly cuts off soon after Mascezel lands in Africa. If the poet ever wrote the story of the ensuing battle, he soon discarded it. Tales in which Stilicho did not personally triumph were not worth the telling. Mascezel had done what Stilicho ordered, no more. "Though Stilicho envied him his great victory," wrote Zosimus, "yet he affected a liking for him, and led him to expect favor."

Mascezel did not help himself by violating the sanctity of a church to drag out some men who for, whatever reason, had claimed asylum there. Church sanctuary could be a great inconvenience to the authorities; recall that Stilicho himself had violated it in the past, and been forced to make amends. That same year, in Constantinople, Eutropius had seen to the passing of a law forbidding sanctuary to criminals. There was always a price for crimes against God, and Mascezel was about to pay it. "This sacrilege was duly rewarded," declared Orosius, "for soon afterward, while the same men whom he had dragged out of the church for punishment still lived, he himself was punished, to their delight."

Late in the year the Berber joined Stilicho and his bodyguards on a walk. Some sources claim this was in Rome, others Mediolanum; it could have been either. At some point they crossed a bridge over a river, the Tiber or the Po. Ever quick to accuse, Zosimus has it, "The guards, obeying Stilicho's signal, tossed Mascezel into the river, where he perished in the turbulence."

That could have been a story concocted by Stilicho's enemies. Mascezel may well have drowned accidentally. But he did drown, and if it wasn't murder, it was certainly convenient for Stilicho's purposes. After all, the whole campaign had been Stilicho's idea. The glory was his.

In his honor the city's fishermen and river boatmen, who transported the foods of Africa from the coastal ports up the Tiber to the city and would have been out of work had Gildo's blockade not been defeated, paid for a modest statue in Stilicho's honor. In 1925 its marble base was found buried a few blocks north of the Forum, damaged and incomplete, but intact enough to piece together some of the inscription (line breaks approximate):

FLAVIUS STILICHO, v.c.*
In honor of Fl. Stilicho, *v.c.* and *inlustri*†
Magistro utriusque militiae

---

*Abbreviating *viri clarissimi*, very famous man
†Distinguished

And *consuli ordinario.**
Out of veneration for great achievements,
Among the other boons which he has bestowed
on the city of Rome,
The river boatmen and related fishermen
of the city of Rome
Who convey food to the city in river boats
Have raised this gilded monument
Because he replenished Rome with food supplies
By subduing Gildo, public enemy.

The modest size of the monument and its out-of-the-way location, of course, indicate that most of the glory actually went to those whom Stilicho served. Until the 15th century a triumphal arch dedicated to Arcadius, Honorius, and Theodosius stood at the eastern end of the Bridge of Nero over the Tiber, and a similar arch was raised to them in the Forum itself. (The irony of Arcadius' Eastern court having actually encouraged Gildo's rebellion was apparently forgotten.) Only the base survives, and that in pieces. It is thought to have been a pedestal for a gilded *quadriga*, a four-horse chariot, supposedly in good condition when excavated in 1549, but the Italian cardinal Alessandro Farnese, the grandson of Pope Paul III, who fancied himself a patron of the arts, had it cut up and remade into a more modern work. The Museum of Naples has one inscribed piece, and the others are still piled in the Forum, where only some of the dedication survives:

The most invincible and prosperous emperors
Our lords Arcadius and Honorius, brothers,
The Senate and People of Rome
Avenged the uprising.
Africa is restored and happy.

Another line, found separately, reads *armipotens Libycum defendit Honorius orbem*, the warrior of Libya Honorius defends the world.

*Consul ordinary, i.e, elected at the start of the year

174

Clearly Honorius was to get the glory, but Stilicho's was the power. He titled his brother-in-law Bathanarius, husband of his unnamed and almost unknown sister, as *comes Africae* and dispatched him to Carthage to rule. He went, however, without a large part of Gildo's fortune. There was no telling when the West might enjoy such a windfall again, and other corners of the Empire needed it more. The Britons, abandoned by Maximus and overrun with the Scots and Picts, had sent emissaries across the Channel to beg for assistance, "like frightened chickens clustering under the protective wings of their hens," wrote Gildas, "that their miserable country might not be totally destroyed, and that the name of Rome, which now was merely a meaningless sound in the ear, might not become an insult even to distant nations."

Stilicho put Rome's money – Gildo's money – to good use. He sent a large part of it to Britannia, to recruit more troops and rebuild and strengthen Hadrian's Wall and the coastal forts. The northern barbarians were made to remember who ruled south of the Wall. "The Romans," wrote Gildas, "roused with compassion as much as men can be on hearing of such horrors, send forward, like eagles in flight, their unexpected bands of cavalry by land and mariners by sea, and bringing down their terrible swords upon their enemies' shoulders, they cut them down like falling leaves."

The coasts were duly cleared and the Picts driven back to Caledonia. The campaign is sometimes referred to as "Stilicho's Pictish War," though there's little indication of any more fighting than usual, much less that the generalissimo journeyed there himself, and actually no hard evidence of decisive victory. Claudian didn't let that stop him. In his poetic way, he has the island, personified, tattooed like a Celt and clothed in Caledonian fur with a blue cloak symbolizing the surrounding seas, praising Stilicho as her deliverer: "Thanks to him I no longer fear the Scottish arms, tremble at the Pict, or keep watch on my coasts for the Saxon who would come however the wind might blow."

As usual, Claudian overstates the situation for his patron's benefit. Even if the fighting died down, Britannia had become an imperial backwater where barbarism remained a constant threat. After almost 400 years the cold, wet, windswept, faraway province that could only be reached by sea was becoming too expensive to maintain, and was garrisoned more as a matter of principle than out of any critical importance to the Empire.

Yet there were already some Britons, whether of Roman or barbarian blood, who had tired of barring the door against invasion and delaying the inevitable. They aspired to greater deeds. Emperor Constantine the Great had begun his eighteen-year campaign for sole rule of the Empire from Eboracum, and Magnus Maximus had acquired his imperial start in northern Wales. Down among the lower ranks, either already serving in Britannia or sent there as part of Stilicho's reinforcements, were men – Marcus, Gratianus, Flavius Claudius Constantinus – who would soon enough make their names famous. Or infamous. Stilicho's infusion of men and money may even have whetted their appetites and helped set them on their path.

For the time being, war in the North was overshadowed by news from the East. Riding on the coattails of his "victory" over the Huns, Eutropius had himself nominated for the position of consul for the year 399, and was confirmed by his loyalists in the Eastern Senate.

When word reached Italia the Western Senate refused to endorse Eutropius, and their disgust extended even to the Eastern court for supporting him. "A eunuch, wearing the cloak of Romulus, sat in the house of emperors," wrote Claudian in disbelief, "the soiled palace lay open to an eager crowd of supplicants. There hurry senators, rubbing shoulders with commoners, apprehensive generals and magistrates of every station. All would be happy to be the first to throw themselves at his feet and to touch his hand. The highest aspiration of all is to press kisses to those repellent wrinkles."

However, not everyone in the Eastern court favored the eunuch. A group of discontents had begun to coalesce around the imperial consort, Eudoxia. Having raised her up to her current high position, Eutropius still regarded her as an underling. Nor did Arcadius stand up for her, lacking the nerve to oppose his chamberlain, no matter how grievous the offense. "Eutropius had once treated his wife with great lack of respect," confided Philostorgius, who lived in the capital at the time, "threatening that he would soon turn her out of his palace."

Eudoxia's position was precarious. She was the imperial consort, but had not yet been named *Augusta*, empress – probably Eutropius' doing as well. She was, however, earning her keep, having that January borne Arcadius another daughter, Aelia Pulcheria. Admittedly, in Roman society daughters were not as important as sons, but in those days when every birth was potentially fatal to mother and baby Eudoxia had proven herself a capable child bearer. Furthermore, she had Arcadius' ear – among other parts – as much or more than did Eutropius, which put them further at odds. Plus, she had barbarian blood on her father Bauto's side, even though Frankish instead of Goth. As Philostorgius put it, "She had in her a good bit of the boldness which is the mark of the barbarian."

And *that* made her and Gainas natural allies.

All across the Empire, barbarians could look up with envy and admiration to Alaric, who had achieved what no chieftain had managed since Fritigern. He had bent the Romans to his will. He had pushed Rome and Constantinople to see which one gave way first, and he had been richly rewarded for it.

His people no longer had to eke a living out of the rocky Balkan soil. His officers were billeted in the finest houses, their wives and children living under roofs like real Romans. They had Greek slaves to labor for them. They had Thracian horses to ride. Roman *fabricae*, armories, turned out Roman swords and spears, Roman armor, and Roman shields for them. Alaric's soldiers were Roman soldiers, organized into cohorts and legions, with Roman tribunes and Roman centurions training them in Roman strategy and tactics. Granted, many of them – Franks, Gauls, Vandals, even a Hun here and there – were as barbarian as the Goths, but it was over twenty years since Adrianople and many of them had grown up not knowing anything other than Roman life and Roman ways. Gone were the days of defending a wagon circle against outsiders; gone were the days of fighting to defend at all. The Goths learned how to circumvallate and starve a city to death. They learned how Romans defeated barbarians...and they learned how to defeat other Romans.

In truth, Alaric the king now had a kingdom. Macedonia, Dacia, and Greece all owed him allegiance. The civic leaders of Naissus, Sirmium, Thessaloniki, and more paid him call to show obeisance, pay taxes, and offer tribute. They were a conquered people, and Alaric was their overlord. From the Julian Alps in the north to the fingertips of the Peloponnesus in the south, he was lord over a domain not only comparable in size to Italia or Byzantium, but strategically placed between them, where Alaric could bully or supplicate either. If one side threatened him, he could call on the other for defense. If he wished to attack one, he could call on the other to back him. He could rightly consider himself the equal of Stilicho on one hand and Eutropius on the other. There was no reason to think he could not still better himself. And every barbarian who knew the name of Alaric could not think but to follow his example.

"The success of his rebellion," declared Gibbon, "encouraged the ambition of every leader of the foreign mercenaries."[1]

In the summer of 399 Tribigild rode from his headquarters at Nakoleia (modern Seyitgazi in central Turkey) 200 miles to Constantinople, seeking imperial remuneration for his people's services and possibly a promotion into the bargain. He was unsuccessful on both counts. "By chance he had just returned from a visit to Eutropius with empty hands," claimed Claudian. "Disillusionment and resentment kindled his anger, and poverty, which can drive the gentlest heart to break the law, inflamed his savage heart."

The poet has the war goddess Bellona assuming the form of Tribigild's wife to scold and shame him, but no divine intervention was necessary. Hell hath no fury like a barbarian's wife. As Claudian depicts it, she rips into Tribigild, calling him a better farmer than warrior, and reminding him that Alaric won the Romans' friendship by being the Romans' enemy: "It is time for you to return to a barbarian life. It is your turn to be a terror, so that men who belittled your virtues marvel at your crimes. Weighed down with loot and spoils, you will be a Roman when you please."

Whether following the orders of a wife or a goddess, Tribigild summoned his men, the soldiers and farmers and townspeople who had with their families tried to settle into a Roman way of life. Arians would have found sympathetic ground in Phrygia, known for its offshoots of Christianity like Monatists, who dabbled in prophecy, and Novatianists, who denied communion to lapsed Christians. Like Arianism, these sects had been declared as heresy by the Roman church, and though their adherents denied each other's beliefs they

[1] *History*, Vol. III, p. 143

had a common foe in Constantinople. Tribigild did not have much trouble stirring up a revolt among his own Goths and the locals who had become their neighbors over the past thirteen years. Though Claudian surely concocted the scene, the result is a matter of historical record: "Defiant Barbary had found a leader and threw off the Roman yoke for all to see."

When news of the uprising in Phrygia reached the imperial palace, both Arcadius and Eutropius were inclined to discount it. The emperor had been about to depart on his annual summer sojourn to Ancyra, and a revolt next door in Phrygia was entirely upsetting to his plans. Still, he had no idea what to do about such matters except to place everything in his minister's hands. For his part Eutropius considered the uprising little more than banditry. Recalling his handling of Alaric, he sent messengers with promises of rank and reward if Tribigild would desist. This was nothing more than the Goth had asked for in the first place, and it was too late for that now. Tribigild was enjoying easy pickings among the defenseless cities of long-peaceful Phrygia, Lydia, Pamphylia, and Psidia. The messengers returned with his refusal, reports of the death and destruction the barbarians had wrought, and word that runaway slaves were joining the ranks of the Goths.

Now Eutropius was worried. This was no disorganized band of Huns harrying the Armenian frontier. This was a barbarian army, like Alaric's, trained in the ways of the Romans, and all too close to the capital. If Tribigild couldn't be bought off, the way Alaric had been bought off, it would come to a fight. Eutropius knew he wasn't up to that challenge.

It's easy to imagine Eudoxia and Gainas exchanging knowing looks as events unfolded. Historians are undecided as to what extent the Goth general had anything to do with Tribigild's decision. They would certainly have crossed each other's paths in Constantinople, and Gainas, as his kinsman's commander, would have lent a sympathetic ear to Tribigild's complaints and possibly even encouragement. Any trouble caused to Eutropius worked in Gainas's favor. Zosimus asserted he was "absolutely Tribigild's master, being superior to him in power and influence." And Sozomen, writing closer to events, declared, "To anyone of perception, it was obvious he was laying the path."

But was Gainas still taking orders from Stilicho? As he has Bellona berating Tribigild, Claudian has Aurora, goddess of the dawn – the

East – begging Stilicho to come save her and recalling the first fall of the West and its savior: "Save me from this slave master's tyranny. Do not condemn us all for the wrongs of a few, do not let recent transgressions void previous merits. Grant my request now. Extreme risk always absolves guilt. Camillus, though rightly angry to have been banished, did not refuse to save his country when it was in flames."

But Claudian, though Egyptian, was a Westerner, putting words in the mouth of the East. Gainas was a long way away. He may have followed Stilicho's orders in killing Rufinus, but now he was on his own. And all that stood between him and Emperor Arcadius was one meddlesome eunuch. As Zosimus put it:

> Gainas, honoring the pact between him and Tribigild and that the time had come to see it to fruition, told Tribigild to march his army toward the Hellespont. Had he hidden his plan against the state, and quietly left Constantinople with his barbarians, his entire plan would have succeeded. There was nothing to prevent him from getting a foothold in Asia and ravaging all the east.

Eutropius seems to have been well aware of Gainas's conflict of interest. He ordered the Goth out of the city, but in the other direction, west, supposedly to protect Thrace, even though Thrace was in no way threatened. Meanwhile, searching among his flock of sycophants for a leader, Eutropius settled on one Leo, a corpulent ex-weaver whom he raised to the rank of *comes rei militaris*. No historian of the time shared a good opinion of him. "Audacious when his foe was nowhere near, full of brave talk, immense of body but small of heart," was Claudian's verdict. Eunapius called him "a tranquil man, easily led due to his love of alcohol. For him being a man meant having more whores than warriors and more drinks than anybody else." Zosimus concurred: "Leo, who was designated to relieve the crisis in Asia, was a man of no military conduct, nor of any qualification entitling him to be raised to such rank, other than he was the good friend of Eutropius."

To his credit, Leo did dutifully cross the Hellespont. On the other side Tribigild was finally meeting some resistance from the locals and might even have been in trouble if Leo had attacked. He did not. Both sides found reasons to avoid engagement. This slow dance, however, was not to Gainas's advantage. To get things moving he sent Leo some reinforcements – Goth reinforcements. On arrival they immediately began sowing sedition among their fellow barbarians in the ranks of the legionaries, which is to say most of them. When Tribigild, perhaps having received word of this, finally advanced, these Goths promptly mutinied, turned on the Romans in their units and slaughtered them. Leo, attempting to escape, was killed. "And so," wrote Zosimus, "Gainas's plan met with success."

Now Eutropius was forced to call on him. Probably just as he had planned all along, Gainas took his army over into Anatolia after Tribigild, and promptly did nothing. While the rebels had their way with more imperial cities, Gainas sent word back to the capital that they were too powerful for him. To avoid risking what was left of the army, he asked permission to negotiate. And when that was granted, he reported Tribigild's terms: that Eutropius, as the cause of all the trouble, be put to death.

Now finally recognizing the stakes of the game, Eutropius surely thought he could bank on the loyalty of Arcadius. But as so many men of this period had or would find out, imperial loyalty was a fickle thing. It was now, according to Philostorgius, that Eudoxia played her part:

> Hugging her daughters to her, she came to her husband in plain dress and, sobbing and offering up her children, she poured out a flood of tears, working in those other tricks which angry women are inclined to employ with feminine wiles to earn their husbands' sympathy. Then Arcadius was moved to pity for his little children, who naturally joined their mother's cries with their own, and he was filled with rage.

Feeling the winds of fortune turn against him, Eutropius realized there was one man who could still save him. He fled to the Great Church of Constantinople, on the site where the Hagia Sophia now stands, and begged the very kind of sanctuary he had outlawed from the patriarch he had personally installed, John Chrysostom. The irony of this was not lost on the priest, who lectured him from the pulpit while the former consul hid himself under the altar. It availed him nothing. The authorities soon found him. (Though even the imperial bodyguards were under Eutropius' command, a special unit, the *comites Arcadiaci*, the companions of Arcadius, had been created, answerable only to him. Since Arcadius himself doesn't seem bright enough to have come up with the idea, it might be put down to Eudoxia and her supporters.) When the authorities came for him Eutropius pleaded for his life, which was granted, on the condition that he would be expelled to Cyprus.

That was not good enough for Tribigild and Gainas. Their "negotiations" had resulted in them combining forces – that is to say, bringing their duplicity out in the open – and dictating terms to Arcadius. The emperor agreed to meet Gainas at Chalcedon, across the Hellespont from Constantinople. Whatever else he was, Arcadius was no coward.

Gainas insisted on being appointed *magister militum praesentalis*, the Eastern equivalent of *magister utriusque militiae*, making him to Arcadius what Stilicho was to Honorius: the power behind the throne. In addition to Eutropius, he demanded the lives of Aurelianus, *praefectus urbanus* (mayor) of Constantinople and head of the anti-German faction, and Ioannes, a court favorite of Arcadius (and, some said, the lover of Eudoxia; if the two were in league, this would seem to be Gainas exceeding their agreement; perhaps he had designs on Eudoxia himself). In effect, the government was to be swept clean of Eutropius' cronies and any who opposed a Goth in charge.

However, the patriarch John Chrysostom again intervened, crossing over to Chalcedon to plead on behalf of the accused. John was Nicene and Gainas was Arian, but it behooved the barbarian to have the official church of state on his side. He relented and agreed to exile for all concerned. Eutropius, though, was to be brought to trial. Arcadius had given his word that the eunuch's life was safe in Constantinople and Cyprus. Therefore he was brought back to Chalcedon instead. "Eutropius was convicted of the crime of which he was accused," wrote Philostorgius, "and suffered the penalty, the loss of his head."

The eunuch was declared *damnatio memoriae*, the very memory of him condemned.* His name was struck from the list of consuls, his property confiscated, and his statues destroyed. It was a bitter end to a hard life. "Fortune had treated Eutropius in a most unique

---

*Though Latin, *damnatio memoriae* is a 17th-century term and not actually used by the Romans, but *damnation of memory* rather captures the meaning well.

manner on both counts," summed up Zosimus, "first in raising him to a height which no eunuch had ever before achieved, and then causing his death, via hatred of enemies of the state."

As the 4th century came to a close, however, exactly who was an enemy of the Eastern Empire, and who was its champion, was a matter of opinion. Almost without notice, what amounted to an imperial coup was nearly complete. For years barbarians had infiltrated and gradually taken over the Army of the East. Now Gainas, the Goth, had control of the capital. All that was missing was a barbarian on the throne.

The literal crowning achievement took place on January 9 of the year 400, when the imperial consort Aelia Eudoxia, herself half-barbarian and five months pregnant with her third child, was officially named *Augusta*, empress. Draped in the purple *paludamentum*, the robe of state, she was now entitled to her own court, and to fill it with her own followers. She could mint her own coins, and pay them out to whom she saw fit. She was, to all intents and purposes, the equal of her husband Arcadius, and in terms of guile and willpower clearly his superior. Her Frankish father Bauto would have been proud of his Roman daughter.

The sons of Theodosius had been made puppets. Instead, the barbarians he had raised to high office had taken over both empires. Gainas held power in the East, and Stilicho in the West, where he had saved Rome from starvation and settled the uprisings in Africa and Britannia. With the death of Eutropius, he was no longer *hostis publicus* in the East. As a result, he had been elected Western consul for 400, endowed with the ivory baton of office and draped in a purple robe trimmed in gold. Not bad for a half-Vandal.

For the occasion Claudian painted his patron a rosy future in verse. Young Maria, her labor eased by Lucina, the goddess of childbirth, bears a son in the likeness of Stilicho, who grows up to become emperor, taught the arts of war at his grandsire's knee. Eucherius lifts the veil from his own blushing bride, who goes unnamed but, described as "daughter and sister of an emperor," can only be Galla Placidia, half-sister of Honorius. "This house now aspires to the crown with people of either sex," declares the poet, "it births empresses and the husbands of empresses."

It was a pretty picture, but only a dream. Conspicuously left out of it was Honorius himself, now sixteen or so and, far from becoming a father, apparently still forbidden by her family to consummate his marriage with Maria, and possibly emasculated by them with drugs. Sexual frustration, envy, and supreme power are not a good combination in a boy emperor. Sitting through a ritual in which his general and father-in-law was acclaimed for victories in which Stilicho had played no greater personal part than Honorius, may have set some imperial teeth on edge. If so, Claudian appears not to have noticed, but went on to proclaim Stilicho "Consul, all but equal of the gods, guardian of a city greater than any the air encompasses on earth."

It seems everyone had swiftly forgotten how recently the consul of the East, that emperor's former favorite, had been sacked and beheaded.

XIII

What's more, the danger to the city was so great that a
comet of tremendous brightness, reaching from heaven down
to the earth, such as had never before been seen,
forewarned of it.

Socrates Scholasticus

Though probably nobody had yet noticed it, a harbinger of doom
had appeared in the sky as early as the end of the year 399. Socrates,
Philostorgius, and Sozomen all recorded it, as well as contemporary
skywatchers in China and Korea. All agreed it was eventually one
of the largest and most spectacular in living memory. By February
its apparent trajectory, as calculated by modern astronomers, led
it closest to the sun and by March it lay near upon the north star,
with its tail descending almost to the horizon. Comets were of course
already a well-known phenomenon, if little understood (Aristotle
had considered them to be atmospheric in nature), and held to be
messengers of the gods, usually heralding disaster. The apparent
magnitude of the comet of AD 400 implied a great catastrophe in the
near future, and in the east at least, the prophecy soon bore itself out.

Though still ruled by a Roman emperor, Constantinople was in effect
an occupied city, conquered as completely as though by assault or

siege, but without a blow struck. Gainas simply ordered the city guard to stand down. He and Tribigild ferried their troops over to the European side and moved them inside the walls. Constantinople only escaped a sack because the occupiers had no need to burn and loot. They could simply demand whatever they wanted, by imperial decree.

"The city was therefore quite overrun by the barbarians," concluded Socrates Scholasticus, who lived in Constantinople at the time, "and its citizens were reduced to a status equivalent to captives."

As Roman writers would have it, the takeover had been entirely too smooth and peaceful for Gainas. He and Arcadius had sworn oaths not to plot against each other. "But Gainas quickly broke his agreement, and did not swerve from his original intent," wrote Socrates. "Quite the contrary, his plan was bloodshed, looting, and holocaust, not only against Constantinople, but also against the entire Roman Empire, if he could in any way carry it out."

Most historical accounts of Gainas's time in power were written decades after the fact, and importantly after an even worse fate befell Rome, by writers who blamed barbarians for everything that had gone wrong and preferred to picture Gainas heading up a bloodthirsty horde of them. A staunch and well-known opponent of barbarians, particularly in Roman employ, the Greek bishop Synesius found much in those days to support his views, but good reason to be discreet in voicing them. More of a philosopher than a historian – and moreover, wary of offending Gainas – he cast his reportage of events as an allegory. *Aegyptus Sive de Providentia*, The Egyptian Tale, is a story of two brothers in an unsuccessful war waged by that country against a rebel army. It's a rather naked *roman à clef* about Romans, specifically the conflict between the pro- and anti-Goth parties in the court of Arcadius during Tribigild's uprising and Gainas's subsequent takeover. Synesius wasn't so much recounting events for his audience, who after all had lived through them as he did, but putting a spin on them to make his point, the same way Claudian never spoke ill of Stilicho, only his enemies. And Synesius' enemies were the barbarians: "Truly it is only foolhardy man or a prophet who sees, yet has no fear of, this horde of foreign-born youth following their own customs, and simultaneously practicing the art of war in this land... For these men will attack us the instant they think they have a chance of success."

The fact that Gainas had not sacked Constantinople when it was easily within his power goes a long way to making him a more sympathetic character than depicted by Synesius, or in history, but he got no fair shake from his critics. They accused him of wanting to steal silver from the bankers and merchants in the city markets who got wind of the plan and outwitted him simply by stashing their wealth away, as if that would have stopped any barbarian worthy of the name. They claim he sent men to burn the imperial palace, without giving the slightest reason why he should want that when practically speaking it was his palace already. They insist that the barbarians were only deterred by a heavenly host, probably a reference to the emperor's personal *Arcadiaci* guardsmen. (Synesius, it should be noted, mentions none of this, even allegorically.) They have it that Gainas, as an Arian, insisted on an Arian church being built for his co-religionists, and weak-kneed Arcadius acceding to the request, only for the patriarch John Chrysostom to advise him to make "no such promise, nor to order holy things given to dogs. I will never permit the worshippers and praisers of the Word of God to be thrown out or their church given to blasphemers." And when Gainas pointed out that in saving Constantinople from Tribigild, he had surely earned the right of free worship, John replied: "You must remember what you were and what you are now – your past poverty and present affluence, what clothing you wore before you crossed the Danube, and what you wear now. Compare, I tell you, your little labor with the magnitude of your reward, and be thankful to those who have given you honors."

As usual, Chrysostom was putting things plainly. Ever since his return to Constantinople, Gainas had been seeking only what he considered his due: rank, recognition, wealth, and power. He even had Arcadius designate him consul, equal to Stilicho, for the following year, 401. All for nothing. Gainas could dress up in a toga all he wanted. To the Romans he was still a Goth, a skin-clad barbarian. That was all he would ever be, he should never forget it, and he should happily accept the scraps they threw him.

It was a lesson Alaric, if not Stilicho, had already taken to heart, but some barbarians had yet to learn.

Murder, in the days of the late Empire, could be quite profitable. Through his killing of Rufinus, and then Eutropius, Gainas had risen to take his place at the side of the emperor Arcadius. His fellow Goth Fravitta, since the slaying of his erstwhile dinner partner Eriulf, had also reaped reward. Theodosius had granted him *conubium*, the right to take a Roman wife, which he had, and glad she and her family were to have him. "The girl's father," wrote Eunapius, "...was happy with the match and considered himself lucky with such a son-in-law."

Both emperor and father showed foresight. At century's end Fravitta was *magister militum per Orientum*, military commander in chief East, with his headquarters in Antioch. It was no inconsequential posting. At the far northeastern corner of the Mediterranean, the city was the extreme outpost of the Roman Empire, on the doorstep of the Persian. Its Christian population alone, according to its former priest John Chrysostom, numbered some 100,000 souls, though Fravitta was not one of them. Eunapius described him as physically frail and sickly, but strong in spirit, "a young man, but most notable of all for his virtue and honesty. He openly admitted that he worshiped the old gods after the ancient manner." Zosimus concurred: "Though born a barbarian, he was a Greek in every other way, not only in his lifestyle, but in his temperament and religion."

Yet Fravitta regarded all of the Antiocheans, pagan and Christian, as his responsibility. "He was a Goth by birth, and pagan in his religion," Philostorgius wrote of him, "but he was true to the Romans, and most talented in military matters." Fravitta had helped stand off the Hunnish invasion of 395, and presumably assisted Eutropius in the campaign of 398, for according to Zosimus he "saved all the east, from Cilicia to Phoenicia and Palestine, from the plundering of raiders."

It's notable that Gainas and Tribigild, in their dealings with Constantinople, did not call on their fellow Goth Fravitta to join their insurrection. Probably they had not forgotten how he had dealt with that earlier disloyal barbarian, Eriulf. And when Gainas finally outstayed his welcome in the capital, it was Fravitta who, in service of Theodosius, had showed no hesitation to kill Goths who went against imperial wishes, who was now called upon in a Theodosian's hour of need.

Over the course of the first half of the year 400, Gainas learned he was no Alaric. It was easier to have taken Constantinople than to keep it. He is thought to have quartered 35,000 troops inside the walls, but even that was a pittance in a city of 300,000. Their presence served mostly to stoke a popular antagonism which, as further stirred by anti-Goths like Synesius, was becoming a political force. The philosopher's advice to Arcadius to divest himself of barbarians in his army did not fall on deaf ears. Even if Arcadius, having all but bent the knee to Gainas, was content with the situation, his empress probably was not. Eudoxia was merely preoccupied. On April 3 she gave birth to a third daughter, Arcadia. This was right about the time the once-blazing comet flamed out overhead, but it seems nobody in Constantinople breathed a sigh of relief.

The Goths did nothing to ease the tension. Synesius – again, writing not to inform but to remind and stir up his audience – has them living it up in town as though they were in an army camp, parading their cavalry through the streets, bullying shopkeepers and merchants, but always careful to move about the city in numbers so they could not be overwhelmed piecemeal. Admittedly, the Goths were armed soldiers, while citizens were forbidden to carry or even manufacture weapons, but not even barbarian warriors could overcome ten-to-one odds, particularly if their numbers were whittled down bit by bit in back rooms and dark alleys with garrotes, clubs, and hidden daggers. In fact at some point in this period Tribigild died, reportedly killed. Like Mascezel's, the timing of his demise is suspicious.

By July the situation was untenable. Unwilling to sack the city, but unable to control it, Gainas issued orders for withdrawal. Feigning illness, he removed himself to a church a few miles outside the walls and waited for his people to assemble there. On the 12th, the Goths collected their women and children, their belongings and weapons and made ready to depart. Zosimus' account is rather confused. He accuses Gainas of wanting to gather his forces outside the city in order to turn around and attack it, which makes little sense. It seems certain, however, that during the barbarian exodus there was some sort of scuffle at the city gates, in which a number of guards were killed. "Immediately there arose a general uproar," wrote Zosimus, "with screams of women intermingled with wailing, as if the city had already been sacked. Soon the citizens got together and attacked the barbarians inside the city."

"From this point the city was full of confusion and tumult as though it had already been captured," agreed Sozomen, who attributed the

189

only clear thinking to the unlikely figure of Arcadius: "One good idea won this dreadful moment, for on the spot the emperor declared Gainas a public enemy, and ordered that every barbarian still in the city should be killed."

That this *hostis publicus* was the same condemnation as bestowed by the East on Stilicho was an irony surely not lost on Gainas. He was now his former commander's equal in every way. At the moment, though, it was small consolation. Only part of his forces had escaped the city. Some of the Goths trapped within – according to Zosimus, 7,000 of them, which does not seem credible – sought sanctuary in a church. For Arians to seek the mercy of God in a Nicene house of prayer hardly justifies the reaction of the mob, who set the building on fire and burned it down along with everyone in it. Even Zosimus had to admit, "This, even in the view of Christian zealots, was a most reprehensible crime to be perpetrated in the middle of such a great city."

By this time Gainas wanted no more to do with Constantinople. Assembling what remained of his forces, he withdrew west, into Thrace. Since the days after Adrianople, however, the cities there had become better prepared for the approach of barbarians. The Goths encountered nothing but walls and locked gates.

Notably, Gainas did not attempt to cross over into Illyricum, where Alaric lurked. The last time the two had met, they had been enemies, and Alaric was now a tool of Constantinople, too powerful for Gainas to risk testing his loyalty. Instead, he circled down around the Sea of Marmara and late in the year arrived on the peninsula of the Chersonese, at modern Gallipoli, where the Hellespont strait separating Europe from Asia is less than five miles wide. His intent was apparently to escape across to Lampsacus, an old Greek city on the Anatolian side. "He believed that if he could land on the opposite, Asian shore," wrote Sozomen, "he could easily conquer all the imperial provinces of the East."

Despite the depredations of Tribigild, Asia Minor still offered plenty of pickings for an army on the loose. Gainas might even link up with Fravitta, if his fellow Goth was willing, and if not, then defeat him piecemeal, one battle at a time, before Fravitta could gather his forces. According to Socrates, Gainas "was aware that the larger part of the Roman army was distant, scattered as garrisons in the Eastern cities."

The Goths had no ships, however, and weren't much in the way of shipwrights either. They hastily fabricated rafts to ferry their people and animals across. They had only made it part way across when fate chose sides.

The *lodos*, a southwesterly wind that funnels out of the Aegean into the Dardanelles strait, is most predominant over the winter months, but can kick up out of a clear sky at any time and frequently attains a rate of nine or ten on the Beaufort scale: gale strength. The winds may not have achieved such force on this day, but they didn't have to, for they drove before them a fleet of Roman bireme galleys, *liburnae*, tipped with rams.

Gainas would not have to meet Fravitta. Fravitta had come to him.

While Gainas had been occupied with Constantinople, messengers had been dispatched to Antioch with orders for Fravitta. Zosimus wrote, "They therefore bestowed command of the army on him, since he had been a famous leader in many wars."

"Although his physical strength was not up to his courage," wrote Eunapius, "still he worked hard, equipping and training his forces for audacious deeds."

To march the length of Anatolia would have taken weeks, but with Antioch lying so near the coast Fravitta had no need. He was a Goth with a fleet. The Roman navy could take him the roundabout seaward route in less time, and its patrol ships soon brought word of Gainas's gathering on the west bank of the Hellespont. Upon Gainas's erstwhile navy putting to sea, Fravitta immediately answered the challenge.

"Seeing the crude barbarian rafts were carried on the current in whichever direction it took them," wrote Zosimus, "he first attacked the nearest of them straight on, and his ship, having a brass ram, overran it, not only breaking it up, but his crew throwing darts at the men aboard it, sank both them and their craft."

Following his lead, the Roman galleys sliced through the helpless Goths, their rams plowing up and riding down every raft they got in front of them. Those warriors who didn't drown in the wind-whipped seas were easy prey for Roman archers and dart-throwers. As Socrates put it, "The barbarians and their horses, with the violent gale tossing them up and down in their rickety craft, were quickly engulfed by the high seas. Many of the rest were slain by the Romans."

Still on the western shore, Gainas witnessed the destruction of his army. In the space of a few months he had gone from ruler of half the Roman world to a hunted fugitive. With his few surviving troops he turned and fled back into Thrace.

Fravitta landed his army on the European bank, but did not pursue. According to Zosimus he was accused, probably by some of the anti-barbarian faction in the capital, of deliberately letting his fellow Goth escape, but Gainas had nowhere to go. The more his strength dwindled, the less hospitable Thrace became. By this time the Goths, having had enough of civilization in general, determined to return to their barbarian homeland north of the Danube. First, though, Gainas took out his frustrations on those few Romans who had stood by him. "Now suspicious of the Romans who were with him," wrote Zosimus, "he killed every one of them, before they even knew what was happening."

Having thus cleansed himself of the last vestiges of civilization, Gainas and his barbarians crossed over the Danube. This was still Hunnish country, but he doubtless hoped to sell his services, and his knowledge of Roman ways, to whoever was the closest thing those most barbaric of barbarians had to a leader.

In 400 that leader was Uldin, though some historians think that may have been his title rather than his name. When Attila probably had not yet been born and was still several decades from making his appearance on the world stage, Uldin was the earliest known ruler of the Huns, or at least some of them. He held sway over the western coast of the Black Sea to the banks of the Danube, making him the first Hunnish leader Gainas encountered after his crossing. He would also be the last.

After years of raiding into Roman lands the Huns had realized, as had the Goths, that dealing with civilized people required the carrot as well as the stick. Gainas arrived at the wrong time to come seeking backers against Arcadius. Zosimus recorded, "After a few battles between the two forces, in some of which Gainas's army triumphed, many of his men were killed, and Gainas himself was finally slain as well, having fought with great courage."

Philostorgius says simply, "His head was preserved in salt and sent to Constantinople."

It arrived at court a few days into the new year. Arcadius returned the favor by giving Uldin a commission, *comes*, making him a Roman officer, and his army a Roman army. Likewise, for his part Fravitta was not only appointed consul for 401, taking the place once designated for Gainas, but Arcadius gave the Goth official permission to worship the old pagan gods. That this was even more than Gainas had desired for himself did not go unnoticed by the anti-barbarians at court, now dependent on not one but two barbarian armies, predominantly Goth and Hunnish, for their security.

"Is it not a disgrace that the empire with the greatest manpower should award the laurel of victory in war to foreigners?" wondered Synesius. "For myself, however many triumphs such men might win us, I will be ashamed of taking their help."

But as Gibbon would note over 1,300 years later, "The court of Arcadius indulged the zeal, applauded the eloquence, and neglected the advice of Synesius."[1]

[1] *History*, Vol. III, p. 143

XIV

THE WORLD TURNS

AD 401

There is kindred joy in heaven. The two Theodosians
and your own protecting gods are glad. The Sun himself,
decorating his chariot with spring flowers,
readies a year worthy of you.

Claudian

Claudian's ode to Stilicho on his consulship of 400 might have applied even more to 401. That spring was one of idyllic rapport in the Roman world. For a change neither empire, East nor West, was striving to exert its will over the other. No one held Stilicho responsible for Gainas's uprising, as the Goth had clearly exceeded any orders he had received years earlier. Indeed, Gainas's defeat was made a cause of common celebration throughout both empires. Though Arcadius had as little to do with it as Honorius had in the defeat of Gildo, it was the closest thing the elder emperor had to a military triumph, and he determined to make the most of it. Seventy years earlier, Emperor Constantine had raised a 160-foot column of solid porphyry to mark the foundation of the city. In 393 Theodosius had built a column almost as tall, but hollow, with a spiral staircase running up the inside. Now Arcadius would build a monument to himself to outdo both. The Column of Arcadius, as planned, would reach nearly 175 feet, with a similar stairway inside leading out onto a viewing deck at the foot of a thirty-foot bronze statue of its namesake. The marble outer shaft would be inscribed with a spiral frieze depicting a Roman triumphal parade, complete with barbarian prisoners, grateful senators, and winged Victories. Arcadius even had Honorius carved into the reliefs of his new column, though the younger brother had even less to do with the victory than the elder. They had not even seen each other in seven years.

It would require years to build, but it's easy to imagine Arcadius, now in his early twenties, excitedly poring over the architects' drawings of what was sure to be the first in a series of inspiring monuments to a long and momentous reign. He was free at last of his overbearing advisors. Or, at least, he could imagine himself so.

In the background, working on her own memorial, was the *Augusta* Aelia Eudoxia with her three little daughters, herself pregnant yet again, the fourth time in six years of marriage. With Eutropius and Gainas gone, at last no one stood between her and her husband. In April she gave birth to a son. They named him Flavius Theodosius II, in anticipation of one day naming him junior emperor to his father, the continuation of the dynasty. Rumor had it that her husband's courtier, Ioannes, was the boy's real father, but the birth was celebrated across both empires.

What this meant, however, was that the empire was now clearly and unequivocally divided. The sons of Theodosius I ruled separately, with no one person in overarching control. Whether that was as Theodosius had intended or not depends on whether Stilicho was telling the truth when he came away from the old emperor's deathbed, and opinions on that are as widely opposed now as they were then. At the time, what mattered was that the dual empires, though not at war, were separate entities, inclined to act as allies but not required to. And perhaps forgotten in all the excitement was that the barbarian threat had not subsided, but simply been handed off to other barbarians.

Since the close call of Gainas's uprising the Eastern Romans had been suddenly awakened to the precariousness of their position. "As things stand," Synesius warned, "we can neither rest at ease nor take steps to improve matters, for right now all men stand on the razor's edge."

As Eastern consul, Fravitta still resided at court, but there is little record of anything he did during his administration, and it's probable he simply kept his head down and attracted as little attention as possible. His major accomplishment was putting down a band of deserters and runaway slaves, probably survivors of Gainas's army who had been running amok in Thrace, in an effort to demonstrate his loyalty. Fravitta, as he had proven again and again, fancied himself Roman, but had forgotten, as Gainas had, that in Roman eyes he would never be more than a barbarian. His troops were largely German mercenaries as well, and had been willing to fight a Roman consul-designate because Fravitta ordered them to. The Romans had to ask themselves, who else might they be willing to fight on Fravitta's command? And to the north, Uldin's Hunnish army, of unknown size and power, was not Roman at all, its loyalty to the Empire hanging on the thread of a Hun's word of honor. With two armies of dubious reliability, Constantinople did not need a third.

In Illyricum, word of Gainas's overthrow and the rise of the anti-barbarian party in the capital must have come as an unpleasant shock to Alaric. First Rufinus, who had given him leave to march into Greece; then Eutropius, who had made him officially its master; and now Gainas, who had been Alaric's commander and mentor at the Frigidus, all gone. And on the death of Eutropius came the worst news of all. The status the eunuch had granted Alaric had been rescinded. He was no longer *magister militum per Illyricum*, no longer the representative of Constantinople, no longer entitled to Roman support. He was once again just another barbarian chief.

That was a perilous position for any man, and Alaric was no exception. There were some among the ranks of the Goths who would eagerly take his place, even over his dead body. There were Sarus and his brother Sigeric, of the powerful Amali clan, which had historically considered themselves superior to Alaric's Balti clan and still opposed it on mere principle. On his side Alaric had his wife's brother Athaulf, a capable warrior and reliable ally. And although we know next to nothing about them, Alaric had a family of his own to protect. Some genealogy sites give his wife's name as Amalaberge, or Eurica, both good Gothic female names, and Alaric may have had more than one wife – Claudian makes mention of Alaric's wives and children – but none are named in the primary sources. There was a boy, Theodoric, who may have been Alaric's acknowledged son, but might equally have been his bastard or his future son-in-law. Nobody knows, and at any rate as king – *rex Gothorum*, King of the Goths – Alaric had to put himself above family concerns, above clan feuds, and think of his people.

Alaric's realm – his former realm – strategically located between the two empires, to this point had been to his advantage, but was now to his detriment. The ground beneath his feet was still property of the Empire, and if either Rome or Constantinople decided to come to run him off it, he was at their mercy. Without Gildo and Gainas to distract them, the empires were now on good speaking terms, and might even come at him from both directions at once.

But Alaric had never been a man to let himself be pushed around. He did the pushing. It was only a matter of the right time.

If there was anything to upset the precarious peace in the East, it wasn't barbarians. It was, as it has so often been, religion.

The antagonism between the various sects was ongoing. Some were already dying out, others were still struggling for supremacy, declaring each other heretics but only able to do anything about it if they attained enough backing and power. At the dawn of the 5th century, the current crisis was with the Origenists.

Their creed was based on the prolific writings of Origen, a 3rd-century Alexandrian scholar, ascetic, and theologian, and a bit of a fanatic. He believed that the Son and the Holy Spirit were subordinate to God the Father, and that all were manifestations of God, who was not some anthropomorphic old man up in the clouds, but invisible, incorporeal, transcendent, and beyond the understanding of mortal beings. Furthermore, he believed the human soul was immortal and could never die. Origenism had captured the attention of Christians everywhere, but was a particularly hot topic in Palestine and Egypt.

Rather than spreading the faith, adherents were reduced to accusing each other of heresy and blasphemy. As late as 399, Theophilus, the patriarch of Alexandria, had agreed with Origen's ideas, but when the city's rabid Christian populace rose up, he backtracked and condemned them. (Like Arian Goths, Nicene Alexandrians had learned they could accomplish much by pushing in the right directions.) In Constantinople, however, John Chrysostom was sympathetic to Origenists, and that's where the story intersects with ours, for John and Theophilus were bitter enemies. Both had realized that, as leaders of the church, they were setting standards it would follow for centuries. Both were determined for their views to come out on top.

John's problem was, he was antagonizing the secular leaders in Constantinople as well. Arcadius seems not to have cared much for matters of religion, but his wife Eudoxia took it very seriously, at least to the extent it served her interests. She supported anti-Arian demonstrations in the city and took prominent part in importing martyrs' remains. None of this curried any favor from John. She had engineered the downfall of his patron, Eutropius. And she was a woman. Willful, extravagant women came in for particular condemnation from his altar, and the most willful, extravagant woman in the city was Empress Eudoxia. Zosimus exaggerated only a little: "For the emperor being no more than an idiot, his wife, the most arrogant of her sex, was devoted to the insatiable greed of eunuchs and her female servants, who greatly influenced her, causing everyone to tire of life, so that to humble people nothing became so welcome as death."

All this might have come to nothing, except that in the year 400 four ascetic Egyptian monks called the Tall Brothers, being dedicated Origenists, were expelled from Alexandria by Theophilus. To his annoyance they sought, and were granted, sanctuary by John in Constantinople.

When this trifling matter came to the ear of Eudoxia, she saw an opportunity to get Chrysostom out of her hair for good. Little did she know that her spat with an obstinate churchman would ultimately cause a rift between the two empires of Rome.

By autumn, the good times were over. Word spread that Alaric's Goths had pulled up stakes, dusted off their wagons, and were on the move. Furthermore, they were moving west, into the Julian Alps.

The news inspired near panic in some quarters of Italy. In Mediolanum, some of Honorius' ministers advised him to abandon the city and move west himself, putting the Alps between him and the threat and perhaps establishing a new capital in Gaul. To go by Claudian, only Stilicho refused to panic.

"Do you consider dishonorable retreat and look to Gaul?" he demanded of the weak-kneed courtiers. "Would you abandon Latium to camp like refugees on the banks of the Saone? Is Rome to be surrendered to boreal tribes, our empire to recenter on the Rhone...?"

He had a point. The Goths had not attacked anyone. They had been living peaceably in Illyricum for several years, and though word had surely arrived in the West of Alaric's dismissal, he had no quarrel with Rome and no reason to start one. The barbarian procession included women and children, plus all their belongings, including the loot of Thrace and Greece. This was not an invasion. It was a migration.

On the other hand, there was more bad news elsewhere on the frontier. Probably because they knew all Roman eyes were on the Gothic incursion, northern barbarians had seized the opportunity to cross the upper reaches of the Danube and invade the alpine provinces of Vindelicia (now southern Germany), Raetia (Switzerland), and Noricum (Austria). These were no minor holdings. The best Roman blades were made of *chalybs Noricus*, Noric steel: manganese-rich, phosphorus-poor and therefore stronger than those from the Mediterranean regions. Such a resource could not be allowed to fall into the hands of outsiders. Furthermore, the interlopers were reportedly Alans and Vandals, Stilicho's father's people, and it was natural that Stilicho should go meet them in person.

For those who insisted that the Goths were closer – essentially only at the other end of the Po Valley – Stilicho could point out that they were as yet no threat at all. He knew Alaric as well as anyone in the West, and was familiar with the Goths' game, going all the way back to Fritigern in Thrace and Alaric outside Constantinople and Athens. The Goths preferred to intimidate cities rather than sack them, relying less on catapults and siege towers than on blockades and time. Stilicho was willing to risk their presence in Italy long enough to put down the northern revolt, betting he could still return in time to deal with the Goths if it proved necessary. He reminded everyone that he was leaving behind his own wife and children with the emperor in the capital: "Romans, hold the fort just a short while, until my return to the sound of trumpets, with the flower of your army."

It was getting late in the year, though, to launch a military expedition, particularly over the mountains. Stilicho's exact route from Mediolanum to the Raetian capital at Augusta Vindelicorum, modern Augsburg, Germany, is not known; there are several passes through that section of the Alps, including the Splügen and the

Brenner. Probably the most direct route was the Via Septimer (from *septimus*, seventh on the list of Alpine routes), but it was not the easiest. Even today the narrow, steep gravel track through Septimer Pass, superseded in the 1820s by a road through neighboring Julier Pass, is little improved from its Roman days: impassable to vehicles, accessible only by foot or mountain bike, subject to landslides, heavy snow, and avalanches, at one point crossing an ancient stone-arch bridge hardly wide enough for an oxcart. Almost 7,600 feet up, sharp-eyed men on the march might have spotted lost, leaden sling bullets inscribed with the insignia of legions – Legio III *Gallica*, Legio X *Gemina*, and Legio XII *Fulminata* – who had threaded the pass before them and still fascinate treasure seekers, historians, and archaeologists to this day. They could look to the nearby streams to know when they crossed the continental divide. Water running south would eventually reach the Mediterranean, but on the other side of the pass, all streams flowed toward the Rhine and the North Sea, or the Danube and the Black Sea. They would have been lucky, and happy, to get down out of the mountains before the first snows fell.

Undoubtedly surprised at the appearance of a Roman army on the north side of the Alps so near winter, the northern barbarians reconsidered following the aggressive example of Alaric. "Do you put your faith in the Goths?" Stilicho demanded. "Is it the Goths who fill your hearts with senseless pride? Rome is not yet so weak that she cannot punish your revolt with a mere fraction of her legions."

Just beyond Augusta Vindelicorum at modern Donauworth, a military trunk road, the Via Iuxta Danuvium, followed the south bank of the Danube, eventually all the way to Singidunum, modern Belgrade. (It still exists, as the German Donausudstrasse.) It marked the northern border of the Empire, and Stilicho paraded his forces up and down it in plain view of those on the river's far bank. The ancient sources make no mention of fighting, because none was necessary. According to Claudian, the very appearance of this most powerful man in the Western Empire was enough to cow the barbarians into submission: "The rebels all feared retribution the minute they saw the commander, the very personification of Emperor, Latium and Rome, before their eyes."

Stilicho and his army spent the winter of 401–402 on the German side of the Alps, reminding the discontented Vandals and Alans of the benefits of civilization. The protection of Rome, the security of Rome, the trade and wealth of Rome were available to everyone, barbarian or not, who accepted Rome's sovereignty. (Except, apparently, the Goths.) Was not Stilicho, himself half-Vandal, proof of that?

This was nothing less than what the barbarians had wanted all along. They willingly acquiesced. Claudian wrote:

> Germania, once home to people so haughty and savage that past emperors could hardly control them even with all of their legions, now offers itself so willingly to follow of Stilicho's guidance that it neither attempts to invade the provinces left weakened by the withdrawal of the frontier garrisons, nor even dares to cross the river, too afraid to land on an undefended shore.

He was only partly correct. It was true that the benefits of Roman citizenship were available to most, but on the frontier of Germania it came at a price. Emperor after emperor had enlisted German manpower into the legions, as Theodosius had done with the Goths on the Danube and Stilicho had done on his last campaign along the Rhine, and then sent those legions away to wherever the next invasion or usurper rose up. As a result, the local economy had suffered a lack of both supply and demand. Barbarians from across the river had been moving in to fill the vacuum, clearing farms, raising villages, growing food, and manufacturing products for sale to the local Romanized inhabitants, who as a result were becoming more Germanized. The once-clear demarcation between civilization and barbarism was becoming fuzzier, more nebulous. It was no longer certain where Rome stopped and Germania started. This latest incursion of Alans and Vandals was simply a sharp spike in what was a kind of ongoing, "soft" invasion.

Unfortunately, Stilicho's return wasn't going to change that. He was going to need all the German troops he could get. For at a certain point that winter, some poor messenger came staggering over the snowy high mountain passes with urgent word from Mediolanum.

Stilicho's wasn't the only army that had crossed the Alps the preceding autumn. Alaric had brought the Goths down out of the Julians and was marching on Aquileia.

That put him closer to both Mediolanum and Rome than Stilicho, who had most of the Western army, including almost all the forces from Cisalpine Gaul, with him on the wrong side of the mountains. There was nothing to stop the Goths from marching the length of the Italian boot, killing, raping, and burning as they went.

As Claudian put it, "Would anyone have believed that, once a transit over the Alps had been achieved, the slightest ghost of Rome's name would survive?"

XV

INVASION

AD 402

Hannibal rode on ahead and found a lookout with a scenic view of the lowlands below. He ordered the army to halt there and pointed across the open country of Italia and the Po Valley plain spread out at the foot of the Alps, proclaiming that at this moment they were not merely crossing the breastworks of Italia, but climbing the very walls of Rome.

Livy

It had been over 600 years since Hannibal led the Carthaginian army down out of the Alps to invade Italy, but Rome had not forgotten. In his account of the Gothic invasion, Claudian frequently compared Alaric to Hannibal, recalling how the Goths triggered similar panic. As the barbarians came down out of the Julians, the outer walls of Rome, built 125 years earlier, were belatedly strengthened, despite which the wealthy hastily packed their belongings and took ship across the water to Sardinia, Corsica, and Sicily to avoid the wrath of Alaric: "It seemed no wall or bulwark was strong enough to withstand his fleeting cavalry's attack."

A force sent to meet him at the Timavus River (modern Timavo), less than ten miles from Aquileia, was brushed aside. Some of the citizens followed the Roman example and evacuated, hoping to lose themselves in the swamps and islands of the vast Marano-Grado lagoon which forms that part of the Adriatic coast. All would have been safer in the city. Aquileia, with a population of 100,000, had been founded on the site of an ancient Celtic village around 180 BC to defend the northeastern rim of the Adriatic against invaders. Fortified with strong walls and situated on a little angle of land where the Natissa and Turris Rivers (modern Natisone and Torre) came together, it was unassailable on three sides. The fourth, landward side proved impregnable to the Goths.

In truth, Alaric probably did not put much effort into a siege. By all appearances, and as Stilicho expected, he was trying to play the old game that Fritigern had played in Thrace, and he himself had played outside Constantinople and Athens. All he wanted to do was to bully some Romans into contributing food, supplies, and money. By now Easterners were familiar with this game, and with their two armies undoubtedly would have called Alaric's bluff. The Aquileians may have done the same. It's unclear what the Goths received, if anything, from their city, but it was not sacked, nor did the barbarians linger there for long. Probably Alaric had learned that Stilicho was over the mountains for the winter, and thought it safe to go in search of easier pickings. Over the next two months, into early 402, the Goths marched through Venetia, up the Po Valley to threaten Mediolanum, and the Empire itself.

Inside the walls the imperial court was in an uproar. Commoners had been pressed into service to defend the city. Ministers and bureaucrats with no military experience argued over strategy, tactics, and the advisability of surrender, again urging the emperor to vacate the capital altogether. (Gibbon asserted that Honorius did in fact try to escape west, only to be headed off and herded south by Gothic cavalry, but this is not supported by Claudian, who was there and places the emperor in Mediolanum throughout the period.) Honorius himself, perhaps for the first time in his life, learned the real risk of being a Roman emperor. Still a teenager, the boy who had been so eager to go to Africa and take on Gildo four years earlier now found himself facing a barbarian horde on his own doorstep, and without his father-in-law and favorite general at his side. His soft upbringing had not prepared him for the very real possibility of his own head being paraded through the streets on the point of a Gothic lance.

Claudian, though, in verse to be recited before Honorius, made sure to write him using brave words: "I had no fear, for I relied on Stilicho to arrive in time."

He has Honorius walking the ramparts, looking down on the Goth army encamped on the plain: "It was night. Wherever I looked I saw enemy campfires glittering like stars." Suddenly there was a commotion along the main road from the east. "The trumpet had already called the guards to the first watch [two hours to midnight] when illustrious Stilicho arrived from the frigid north."

It was not Alaric but Stilicho who played the role of Hannibal, crossing the Alps in the dead of winter. And in true form he returned with more troops than he had taken with him. Over the autumn he had summoned the garrisons of the Rhine fortresses and, if Claudian is to be believed, even pulled a legion off Hadrian's Wall in Britannia. The poet also declares that many of the former rebels and invaders among the Alans and Vandals had signed up for Roman service: "Stilicho both halted the looming war and won new allies, recruiting them at their own bidding in such numbers as was most proper – neither a burden to Italia nor a menace to its emperor."

Stilicho's problem was that the majority of his new army was behind him, possibly still bogged down in the mountains, while he raced to the rescue with his vanguard to arrive on the banks of the Adda River. This runs down out of Lake Como to cross the main road to Mediolanum from the east. The Goths held the only bridge. Stilicho had too few troops with him to defeat the Goth army, but enough to force the crossing in a surprise attack. "Regardless of risk to himself," declared Claudian, "he broke through the enemy lines and, sword in hand, cutting down anyone who got in his way, struck like lightning through the barbarian camp."

Of the following day in Mediolanum the poet recalled, "From the heights of the battlements we sight a cloud of dust in the distance, not knowing whether it hides friend or foe. Suspense renders us all mute. Then suddenly from that dusty cloud appeared the helmet of Stilicho, shining like a star, whom we recognized by his brilliant white hair." (This is a telling detail, which would have been familiar to Claudian's immediate audience, but reveals much to posterity: Stilicho was in his early forties at the latest, and for his hair to have gone white surely indicates the stress of his job.) "Here is Rome's true strength, her true leader, the god of war in human form."

As morale in the city rose high, that in the Gothic camp sank low. The ease with which Stilicho had cut through their lines shows how little Alaric was expecting, or seeking, a fight. His bargaining position had just weakened considerably. With his old friend/foe inside the walls, Mediolanum was unlikely to open its gates to any appeal from the Goths, especially not with a Roman army bearing down on them from out of the mountains. To remain beneath the city walls invited a two-front battle, against the approaching forces and against city defenders who would certainly sally out to attack from behind. Julius Caesar had managed to win such a battle, against the Gauls of Vercingetorix at Alesia in 52 BC, but Caesar had fought from inside miles of trenches and battlements of circumvallation and contravallation around the hilltop town. There is, again, no evidence that the Goths put such effort into a siege of Mediolanum. They had simply camped outside the walls to provoke a reaction, and now they had it.

Alaric called a council of war among his ranking chieftains, or as Claudian put it, his "senate of long-haired, skin-clad Gothic captains." Some of these venerable old warriors had served under Fritigern in that first crossing of the Danube, a generation gone. Now one of them, in a scene almost certainly concocted by Claudian but for all that believable enough (it's conceivable he and Alaric may have met on occasion and traded stories), stood to address the king:

If the impetuosity of hot-blooded youthfulness hurried you into war, now at least, I beg you, if you have any love left for your people, make good your escape from out of this trap. The enemy army is far away. You have a chance. Retreat in haste from Italia before, in your desire for fresh spoils, you lose even what you have won, and like a wolf pay for former thieving from the shepherd by being killed within the flock... If you don't fear the gods, beware the power of Stilicho. Luck is always on his side against attackers. You yourself know how high he piled bones on our funeral pyres in Arcadia, and how he made the rivers of Greece run warm with our blood; and you would have been slain if not protected by treason disguised as law and the benevolence of the eastern emperor.

What's interesting in the quote is not only Claudian's depiction of the scene, but that he practically accuses Emperor Arcadius of treason in ordering Alaric's freedom, which from the western perspective he did, twice. Perhaps some hard feelings still lingered between the two imperial courts. At any rate, the Goths could no longer depend on such an imperial decree.

Alaric's response, at least as written for him by Claudian, is one of the longest speeches attributed to him, and whether or not he ever actually spoke the words, they have come to define him for posterity:

> If old age had not deprived you of reason, old fool, I would make you regret such insults. Should I, who have caused so many emperors to flee, listen to you prattle on about peace? No. I will rule this land or, in defeat, be buried in it. The Alps have been crossed, the Po has witnessed our victories. Only Rome is left to overcome.

He goes on to reveal that, having once paused in a sacred grove (like many Germanic tribes, and even the ancient Greeks and Romans, the Goths put stock in the sanctity of certain copses), a voice spoke to him: *Do not hesitate, Alaric. Be bold, cross the Italian Alps this year and you will reach the City.* "So far the road is mine," he declares. "What coward hesitates after such encouragement, or hesitates to obey the word of God?"

This last episode is certainly spun by Claudian in order to depict Alaric as foolish.* And yet Alaric may have indeed felt himself to be the tool of a greater power.

He was not immediately intent on Rome, and was still seeking to avoid a fight. Before the bulk of the Roman army arrived down out of the Alps, the Goths abandoned Mediolanum and moved, notably not south toward Rome, but west. The assumption is that Alaric was making for Gaul via the western Alpine passes, probably by the same routes that had enticed Honorius to escape there, but before he reached the

---

*There was a river in Italy called the Urbis, "of the City." At the turn of the 20th century it was thought to correspond to a stream near Pollenzo called the Borbo, which does not appear on modern maps. There's an Orba River, but it's about forty miles to the east. The town of Pollenzo fronts on an oxbow lake of the Tanaro, which may once have been a tributary stream. Claudian made a play on words, having Alaric set on Rome but reaching a different "city," to please his Roman audience.

mountains Alaric did turn south and crossed the Po. Some historians think Stilicho's Britannic legion may have been coming his way over those same western passes and that Alaric feared being caught between them and Stilicho. Yet he seems to have been in no particular hurry, since he stopped to "besiege" Hasta, where Gibbon would have it that Honorius had holed up. Stilicho really was in pursuit, though, and before long the Goths gave up the fruitless delay and continued southwest into today's Piedmont (Latin *Pedemontium* or *Pedemontis*, from *ad pedem montium*, "at the foot of the mountains"). If Alaric was looking to bypass the peaks via the Azure Coast to reach southern Gaul, he never made it.

Retreating southwest along the Tanarus River (modern Tanaro), by the beginning of April the Goths had reached Pollentia (modern Pollenzo, a subsection of the city of Bra). That year Easter fell in the first week of April. In the certainty that Stilicho would not violate the holy day, the Goths paused in their retreat to celebrate Mass. Jordanes, the Goth, wrote, "This Stilicho, I say, traitorously hastened to the city of Pollentia in the Cottian Alps. There he attacked the unwitting Goths, to his own disgrace and the ruin of all Italia."

Before battle Stilicho addressed the troops, reminding them how Alaric had previously slipped out of his grasp: "This is the enemy you so often defeated on the plains of Greece. That they still live has nothing do to with their own bravery, but that the empire is torn in two. They disregard treaties at will and traffic in lies with the West, then the East."

Stilicho's Alans were under the command of Saulus, the Alan who had been Theodosius' cavalry commander at the Frigidus. "He was physically small," wrote Claudian, "but his soul was great, and his eyes blazed with anger. He was covered with old wounds and his face was all the more glorious and proud because of the scar some spear-thrust made." Saulus was a pagan, and cared not a whit whether he fought and killed on some Christian holy day. In the first day's fighting at the Frigidus, he had escaped when his commander Bacurius was killed, and he seems to have been accused of cowardice or even treachery. He was eager to prove himself – perhaps too eager. Orosius claimed he "wickedly demeaned the most sacred holidays, even holy Eastertide, and though the enemy declined to fight for religious reasons he left them no choice but to fight."

Saulus led the screaming Alans in a cavalry charge, probably in an attempt to turn the Goths' flank as the Romans had tried at Adrianople, and possibly against the orders of Stilicho, who according to Claudian had hoped to complete his victory with the capture of the Gothic king himself. "You would have captured Alaric and put him to death," the poet assured him, "if not for the hasty zeal of the reckless Alan chief upsetting your carefully laid plans."

"When the Goths first saw him, they were terrified," admitted Jordanes, but they soon recovered. "Quickly regaining their courage and inspiring each other with their shouting, as is their way, they put Stilicho's entire army to flight and nearly exterminated it."

Saulus was killed and, just as at Adrianople, the barbarians threatened to turn the tables on the Romans. "Reduced to turmoil by their leader's death, his cavalry reined about," declared Claudian, "and with its flank exposed, the whole army would have given way had not Stilicho quickly ordered up a legion and, rushing to the spot, supported the horsemen with infantry."

Stilicho proved to be a better general than Valens. With his barbarian cavalry recovering and holding their ground instead of fleeing as at Adrianople, the Roman line not only advanced, but actually overran the barbarian camp. The fleeing Goths left behind the spoils garnered over half a decade of conquest: wagons full of gold and silver, Greek statuary, clothing, slaves from across the East, and even their families, including Alaric's own wife and children. They would be lucky not to end up enslaved.

The Romans counted Pollentia as a great victory. The contemporary lawyer, politician, poet, and ascetic Aurelius Prudentius Clemens recorded, "A race that had menaced Pannonia for thirty years finally paid the penalty and was massacred. Bodies once rich with ill-gotten loot lie piled in heaps. In years to come posterity will wonder at the scattering of corpses which cover the fields of Pollentia with their bones."

"Never before was the sword of Rome stabbed so deep in the barbarians' throat," gloated Claudian. "…Your glory, Pollentia, will live forever. Your name is worthy to be celebrated in song, a theme fit for rejoicing and triumph."

Claudian's propaganda aside, many historians regard Pollentia as a drawn battle, because Stilicho once again failed, or neglected, or decided not to finish off Alaric. True, the Romans had won the ground, booty, and Gothic prisoners, but they had not ended the Gothic threat. Alaric still had much of his army, particularly his cavalry, intact. The barbarians had the capability and every reason to strike back and reclaim their losses, or else to run rampant over northern Italy while the Romans gave chase. Even if he finally destroyed them, Stilicho might yet lose most of his army in doing it. There were still plenty of barbarians north of the Rhine and Danube and Hadrian's Wall who would jump at the chance to attack a weakened empire.

Stilicho the general now had to be Stilicho the politician. So, in a very Theodosian move, he negotiated a peace with Alaric. Claudian admitted, "Policy dictated that he should live."

Not everyone saw it that way. The agreement stirred discord in both camps. From the Roman view, Stilicho had already let Alaric slip through his fingers twice, in Greece. That had been on the orders of the government in Constantinople, but this time it was his decision, made on Western soil, as the head of the Western government. Ministers and senators began to wonder if there was more to the relationship between Stilicho and Alaric than there appeared. The same questions were undoubtedly being raised in the Gothic camp as well, where Alaric's enemies could point to the dead of Pollentia, the outrages inflicted on their women, and the riches lost to the Romans, and reasonably ask what had been gained in this venture. The good faith of Rome? The Goths knew what that was worth.

Divisiveness in the barbarian camp is evidenced by the fact that the Goths didn't even make it out of Italy before breaking the terms of the agreement. Alaric may have been pondering a turn north, over the Alps into Raetia. It was summer now (some historians, lacking any dates to go on, have put the battle off until 403) and the alpine meadows were more easily passable. More likely, though, some of his more insubordinate underlings were clamoring for loot, for at least something to show for their trouble. In the foothills southeast of Lake Garda, where the Adige River winds down out of the Alps, the Goths couldn't resist stopping to bully concessions from Verona, a road junction that for centuries had been a frequent residence and battleground of emperors. "Here," Claudian derided Alaric, "he broke his oath again and, driven by his losses, risked everything trying to improve his luck. Alaric learned that his demented betrayal won him nothing and that changing scenery does not change destiny."

Stilicho had been closely shadowing the Goths on their march, and wasted no time in underlining the terms of the treaty – and that on the battlefield he was more than a match for Alaric. "The vultures fed on the innumerable corpses," wrote Claudian, "and the Adige, washing the bodies of Rome's enemies downstream, turned the seas red with blood."

If the poet can be taken literally, Stilicho appears to have once again surrounded the Goths on a hilltop and settled in to let famine, disease, and desertion finish them off. By this time it had occurred to some of the barbarians that they might be following the wrong leader. In all their encounters, Alaric had never overcome Stilicho in battle. The benefits of being a legionary, even a *foederatus* or auxiliary, outweighed the prospect of starving on a hill for a leader who had lost nearly everything. "And now scores of deserters began to drain his already weakened army," wrote Claudian, "and daily his numbers grew smaller. Surrender was no longer the secret of a few, but involved the open decamping of whole cohorts and maniples. Their chieftain rides after them and with irate curses and vain shouting seeks to rein them in, now waging war on his own warriors."

Among these, it is believed, were Sarus and Sigeric, those brothers of the rival Amali clan, who had had enough of this Balti upstart and, possibly hoping to have a hand in his end, signed on with Stilicho instead. It wasn't to Stilicho's advantage, however, to have Alaric's forces bled white, making them useless to him as a buffer against the East. Accordingly, before he lost too many warriors, peace was declared and the Goth spared yet again. "He had deserved the esteem," wrote Gibbon, "and he soon accepted the friendship, of Stilicho himself."[1]

Friendship was probably not a term the ancients, let alone Stilicho and Alaric themselves, would have used in this situation. Neither could afford to look weak in front of his men, and they may have even carried on their old grudge for that purpose. Yet clearly there was something more than just antagonism between them. Perhaps because of his barbarian blood, Stilicho appears to have been the only Roman who could reliably defeat Alaric, yet he was the one Roman who repeatedly let his foe live to fight another day. What

[1] *History*, Vol. III, p. 178

other Roman general was so magnanimous? After so many clashes, the two must have come to respect each other's abilities. It would seem that Stilicho had come to regret ever banishing Alaric from Roman service, and to serve Rome was what Alaric had wanted all along. In the rapidly changing conditions of the Empire, allies were hard to come by. General and king, Roman and barbarian, there was no telling when one of them might have need of the other. *The enemy of my enemy is my friend.*

For his Roman audience, though, Stilicho's panegyrist Claudian did not wax too warm and affectionate for the king of the Goths. "He was forced out of Latium," he reminded his readers, "retracing his steps in failure and shame. Such was the complete turnabout of his luck."

He has Alaric morosely regretting his fate, recalling the distant sight of the northernmost Appenines and wishing he had marched on Rome when he had the chance:

This range stretched from the border of Liguria all the way to the heights of Pelorus in Sicily and was known to all the peoples of Italia, its unbroken peaks dividing the seas that lap their country's shores. If I had followed the plan that anger first inspired in me and continued my desperate march along its crest, what might have been? Consigning everything to fire, I might have died with greater fame. Aye, and my dying eyes would have beheld you, Rome…

Claudian didn't know how prescient he was.

XVI

DEATH RENDERS ALL EQUAL

AD 404

No one is greater than you, Stilicho. Your only rival is Camillus,
whose arms broke Brennus's reckless power
as yours have broken Alaric's.

Claudian

In January 404 the Eternal City was treated to a spectacle its citizens had not enjoyed in years: a Roman triumph. Emperor Theodosius had staged the last such parade after his defeat of Eugenius in 395. The triumph of 404 was even more joyous, since it did not celebrate a decision of one emperor over another and therefore a defeat of Romans, but a victory (even if not clear-cut) over outsiders and barbarians, the Goths of Alaric.

Uncertainty over the date of the battle at Verona, whether summer 402 or summer 403, means as much as a year and a half may have passed. The imperial court, it would appear, was not so certain of the totality of victory. The Gothic encirclement at Mediolanum prior to Stilicho's arrival had given Honorius a fright. For the emperor's peace of mind Stilicho had ordered the capital moved to a new home, in the coastal city of Ravenna. With rivers, swamps, and ocean on all sides, it was possible, but next to impossible, to take the city. Ravenna's port ensured that, like Constantinople, it could be supplied by, and maintain contact with, the Eastern capital.

What nobody at the time seems to have realized is that Rome, now twice removed as the Western imperial capital, was increasingly in strategic terms of only symbolic importance. Symbols, though, mean everything. The threat of Gothic assault had spurred the inhabitants to upgrade the city's crumbling defenses. The Servian Wall that had protected it in Camillus' time – that is, when the citizens didn't leave its gates open to barbarian incursion – had long since been overflowed by the expanding city and was ultimately torn down for its stone and to make room; today only a few stretches and a gate survive. The Aurelian Walls, built to fend off an invasion of Germanic tribes during the crisis-ridden 3rd century, were already 125 years old, but had been restored to their former glory and raised ten or twelve feet above their previous level.* "Terror was the builder of that monumental work," admitted Claudian, "and, by an odd twist of fortune, war ended the decay that peace had wrought. For terror caused the sudden raising of all those towers and replenished the vigor of Rome's seven hills by encircling them all within a single long wall."

But Rome had so long depended on its armies, rather than its walls, to hold its enemies at a distance that everyone had forgotten the essence of siege warfare: Walls not only keep enemies out, but keep inhabitants in.

"The avid wish of both senate and people to see their emperor," wrote Claudian, "requires his oft-refused return." Symbolic or not, the heart of the Empire was still the Eternal City, where the Senate resided, even if the mob ruled. Whether all insisted on Honorius putting in an appearance, as Claudian had it, or the people simply needed another excuse for celebration, the emperor had finally bowed to demand. He had less to do with the victory over Alaric than the lowliest bureaucrat in Rome, but the victory had been accomplished in his name, and his was the glory of the triumph. For 404 he had also been honored with the title of consul, again, his sixth one-year term in his nineteen years.

---

*The 19th-century Italian archaeologist Rodolfo Lanciani pointed out that the raising of the walls was made easier by the leveling and spreading of the layers of city rubbish which, over generations, had been thrown over and piled up outside them, but that made them no less imposing.

If the old traditions were followed, Honorius donned a laurel crown and a purple toga trimmed in gold, and mounted a four-horse chariot in the Field of Mars, a complex of temples and public monuments which had not been an actual open field since the earliest days of the city. Triumphal parades were usually preceded by prisoners – captive enemy leaders, soldiers and sometimes their families – and rolling displays of captured weaponry, followed up by the senators and magistrates of Rome, walking before the emperor in his chariot. Honorius, however, had excused – Claudian said forbidden – the senators from taking part. How much of that decision was Stilicho's is left unmentioned. The interests of the Senate, in Rome, increasingly differed with those of the imperial court, whether in Mediolanum or Ravenna. It was Stilicho, by whose martial skill the victory had been accomplished, who rode in the chariot beside his son-in-law, with his daughters following on foot and his son Eucherius marching along like a true soldier. As for the prisoners, they must have been relatively few and unimportant, as most had been released and many of the Goth deserters were now passing in formation behind the imperial chariot, along with the former rebel Alans and Vandals, all now members of Stilicho's legions.

Many of the senators, watching the slow parade pass, but denied the adoration of the crowd and the association with Roman victory, were doubtless grumbling among themselves to see so few barbarian prisoners and so many barbarian legionaries. Were they, as good Romans, supposed to celebrate a campaign by a semi-barbarian general leading a mostly barbarian army to an at-best partial victory over more barbarians? Had this campaign of Stilicho's been a military operation or another recruiting tour? How many barbarians in the army were enough?

Still, if the choice had to be between barbarian mercenaries and pilfering the senators' own properties for manpower, their answer was unequivocal. One didn't become a Roman senator in the first place if one did not have the financial wherewithal to provide public games and entertainments, thereby gaining political favor and office. Where was such income to be derived, if not from properties, villas, and land? And all that required workers, whether free or enslaved. If the military was allowed to conscript manpower from landowners, where would it all end? Taxes? Taxes were for plebeians. If the patrician class were expected to provide bread and circuses out of their own pockets, they could not be expected to pay taxes as well. The former consul and urban prefect of Rome, Senator Quintus Symmachus, explained the aristocrats' predicament when he complained to a friend, "I must now exceed the reputation my own shows have garnered. Our family's benevolence during my recent consulship and the official games held in my son's honor preclude any mediocrity."*

When his son was named *praetor* in 401, the obligatory games are estimated to have cost Symmachus 2,000 *solidi*, gold coins, a year's income. He hoped to hold them in the Colosseum in Rome, then called the Flavian Amphitheater, which sat 50,000. Permission from the current urban prefect needed ratification by the court and was slow in coming, so Symmachus had written Stilicho, requesting special authorization. Ever since Theodosius had seen fit to pardon Symmachus for his misguided support of Maximus, the politician and the general had enjoyed a special relationship. Pagan though he was, Symmachus was Stilicho's spokesman in the Senate, in return for which Stilicho had restored some of that body's legislative powers. Permission was duly granted him, and the games held. A statue in the Centrale Montemartini Museum in Rome is thought to be of Symmachus, holding up a *mappa*, a cloth to be thrown down to signal such contests to begin. Consul, urban prefect, senator, entitled *vir clarissimus* – very famous man – Symmachus apparently chose to be remembered instead for his contribution to the games. Such was the life of a Roman aristocrat.

Games also played a role in the conflict between Christians, who for so many years had been fodder in the arena, and pagans, who now found themselves fighting for their faith. In this period always simmering just beneath the surface, the struggle reached a flashpoint

---

*For the games concerned, on the occasion of the elevation of Symmachus' ten-year-old son Memmius to the quaestorship in 393, he acquired a number of Saxon slaves, probably prisoners captured by Arbogastes in his campaign in Germany the previous year, to be executed in the arena for the pleasure of the crowd and Emperor Eugenius. Much to his dismay, twenty-nine of them defied his plans by strangling each other to death, by hand, in their holding pen. "So I think no more of a gaggle of slaves more useless than Spartacus," he wrote in spite, "and I wish, if it could easily be done, that the beneficence of the Emperor be exchanged for a present of African animals."

during Honorius' triumph. Gladiatorial games were of course part of the celebration. Telemachus, also called Almachius, a Christian ascetic out of the East (where asceticism seems to have been rampant), was in town. According to Theodoret, "There, when the loathsome show was playing out, he went into the arena himself."

There are several versions of the story, but all end the same. According to one, Telemachus decided to take advantage of the ready-made congregation to proselytize, rising up to proclaim against the slaughter: "Today is the Octave of our Lord's birth.* Be done with idol worship, and abstain from pagan sacrifices." Others say his message was much more straightforward: "In Jesus Christ's name, stop!"

Theodoret claimed that he, "going down into the arena, tried to stop the men who were using their weapons on one another." Other versions have it that Alipius, governor of the city, ordered him thrown in the arena. One of the gladiators fatally stabbed him or, as Theodoret tells it, "The fans of the games were angered, and driven by the madness of the devil, who delights in such bloody deeds, stoned him to death."

Other versions have the crowd, stunned speechless by his sacrifice, leaving the stadium in silence, but the influence of Telemachus' death on the mob is not as important as its effect on Emperor Honorius, who witnessed it from the imperial box in the southwest gallery of the stadium. He was not the first emperor to realize the incompatibility of Christian faith with gladiatorial combat, which over the centuries had seen perhaps half a million people and millions of animals dead on the Colosseum floor. Constantine the Great, who first established tolerance of Christianity in the Empire, and Theodosius, who made it the official religion, had both tried to abolish the games, but the bloodthirst of the mob always won out. No more. It was timid little Honorius who finally put a foot down, forbade death matches, and declared Telemachus a saint. According to Theodoret, "He included Telemachus in the list of triumphant martyrs, and called a halt to that godless spectacle."

Gibbon, at least, felt the decline of the games contributed to, or was symbolic of, the decline of Rome: "The citizens, who adhered to the manners of their ancestors, might perhaps insinuate that the last

*The feast day of Jesus's circumcision and naming.

217

remains of a martial spirit were preserved in this school of fortitude, which accustomed the Romans to the sight of blood, and to the contempt of death."[1]

Some sources claim Telemachus' martyrdom took place in the year 391, but though man versus animal fights would continue, the last recorded gladiatorial games in the Colosseum took place on January 1, 404 – the date of Honorius' triumph.

It's thought Symmachus did not live to see it. His last known letter dates from 402. Without him to act as a go-between, Stilicho and his barbarian army were bound to come into conflict with the anti-barbarian faction among the aristocrats. And Stilicho had offended the Christians among them as well, by his attack on Alaric at Pollentia on Eastertide. With the death of Symmachus, he may have lost his last friend in the Senate.

Even without Symmachus, Stilicho still had a good friend, and silver-tongued spokesman, in Claudian. The poet had risen high in imperial estimation as well, so much so that he had been honored with his own statue. It no longer survives, but the base on which it stood still resides in the National Archaeological Museum, Naples. At the bottom, an inscription in Greek proclaims the poet equal to the talents of Homer and Virgil combined. The main Latin dedication, somewhat chipped and interrupted with age, reads:

> To Claudius Claudianus, tribune and notary, and among other good deeds, the most excellent of poets. Though his own poems are enough to make his name immortal, as a testament of their approval, the most studious and grateful emperors Arcadius and Honorius have, at the request of the senate, ordered this monument to be raised in the forum of Trajan.

Let it never be said Claudian's work was not appreciated by Stilicho and his family, though he seems to have enjoyed little wealth or female companionship in their service. "Grinding poverty and pitiless Cupid are my enemies," he once wrote. "Hunger I can live with, but love I cannot."

[1] *History*, Vol. III, p. 157

That year, 404, Serena solved both problems for him, arranging a marriage for the poet to a wealthy bride of Libya. In proper gratitude Claudian wrote her, "The word of a goddess sufficed. Your recommendation, Serena, does more for me than flocks, harvests, or palaces. The mention of your name has persuaded her parents and an imperial prayer disguised my poverty. When Serena writes, what could the imperial spirit or dutiful love not accomplish with her words?"

Unfortunately it appears to have been agreed the wedding would take place in the home of the bride's family, across the Mediterranean, a source of regret for the Egyptian:

> I wish heaven had permitted me to make the long-awaited day official in the light of your presence, in your lord's camp, before your son-in-law's throne. Imperial purple would have been a good sign for our union, the distinguished assembly of the court would have dignified the proceedings and the hand which, in writing that letter, assured me of my bride would have lit the torch to guide her to the altar. Now that the covetous sea deprives me of my fondest wish and stretches between you and the Libyan coast, though distant, be gracious to me, my queen, and out of your kindness grant my safe return, as by a nod of your head you, a goddess, can do.

Claudian apparently set sail for Libya, and nothing more is ever heard of him. He is presumed to have died, whether at sea, in Africa, or soon after his return. He was probably in his mid-thirties, at the peak of his ability. In one of his last works he had unknowingly written what might have been his own epitaph: "To your feet shall come purple-clad kings, stripped of their majesty and mingling with the common throng, for death renders all equal."

Symmachus and Claudian weren't the only ones having statues dedicated to them. In August 403 Simplicius, the urban prefect of Constantinople, had made a name for himself by raising a statue of the *Augusta* Aelia Eudoxia in the market square in front of the senate house. Like Claudian's, only the base survives, a single block of white marble. Luckily, its inscriptions reveal the monument's design. One side is inscribed in Latin, *To our mistress Aelia Eudoxia, forever Augusta. Simplicius, of clarissimus rank, prefect of the city, dedicated [this]*. On the opposite side, four lines in Greek hexameter read: *Look upon this porphyry column and silver empress, placed where the emperors rule the city. What is her name, you might ask? Eudoxia. Who raised her? Simplicius, son of mighty consuls, the noble prefect.*

A shaft of priceless purple stone, topped with a figure of the empress, in silver? The unveiling of such a monument was a cause for celebration in the city. The market square would have been jammed shoulder to shoulder with citizens eager for their first glimpse of the gleaming statue of Eudoxia.

In the *Magna Ecclesia*, the Great Church which also fronted on the square, the commotion disturbed John Chrysostom in the midst of a sermon. For him, it was the last straw. He and the empress had been aggravating each other for years. John thought women should stay in the background and keep their mouths shut: "Women should be silent to the point that they are not permitted to speak of earthly topics, or even of spiritual matter, in the church. This is order and modesty." His ideal women were "devout, restrained, caring nothing for wealth, refusing decoration."

Eudoxia at least pretended to piety, but not as John defined it. "The people thought that his sermons were obliquely directed against the empress," wrote Sozomen. When he made these claims in his sermons, Chrysostom would turn toward the empress and her ladies sitting in their imperial gallery. At one point, after it was said Eudoxia had expropriated a dead man's vineyard from his widow, he went so far as to compare her to Jezebel, the biblical princess who had a subject executed so her husband Ahab could confiscate his vineyard. "The bishop's enemies did not hesitate to report his words to the empress," continued Sozomen, "and she, believing herself insulted, complained to the emperor."

The previous June, Arcadius – Eudoxia – had summoned John's rival, Theophilus the pope of Alexandria, and other churchmen hostile to John to a synod to charge him with Origenist sympathies. John had many enemies in the church. Theodoret wrote, "I think it pointless to drag out my story by listing how many bishops Chrysostom had cast out from the church and banished to the far ends of the earth, or how many religious scholars were likewise treated."

Denied the use of his golden voice in his own defense, indeed not even informed of the specific charges, John was found guilty in absentia, deposed, and banished. That night, however, an earthquake rattled Constantinople. Theodoret reported, "The empress was stricken with fear. At dawn messengers were sent to the exiled bishop, pleading with him to return as soon as possible to Constantinople and save the city from its peril."

The victory had only encouraged John to more emphatic harangues. Now he railed against those celebrating the empress's statue, as though they were no more than pagans worshiping a false idol. "The empress once more took his condemnation as sign of his contempt toward her," recorded Socrates, "so she set about convoking another ecumenical council against him."

When John heard the news, he started his next sermon by comparing Eudoxia to Herodias, the wife of Herod and mother of Salome, who in the gospels was responsible for the beheading of John the Baptist: "Again Herodias rants, again she is distressed, again she dances, and again desires to have John's head on a platter."

This, naturally, drove Eudoxia into a rage, for she had already felt the wrath of God. In 403 the normally fecund empress had suffered a miscarriage, as an anonymous follower of John ungraciously put it, "using the first swaddling clothes as the final burial shroud and becoming a mother and childless at the same time." (Simplicius' statue might have been raised in an effort to console her.) By early 404, though, she was pregnant again. Her hold on Arcadius was as strong as ever; in 402 their son, Theodosius II, had been proclaimed co-*Augustus*, the youngest person in Roman history to bear the title. The wife and mother of emperors, herself equal to them, could not be seen to be browbeaten by a mere cleric. Arcadius ordered Chrysostom removed from his church.

John refused to go. Finally, during the celebrations of Easter, imperial guards dragged him out and placed him under house arrest. As he himself put it in a letter to Pope Innocent I in Rome:

A detachment of soldiers invaded the Church on the evening of the Great Sabbath, forcibly threw out all the clergymen with us, and surrounded the chancel with armed men. Women who were in the prayer houses, unclothed in preparation for baptism that day, fled naked before this unbidden attack, not even permitted to cover themselves as female decency required. Many of these were injured in their travails, blood filled the fonts and the holy water was tainted red from their wounds. Even then the horror was not done. The soldiers, some of them we know to be pagans, broke into the room in which the sacred vessels were kept, and cast eyes on everything inside. In the commotion the most holy blood of Christ was spilled on the garments of the women of whom I spoke. It was exactly like a barbarian slave-taking raid.

John's followers were hunted down and imprisoned. Finally, in June, Chrysostom was banished again, this time for good, to remote Cucusus in Cappadocia (modern Goksun in southeast Turkey). No earthquake signaled God's wrath, but John's congregation did. A riot broke out between his supporters and his opponents. Somebody set fire to his church, the Great Church. Whipped by the wind, the flames spread to the senate house on the adjacent side of the square, which burned as well, except for two statues of Zeus and Athena. That was not enough of a sign for John to be recalled again, but the gods exacted vengeance soon enough.

That autumn, Eudoxia's child was stillborn. Doctors were unable to stop the mother's bleeding. Infection set in. John's sycophants grotesquely claimed that, while holding her dead child, Eudoxia received Eucharist – "the only sin she had yet to commit" – and that, on tasting the holy wine, "she immediately vomited her soul out along with the communion."

The *Augusta* died on October 6.

From the death of her father Bauto, and the death of her adopted father Promotus, Eudoxia had made her way in a man's world, willing and able to use her beauty to get what she wanted, and to eliminate anyone who got in her way, and unlike most of them she was not struck down by a more powerful man, but by fate. Almost everything we know about her was written by her detractors. The degree to which she controlled the Eastern Empire during her reign as *Augusta* is open to dispute, but she surely had a certain degree of control over her husband.

And now that she was gone, who was there to take her place?

XVII

"EVERYTHING WILL FALL TO PIECES"

AD 405

About this time the disputes troubling the Church were followed,
as is often the case, by disorder and tumult in the state.

Sozomen

Exile did not silence John's golden tongue. Thus far the contest had been between the prelates and politicos of the Eastern Empire. Having come out on the losing end of it, he determined to embroil the Western church, and Empire, in the fray. He wrote letters to the bishops of Mediolanum and Aquileia and to Pope Innocent I in Rome, protesting his treatment and requesting their intervention: "If these proceedings set a precedent, if the powers that be are able to use force against whomever they wish, however far from home, and banish whom they wish, and do whatever they want on their own authority, then be sure everything will fall to pieces and the world will be overwhelmed by unstoppable war."

In the early 5th century, however, the pope had even less power over the Eastern church than he does today. (Recall that Chrysostom's rival Theophilus was the pope of Alexandria, actually the 23rd such.) In AD 325 the Council of Nicaea had designated the bishops of Rome, Alexandria, and Antioch as church patriarchs, with the bishop of Rome, if not declared, then regarded as merely "first among equals." Innocent had no authority over religious squabbles in the East. "What are we to do to oppose such matters now?" he inquired. "A synodical decision of them is required, and we have long said that a synod should be convened, as it is the only way to allay the turmoil of such ferments as these."

Alexandria was to Constantinople what Rome was to Mediolanum or Ravenna: an old, traditional capital of the past, secondary and subservient to a modern imperial one. Eudoxia, and so Arcadius, had taken the side of Theophilus. Therefore, writing to John in Cucusus and his followers in Constantinople and urging them toward calm and patience, Innocent went over Theophilus' head and sought to bring in Honorius on the side of John. Sozomen reported, "He sent five bishops and two priests of the Roman church, with the eastern bishops who had been sent to him as envoys, to the emperors Honorius and Arcadius, to petition the convocation of a council, at the time and place of their choosing."

These papal ambassadors were very welcome at the imperial court in Ravenna. Honorius, doubtless at Stilicho's instigation, had been complaining in writing to his brother about various offenses, real or imagined, by the East against the West, from the nomination of Eudoxia as *Augusta* and the brothers' equal, to the treatment of Chrysostom, to no avail. From the Western point of view, Arcadius was out of touch, losing control of his court. He was parading statues of his dead empress through the realm as though she was a pagan goddess, despite the rumors of her cuckoldry and that his own son and heir Theodosius was born of another man's seed. Perhaps out of shame, or simply from grief, the elder emperor withdrew from public life, leaving his government in the hands of his consuls, Aristaenetus in 404 and Flavius Anthemius in 405. Stilicho, himself named Western consul for the year 405, had declined to confirm either, not that they cared. Aristaenetus had been a supporter of Rufinus. Anthemius, like Arcadius, was anti-Chrysostom; it was he who had permitted John's enemies to turn troops loose on the bishop's followers. And he was a member, perhaps the leader, of the anti-barbarian faction at the court.

It's no wonder that about this time Uldin, lord of the Huns, made a break with the Eastern court. The Huns may have found themselves under pressure from the Tartars, who are thought to have defeated them in battle on the upper Volga at about this time. As they had once pressed the Goths, now they were being pressed. Help was not forthcoming from Constantinople, so Uldin considered their pact void. "The Huns crossed the Danube," confirmed Sozomen, "and devastated Thrace."

Uldin was not the only barbarian offended by Anthemius. For him to assume the position of de facto emperor was practically an insult to Stilicho. Rather than work directly with his own brother-in-law on the throne, putting their family interests and by definition imperial interests at the forefront, he had to deal with another Rufinus, another Eutropius, whose personal aspirations might not coincide with those of the Empire, or at least Stilicho's view of the Empire. In his defense, Anthemius seems to have been less self-serving than those two, but he was not about to let Stilicho and the West interfere in Eastern affairs.

As a result, the embassy sent by Innocent, with the approval of Honorius and Stilicho, ended up exacerbating matters. "The enemies of John at Constantinople claimed these men were sent to humiliate the Eastern emperor," wrote Sozomen, "and saw to it the envoys were summarily thrown out, as though they represented an invading power."

Wars had started over less. The disagreement between Chrysostom and Theophilus had flared into a rift between Ravenna and Constantinople. In response, Stilicho broke off relations and closed the Italian ports to Eastern shipping. That was not enough. The situation in the East could not be allowed to stand. Arcadius had to be put back in charge, by force if necessary. As Sozomen put it, "Honorius' general Stilicho, a man who had attained supreme power as no one ever had, and had under his command the best of the Roman and barbarian troops, developed a hate for the courtiers under Arcadius, and determined to set the two empires at odds."

Like Innocent, however, Stilicho was as yet powerless to intervene in Constantinople. It was a long time since Gainas had served as his sword in assassinating Rufinus. The barbarian general Fravitta did not have the solid grip on power that Stilicho did. As a Goth, he was naturally at odds with Anthemius, but according to Eunapius he also called out the courtier Ioannes, the purported lover of Empress Eudoxia and father of Theodosius II, who had taken over the consul's former post as *comes sacrarum largitionum*, minister of finances, for his meddling in imperial affairs. "It is you who are the cause of all these troubles," he accused, "you who break the peace between our emperors, undercutting, dismantling, and putting an end to this most blessed and godly organization with your plotting. It is a most sacred thing, an unshakable and enduring safeguard, when emperors in two separate states rule a single empire."

Unfortunately, but intriguingly in this case, much of Eunapius' work is lost and only a fragment of this scene survives.* No exact date is mentioned and it's not even certain exactly whom Fravitta is lecturing. Ioannes is the Greek form of the name John – in his day John Chrysostom would have been addressed as Ioannes – and pagan Fravitta might equally have been accusing the bishop of overstepping his ecclesiastical boundaries, prior to his banishment. That would have won him approval in the court of Arcadius and Eudoxia. In the court of Arcadius and Anthemius and Ioannes, though, such plain speaking reaped a different reward. Fravitta was accused of treachery, and executed.

There's no evidence the last barbarian general of the East had any ties to Stilicho beyond perhaps having known each other in the old days under Theodosius, but there could be no plainer demonstration of Eastern attitudes toward barbarians. Every one of them who had risen to prominence there met an untimely end, like Gainas and Fravitta, or were pushed out like Alaric and Uldin. And, for that matter, Stilicho.

But the thing is…*Constantinople had resolved its barbarian problem.* The Eastern Roman Empire, to be known as the Byzantine Empire, would endure for over a thousand years. Its army, its government, would welcome foreign mercenaries and leaders, but never let them achieve positions of power unless they were thoroughly assimilated, becoming Byzantine themselves. The Byzantines recognized the basic Greco-Roman traditions that had made them, and went to great lengths to preserve them.

In the West, Stilicho's continued inability, or unwillingness, to subdue Alaric and his Goths was increasingly seen by some as treachery, as colluding with barbarians, and heretical ones at that. And the old traditions were not above sacrifice to his cause.

"Nor was it only through the Goths that the traitor carried out his plans," accused the contemporary governor and poet Rutilius Claudius Namatianus some years later, "before this he burned the holy books which invoked the Sibyl's aid." These Sibyllene Books were

---

*Though Eunapius lived several more years in Athens, his *Universal History* ends circa 404 and Zosimus resorts to other sources to continue his coverage.

a 900-year-old collection of pagan rituals originally set down by a sibyl, a prophetess of ancient Greece, and purchased at great expense by Tarquinius Superbus, the last king of Rome. They were kept under guard in the Temple of Apollo on the Palatine Hill and traditionally consulted whenever Rome faced some crisis, in order that the correct religious ceremonies be performed. That they come up in connection with Stilicho – only Namatianus, himself a pagan, mentions the story – implies that many in Rome believed a crisis was imminent. That they were burned on Stilicho's orders also indicates that the perceived crisis involved him, and further that whatever answer they advised was to his detriment. Namatianus doesn't mention the nature of the crisis, but rather obviously the potential war with the East, and Stilicho's means of waging it, was causing unrest in Rome. And those anti-barbarians who accused Stilicho and Alaric of collusion were about to have their eyes opened, for according to Zosimus, "Stilicho, seeing that Arcadius' ministers were hostile to him, intended, with Alaric's help, to add all the Illyrian provinces to Honorius' empire."

We know very little of Alaric's doings in this interim. Dismissed by the East, defeated and expelled by the West, lacking manpower and any imperial authority, he was almost certainly trying not to be noticed by either side as he started over from scratch. Sozomen placed him in "the barbaric regions bordering on Dalmatia and Pannonia," which would seem to indicate that he and his people had crossed the Danube and weren't even part of the Empire anymore. Uldin's depredations in Thrace almost certainly threatened them with the same Hunnish destruction they had been trying for generations now to evade.

Imagine the commotion in the Goth camp when a messenger arrived with word from Stilicho in Ravenna. Sozomen wrote the breathless headline: "He had Alaric, the Gothic leader, appointed by Honorius as a Roman general, and sent him into Illyricum."

Stilicho meant to reclaim Dacia and Macedonia from the East. If the senators representing Italy, Sicily, Africa, and Gaul – more precisely, representing their estates in those provinces – would not yield up their workers to be his soldiers or their tax dollars to hire more, then Stilicho would use Alaric's. Alaric's warriors would be Roman soldiers again, his army a Roman army. With the Goths' help,

Dacia and Macedonia would not come under senatorial control. They would be under Alaric's control, which meant Stilicho's control. All that tax money would come through Alaric to Stilicho, to the detriment of the Senate, to the detriment of the East. Stilicho and Alaric had been fighting each other for years. What was the point, when what they both wanted was right there, in the East?

For now, Stilicho's plan was for Alaric to get a head start and march his warriors down the eastern Adriatic coast. Stilicho, as he had done in 397, would take the shorter, quicker route, by sea. "He also sent ahead Jovius," wrote 5th-century Roman diplomat, poet, and historian Olympiodorus of Thebes, "appointing him praetorian prefect of the province, promising that to quickly join him with the western army, in order to bring the population there into Honorius' dominion."

This is Jovius' first appearance in our story, but he was to prove an ally, if not an unwavering one, of both Stilicho and Alaric, and would play a critical role in the crucial few years ahead. And they would be crucial. This would not be just another chapter in all those years of East and West using Alaric and the Goths to annoy each other. Nor would it be a proxy fight, as with Gildo and Mascezel in Africa. There could be no disguising it anymore: this invasion of Illyricum would be an act of war. As *praefectus praetorio Illyrici*, Jovius would represent the government of Honorius over territory rightfully bequeathed by Emperor Gratian to Emperor Theodosius I and the East, and thus to Arcadius. The cold war between the empires was about to go hot.

But for a generation now, from Theodosius with the Goths to Rufinus with the Huns, the East had shown a preference to avoid conflict and instead buy off its enemies. Its best generals, like Gainas and Fravitta, had been purged. Stilicho could be reasonably confident that the East would not fight for Illyricum, but simply let him have it.

"Having allied with Alaric to this purpose," wrote Zosimus, "he expected to soon put his plan into action."

Of course Alaric agreed. As *magister militum per Illyricum*, he would achieve the objective of his invasion of Italy a few years previous. This Jovius aside, his private domain was to be his again. All he had to do was help Stilicho take it, and he would once again be, in title and reality, King of the Goths.

What he and Stilicho perhaps didn't realize, was that Alaric wasn't the only king of the Goths.

XVIII

RADAGAISUS

AD 406

*In those days there were two Gothic peoples running wild
through the Roman provinces, led by two mighty kings. One of
these kings was Christian and more like a Roman, a man who,
through respect for God, as shown by his deeds, was willing to
let men live. The other was a pagan, barbarian, and true monster,
who in his ravening brutality killed less for renown
or profit than for the simple love of killing.*

Orosius

Maybe it was an indication that Roman civilization was merely a thin
veneer over what was essentially pure barbarism: just as any usurper
with enough soldiers at his back and willingness to bet his life could title
himself emperor and try for an imperial throne, barbarian warlords
were in a constant survival-of-the-fittest struggle to stay on top. They
might not have been constantly battling underlings in death matches,
but their people were free to simply pack up and leave, following any
leader perceived to be better. Back in the days of Adrianople, Fritigern
and Athanaric had vied for the Gothic kingship. The title of *reiks* had
been bestowed on Alaric because he displayed leadership. But after a
string of defeats by Stilicho and effective banishment for him and his
people to the backwaters of the empire or beyond, it's no surprise that
another *rex Gothorum* appeared.

The origins of Radagaisus are a complete unknown. Even his name is a Latinization of his real, German one, which may have been Rhodogast, Radegis, or Ratchis (none of which, notably, have the -ric suffix). Some historians have surmised that Radagaisus had been part of the Vandal and Alan uprising north of the Alps in 401, which seems likely even if not confirmed in the sources. If so, and perhaps because of the prospect of fighting other Goths, he had not joined Stilicho's legions to come south against Alaric, but had been biding his time to see how the fighting went and how Stilicho treated barbarian enemies. Evidently he liked what he saw. By the autumn of 405, with Alaric under Stilicho's command, Radagaisus had gathered enough manpower to him from the barbarian lands across the frontier to try his hand. He had nothing to lose. Even if defeated on the battlefield, he could look forward to the benefits of becoming a Roman *foederatus*. And if he was victorious, Radagaisus would be the first barbarian to conquer Rome.

"While Alaric awaited Stilicho's commands," wrote Zosimus, "Radagaisus, having assembled 400,000 Celts and Germanics from beyond the Danube and the Rhine, prepared for the march over into Italia."

Besides the Vandals and Alans with him, these Celts beyond the Alps – the Gauls – were long since almost totally Romanized, and if Zosimus is right Radagaisus' "army" included families from both sides of the frontier, which makes his movement, like Alaric's, less of an invasion than a migration. Zosimus furthermore almost certainly overstates their numbers. Orosius counted them at 200,000, probably still twice the actual total, but even that would give Radagaisus a warrior strength of up to 40,000.

Therefore, in late 405, as the *Gallic Chronicle* succinctly puts it, "Radagaisus, the king of the Goths, crossed the border of Italia, intending to lay it to waste."

To his discredit, the sudden invasion appears to have caught Stilicho completely off guard. His plans for the invasion of Illyricum had to be put on hold. Worse, even with his new barbarian recruits from among the very tribes that now supported Radagaisus, Stilicho had no army capable of countering such a large invasion force.

He did not, however, resort to calling on his new ally Alaric. The Goth had reneged on their peace agreements once already, in attacking

Verona. On meeting Radagaisus he might well forget his new pact with Stilicho and throw in with his fellow barbarian. Neither could Alaric be permitted to march south as originally planned. On his own, he would be at the mercy of a counter stroke from the East, which might well take advantage of the situation to defeat him and Stilicho piecemeal, or even re-enlist him to that side. So Alaric stayed where he was.

Instead, as Radagaisus' horde moved down over the Alps, Stilicho sent word over the mountains the other way, summoning Rhine garrisons and reinforcements from Britannia. It was late in the year, however, and there could be little hope of help before spring.

The fact that Radagaisus did not drive directly on Ravenna or Rome demonstrates that his campaign, like Alaric's, was probably not one of conquest, but of intimidation. But intimidate the Romans he did. Over the first half of 406 he had his way with northern Italy. He was "by far the most murderous of all our enemies, today or yesterday," wrote Orosius. "...Aside from the fact of his own indomitable courage and the support of vast manpower, he was a pagan and a barbarian, who, according to barbaric tradition, had vowed to offer the blood of the entire Roman race to his gods."

The approach of another barbarian army into Italy, the second in just a few years and this time a very un-Christian one, caused Honorius to take fresh shelter in Ravenna and stirred a fresh panic in Rome. "For had such an ungodly man, with such a huge and ungodly host, entered the city, whom would he have let live?" wrote Augustine of Hippo. "What martyr's tombs would he have not defiled? Through what actions would he have shown the fear of God? Whose blood would he have not shed? Whose chastity would he have not taken?"

The pagans in the city claimed the old gods had taken the side of Radagaisus and abandoned Rome, which would soon regret renouncing their worship. They clamored for the return of pagan sacrifices. Christ's name was uttered in curses.

By spring Stilicho, making his base in Ticinum (modern Pavia), twenty-odd miles south of Mediolanum, had resorted to paying two gold coins for every slave taken into the army. As the weather warmed and the Alps became passable again, his reinforcements arrived from

Gaul and Britannia. Moreover, to help fight the barbarians Stilicho found yet more barbarians. "God granted that former enemies agreed to lend us their forces," recorded Orosius. "Uldin and Sarus, leaders of the Huns and the Goths, came to the rescue of the Romans." Sarus had been a mutinous rebel under Alaric, but under Stilicho he was commander of the Goth contingent in the Roman army, as Gainas had once been (though Stilicho probably trusted him little more than he did Alaric). And Uldin, feeling himself jilted by Anthemius and Constantinople, abandoned Thrace to answer Mediolanum's call for troops.* With these reinforcements Zosimus counts Stilicho's army as thirty cohorts, but that was probably not more than 20,000 men, only about half of Radagaisus' force.

Radagaisus' problem, though, like Fritigern's in the run up to Adrianople, was that he had assembled this massive throng of barbarians, but couldn't keep it in one piece. It was simply too large to be supported anyplace that wasn't a major city. To live off the land, Radagaisus had to split up his army and let two-thirds of it go their own separate ways. The *Gallic Chronicle* reveals, "Dividing his army into three under various chiefs gave the Romans a fighting chance."

With his third, Radagaisus had marched down the Via Cassia, the main road through the Italian interior, toward Rome. In Tuscany he stopped along the way to lay siege to Florentia, modern Florence, then already a major city less than 170 miles from the capital. Founded on the site of an old Etruscan village by Julius Caesar in 59 BC as an army camp, in growing up the city had retained its military layout and defenses. There was only a small garrison but, like Alaric, Radagaisus had little experience of siege work and settled in for a blockade to starve the Florentines into submission. The defenders' fortitude was strengthened by the spirit of St. Ambrose, who according to his biographer Deacon Paulinus of Milan appeared before the altar in the basilica he had founded in the city, promising relief would come the next day.

---

*Historians dispute whether Radagaisus' advance was originally to escape Hunnish pressure. Uldin's domain may well have extended the length of the Danube, and war on Goths beyond the bounds of the Empire was not in violation of his agreement with Constantinople, but despite the Tartar presence to his own rear there's no evidence he was pushing Radagaisus from behind.

Sure enough, Stilicho's army arrived on cue. Suddenly outnumbered, Radagaisus immediately abandoned the siege. Orosius, a better priest and theologian than historian, attributed the victory to the power of God: "No army formed up for battle, the fight was not dragged out in fury and fear, no killing was done; no blood was shed; nor in the end was there even what is usually thought of as cause for celebration – a decision in battle resulting by the fruits of victory."

To judge by Radagaisus' response, and by Alaric's past maneuvers, the natural instinct of barbarians on the defensive was to seek high ground and dare their enemies to climb it. The Goths retreated to the heights of Faesulae, modern Fiesole, on a scenic but rugged ridge crest which overlooks Florence. "Downtrodden with worry," wrote Orosius, "the army that had only recently thought Italy too small was crowded on one small hilltop, where it hoped to escape notice."

As at Pholoe in Greece and Verona in Venetia, Stilicho found himself encircling a Goth-infested hill with entrenchments, and if his barbarian legionaries were loathe to engage in such grunt work, the Florentines and local peasantry could supply vast numbers of diggers. The besiegers were besieged, their numbers working against them. Meanwhile the Romans, in the heart of their own territory, enjoyed the full support of the Tuscans. Orosius continued, "Our men enjoyed plenty to eat and drink, while the enemy, so great in number and so rapacious, were worn down by hunger, thirst, and weariness."

At some point Radagaisus had to come down and try to force a way out, in another of these strange and increasingly frequent battles in which the future of Rome was decided by barbarians fighting barbarians, while the Romans looked on. As Orosius put it, "Two armies of the Goths, and then the Alans and Huns, mutually exterminated each other."

Radagaisus' forces may have actually broken through, only to be cut off by those of Uldin. The *Gallic Chronicle* reports, "In an outstanding victory Stilicho wiped out the army of the enemy third after the cavalry of the Huns were employed to surround them."

"After many thousands of Goths were slain," wrote Prosper of Aquitaine, "Stilicho, commander of the army, pursued Radagaisus and captured him in Tuscany."

Like the Gaulish chieftain Vercingetorix coming down from Alesia to surrender to Julius Caesar in 52 BC, Radagaisus was forced to submit to Stilicho. Caesar had kept his barbarian trophy alive, to show him off in his triumphal parade and then, his usefulness at an end, have him imprisoned and strangled. Surely Radagaisus was still hoping for better treatment, to become a *foederatus* like Alaric, a general of Roman legions. In the terms of surrender, Stilicho did agree to accept 12,000 of the Goth's warriors into his army, probably his nobles, their families, and retainers. They owed no loyalty to the man who had gotten them into this spot, nor to the vast majority of commoners who had followed him, and them. On August 23 Radagaisus was summarily executed, and the remainder of his people taken captive, to be sold as slaves.

"The Gothic prisoners are said to have been so plentiful that they were sold everywhere in droves like the cheapest cattle, for a gold coin apiece," wrote Orosius. (Half what Stilicho had paid.) The sudden increase in supply, and resultant drop in price, of slaves is said to have temporarily crashed the market in Rome. Yet Goths made poor laborers and even poorer slaves. According to Orosius, like wild animals, unable to be domesticated, most would soon die in captivity, and the masters who had saved money in purchasing them would lose it in disposing of their bodies.

The other two-thirds of Radagaisus' army, bereft of a leader and in no way willing to face Stilicho, the scourge of the Goths, fled of their own accord back over the Alps. Stilicho let them go. There were no garrisons to speak of along the Rhine, the brunt of them having been summoned to him that spring, but surely the barbarians had been taught a lesson they would not soon forget. The triumph was total, and nearly bloodless. Zosimus wrote, "Stilicho, as might be expected, was very pleased by this victory, and as he led back his army received garlands from the people everywhere, for having so safely delivered Italia from the dangers which she so much feared and anticipated."

Now, finally, the generalissimo received his own statue in the Forum, from the prefect of Rome, Psidius Romulus, in the name of the *populus Romanus*, the people of Rome. Admittedly, it was a very modest statue. A marble block, though mounted on a base of travertine, had been repurposed from an earlier equestrian monument, with the bronze horseman removed – the sockets for the horse's feet were still visible – and the block simply tipped up on end. The old inscription had been chiseled off and a new one carved (line breaks approximate):

> To the honor and virtue
> of the most loyal soldiers
> our lords Arcadius, Honorius and Theodosius,
> lifelong Augusti,
> after the end of the Gothic War
> through the good providence of the perpetual ruler,
> our lord Honorius
> and the strategy and bravery
> of the illustrious Count
> and Master of Horse and Foot in
> Attendance of the Emperor, Flavius Stilicho.
> [signed]
> The Senate and People of Rome.
> This monument's preparation
> accomplished by Psidius Romulus, v.c.,
> Prefect of the City, and deputy
> in charge of judging imperial considerations.

One gets the impression that Psidius, who gave himself as many lines as he gave Stilicho, intended the monument to immortalize his name as much as the general's. No matter. By this time Stilicho was accustomed to others getting the glory. He satisfied himself with having the power, knowing as he must have how fleeting the grasp of it, and even the memory of it, could be. The fate of Eutropius, damned for all time, attested to that. Marble is a stone as soft as history, easily erased and rewritten.

With yet more barbarian recruits in his ranks, and Uldin's Huns and Alaric's Goths as well, Stilicho had at his command probably the largest army of his career. Given the intransigence of the Roman aristocracy when it came to supplying him with manpower, and his recent recruiting strategy of hiring mercenaries from every barbarian army he defeated, it seems certain that the *vast* majority of his troops were barbarians of various stripes, with only a minority of blood-Romans, and those not necessarily at the top levels of command. By this time, like Rufinus before him, Stilicho even had a personal bodyguard of *bucellari*, Goths or possibly even Huns.

Picture these Roman magisters, tribunes, and centurions, completely outnumbered by their barbarian counterparts, taking part in Stilicho's *consilia*, his war councils, while he went back to plotting the conquest of eastern Illyricum – imperial Roman territory – in concert with the army of the notorious barbarian, Alaric. In the Senate and among the aristocratic class, too, wealthy and powerful men whispered to each other. They had feared a barbarian invasion, but the invasion had already happened. Much as Gainas had mounted a soft coup and, however briefly, taken over Constantinople, Stilicho, the half-breed barbarian in command of what now amounted to a barbarian army, had effectively put the Western Empire into barbarian hands.

And from Stilicho's viewpoint, why stop there? It was not inconceivable that, once he and Alaric had conquered Dacia and Macedonia, they might continue eastward to Constantinople itself, oust the troublesome minister Anthemius and his ilk the way Rufinus and Eutropius had been ousted, and reunite East and West again, as Theodosius had always intended, into one Roman Empire. There would be no such thing as barbarians and *foederati*, only Roman citizens, from the shores of Britannia to the deserts of Egypt.

In the spring of 407 Stilicho was in Ravenna again, assembling another fleet large enough to take this huge army of his across the Adriatic to his rendezvous with Alaric. Sozomen confirmed the plan was in motion: "Alaric led his troops out of the barbaric regions bordering on Dalmatia and Pannonia, down to Epirus [northwest Greece]."

Too late. Honorius, then in Rome, sent word to Stilicho commanding him to call off the invasion. New developments in the north required his immediate attention.

War had broken out again among the barbarian tribes along the Rhine.

The legions in Britannia had mutinied.

But for Stilicho this news mattered little, compared to that from across the Adriatic.

Alaric was dead.

XIX

ANNUS HORRIBILIS

AD 407

*Barbarian tribesmen have overrun all of Gaul in countless
numbers. The entire land between the Alps and the Pyrenees, the
Rhine and the Ocean, has been ravaged... except for a few cities,
a scene of widespread destruction. And those which are spared
the sword from outside, are inside taken by famine.*

Jerome

By the time Stilicho, in Ravenna, received word of events north of
the Alps, things were already out of control. The only attention he
had paid to Britannia and the Rhine frontier of late was to strip
them of legions for his battles against Alaric and Radagaisus. But
while Stilicho was doling out gold to fill his ranks with slaves,
the frontier legions had not been paid in months, possibly years.
(To judge by archaeological finds, or lack thereof, Roman coinage
in Britannia dropped off precipitously after about 402, or may
have been hoarded.*) The island province, its garrisons forged by
generations of fighting the Irish, Picts, and Saxons, had become
almost a separate state. It had been from Britannia that the emperors

*In 1992, while searching for a lost hammer with a metal detector, two men of the village of Hoxne,
Suffolk, uncovered an oaken chest containing almost sixty pounds of silver tableware, gold jewelry,
and almost 15,000 gold, silver, and bronze coins dated no earlier than AD 407. Altogether the largest
trove of Roman-era treasure ever found within the bounds of the Empire, the "Hoxne Hoard,"
worth about $5.3 million in 2021, is now on permanent display at the British Museum in London.

Constantine the Great and Magnus Maximus had launched their bids for imperial thrones. Leaders there had become used to running their own affairs and, with hardened troops at their command, saw no reason not to extend their authority as far as it would reach, even over the decadent sybarites south of the Alps. As a result, Britannia had turned into a hotbed of mutiny and counter-mutiny.

In July of 406 the remaining legionaries had proclaimed another of their officers as emperor. Known to history only as Marcus, he was probably a commander of some rank, a *comes litoris Saxonici, comes Britanniarum*, or *dux Britanniarum*, but his new title was *Imperator Caesar* Marcus *Augustus*. Little is known about him, because he was only in power for a few months. Whatever it was that the rebellious legions wanted of him, Marcus failed to deliver. So, in or around that October, they killed him.

His replacement, Gratian, was little better. He may not have even been Roman. Orosius called him "a townsman of Britain." Why legionaries would put a civilian, possibly even a Celt, in charge is unknown. Considering the brevity and results of Marcus's usurpation, there were probably several factions among the legionaries battling for supremacy, and Gratian may have been viewed as a neutral intermediary.

By the winter of 406–407 the political discord and utter weakness of the imperial forces, from the Irish Sea across the English Channel to the banks of the Rhine, made it obvious to everyone that Ravenna had in all practical terms given up responsibility for government north of the Alps. Without legions to keep the lid on the pot, all the old antagonisms between the Germanic and Celtic tribes flared up anew. Add the escaped two-thirds of Radagaisus' Goth army – perhaps 60,000 souls – into the mix, and matters swiftly came to a head. Orosius, for one, laid the fault for the upheaval at the feet of the most powerful man in the West, claiming the barbarians all "were incited by Stilicho to take arms on their own behalf and rose up as soon as their fear of Rome abated."

"Quadi, Vandals, Sarmatians, Alans, Gepids, Herules, Saxons, Burgundians, Allemanni and – alas for the state – even Pannonians," lamented Jerome. He had lived in Rome and Constantinople before moving to Bethlehem, but had been born in Illyricum, and was familiar enough with the wild tribesmen across the rivers to the north and the travails they had been inflicting on civilized world ever since the buildup to Adrianople. "For thirty years the barbarians burst the barrier of the Danube and fought in the heart of the Roman Empire. Long use dried our tears."

The worst of these were the Vandals, the untamed ones who had last risen up in 401 when Stilicho marched over the Alps and, instead of vanquishing them, recruited large numbers into his legions. By the summer of 406, when they were possibly under Hunnish pressure to their rear, those who had remained behind were ready to rise up again. Their king, Godegisil, led them against the Frankish *foederati* who dwelt along the Rhine.

Territory or treaty, whatever the Vandals wanted, the Franks were unwilling to give. Little is known of this Vandal-Frankish War, except that the Vandals were defeated. The 5th-century historian Frigeridus recorded, "The Vandals were beaten in the war with the Franks, losing their king Godegisil and about 20,000 of their army, and all of them would have been wiped out if the Alans had not come to their aid in time."

These Alans had also taken part in the uprising of 401, but were now divided into factions. One, led by the king Respendial, came to the Vandals' aid, while the other, under a chieftain with the splendidly barbarian name Goar, may not have sided with the Franks but at least sided with the Romans. Over the autumn of 406, Respendial and Goderic, the son of Godegisil, prepared for war, and on the last day of the year they attacked. The Christian writer Prosper of Aquitaine had to flee that province ahead of the barbarian invasion. In his *Epitoma chronicon*, a chronological summary of the years 379–455, his entry for the year 406 states simply, "The Vandals and Alans crossed the Rhine and entered Gaul on December 31."*

---

*Just as the Huns were said to have crossed the frozen Danube in 395, this winter crossing is often said to have been made directly over the frozen-solid Rhine, and though the river had often frozen in the past, none of the original sources make that claim for the end of AD 406. It seems to derive from some speculation by Gibbon that "the waters of the Rhine were most probably frozen." (*History*, Vol. III, p. 170) But Gibbon was writing at the height of the Little Ice Age (circa 1300–1850), when European temperatures were much colder than the early 5th century, or today. Between 1400 and 1835, the Thames River froze over two dozen times. Three-year-old Gibbon and his family probably took part in the "Frost Fair" in the winter 1739–1740, when Londoners held public festivals and fairs right on the iced-over river (and would do so again in 1789); during the winter of 1780 New Yorkers could walk completely across their frozen harbor from Manhattan to Staten Island. For Gibbon, frozen rivers were the norm. But the early 5th century was still the close of the Roman Warm Period, when temperatures were comparable to, or even warmer than, today. As of this writing in 2021 the Rhine has not frozen over since 1963.

However the barbarians crossed the river, the initial attack, according to Jerome, came at Moguntiacum, modern Mainz, at the confluence of the Main and Rhine Rivers. In the past the city had been the headquarters of up to three legions at a time, as well as the *Classis Germanica*, one of the largest riverine fleets in the provinces, but as of Stilicho's recall it probably hosted only a skeleton garrison. The Franks, still recovering from the summer's battles, were unable to resist the combined might of the Vandals and Alans, who stormed the Pons Ingeniosa bridge over the Rhine and laid waste the town. "The once great city of Moguntiacum has been taken and devastated," reported Jerome. "Many thousands have been massacred in its church."

It's indicative of the barbarians' goal that they did not proceed downriver along the frontier, but turned south, upriver, toward the heart of the Empire. They sacked Augusta Vangionum (modern Worms) before turning west, into Gaul. According to legend, Nicasius, the bishop of Durocotorum (Reims) who had founded that city's cathedral just a few years earlier, foresaw the Vandals' attack and tried to warn his congregation. Depending on the story – no dates are given and some sources set it the next time the city was sacked, in AD 451 by the Huns – the barbarians came upon him in the door of the church or at the city gates, trying to slow them while the people escaped. He was said to have begun reciting Psalm 119, "I am laid low in the dust," when they struck off his head, which finished, "Revive me, Lord, with your words," as it lay on the ground. His lector and deacon were slain with him, as well as his sister, who fought to the death rather than surrender her virginity. All would be named saints.

News of the barbarian conquest of Gaul had to be, to say the least, disconcerting in Britannia. If, as they seemed intent on doing, the invaders swept across the entire province to Hispania, they would cut the island off from whatever little support it still received from Rome. And Rome appeared to be leaving the provinces to their own defense. The new Britannic emperor, Gratian, had done as little as his predecessor Marcus to address the concerns of the troops. As a result, in February 407 they rose up and killed him as well. Orosius wrote, "In his place Constantine, a soldier from the lowest ranks of the army, was chosen simply because his name [being that of two previous emperors] inspired confidence, without any other qualifications to commend him."

Procopius, on the other hand, called him "a man of no low station," and for a soldier to rise so high without starting from high rank indicates that Constantine didn't do it strictly on his good name, which was rather a mixed bag. Named emperor almost exactly a hundred years earlier, Constantine I, the Great, had of course set out from Eboracum in Britannia to conquer the entire Empire and rule it benevolently for some thirty years, founding Constantinople along the way. His son, Constantine II, reigned only a tenth as long, dying in AD 340 in an ambush at Aquileia while bickering with his brothers, Constantius II and Constans, over the redivision of their father's empire. It remained to be seen how well this Flavius Claudius Constantinus, henceforth to be known as Constantine III, would live up to his name. The beginning of his reign was hardly auspicious, since his first move as emperor was to finally admit that Britannia could no longer be supported. Gildas wrote:

> The Romans abandoned the country, making it known that they could no longer undertake such punitive expeditions, or suffer their standards and their large and brave army to be wasted at sea and on land by battling these cowardly, thieving bandits [the Picts and Scots]; but that the Britons, hardening themselves to fighting weapons, and bravely making a stand, should bravely protect their land, their property and families and, what is more, their freedom and lives.

Gathering a fleet, Constantine crossed the English Channel to land at Bononia (Boulogne), along with about 12,000 troops, meaning practically every able-bodied legionary in Britannia. His stripping of Hadrian's Wall and indeed the rest of the island of Roman garrisons is considered the final abandonment of the province by Rome. The island would be fought over by Britons, Angles, Saxons, and Norsemen for the next 600 years.

On the other hand, the Roman troops remaining in Gaul were desperate for a leader. Constantine demonstrated his sympathy for both Gaul and Britannia by appointing two barbarians, the Frank

Nebiogastes and the Briton Justinianus, as his *magistri militum*. Given his willingness to trust loyal barbarians, and to fight disloyal ones, the Spanish and Gallic legions joined the Britannic ones in declaring Constantine as their emperor. This in itself meant nothing, however, unless Constantine earned recognition from – or imposed it on – Emperor Honorius. And Stilicho.

"The rumor of Alaric's death appeared dubious," wrote Zosimus. "...But the report that Constantine had risen up against the Empire was widely believed. Stilicho, his planned invasion against the Illyrians quashed, went to Rome to discuss matters with the politicians of the Empire."

The initial reports, of the defeat of the Vandals by the Franks, would have reassured Stilicho and his generals that the frontier was holding and only required reinforcement. On the other hand, if Alaric was indeed dead, the loyalty of his Goths was in question. They might well come marching back up out of Epirus and around the Adriatic to try another invasion of Italy. And Constantine's landing in Gaul could not be ignored. If he, and not Stilicho, was seen to be rescuing Gaul from the barbarians in the name of the Empire, his usurpation would gain followers. All this meant Stilicho was possibly facing a three-front war: in Illyricum against the Goths, along the Rhine against the Vandals and Alans, and in Gaul against Constantine.

As commander in chief, he elected to stay in Italy, centrally located to direct operations against the usurper, barbarians, and Goths. To reinforce the loyal Franks along the Rhine against the Vandals and Alans, he sent a contingent of Vandal legionaries he had recruited in the campaign of 401, who would know best how to deal with their errant brethren, whether to fight them or recruit them. Stilicho also had those loyal Goths under his command, led by Sarus, the Amali chieftain, but with his old rival Alaric out of the picture Sarus was more likely to join the Goths than fight them, and Stilicho evidently didn't trust him that far. By remaining in Italy Stilicho could defend against the Goths if necessary; he sent Sarus, appointed *comes rei militaris*, against Constantine and the Gauls.

It was not a great operational strategy, but probably the best that could be done under the circumstances. It was just a shame things didn't work out according to plan.

By the time Stilicho's Vandal reinforcements crossed the Alps, Constantine and his Gaulish legions had already driven the invaders back toward the Rhine. "A vicious battle ensued between them, in which the Romans prevailed, killing most of the barbarians," wrote Zosimus. "Yet by not running down those who fled, by which they might have exterminated every man, they gave them the chance to rally, and by summoning more barbarians, to fight again."

With the Britannic usurper acting to protect the Empire, the Gaulish locals didn't need Stilicho's help. His Vandals, attempting to victual and supply themselves at the expense of the people they were sent to defend, were taken for simply another set of Vandal raiders, and treated as such. As a result, in a short while they simply went over to the other side and joined up with their outlaw brethren.

Meanwhile Constantine, having secured the Rhine frontier from the barbarians, now undertook to secure Gaul from the Romans. He captured the provincial capital of Lugdunum, modern Lyon, and evidently took a cache of gold with it, because he immediately set about asserting another right of a legitimate emperor: minting coins. (Notably, the mint marks on Constantine's coins indicate he saw himself not as a usurper, but as a Western co-emperor, not overthrowing Honorius but ruling with him.) Continuing south, he moved into Valentia, modern Valence, sending his lieutenants Nebiogastes and Justinianus ahead to secure the alpine passes. They did not arrive in time to stop Sarus and his Goth mercenaries from coming through. "Having come up against Justinianus' faction," wrote Zosimus, "he slew that commander, along with the greater number of his men. Capturing great spoils, he moved up to besiege Valentia, where he knew Constantine to have taken shelter, it being strongly fortified and secure."

With Sarus investing the city, Nebiogastes hurried back, but rather than lift the siege by arms, he sought to negotiate. Whether he intended to speak on Constantine's behalf, or switch sides and offer his services to Sarus, will never be known. Sarus guaranteed the Frank's safety and, the minute he set foot in the Goth camp, had him executed.

Luckily Constantine was not short of barbarian commanders. In a move very reminiscent of Theodosius and Stilicho himself, he had left another Frank, Edobichus, and Gerontius, a Briton of Frankish descent, behind to raise troops among the barbarians. As usual, they were as willing to fight against Rome as for it if the pay was better, and unlike Stilicho, Constantius was able to pay. Valentia was under siege for only a week before these two came down from the north with reinforcements and no need to negotiate. Sarus had been able to defeat Constantine's generals one at a time, but with Nebiogastes' troops allied with those of Edobichus and Gerontius, and furthermore eager to avenge their late commander, Sarus was outnumbered.

"Constantine's forces attacked him so vehemently," wrote Zosimus, "that he barely escaped with his life." The Goths beat a hasty retreat back into the Alps. Unfortunately, the anarchy overtaking Europe had reached the mountain peaks and passes as well. They were infested with *bacaudae* (the term is probably from the Gaulish for "fighters") – brigands and bandits, escaped slaves, and deserters from the legions. When Sarus had come through the first time, at full strength, they had kept their heads down. When he came reeling back, his forces depleted and weighed down with booty, they were strong enough to demand a price for his passage. After his treatment of Nebiogastes, Sarus couldn't let Constantine, Edobichus, and Gerontius catch him alive, wrote Zosimus, "and was forced to hand over all his spoils to the *bacaudae*, a tribe of freebooters, to gain passage into Italia."

Many Roman generals would have paid with their lives for such a defeat, but Sarus had at least managed to halt Constantine north of the Alps. It was just one of many setbacks Stilicho faced in that horrible year. He was even accused of orchestrating the whole thing. "It was Stilicho's plan to weaken the Rhine frontier," declared Orosius, "and make war on both Gauls [Cisalpine and Transalpine]."

Worst of all, it turned out that Honorius' letter forbidding Stilicho to invade Illyricum had been written at the urging of his own wife.

"Serena was the cause of all," admitted Zosimus, "wishing to preserve an inviolable connection between the two emperors." Knowing her husband's attack would instigate a war between her adopted brothers, and fearing the outcome meant the violent overthrow and possibly the death of one of them, she had gone behind Stilicho's back to prevent it. Whether he understood her motives, or took it as his wife choosing her brothers over him, is unknown. At this point he and Serena had been married more than twenty years. Much of that time he had been away on campaign, and it's possible they had grown apart. This was not the last public disagreement they would have.

What Serena may not have appreciated, however, was the degree to which Honorius' orders – her orders – undercut Stilicho's authority. For him to be seen as not having the emperor's total and complete support left him vulnerable to his opponents in the Senate and among the aristocracy, of which there were more every day. Senators from Gaul and Britannia had lost their estates to the invaders, or to Constantine. Wasn't Stilicho supposed to be defending the provinces, instead of sending troops to take part in their destruction? Had Sarus really lost to Constantine, or struck a devil's bargain with him, and on Stilicho's orders? What good did it do Rome to have an army full of barbarians, if it came to war with barbarians? And nobody ever forgot that Stilicho was half-barbarian himself.

Nor was anyone relieved by the news that Alaric wasn't dead after all. All this time he and his Goths had been waiting in Epirus for the rendezvous with Stilicho that never came. If the rumor had been some kind of disinformation campaign out of the East, or by Stilicho's enemies at court, to delay or upset his invasion plans, it had worked admirably. Constantinople had sent no army to interfere. It didn't have to. Constantine had provided enough distraction and delay that Stilicho's invasion had to be called off. Keeping his huge navy, including cargo vessels that would normally be engaged in trade, on standby in Ravenna was prohibitively expensive for a populace already groaning under the tax burden of supporting his army. Stilicho released the ships, prepared his troops to move toward Ticinum (modern Pavia), and sent fresh orders to Alaric to move north, where he might be called upon to face Constantine if the usurper crossed the Alps. Alaric obeyed, but like the troops in Britannia and Gaul, had expenses to meet and had not been paid for his trouble. "Alaric advanced to Noricum [modern Austria]," wrote Zosimus, "and from there sent messengers to Stilicho, desiring a sum of money not only to compensate him for his stay in Epirus, which he said was done at Stilicho's orders, but also to offset the cost of his journey into Noricum and Italy."

Alaric requested 4,000 pounds of gold. Implicit in this message was the threat that if he did not receive it, he would come to Italy to get it.

And even this was not the worst news of 407. At some point in the year (the exact date is unknown, and it may have been early 408) came word from the imperial court: the empress Maria had died.

XX

Contenders for the Throne

AD 407–408

There now shone forth but one hope of salvation – Stilicho.
Him the expectation of whose visits the consciousness of deeds
ill-done had ever rendered bitter and unpleasant, him whose
approach even as far as the Alps afflicted the Byzantines with
fear of death and punishment, all now wish to come,
repentant of their former wrongdoing.

Claudian

In the mid-1500s construction of a new Basilica of St. Peter in Rome had been going on for almost a century since the first architectural plans had been drawn up, and it would be well over a century more before the final touches were completed. The old basilica, built over the saint's tomb, had been started by Constantine the Great on the site of the old Roman racetrack, the Circus of Nero. Saracen raiders had looted and pillaged the cathedral in the year 846, and during the Western Schism of the church (1378–1417), when French popes ruled from Avignon, it fell into near ruin. In 1505 Pope Julius II decided to demolish it altogether and build a monumental new basilica, in part to house his own tomb as much as St. Peter's. Work was delayed due to the sack of the city in 1527 by the mutinous army of Holy Roman Emperor Charles V, which killed eighty percent of the population and is often said to mark the end of the Italian Renaissance.

Seventeen years later, in February 1544, workmen digging in the shadow of the Vatican Obelisk (forty-two years before it was moved to its current location in St. Peter's Square) cut into the floor of the Chapel of St. Petronilla, the saint's daughter. The building, a rotunda with a dome roof, had been demolished in 1519. On that occasion several sarcophagi had been discovered, one of which contained bones and jewelry wrapped in eight pounds of cloth of gold.

Now, six feet under the rotunda floor, the workers broke into a forgotten, vaulted brick crypt with another sarcophagus, and an even greater treasure. In a coffin of red porphyry, a body lay wrapped in a cloth-of-gold robe of state, veil, and shroud weighing in total over forty pounds. On one side of the body, a silver casket held thirty cut-crystal goblets and gold vases. Another casket on the other side held 150 pieces of jewelry: gold rings, earrings, brooches, necklaces, buttons, and hairpins, all set with sapphires, pearls, and emeralds. Many of the pieces were inscribed *Domina Nostra* Maria and *Dominus Noster* Honorius – Our Lady and Our Lord – making it certain this was the tomb of Maria, daughter of Stilicho and Serena, filled with her personal trinkets and toiletries.

Today the Louvre displays a *bulla*, an amulet from this trove, inscribed with the names Honorius, Maria, Stilicho, Serena, Thermantia, and Eucherius, plus the blessing *Vivatis*, "Live," all arranged in the form of a Chi-Ro (☧, combining X and P, the first two letters of the name of Christ in Greek). Of all that treasure, only the amulet remains. Everything else disappeared. Maria's cloth-of-gold raiments and the silver jewel boxes were all melted down. The jewelry, including an emerald carved with a bust of Honorius, was all broken up and sold. Even the cut-crystal vases and goblets, gone. Maria was buried by people who loved her enough to have her favorite things, a fantastic trove, interred with her on a holy site. Yet once discovered, not even her body survived.

Stilicho was wealthy, but not even he had the riches to meet Alaric's demand for two tons of gold. He had to take the issue before the Senate in Rome. The dribs and drabs of power he had awarded that body in the past counted for nothing when he informed them of Alaric's ultimatum, and that to refuse it meant bloodshed. As Zosimus attested, when the Senate assembled to choose war or peace, "most of them were inclined toward war."

Not since the days of Brennus and Camillus had Rome bargained with barbarians. In the senators' view, of the two threats facing the Empire, Constantine and Alaric, the former was surely the lesser. Alaric had already invaded Italy once, and even if paid his extortion fee, might well do it again. Constantine had shown no desire to overthrow Honorius, only to rule beside him. He already ruled, in effect, half the Western Empire. If Alaric tried to mount another invasion, better to have him face two emperors and a united empire. To buy peace was to dishonor Rome.

Stilicho advised them to think again.

"All this time Alaric spent in Epirus in order to join with me against the emperor of the east," he told them, "to cut the Illyrians from that domain, and make them subjects of Honorius." He admitted the invasion had been called off by imperial command, at his own wife's bidding, but that didn't mean Alaric wasn't a *foederatus*, an officer of the Empire. For the senators to deny him remittance out of imperial tax revenue would be the same as Rome had done to Britannia, and turn out the same way.

To the implicit threat of war, Stilicho added his own threat, though it wasn't recorded in words and probably wasn't expressed as such. It didn't need to be. Stilicho was no senator. If anyone had forgotten, he was *comes et magister utriusque militiae praesentalis*, supreme military commander in the name of the emperor. Some of these aristocrats and patricians had lost their estates in Gaul. They and all the rest stood to lose much more if Alaric invaded Italy, particularly if Rome's mostly barbarian legions decided to go over to his side. Roman democracy was not the barbarian way. Goths had little use for senates. Or senators. At times like this, neither did Stilicho.

Suddenly deciding the semi-barbarian generalissimo of Rome was being more than reasonable, the rest of the Senate voted to give in to Alaric's demand, although as Zosimus admitted, "most consented more in terror of Stilicho than because of their own decision or feeling."

Many of these senators and patricians owed their position to Stilicho, but even they were having second thoughts. Lampadius, a nobleman by birth, had been named *praefectus urbis Romae*, prefect of the city of Rome, by Stilicho back in 398 to enforce conscription of slaves in the campaign against Gildo. From that humble start in politics he had since risen to senator, just in time. Seeing the Senate of Rome – which had endured for over 1,100 years, through the kingdom, the Republic, and the division of the Empire – voting to pay off barbarians, he famously declared aloud, "*Non est ista pax, sed pactio servitutis.*"

This is not a peace, but a pact of servitude.

Then, as soon as the session gave out, he fled to the nearest church to plead sanctuary before any of Stilicho's barbarian legionaries could further discuss the matter with him.

Another officer of the court, Olympius, had been elevated by Stilicho to *magister scrinii*, master of secretaries, and in that capacity was doubtless present when the decision was made to appease Alaric. His opinion at the time, ironically, was not recorded by any imperial secretary, or at least has not survived. Olympius very likely kept it to himself, but he would not do so much longer. According to Zosimus, he was now in charge of both the emperor's communications and security. It was a dangerous combination: "Olympius, a native of the shore of the Black Sea, and a high-ranking officer of the court guards, concealed under the guise of Christian faith the most wicked plans in his heart."

With his Illyrian flank secured (but leaving a garrison in Ravenna under Sarus, just in case), over the winter of 407–408 Stilicho marched his army up the Po Valley to Ticinum (modern Pavia), where they would be ideally located to launch an invasion in the spring, or meet one by Constantine. To judge by later events, the Ticinum garrison were primarily Roman, that is to say not barbarian *foederati*, which were still manning Ravenna. They might well have been asking themselves why they were following a half-barbarian's orders against a Roman emperor, one self-proclaimed but who had shown willingness and ability to run the Empire, perhaps better than Stilicho was running it.

For the moment Constantine was less concerned with invading Italy than on securing his own flank, in Hispania. The provincial governors there had declared for him – as well they might, considering that by occupying Gaul he had cut them off by land from Italy – but the Theodosian family still had relatives and strong ties there. "Constantine was apprehensive," wrote Zosimus, "that when they had assembled an army of the soldiers manning that province, they might soon cross the Pyrenees against him, even as Honorius sent an army from Italy, and by approaching him on either side, deprive him of his throne."

In other words, a pincer attack. Honorius and Stilicho tried to engineer one. Messengers were sent, almost certainly by water across the Ligurian and Balearic Seas, to contact the emperor's cousins and encourage them to rise up. Two, Theodosiolus and Lagodius, abstained, but according to Orosius two others, Didymus and Verenianus, "who were young, aristocratic, and rich, agreed not only to march against the usurper, but to protect themselves and their land in the emperor's name against usurper and barbarians alike."

"Didymus and Verenianus had often argued with each other," confided Sozomen, "but came to agreement when threatened by a common danger."

Like the younger generation of Theodosians, however, the brothers had little military acumen. "Just the opposite," wrote Orosius, "they took a long time simply mustering the slaves from their own estates and arming them out of their own pockets. Making no effort to hide their intentions, they proceeded up the Pyrenean passes without intimidating anyone."

Meanwhile Constantine had called upon his own blood relatives to join him. He summoned his eldest son, Constans, from the monastery where he was living as a monk. A man of peace, perhaps, but Constans was the son of a soldier and of no small talent himself in that regard, particularly when his father raised him to the rank of *Caesar*, junior emperor.*

So titled, Constans and his *magister militum* Gerontius marched over the Pyrenees into Hispania. They set up their new capital at Caesaraugusta (modern Zaragoza or Saragossa) on the Ebro River. Sozomen wrote, "Constans, after mastering this province and naming his own governors over it, ordered that Didymus and Verenianus, the relatives of Honorius, should be brought before him in chains."

---

*This indicates that Constantine had given up trying to reassure Honorius of his intentions. To this point he had been lobbying for the position of junior emperor himself. There was no such rank as junior-junior emperor, and by so elevating his son Constantine seems to have become resigned to war.

To their credit, the Theodosians made good on their promise to cousin Honorius. "They combined their armies, made up mostly of armed farmers and slaves," reported Sozomen. "They attacked Lusitania [modern Portugal and western Spain] together, and killed many of the soldiers the tyrant sent to capture them."

In response, according to Orosius, Constans turned loose "certain barbarians, who had earlier been enlisted as allies, called *Honoriaci*." The name, ironically, indicates the unit had been named in honor of, or even created by, Honorius (ergo, Stilicho), probably out of some of the barbarian bands the general recruited on his first campaign through Gaul in 396 to garrison the Rhine, but now re-recruited by Constantine. For them, one Roman emperor was as good as another, if he gave them an opportunity to loot.

"They were the cause of the first disaster that befell Spain," claimed Orosius. "…These barbarians were permitted to loot the plains of Pallantia [modern Palencia in northwest Spain] as their prize for victory. Later, when the loyal and well-regulated peasant guard was removed, they were assigned to the defense of the mountain passes." This placement of barbarians to guard the key Pyrenees routes between Gaul and Hispania was to have severe ramifications in the future.

For now, the Theodosians' army of servants, slaves, and field workers quickly fell before the barbarian onslaught. "Didymus and Verenianus, along with their wives, were taken prisoner, and eventually put to death," reported Sozomen. "Their brothers, Theodosiolus and Lagodius, who were living elsewhere, fled the province." Despite having taken no part in the fighting, Theodosiolus took a ship to Italy, and Lagodius to Constantinople. The reign of the Theodosians in Hispania was at an end. Leaving Gerontius in charge, Constans returned triumphantly over the Pyrenees to his father, who now held two-thirds of the Western Empire.

Dynasties are not only maintained through warfare. It was Stilicho's responsibility to maintain the imperial family's legacy in the face of all challenges. Still in his early twenties, Emperor Honorius was a widower, and a childless one at that. For the future's sake, such a situation could not be allowed to stand, particularly with Constantine already naming his own successor. The choice of imperial consort was a matter of state, and Stilicho had to resolve it like any other. If he didn't provide the emperor with companionship, someone else at court would, the same way Eutropius had outmaneuvered Rufinus at the court of Arcadius.

One would think there would be any number of women eager to fill the void beside the imperial throne. Then again, Honorius had grown into the kind of man that women had to be compelled to love. The teen who, according to Claudian, had so ardently desired Maria's hand had, according to Zosimus, left her to die still a virgin. Whoever had been satisfying the emperor's carnal desires, if indeed anyone was, was too inconsequential to be mentioned in the accounts of the time. Perhaps because of losing so many loved ones so early in life, Honorius seems to have reserved his love for his pigeons and chickens. He had named one of his roosters Rome, and cared for it more than he did the city.

The task was made more ticklish by the fact that Honorius, bowing as always to his advisors, acknowledged the requirement for marriage, but with his pick of all the women in the world, was too lazy – or too amoral, or too scornful of lesser beings – to look any further than his own household. Zosimus wrote, "Honorius, having long since lost his wife Maria, wished to marry her sister Thermantia."

In 408 Thermantia was probably sixteen or seventeen, a good bit older than Maria or Serena at their weddings, with a better idea of what she was getting into. If her sister had died a virgin, her own virtue was at less risk from the emperor than from her own mother, who took a completely different view of this daughter's matrimony from the previous one. Zosimus wrote, "Serena, who, as may easily be believed, wished to become the grandmother of a young emperor or empress, for fear of her losing influence, used all her wiles to marry her other daughter to Honorius."

Romans took a dim view of incest, considered it barbaric behavior, and had a broad definition of it. Besides sex between relatives closer than cousins, acts of *incestum*, impurity or sacrilege, extended to defiling Vestal Virgins, and even men intruding on the all-female *Bona Dea* (Good Goddess) religious rites. Roman civil law forbade marriages within four degrees of consanguinity. Serena, though his adopted sister, was Honorius' cousin, the fourth degree. Her daughter Maria had been Honorius' first cousin, once removed – the fifth degree.

Their marriage had made Thermantia the emperor's sister, but only in-law, a kinship of affinity rather than consanguinity. Such marriages were forbidden in many Western nations right up to the Great Britain of Gibbon's day, but not under Roman law, and anyway emperors all the way back to Caligula, Claudius, and Nero had engaged in incest in the first degree.* If they were smart, courtiers and senators – and generalissimos – would not object to Honorius marrying anyone he desired. The emperor's favor was as fickle as his love, and despite becoming more willful, he was no less susceptible to whoever had his ear at the moment. One would think that Stilicho would want that person to be Thermantia, but Zosimus asserted, "Stilicho, it appeared, did not approve of the idea, although it was pressed by Serena, who wanted it out of ulterior motives."

If true – and skepticism of Zosimus is always wise – this is an interesting observation. It was to Stilicho's advantage to have his daughter at Honorius' side, for the future of the imperial dynasty and his own. It may be, however, that he was beginning to have doubts that feckless Honorius was the future. Stilicho had other options, other paths to putting a descendant on the throne.

Though it had not yet come to pass, it was widely assumed his son Eucherius would be betrothed to his own first cousin once removed, Honorius' half-sister Galla Placidia. She was about Thermantia's age, and that she was not yet married would seem to indicate that Stilicho, as her *pater familias*, indeed had special plans for her. Why he waited is another issue altogether. Perhaps Eucherius was simply not yet worthy. He almost certainly attained a rank higher than entry-level *tribunus et notarius*, tribune and notary, but none is recorded. Zosimus claimed that Stilicho had cautioned the boy "neither to want nor try to achieve any other office or authority," possibly to hold him safely aloof of court politics.

And until Honorius had an heir, a child born of Eucherius and Galla might be portrayed by Stilicho's enemies as a threat to the emperor's reign. Such a match could only be a safeguard, a backup plan, in the case that Thermantia never bore the emperor children.

---

*Though since these three all committed incest with the same woman, Julia Agrippina the Younger – respectively their sister, niece, and mother – it might have said more about her than them.

Or if, say, the imperial throne suddenly became vacant.

In the end Stilicho, like Honorius, bowed to the pressure of his own advisor, Serena, and very likely submitted to the wishes of his increasingly imperious emperor. In May of 408, Honorius and Thermantia were wed.

Funny how things work out. The exact date of the wedding that month is not known, but the timing was either highly coincidental or rushed in response to events. Travel time from Constantinople to Ravenna or Rome by sea being on the order of three weeks, it was late that same May when word arrived that on the first of the month the emperor Arcadius had passed away.

He was interred, like his father, in a tomb of purple porphyry in Constantinople's Church of the Holy Apostles, though not in the east wing but in the south, next to the tomb of his empress, Eudoxia. "This prince was a kind and forgiving person," wrote Socrates Scholasticus, "and by the end of his life was judged to be fondly beloved of God."

And now the Eastern throne was occupied by his and Eudoxia's seven-year-old son, Theodosius II.

XXI

OVERTHROW

AD 408

*It is clear from the order of events, that every usurper quickly
devises his plans before secretly seizing power and publicly
displaying it. Success is in being seen with the crown and the
purple before being discovered.*

Orosius

When word of young Theodosius' accession reached Italy, Stilicho
was in Ravenna, seeing to the defense of Cisalpine Gaul in case either
Constantine or Alaric pursued the idea of invasion. Honorius was
on his way from Rome to join him. Stilicho had strongly advised
against this trip, as it put the emperor in closer proximity to Alaric,
but Serena had just as strongly urged Honorius to go.

"She wanted him to live in a more defensible city," wrote Zosimus,
"so that if Alaric broke the treaty and attacked Rome, he would not
capture the emperor. She was the more protective of him because her
own safety depended on his."

Lately Stilicho and Serena were working more and more at cross
purposes. To do so with a fickle emperor was like juggling axes and
swords.

Honorius had only got as far as Bononia (modern Bologna), about
seventy miles short of the capital, when news arrived from Ravenna
that the troops were in an uproar. The cause of the commotion is

unclear. Zosimus accused Stilicho of having Sarus stir up a mutiny in order to frighten the emperor out of making the trip, which seems excessive. What's more likely is that word had got out about the two tons of gold Alaric was supposedly getting for nothing more arduous than marching down to Epirus and back up, and that Sarus's barbarians were wondering whether they had backed the right Goth.

In any case, Stilicho again advised Honorius to stay well clear in Bononia until the fuss died down. But Honorius, who on Arcadius' death had suddenly become senior emperor, chose this moment to act imperiously.

He ordered Stilicho to have the mutinous legions undergo *decimatio*.

This punishment, dating back to the early days of the Republic and even Alexander the Great, called for the perpetrators to draw lots by tens. The man who drew the short straw was to be clubbed, or stabbed, or stoned to death by his nine former compatriots.

Decimation had been carried out several times during the Republic, and a few times at the dawn of the Empire, but thereafter the practice had died out. It was said the emperor Macrinus, who ruled for little over a year in AD 217–218, had ordered his men to undergo *centesimatio*, the death of every hundredth man. His legions soon revolted and delivered Macrinus' head to his successor, who furthermore had Macrinus declared *damnatio memoriae* and erased from the historical record.

The decline of decimation rather obviously coincides with the increase in barbarian recruits among legionaries. Civilized soldiers might stand for such punishment, even participate in it. Barbarian *foederati* would not. Stilicho must have known full well that to carry out Honorius' orders was less likely to quell a mutiny than cause one. It might even be that he came up with the idea himself, in order to make himself a hero to his men. "They were in such a state of alarm that they burst into tears," wrote Zosimus, rather implausibly of a bunch of barbarians, "and wishing him to take pity on them, persuaded him to promise them the emperor's pardon."

Having so agreed, Stilicho departed for Bononia, where he told Honorius the problem had been resolved without requiring punishment. In this he essentially disobeyed a direct order from his emperor. Whether Honorius believed his excuse remained to be seen.

Olympius, as court secretary and imperial bodyguard, would have accompanied the emperor on his journey and was doubtless taking notes at the meeting. The matter was let rest, however, in favor of a more pressing one: what to do about young Theodosius and the East.

"Stilicho still desired to go east," wrote Zosimus, "and take over the affairs of Theodosius the son of Arcadius, who was still very young and needed a guardian." The problem was, the emperor had the same idea: "Honorius himself was also inclined to go, with the idea of securing those dominions on behalf of Theodosius."

It was obvious Honorius' nephew was not yet old enough to rule by himself. If left to their own devices, the praetorian prefect Anthemius and his chamberlains would quickly take over. This was a prime opportunity for the West to finally exert a little control over goings-on in the East. Someone would have to go there, take up the reins of power, and see to it that the concerns of Ravenna were properly considered in Constantinople. Honorius, as senior emperor, had decided he should be that someone. He would dictate to both imperial courts the way Stilicho never could. Therefore, Honorius would take a ship to Constantinople, supervise the early months and years of Theodosius' reign, and make sure he grew up knowing who were his true friends and family. Groom the boy, as it were, to become a responsible, capable emperor. A Theodosian.

Stilicho opposed this idea even more strongly that he had opposed the emperor's trip to Ravenna. As Zosimus put it, "Stilicho, being unhappy with this, and explaining to the emperor what an immense amount of money such an expedition would cost, put him off the idea."

It was a flimsy excuse. The fact was, leaving matters of state to Honorius was inviting disaster. Without Stilicho to advise him, there was no guarantee that on arrival in Constantinople, Honorius would handle things at all. Instead there was a high probability that he would let himself become a tool, the way his brother had, of the praetorian prefect Anthemius, who would then control both emperors.

Anthemius was at the time busy appeasing foreign enemies. Uldin, having proven himself an ally of the West, was back to making trouble for the East. That summer his Huns crossed the Danube to occupy the Castra Martis (Castle of Mars, modern Kula, Bulgaria), which they used as a base from which to launch raids down into Thrace. An imperial envoy arrived to make overtures of peace, but Uldin, according to Sozomen, gestured at the sun, "declaring that he could, if he wished, easily conquer every land on earth that it shined upon."

As if that wasn't humiliating enough, Anthemius had also concluded a peace with the Persian Empire, which might more correctly be termed a submission; it was rumored that King Yazdegerd I had even been named executor of Arcadius' will and protector of his son, an affront to the honor of the Theodosian house and of Rome itself.

No, Stilicho insisted, Honorius should not be the one to go to Constantinople, not with Alaric at one end of the Alps and Constantine the other, both threatening to invade. It would be seen as a retreat, a surrender. As had just been proven in Ravenna, without their emperor to lead and inspire them, the Western legions might well mutiny and go over to one or another of the outsiders.

Instead Stilicho sketched out an admirable plan of divide-and-conquer. Alaric wanted to be known as an imperial general, and earn more imperial largess? Then appoint him *magister militum* and let him lead his army in the emperor's name, against Constantine. The two troublemakers could keep each other busy in Gaul until Stilicho's return. Honorius would reap the glory of defeating Rome's enemies, while Stilicho went east and handled the humdrum affairs of Theodosius' accession in his name.

For Honorius to put his best general in charge of politics while he himself played army demonstrates just how weak-willed and easily led he truly was. Zosimus wrote, "The emperor, falling for these contrived explanations by Stilicho, wrote letters for him to give to the emperor of the east and to Alaric, and set out from Bononia."

With Olympius in tow, the emperor duly departed for Ticinum to review and inspire the troops. Yet Stilicho, fearing Honorius would be led by the nose in Constantinople, neglected that he might be equally led in Italy.

According to Olympiodorus, Stilicho ordered up four legions, perhaps 4,000 men, for the trip. It was not an overwhelming force, but Stilicho was hoping for this to be a diplomatic mission, not an invasion. If Constantinople offered resistance, he could always call upon Uldin's Huns again.

It's known that Serena did not accompany Honorius and Olympius to Ticinum. (Of Thermantia and Galla's whereabouts at this time, we know nothing. They could well have still been in Rome.) She may have continued on her way to Ravenna as planned, but one would like to think she tarried a few happy weeks in Bononia with her husband, given everything about to ensue.

The most direct route from Bononia to Ticinum was some 125 miles by road, but the cheapest was by boat, 220 miles up the coast and the winding Po River to where it converged with the Ticino. As both routes took about a week, the cash-strapped court probably saved some money by taking the water route. Either way, that was a week for Olympius to bend Emperor Honorius' ear.

"It being normal, because of his faked modesty and gentle manner, for him to talk often with the emperor," wrote Zosimus, "he spoke in bitter terms of Stilicho, stating that he wished to proceed east for no other reason than to remove young Theodosius, and put the empire in the hands of his son, Eucherius."

Olympius' reasoning was a bit specious. Stilicho would not have had to remove Theodosius to put Eucherius on a throne. If Stilicho had wanted a throne, with his barbarian army at his back, he could have usurped and overthrown Honorius any time he wanted. He could have overthrown Arcadius after his *foederati*, under Gainas, had paved the way by killing Rufinus. With little choice, the compliant Senates of East and West would have acclaimed Stilicho emperor, as they had acclaimed usurpers before him.

Yet he had not.

He had not, because in the end he was still carrying out the elder Theodosius' wishes.

Historians have debated that point to this day, much as they have Stilicho's claim to guardianship of Honorius and Arcadius on the elder Theodosius' death. In part this is because, like that earlier claim, not even anyone at the time knew Stilicho's heart. Plainly he was still determined to gain control of the East, but what would he do when he had it? Sozomen recorded the most popular theory, the one Olympius put forward: "Stilicho, commanding the troops of Honorius, was suspected of plotting to proclaim his son Eucherius as emperor of the East."

Orosius concurred: "This wicked man believed that in this dangerous state of affairs he could seize the imperial title from his son-in-law and award it to his son, and that he could put down the barbarian tribes as easily as he had roused them."

Eucherius didn't help matters. Orosius held that, "in hopes of getting pagans [senators] on his side, he had promised that he would, on the beginning of his reign, restore the temples and overthrow the churches."

But given Stilicho's actions for the preceding thirteen years, does that make sense, or was it just the accusation put forward by his enemies?

It's true that once Stilicho took control of the East, eliminated Anthemius and any other rivals, and joined its army to that of the West, no one would be able to stand against him. Not Constantine, not Alaric, not the Senates of Rome or Constantinople, not even Honorius and Theodosius. The Empire would be united again. The two boy emperors, the Theodosian dynasty, would be secure under Stilicho's dominion. And he still had Eucherius and Galla Placidia waiting in the wings. If Honorius and Theodosius remained on their thrones, what better place for Eucherius than on Stilicho's, as overall master of the Empire?

All these years, Stilicho had sought to make himself what Theodosius the Great had so briefly been, what the old emperor had desired him to be. More than a *Caesar*, more than an *Augustus*: *pater patriae*, the father of the country, supreme ruler over the boy emperors. By clever battlefield strategy and artful political maneuver Stilicho had kept the Western Empire alive while Honorius was cowering in his throne room in Mediolanum. And it was Stilicho's army, under Gainas, that had defended the East against the Huns – as well as against Rufinus and Eutropius. Stilicho was already Western Emperor in all but name, lacking only imperial blood. And in the Roman Empire, by sufficient expenditure of common blood, common blood could be made imperial.

Of course, all that may have been part of Olympius' argument. As had Gainas and his barbarian army in Constantinople, Stilicho and his barbarian army had, for all practical purposes, staged a soft coup in the West. Now, Olympius could point out, he was about to complete it in the East. With Eucherius wed to Galla Placidia, a daughter of both the Valentinian and Theodosian dynasties, their child would have at least as strong, and possibly stronger, claim to overall rule than either Honorius or young Theodosius, all owed to his illustrious grandfather. *Pater patriae.*

But in ancient Rome, East or West, true power always derived from one source: command of the legions.

Little remains of Roman Ticinum under the modern city of Pavia. The town originated as a military camp founded at the northern end of a wooden bridge over the Ticino, both built by the consul Publius Cornelius Scipio in his ill-fated attempt to hold off Hannibal and the Carthaginians in 218 BC. Of the stone bridge that replaced the wooden one, only a partial pillar remains in the middle of the modern span, built in 1351–1354 (and rebuilt after it was bombed in World War II). The original fortified Roman camp, in its day the most far-flung military outpost in the northern Republic, somehow survived Hannibal's victory, but today is thought to lie under the *piazza* of the Duomo di Pavia, the city cathedral. It was probably there that Honorius addressed the troops. Zosimus wrote, "When the emperor had been in Ticinum four days, all the soldiers being assembled in the court, he appeared before them, and called on them to war against the rebel Constantine."

These troops knew more about Constantine than Honorius did, or for that matter Stilicho. Limenius, the praetorian prefect of Gaul, and Chariobaudes, its *magister militum*, had both escaped ahead of the usurper's invasion the previous year and would have already told anyone who cared to listen to everything they knew of it. (Whether their tales of Constantine's prowess impressed the rank-and-file soldiers as a threat, or a hope, is an open question.) They and the *magister equitum* Vincentius and Salvius, commander of the *domestici*, the imperial guards (which might have made him Olympius' superior in that regard; *domestici* often held down other jobs in the civilian sector or even other military postings), were all Stilicho loyalists; Chariobaudes' name indicates he was probably a German. All were ready, however, to do whatever their emperor commanded.

The legions in Ticinum would also have been aware of the rioting among the barbarian troops in Ravenna, not least because Olympius would have been telling them all about it, and about the suspicions of Stilicho he had imparted to the emperor. "A rumor was making the rounds," confided Olympiodorus, "that Stilicho was conspiring against the Emperor and, together with his top officers, was planning to elevate his son to the throne."

The dissension between Romans and barbarians in the legions was open to exploitation. Zosimus recorded, "Olympius, making sure to visit the sick soldiers, which was the height of his hypocrisy, made similar insinuations among them."

Olympius had been doing more than just insinuate. He had been laying groundwork, giving orders. And now, when Stilicho's officers were all assembled in one place, was the time to act. When Honorius' address failed to stir them, the legionaries needed only a signal. "Seeing that none of them were moved in regards to Stilicho, Olympius was seen to nod to his soldiers, as though to remind them of their private talks."

Thirteen years earlier, in Constantinople, Gainas and his Goths had slain Rufinus at the feet of Emperor Arcadius. Here, at last, was vengeance against the hated barbarians and their sympathizers. Olympius' Romans drew their swords.

"The troops revolted," wrote Olympiodorus, "and slew the prefects of Italia and Gaul, the commanders and other palatine officials."

The barbarian Chariobaudes was among the first to die, and with him Limenius, Vincentius, and the guard-captain Salvius. With the *domestici* leaderless, someone needed to protect the emperor. We can be sure Olympius saw to that. Honorius swiftly fled the scene, or more likely was spirited away in numbed shock. Never since Alaric's advance on Mediolanum – actually, never at all – had physical harm come so near his imperial person. With the passing of his father and more recently his empress, Honorius was no stranger to death, but violent death was something else, something he would seldom have witnessed outside the arena, certainly not with his own life in the balance. In this instance one of his *quaestors*, his court lawyers, had resorted to clutching the emperor's knees – in any other circumstances, a crime in itself – pleading for his life, only to be dragged off and butchered. The screaming, the dying, the *blood* was a dose of hard reality for Honorius.

With the emperor safely out of the way, the mutineers – who, thanks to Olympius, were almost certainly under the impression they had imperial blessing – went on a rampage. Zosimus recorded, "The soldiers, spreading throughout the city, killed every civilian official they could find, tearing them out of the houses where they had sought safety, and looted the entire town."

Events had progressed nearly out of Olympius' control. Only Honorius himself could stop the massacre. When he finally worked up the courage to call a halt to the slaughter – or was pushed out in front of the mob by Olympius – he did it in the guise of a common soldier, bereft of his crown and toga, wearing only a short tunic. Rather than attempt to dissuade the rebels, he assured them he had been on their side all along. Even so, wrote Zosimus, he had "great trouble conciliating and calming their rage."

The coup was almost complete. Stilicho's officers and loyalists in Ticinum were dead. The legions there were under Olympius' control. There remained only one final step to complete the overthrow.

Stilicho himself.

XXII

DOWNFALL

AD 408

The tallest tree is most often bowed by the winds,
high towers fall with a greater din,
and the lightning strikes the loftiest mountain.

Horace

Two or three weeks after Honorius' departure, Stilicho had not moved from Bononia. It's likely he was hearing whispers of discontent from all sides and belatedly realized it would be dangerous for him to leave the West unattended. The Senate, his rivals at court, even his own mutinous Goths, all sensed weakness and were ready to pounce.

The *magister utriusque* had boxed himself into a corner. If he went to Ravenna and mustered four legions to go east, as Olympiodorus claimed, his enemies would accuse him of fomenting civil war or, worse, carrying out his rumored plans to put Eucherius on the throne in Constantinople. If he stayed, he would be disobeying imperial orders. If he went to Ticinum, he would be accused not only of disobeying, but of trying to regain control of the troops from Honorius and possibly even attempting to usurp the Western throne himself. Uncharacteristically, he did the worst thing of all: he dithered.

On his arrival in Bononia, news of the uprising in Ticinum would have been about a week old. By that time the situation at the imperial court would have stabilized one way or the other, but Stilicho as yet could have no idea which way things had gone. "So, convening all the commanders of his allied barbarians who were on hand," wrote Zosimus, "he consulted them as to the most prudent plan to adopt."

Everything depended on whether Honorius was alive or dead. To judge by the casualty list, the revolt plainly targeted Stilicho, but was it also against the emperor? If Honorius was dead, the decision was easy: civil war. Instead of Constantinople, Stilicho would lead the *foederati* to Ticinum and crush the rebels, after which they could beg him the favor of *decimatio*, of only executing one in ten. The Goths in Stilicho's staff were already clamoring for vengeance. If Honorius had been spared and was not held hostage, then Stilicho would still lead the Gothic legions to Ticinum, but contain his punishment to the ringleaders of the revolt.

But what if the revolt had Honorius' approval? What if he had ordered it?

As updates arrived from upriver via escapees and refugees of the massacre, it became plain that the emperor was not only still alive, but still in at least nominal command. It would not have been tough to guess, however, that it was Olympius who was actually in charge. That changed everything. Zosimus wrote, "Stilicho decided to do no more to punish or rectify the soldiers, but to go to Ravenna, in light of both the numbers being against him, and that the emperor was not on his side."

It was a fateful decision, Stilicho's make-or-break moment. Yes, to march on Ticinum meant civil war, and certainly a murderous fight between Roman and barbarian legions, while Alaric and Constantine waited to pounce on the bloodied victor. But if Honorius was already against him, Stilicho had nothing to lose and everything to gain, including the throne of the Western Empire. Everything depended on who had command of the legions.

It may be that he doubted the Ravenna troops – so recently mutinous, and with Alaric lurking just offstage – would fight for him unless he went there personally to lead them. It may be that he hoped to send a message from Ravenna to summon Alaric, and Alaric's Goths, to his side before marching on Ticinum. And, it must be said, Stilicho may simply have felt it was treason to march against his emperor. Even Zosimus admitted, "He believed it would not be honorable or safe to lead barbarians against the forces of Rome."

In the end, Stilicho's barbarian half submitted to his Roman half. He had the loyalty of the legions, of the *foederati*…until he declined it.

"Instead of executing a resolution, which might have been justified by success," judged Gibbon, "Stilicho hesitated till he was irrecoverably lost."[1]

To submit without a fight was not good enough for the barbarians on Stilicho's staff. With their vengeance denied – and to whom they owed loyalty now in question – they had their own decisions to make. They had urged Stilicho to avenge their dead brethren, and would have gladly followed him in doing so, but he had decided against it. If he was not going to fight, and if Honorius was still their lawful emperor, then what good was Stilicho to them? "Unable to get anywhere with him," wrote Zosimus, "they all decided to stay where they were until they learned the emperor's attitude toward Stilicho."

It was Sarus of the Amali clan, who according to Zosimus "exceeded all other *foederati* in power and rank" – but who had deserted Alaric at Verona back in 402 to enter Stilicho's service, in which he had risen far – who first betrayed his commander. That night he and his men crept into Stilicho's quarters and killed his *bucellarii*, his Hunnish bodyguards. Yet Stilicho himself was either not present (unlikely, if unaccompanied by his guards) or, amid the confusion as his guards were slain, escaped. He must have already sent Serena and Eucherius away. Sarus and his warriors had to content themselves with looting their general's baggage and returning to their tents to await, like the rest of the Goths, their emperor's pleasure.

"Stilicho, seeing that his barbarians were battling each other, fled to Ravenna," wrote Zosimus, "and warned the cities in which lived any barbarian women or children, not to admit any barbarians if they should wish entry." Any *foederati* now on the move were doing so without his orders – meaning they were operating on either Sarus's orders, or those of Olympius, which might be the same thing – and Stilicho was determined to treat them as the enemy. Whether their families obeyed him, though, would be doubtful.

Stilicho had let matters get away from him. Clearly at this point he had no idea how many of his men he could trust. The *foederati*

[1] *History*, Vol. III, p. 183

had signed on to serve the Empire, but whether they served their emperor or their general remained to be seen. Stilicho must have gained new respect and sympathy for those usurpers of the past – Maximus, Arbogastes, and even Constantine – who had made certain of their troops' loyalty before launching their campaigns. His lack of control over events is evidence that he was not in fact planning a usurpation, at least not in the West. That mattered not in the least to his enemies.

"Meanwhile," wrote Zosimus, "Olympius, who was now in charge of the emperor's decisions, sent imperial orders to the soldiers at Ravenna, ordering them immediately to arrest Stilicho and to hold him in prison, though not in irons."

Soon after Stilicho's arrival at Ravenna, sympathetic followers must have received word of his impending arrest and passed it along to him. With his bodyguard dead and most of his barbarian troops unwilling to back him, he was powerless to resist. His only haven was the one he himself had violated in the past: holy sanctuary. "That night he took refuge in a nearby Christian church," wrote Zosimus. "Seeing this, his barbarians and his other men and servants, all armed, knew what to expect."

In the six years since Alaric's invasion and defeat in 402, when the imperial court had moved from Mediolanum to more easily defended Ravenna, the city had undergone something of an architectural renaissance. Many of its finest, most famous monuments date from this period. The octagonal *Battistero Neoniano*, Baptistery of Neon, was completed by the city's Bishop Neon in the late 5th century, but founded by its bishop, Ursus, at the century's beginning, on the former site of a Roman bath. It is the only surviving part of his Basilica Ursiana, a typical Roman church, rectangular, divided inside by rows of columns into four aisles and a nave.*

One can imagine the whisper of sandals echoing among the candlelit columns as Stilicho and his few remaining followers hurried inside, barred the doors behind them, and sought the mercy of Bishop Ursus. Among Ravenna's many artworks (it's known as Italy's City

---

* It was knocked down in 1734 and replaced by the modern Ravenna Cathedral, a baroque design but based on the original.

of Mosaics) an image of Ursus survives in the rear of the apse of the Basilica of Sant' Apollinare in Classe, the old seaport section of town. Probably not done from life, but possibly from memory – Ursus is thought to have died around AD 431, almost twenty years before the basilica was consecrated – it depicts a typically priestly old man with a white, neatly trimmed beard and what appears to be a tonsure: the crown of his head shaved, a practice then only recently undertaken by Catholic priests. Ursus would have been twenty years younger yet, his beard and hair darker and probably unshaven, when Stilicho came seeking sanctuary.

The original *asylum* was the temple of the god Asylacus founded by Romulus between the two summits of the Capitoline Hill in Rome, but the concept of *asylia*, territorial inviolability, came down to the Romans from the Hellenistic Greeks. Since pagan temples offered sanctuary to fugitives, Christian churches with their ethos of mercy could do no less. In theory even a murderer could find forgiveness and safety within church walls. In practice though, as Stilicho himself had proven in his day, the term "sacrosanct" was subject to interpretation.

Ursus, who would certainly have known Stilicho from their service together in the capital, must have been shocked and surprised to find the former most powerful man in the Empire seeking sanctuary, but like a dutiful priest admitted his new supplicant into the safety of the church.

Who can know Stilicho's mind on that loneliest of nights? Certainly he still harbored some forlorn hope that Honorius, his adopted son, would come to his senses and intervene on his behalf. But Honorius was under the thumb of Olympius now. No reprieve would come from that angle. There was only regret for what might have been.

"He had achieved almost total power," wrote Sozomen of Stilicho, "and all men, Romans and barbarians, were under his command."

Almost total power. Surely the greatest woe was that the name Stilicho might be added to the long list of men who had competed for such power, ultimately died in its pursuit, and been reviled. Maximus. Arbogastes. Eugenius. Rufinus. Eutropius. Gildo. Mascezel. Radagaisus.

Alaric?

There was a chance that if Stilicho got word to his erstwhile compatriot, he and his Goths might march to the rescue. Stilicho had, after all, spared Alaric's life multiple times.

But who could he trust to bear the message? No one.

Stilicho had thrown himself on God's mercy, and would have to trust in it. "If a man knows himself, his deeds, and his own beliefs, and fears God's judgment," wrote Orosius, "would he not concede that all his suffering is justified, even unimportant? Or, if he does not know himself and does not fear God, how can he insist that his sufferings are not justified and unimportant?"

But what if a man acts on behalf of another? A man, even the most well-intentioned, right-acting man, is no better than the man to whom he is loyal. Stilicho had been loyal to Honorius – to old Theodosius – until it was too late.

But Stilicho did not fear judgment. His final actions attest to it.

At dawn a squad of legionaries showed up at the church doors, demanding that Stilicho come out. As was his duty, Bishop Ursus admitted them inside, on the condition that no violence would be committed on sacred ground. According to Zosimus, "The soldiers, on entering the church, swore to the bishop that they had orders from the emperor to take Stilicho into custody, not to kill him."

Their commander, Heraclianus, was looking to make a name for himself by arresting the father-in-law of an emperor. Jerome, who probably never met the man, but later knew of him by reputation, wrote, "...it would be difficult to say whether he was more greedy or merciless, caring for nothing but drink and wealth."

Heraclianus produced his orders specifying that Stilicho was not to be killed, and not even put in irons, but simply to be detained under guard until the situation could be worked out. With these assurances, and with Eucherius safely beyond their reach on his way toward Rome, Stilicho agreed to come forth. As soon as he was outside, beyond the safety of the church, he was seized. Heraclianus now produced a second set of orders countermanding the first, and dictating that Stilicho was to be executed for "crimes against the state."

For a civilized people, the Romans had many imaginative methods of execution, with special punishment reserved in cases of treason.

In Rome itself, it was common for traitors to be thrown from the Tarpeian Rock, the eighty-five-foot cliff on the south side of the Capitoline Hill, or else down the Gemonian Steps, which led down another side of the hill from the Arx to the Forum, in either case the body being left to rot or be defiled by vultures or dogs before being thrown into the Tiber. Outside the city, besides the famously popular crucifixion, the condemned might be whipped to death or burned alive, beheaded, strangled, drowned, or torn to pieces by animals in the arena. Most of the more violent punishments were reserved for slaves and the lower classes, however, and crucifixion was for non-citizens. Patricians and equestrians were given the benefit of quicker deaths, and even encouraged to commit suicide as a more honorable alternative.

Stilicho was not to be given that option, but he was also to be spared the more gruesome executions. The Romans considered decapitation to be among the most honorable punishments.

The sentence was not universally acclaimed. According to Zosimus, besides Stilicho's retainers and servants, there was a "vast number" of people present outside the church, not all of whom were there to see the high and mighty fall. Many of them sympathized with Stilicho, and even threatened to put up a fight and set him free. In a scene reminiscent of Christ in the Garden, Stilicho forbade violence. It doesn't even seem he had to be forced to his knees as Heraclianus drew his sword – not the short stabbing blade of the old days, the *gladius*, but the longer, heavier, barbarian-style *spatha* – and raised it high.

No final words were recorded, no reflections on the justice of the sentence or lack thereof, no last-minute summation of a life spent in the service of Rome. Zosimus recorded only that Stilicho "calmly submitted his neck to the sword."

It was August 22, AD 408. Stilicho was about fifty years old.

"So perished Stilicho," summed up Sozomen, "accused of having plotted against the emperors."

Orosius was less kind. In his view Stilicho, "in order to clad one boy in the imperial purple, had endangered the whole human race."

"Of any man of power in his day, he was the most even-handed and fair-minded," opined Zosimus. "Even though he was married to the niece of the first Theodosius and was entrusted with both his sons' empires, and had served as a commander twenty-three years, still he never sold military rank for profit, nor withheld his soldiers' pay for his own use."

Olympiodorus, who asserted Stilicho's execution was directly attributable to "the homicidal, heartless schemes of Olympius, who he himself brought into imperial service," conceded of Stilicho, "He won many wars for Rome, against many enemies."

And for Gibbon, Stilicho, the half-barbarian, was simply "the last of the Roman generals."[1]

[1] *History*, Vol. III, p. 184

PART THREE

AD 408–410

Now while Honorius held the imperial power in the West,
barbarians took over dominion of his land;
and I will tell who they were and how they did so.

Procopius

XXIII

The New Order

AD 408

A nation can outlive its fools, and even ambitious men.
But it cannot outlive traitors. An enemy at the gates is not
as dangerous, for he is recognized and waves his flag openly.
The traitor, though, moves freely among those within,
his schemes murmured on every street,
heard even in the halls of government.

Cicero

"After Stilicho's execution," wrote Zosimus, "Olympius managed all the affairs of the court as he saw fit. He took on the office of *magister*, governor of the court, as well, while the lesser offices were terminated, at his suggestion, by the emperor."

As *magister officiorum*, master of offices, Olympius moved quickly to consolidate his grip on power. Orders went out from Ticinum in the name of the emperor, though whether or not Honorius ever saw them, or simply signed them under duress, is unknown.

Like Eutropius before him, Stilicho was declared *damnatio memoriae*. All property belonging to him was immediately confiscated by the state. Any mention of his name on monuments and statues was to be erased. His supporters and defenders were to be immediately detained. Deuterius, the *praepositus sacri cubiculi*, commander of

275

the emperor's bedchamber guards, was arrested, as was Petrus, the *primicerius notarium*, the head of notaries, presumably Eucherius' former boss.

Eucherius himself was on the run. With a handful of barbarian bodyguards, he made for Rome. Olympius was ahead of him. Word of Stilicho's arrest and orders for his son's apprehension had gone out to Rome at the same time as they went to Ravenna, and the authorities were on the lookout for him. Outside the city his men found a safe place to hide. Photius wrote, "When they were nearing Rome, they agreed to let him take refuge in a certain temple which offered the privilege of sanctuary."

Word, or at least the details, of his father's fate had evidently not caught up to Eucherius.

The rest of his family fared little better. Heraclianus was rewarded for his treachery with the title of *comes Africae* and sent to Carthage to depose Stilicho's brother-in-law Bathanarius, who could scarcely have heard the news of the family's downfall before his replacement arrived with orders for his own execution. According to Zosimus, Olympius even saw to it that the empress consort Thermantia was banished from the imperial household: "Even though she was not suspected, the emperor Honorius ordered his wife Thermantia removed from the imperial throne and sent back to her mother." Serena and her daughter, whom Zosimus claimed was still a virgin, were safe for the time being. Not even Olympius would stoop to killing women.

Not all Romans felt the same.

In these early years of the 5th century Virunum, for centuries the capital of Roman Noricum in modern Austria, was a prime example of the downward slide of the Empire. Unfortified and lying in a valley, it was wide open to barbarian incursions from across the Danube. In the past that had not been much of a problem, but Virunum could no longer depend on the Empire's protection. Much of the population had moved to nearby Teurnia (Tiburnia), on a hilltop beside the Drau River (modern Drava). At one time home to 30,000, even Teurnia was being gradually abandoned, its deserted houses torn down for their stone to be used in the city walls as the countryside gradually sank into barbarism. Unimpressive as it was, this is likely where Alaric and his Goths had made their capital since his return from Epirus. Whether they resided as representatives of the Empire, or just another wave of barbarians, is an open question.

Travel time from Ravenna was about a week, so word of Stilicho's execution most likely arrived that September. Probably there was no great grief on Alaric's part. Death was too familiar to men of his time to waste much time on mourning. He and Stilicho had been opponents on the field, with Alaric coming out on the losing end, too often for that. Yet they had known each other since that first treaty, struck in the passes of the Rhodope Mountains back in 391, when Alaric had been a bandit chieftain bargaining to become a Roman soldier. Fallen foes were due respect. Furthermore, the treacherous manner of Stilicho's death offered a lesson.

Romans could not be trusted, even by other Romans, and particularly not by barbarians.

It must have seemed unbelievable to Alaric that his old nemesis and recent commander could possibly have fallen to such a fate, particularly at such a critical time. With Constantine lurking just over the western Alps and Alaric of uncertain loyalty, the Western Empire was surrounded by threats. To put down its foremost general and primary defender in such a situation was the height of folly. Olympius might be chief of the imperial guards, but he was a glorified secretary, not a military man. He could take Stilicho's place at the head of the legions, but he would never replace him. There was no one in the West who could.

Alaric was a Roman officer, but he was a Gothic king. His first duty was not to an untrustworthy emperor, but to his own people. The gold the Senate had reluctantly granted him had not been delivered, and with Stilicho gone, would not be. If food and clothing, supplies and staples, could not be bought, even with blood, they would have to be taken. And it would be easier to take them from weak Honorius and his master of secretaries, Olympius, than from a seasoned war leader like Constantine.

Constantine was finding it easier to be a usurper than an emperor. Having assumed the rulership of Gaul, and quashed the resistance of the Theodosians in Hispania, his task now was to hold onto his gains. As soon as he and his legions had vacated Britannia the barbarians, as they had after Maximus' departure, rushed back in to fill the power vacuum. Gildas wrote:

> No sooner had they departed than the Picts and Scots, like worms which the heat of day bring out of their holes, quickly landed again from their ships, in which they had sailed beyond the Cichican valley.* They differed from one another in manner, but were avid for blood, and all more eager to cover their evil faces with unkempt hair than to clothe those body parts which decency demanded. Moreover, having heard our friends were gone and never coming back, with even greater audacity than before they seized all the country in the extreme north right up to the wall.

To compound the island's misery, the Saxon pirates stepped up their depredations along the Channel coast, where the old Roman fortifications lay abandoned. Britannia sank into an anarchy of which little written record survives. It would be several decades before the semi-mythical king of the Britons, Vortigern, enlisted one enemy, the Saxons, to fight off the others, the Picts and Scots, in return for land, thereby giving the Germanics a foothold they would retain, and expand, for the next six centuries.

Constantine had already given up Britannia as a lost cause. Gaul was another matter entirely. He had driven the hostile Vandals back over the Rhine, but they still prowled its far bank, awaiting an opening. With his new capital in the south, his rear lay unguarded. Even Hispania threatened to shake loose. His general Gerontius, a Briton effectively ruling a foreign land, had begun to wonder why he should not rule it in fact. If Gaul could be usurped from Honorius, Hispania might just as easily be torn from Constantine. And as Vortigern would, Gerontius had an idea to enlist one enemy against another. The Vandals only needed encouragement to try again.

Olympius sent two court eunuchs, Arsacius and Tarentius by name, with men to search out Eucherius. They soon found his hidden sanctum. "Having located him in a church at Rome, in which he had

---

*A location lost to time, but which may refer to the Irish Sea or some vale in the lands beyond Hadrian's Wall.

taken refuge," recorded Zosimus, "they did not pursue him within, out of respect to the place."

As with Stilicho, that situation did not last, and it's likely the same ruse was employed to coax Eucherius into giving up his refuge. "Eucherius was also killed," attested Orosius, "who, merely to gain the favor of the pagans, had boasted that he would celebrate the commencement of his reign with the reopening of the temples and the closing of the churches. Several accomplices were punished for their evil plotting as well."

Olympius had no actual proof of these conspiracies by Stilicho, but didn't let that stop him. Examples were made of Deuterius, the *praepositus sacri cubiculi*, and Petrus, the *primicerius notarium*, the head of notaries. Roman inquisitors lost nothing in comparison to their medieval counterparts. Beating, boiling, breaking bones, hot tar, red-hot metal plates, and plain fire had their uses. Though legally required when extracting testimony from slaves, torture was technically illegal to use against Roman citizens. In special cases, however – at imperial whim – the law was ignored. Olympius considered Deuterius and Petrus to be special cases. "These were publicly tortured to force confessions regarding Stilicho," wrote Zosimus, "yet since they would say nothing to incriminate him or themselves, Olympius was disappointed. He instead ordered them beaten to death with cudgels."

Orosius shrugged, "In this way the churches of Christ and the holy emperor were freed and avenged with very little effort and with only a few persons punished."

Olympius wasn't through yet. Anyone remotely associated with Stilicho was brought in for interrogation. He conducted a veritable witch hunt against those who might have sympathized with the late generalissimo. It gained him nothing. Zosimus wrote, "Although many others who were suspected of being followers of Stilicho and familiar with his plots, were interrogated and tortured to force them to confess knowledge of his imperial ambition, none of them would confess, and the inquisitors finally gave up their line of questioning."

Honorius and Olympius are sometimes accused of ordering what happened next, but Zosimus does not credit them with it. The example they set, of imprisoning, torturing, and killing anyone and everyone who had anything to do with Stilicho, was enough. The general anti-barbarian fever that had been simmering just beneath

Rome's civilized veneer ever since the disaster at Adrianople was now given voice. How dare that half-barbarian *magister* of theirs think he could put his son on a Roman throne? How dare those dirty *foederati* forget their place? It was their duty to defend the Empire from the uncivilized rabble beyond, nothing more. Let there be an end to wasting bread meant for Roman citizens on barbarian whores and their brats. The slaughter of the citizens of Thessaloniki by the Goth garrison was not so long in the past that it would not be recalled in the forums and taverns and barracks of Ravenna, Aquileia, and Rome. Zosimus wrote, "The soldiers in the city, hearing of Stilicho's death, attacked all the barbarian women and children in the city. Killing every one of them as though by a prearranged signal, they robbed them of everything they owned."

Stilicho's last order, to bar the entry of barbarian forces into the cities where their families lived, now had brutal counter-effect. Unprotected, those barbarian families living among Romans – living as Romans – now felt the wrath of Rome again, as their people had felt it along the banks of the Danube, in the forums and town squares of Asia Minor, and in the burning church in Constantinople.

The number of barbarian women and children living among the Romans at this time can only be guessed at. Zosimus numbered the barbarians in the army of Rome at 30,000. The average Roman family had five or six children, half of which died by age ten. Assuming the barbarians, wishing to be Roman in all things, did the same, their population was likely near, and possibly over, 100,000. What had happened in Thessaloniki was a massacre. This was genocide, one culture wresting itself free of another and venting murderous rage on it, with the goal of annihilation, extinction. And as the streets rang with the screams of the fleeing and dying and the gutters ran red with blood, one would have to ask which culture was the barbarous, and which the civilized.

"When this became known to the relatives of those murdered," wrote Zosimus, "they gathered together from all directions."

The *foederati* in their various camps outside the cities, grieving for their families and stunned by the Romans' duplicity, all arrived at a common conclusion: their duty to the emperor was at an end. They had lost their leader, Stilicho. They needed another, a man not in league with the hated, scheming Romans. Such a man was readily available, and known to all. Zosimus concluded, "They all decided to go to Alaric, and to join him in war on Rome."

Thirty thousand warriors, trained in the ways of the Roman legions, went over to Alaric.

Olympius had wanted a mutiny. Now he had one.

XXIV

The March on Rome

AD 408

After the death of Stilicho, Alaric, the leader of the Goths,
sent an embassy to Honorius to treat for peace, to no avail.

Sozomen

Historians question Zosimus' estimate of just how many *foederati* joined Alaric's army, in part because the scribe is as loose in throwing around his numbers as with any other of his facts. It may only have been some 12,000, the remnant of Radagaisus' army that had joined Stilicho's, bringing Alaric's manpower to 30,000. They, however, were only a small fraction of the Goths' total population, as many as 150,000 men, women, and children. Regardless of the exact number, all those new mouths to feed put fresh pressure on Alaric.

To his credit, he did not act in haste. In one sense Stilicho's death had rendered Alaric nothing more than an unemployed mercenary, but in another it had made him more than a leader of *foederati*. He was, more than ever, like Fritigern and Athanaric before him, the *reiks*, the king of the Goths. He had to consider the clamoring of his warriors for vengeance, but also to act as he thought best.

"Not even these men were enough to get Alaric to declare war, as he still preferred peace, remembering the bargain he had struck with Stilicho," wrote Zosimus. "He therefore sent envoys with the goal of procuring a peace, even if it meant only a small sum of money for him."

By not demanding another few tons of gold, Alaric showed himself willing to work with Honorius – with Olympius – to come to a mutually beneficial deal. By merely giving the Goths enough money to live on, the Romans would retain an army capable of standing against Constantine. Otherwise, Italy, with its own army suddenly and severely down on manpower, was looking at a two-front war.

It was an amazingly charitable offer from a ruler who was himself under some duress from his own people, all clamoring for immediate war with Rome. A competent emperor, even intending to renege on the deal later, would have been well advised to accept.

Honorius was neither competent, nor well advised.

Contempt for barbarians colored the Romans' thinking. "The modesty of Alaric," wrote Gibbon, "was interpreted by the ministers of Ravenna as sure evidence of his weakness and fear."[1] The Goth had tried to bully Italy before, and had ended up running back over the Alps with his tail between his legs. Let him try it again, and good Roman legions would send him and his barbarian army packing once more. "When Alaric agreed to peace with those conditions, the emperor refused," wrote Zosimus, admitting, "although if he had handled his business with acumen, he would have picked one or the other choices before him."

Either buy peace with Alaric, or prepare for war. And if it was to be war, then gather what remained of the army and appoint a general to lead it. The most likely candidate, Zosimus admitted, was Sarus, from years' experience well acquainted with Alaric, a capable commander in his own right with his own army, who furthermore might be able to lure the *foederati* away from the Gothic king.

But Sarus was a barbarian. Honorius and Olympius, having rid themselves of one barbarian leader, would not install another. So the emperor opted for the third strategy, his usual choice when action was required. He did nothing.

"The emperor, quite the contrary," continued Zosimus, "neither making peace, nor befriending Sarus, nor assembling the Roman army, but placing all his faith in Olympius, brought on the uncounted disasters by which the state was undone."

[1] *History*, Vol. III, p. 192

Part of the reason Honorius and Olympius rejected Alaric's offer may be that they felt they would not have to fight a two-front war after all. Their other nemesis, Constantine, had his hands quite full just trying to maintain himself in Gaul. His son, the *Caesar* Constans, having delivered Honorius' cousins Verenianus and Didymus (and having put them both to death), was sent back to Hispania to rule that province in his father's name. By this time, however, the Briton general Gerontius had become accustomed to ruling there on his own, and had come to see Constans not as a superior, but as a rival. Zosimus wrote, "Gerontius, not happy with this, and having gained the backing of the soldiers in that province, stirred the barbarians who were in Gallia Celtica [modern Belgium, Luxembourg, and northern France] to rebel against Constantine."

Constantine had recruited heavily in this region on his way south to engage Honorius, but had left few troops behind in his absence. Most of his legionaries, in fact, had gone to Hispania to put down the Theodosian rebellion, and were still there under Gerontius' command. The Vandals, Alans, and other Germanic tribes he had driven beyond the Rhine now took advantage of Constantine's neglect, and marched down through western France. Getting no more protection from Constantine than they had from Honorius, the native Celtic tribes finally revolted. Western Gaul, like Britannia before it, descended into anarchy, a struggle of rebels against invaders in which it's difficult to determine a winner. The Vandals, at least, either drove or were driven down across Armorica (west-central France) toward the Pyrenees. The mountain passes were still guarded by the barbarian troops Constans had posted there, which is to say not guarded at all. They had not so long ago enjoyed looting Hispania themselves, and were eager to do it again. Sozomen concluded, "And since those who Constans had trusted with guarding the passage neglected their duties, the invaders passed through into Spain."

Though Honorius would not have to fight a two-front war, neither would Alaric. The emperor's refusal to accept his generous peace terms gave him, as a leader of barbarians, no other option than war. And with Constantine occupied in Gaul there was no better time to strike than right away.

So in the waning months of AD 408, before winter snows blocked the Alpine passes, Alaric, King of the Goths, led the army of his people out of Noricum, down into the plains of northern Italy. "Being unwilling to enter on such a crucial business without forces nearly equal to his enemy's," wrote Zosimus, "he summoned Athaulf, his wife's brother, from Upper Pannonia, to join with him on the campaign, with his very substantial force of Goths and Huns."

By now Honorius and Olympius realized the real threat was not from Gaul, but from the Goths. They and their legions abandoned Ticinum and retreated behind the swamps and waterways of Ravenna, making ready to withstand the siege to come. In hindsight their preparations were not up to the requirements of events. "For the command was given to men whom the enemy considered were contemptible," wrote Zosimus. "Turpilio was named commander of the cavalry, Varanes of the infantry, Vigilantius of the domestics."

These men are distinguished mainly by how little we know about them. Varanes, whose name is likely Persian, probably arrived at the court of Theodosius after the treaty which Stilicho helped to arrange. He is thought to have been involved in the campaign against Eugenius, and since then had lurked around the court of Honorius, but made no name for himself until the purge by Olympius created job openings at the top. At first he was appointed *magister equitum*, but against barbarians cavalry would be key, and on second thought he was made *magister peditum* and Turpilio was given the cavalry posting. Of him we know almost nothing, except that he was one of Olympius' men, and probably chosen for that reason. Of Vigilantius we really do know nothing, except that as head of the domestics, the imperial guard, he must have enjoyed Olympius' complete trust, hardly a good recommendation.

"For these reasons everyone despaired," admitted Zosimus, "already foreseeing the complete destruction of Italia."

As it turned out, the military postings by Olympius were moot. Having asked Ravenna nicely for concessions, Alaric was not going to try, as he had in the past, to bully that city into giving him anything. He recognized what Honorius and Olympius did not: that having an emperor in residence did not make Ravenna important. The Goths marched right past it and continued south. There was no one now between them and the ultimate prize.

Rome.

Not waiting for Athaulf to join him, but leaving him to catch up, Alaric and his Goths proceeded down the back side of the Italian boot, wrote Zosimus, "as if they were in a parade, with no enemy to stop him."

From Bononia, where Stilicho had made his fateful decision not to usurp the Western throne, they marched down the Via Aemilia to Ariminum (modern Rimini) on the Adriatic shoreline. From there they took the Via Flaminia, the 630-year-old Roman road down the coast to Fanum Fortunae (modern Fano). Any pagans among them, and many Christians as well, might have visited the city's Temple of Fortuna, the blindfolded goddess of luck who remained popular even into the Renaissance, to invoke her blessing for their venture.

They would need it. From Fanum Fortunae the Via Flaminia ran 180 miles almost due south, up over the Apennines toward Rome. The closer the barbarians came to the heart of the empire, the more evidence they found of its technological superiority: the Intercisa, a tunnel chiseled through 125 feet of solid rock under the emperor Vespasian; the Pons Augustus, a four-arch, 520-foot stone bridge of cut white marble, built under emperor Augustus. Such works, already centuries old, were still beyond the barbarians' abilities, and Alaric might well have had second thoughts, daring to conquer such an ancient, advanced civilization.

He did not. Alaric had not come to build. He had come to destroy. Zosimus recorded, "marching on Rome, he sacked every castle and town in his way."

Procopius concurred: "The barbarians, finding that they had no hostile force to encounter them, became the most cruel of all men."

Terror tactics. Word of the rampage would spread ahead of the Goths all the way to Rome, paving the barbarians' way with fear. Yet Alaric, who had so long aspired to be a citizen of Rome, did not wish to be its destroyer. He would not be, if the Romans would simply submit to his demands. Still, having come this far, nothing less than Rome's total capitulation would suffice. And if he could not have that, the only result could be its destruction.

Both Socrates Scholasticus and Sozomen relate that, as Alaric was closing on Rome, a local monk appeared to plead with him to spare the city. The king reportedly replied, "I am not set on this path of my own will. There is something irresistible that compels me every day, telling me, 'Go to Rome, and desolate that city.'"

Six years earlier, during his previous invasion of Italy, Claudian had depicted Alaric as a foolish barbarian, obeying voices that spoke to him from a sacred grove. Yet Alaric in reality did seem to feel himself a tool of a greater power...or perhaps he was already trying to absolve himself of the inevitable.

If Rome had to be destroyed, it would be God's will, not Alaric's.

In their first invasion of Italy, the Goths had come nowhere near Rome, but the mere threat of them had been enough to throw the city into a panic. Just a few years later, there's little record of similar alarm overtaking the Romans even as the barbarian army arrived down out of the Appenines. They had their newly strengthened walls to protect them, and the Goths had repeatedly proven that storming a city was quite beyond them. The only way Rome would fall was if it was betrayed from within. Any barbarian sympathizers, any possible traitors, had to be rooted out before they got the chance.

As always in a crisis, politicians must be seen to do something, anything in response. In the absence of any effective alternative, that response is usually to lay blame on a scapegoat, and so it was in the autumn of 408.

"When Alaric neared Rome to besiege its people," wrote Zosimus, "the Senate suspected Serena of summoning the barbarians against their city."

What reason the wife of Stilicho would have to betray Rome to the Goths is a complete unknown. She and Alaric had probably never even met, much less ever had a chance to plot the city's destruction. Her fault lay in being married to a half-barbarian traitor, and that was enough. Zosimus certainly thought the senators trumped up the charges: "They calculated that 'Alaric, with Serena gone, will retreat from the city, because there would be no one who could betray the city to him.' This suspicion was actually groundless, as Serena never had any such intent."

The senators and patricians had effectively done more to betray the city by doing everything they could to prevent Stilicho from drafting Romans into the military, forcing him to turn Rome's army into a barbarian army. That mattered not at all while they were deciding Serena's fate. What did matter, however, was that Honorius and Olympius, in Ravenna, had already decreed she should be spared. To punish her now would require imperial blessing. And the only member of the imperial family in Rome was Honorius' half-sister – and Serena's stepdaughter – Galla Placidia.

Galla was then at most about twenty years old. Being raised among Roman aristocracy would certainly have hardened her to the death of underlings. To condemn her own stepmother, however, seems remarkably inhuman even by Roman standards (though possibly not by the standards of Roman imperial families). Perhaps she, having gone unmarried so long, harbored some grudge toward her stepmother. Perhaps, being so closely associated with the traitor Stilicho, she was under some duress herself and needed to prove her own innocence. Perhaps she was simply a craven coward, looking to save her own skin. Future events would prove Galla to be first and foremost a survivor at all costs. In any case, she gave her approval to the Senate's decision regarding Serena's fate. Zosimus recorded, "So the whole Senate, along with Placidia, uterine sister to the emperor, thought it justified that she should be put to death, for having brought on the current disaster."

Executions of Roman citizens, considered more shameful than mere death, were rarely held in public. Serena was probably not held in the Tullanium, the 1,000-year-old prison on the northeastern slope of the Capitoline Hill, but as was more usual for upper-class Romans, under house arrest, and it's probably there that her sentence was carried out. She likely even had time to bid farewell to Thermantia and even to Galla, if she so wished. One wonders if she wore the jeweled necklace she had stripped off the statue of Vesta all those years earlier, on the occasion of the executioner arriving at her door with the *laqueus*, the garrote.

XXV

FIRST SIEGE

AD 408

*Serena was ignominiously strangled; and the infatuated
multitude were astonished to find that this cruel act of injustice
did not immediately produce the retreat of the barbarians and
the deliverance of the city.*

Gibbon[1]

It was said that after Hannibal's bloody triumph at Cannae, where
his army surrounded and destroyed eight Roman legions, his general
Maharbal urged him to march directly on Rome, predicting that in
five days the Carthaginians would enjoy a victory feast in the city.
Hannibal, however, sent a delegation to the city to negotiate terms
of peace. The Senate did not even give them a hearing. Maharbal
lamented that Hannibal knew how to win a victory, but not how
to use it. Despite the warning *Hannibal ad portas*, with which
Roman parents frightened misbehaving children, Hannibal felt he
could win by crushing Rome's armies, and never attacked Rome
itself.

In October 408 Alaric led the march of his people down out of
the Sabine Hills north of the city to behold the sight that had eluded
Hannibal six centuries past. The barbarian king had seen plenty of

---

[1] *History*, Vol. III, p. 220

walls in his day, including those of Constantinople, as a boy in 378 after the battle of Adrianople and again in 395, when dealing with Rufinus. The Eastern capital's most imposing walls had not yet been built by Theodosius II, but the walls of Constantine the Great had been enough to give pause to Fritigern and to Alaric himself. Even the walls of cities like Ravenna and Mediolanum were enough to keep barbarians out. And these weren't just any walls before Alaric now. This wasn't just any city. It was the Eternal City. This was Rome.

Its Aurelian Walls, raised in AD 271–275 and strengthened just years previously by Honorius, stood over fifty feet high and ran for twelve miles through and around the city limits. Kiln-dried Roman bricks (longer and lower than modern bricks) fronted almost indestructible Roman concrete, more than ten feet thick. There were no catapults on earth capable of breaking a hole in those walls, and the Goths had no siege towers capable of reaching over them.

Then again, Alaric had no intention of going through or over those walls. It would be enough to go around them. The Romans did not seem to understand that their walls' weak point had nothing to do with height and thickness.

The Tiber both entered and exited the city, permitting boat traffic from the coastal towns fifteen miles downriver, Ostia and Portus, to flow to Rome and keep it fed. No more. The riverbanks and bridges downriver of the city were lined with archers and torchbearers to rain destruction on any boats that dared the passage. The stream of food into the city was abruptly cut off. "By stationing a large force of barbarians on the Tiber's banks," wrote Sozomen of Alaric, "he effectively blocked the import of all supplies into the city from Portus."

"He blockaded the city gates," agreed Zosimus, "and, having taken control of the Tiber, prevented the port from sending any essentials to the city. The Romans, on seeing this, nevertheless determined to maintain their defense, expecting to welcome reinforcement from Ravenna any day."

The problem for the Romans was that to both Alaric and Honorius, Rome – along with the hundreds of thousands of people living in it – was nothing more than a bargaining chip. This contest was, in effect, to determine which of them valued the city least. Alaric was betting Honorius would find himself, as emperor, duty-bound to save it.

Honorius, on the other hand, had spent very little of his life in that teeming cesspit, which for his court, particularly under Stilicho, had mostly been a source of senatorial interference in imperial affairs. From his point of view it might even do those rich patricians some good to stew in their own juice a while, and realize how badly they needed their emperor. As for those hundreds of thousands of clamoring poor, well, their lives were worthless anyway. For that filthy herd to be thinned a bit would be no great loss. Secure in Ravenna, Honorius and Olympius were far from the strife. Little good it would do them to send their little city garrison against Alaric's superior force. Nor were they under any particular compulsion to resolve the matter by negotiation.

So Rome was left to wither, while outside the lines of the Goths tightened around its walls like the strangling cord on Serena's throat. Its people needed the better part of 500 tons of grain per day, just to survive. Their warehouses were not of infinite capacity and could not maintain those deliveries very long. The city fathers ordered the daily grain rations cut in half, and then to a third, which only delayed the inevitable. People went hungry, then began to starve, which created a new problem. Zosimus wrote, "With all their provisions eaten, and no relief in sight, the shortage of food, as might have been expected, gave rise to disease."

During a typical famine, only a minority of victims die of actual starvation. It's the effects of malnutrition on the immune system that cause the vast majority of deaths. In Rome malaria, cholera, dysentery, and plague always lurked in the shadows. Given half a chance any of them might take hold and then, in the tight-packed, unsanitary slums, run wild through the populace. As the weakest of the people – infants, children, the elderly – began dying off, the pressing issue was what to do with their corpses. As Augustine heard it, "In such a holocaust as that, the dead could not even be buried."

With Goths barring the gates, the bodies could not be removed from the city. Under Christianity burial had become the standard funerary practice, but there was little room within the walls for graveyards. Cremation was still an option for the rich (wood being an expensive commodity), but a mass pyre inside the city limits risked a conflagration. As a result of this perfect storm of troubles, Zosimus continued, "every place was filled with corpses."

Not all the senators and upper class were heedless of the suffering. The late emperor Gratian's widow Laeta (for whom he had mistakenly crossed the river to his death a generation gone) had been awarded a stipend out of the imperial treasury by Theodosius. She and her mother are remembered for using it to feed as many people as they could, while they could. Money, however, can't be eaten. The food would run out before the gold.

"They say the lengthy famine laid low many a Christian," admitted Augustine, looking hard for a silver lining. "But in this, too, the faithful gleaned a good lesson through their pious perseverance. For those who died of famine were saved from the evils of this life, as a gentle disease might have done, and those who only somewhat starved learned to live more frugally, accustomed to longer fasts."

Small consolation indeed from a man who didn't live through it. There were rumors of cannibalism before the Senate finally resorted to negotiation. "They resolved to send an embassy to the enemy," wrote Zosimus, "to let him know they were willing to accept any reasonable conditions for peace, but were also prepared to fight, because the people of Rome had taken up weapons, and through constant military training were becoming inclined for action."

Imagine Alaric, the barbarian king, having attained his crown and kept it on the strength of his sword arm, as these preening, somewhat emaciated patricians attempted to intimidate him. According to Zosimus, he laughed right in their faces.

"Thick grass is easier to cut than the thin," he told them, and dictated his terms. He would not give up the siege until all the city's gold and silver, household goods, and barbarian slaves were surrendered to him.

This was basically all the property in Rome. The city would be left an empty shell. One of the ambassadors dared to ask, "If you confiscate all that, what will you leave the people?"

One wonders if Alaric was well-read enough to have recalled Brennus in his negotiations with the Romans.

Vae victis.

He replied, "Their lives."

The envoys pleaded for time to take his offer before the citizenry, to which Alaric – time being on his side – agreed.

By citizenry, of course, the ambassadors meant the Senate. To the pagans among them it seemed obvious that the people had invited this disaster by abandoning the old gods. There was a rumor that one of the more northern cities had avoided a sack by the passing Goths by invoking said gods. The town in question, Narnia (modern Narni), was a hilltop village that Alaric probably considered not worth the effort, but the civic leaders were open to all suggestions. Sozomen recorded, "Those senators who still believed in paganism offered to conduct sacrifices in the Capitol and other temples."

They asked permission of the pope, Innocent I, to perform the necessary rites. "Favoring the salvation of the city to his own private beliefs," wrote Zosimus, "he permitted them to do whatever they thought appropriate, in private," which is a rather nice way of saying he abandoned his faith when necessary. Unfortunately the rites had to be conducted in public, atop the Capitoline Hill for all to see, and as no one wanted to be seen doing them, the idea was abandoned. It was decided to try talking Alaric to death.

Letting the hourglass run to his advantage – the siege ran over into early AD 409 – Alaric dragged out the negotiations until the Romans, with the stench of the city's dead in their nostrils, finally agreed on solid numbers: two and a half tons of gold, fifteen tons of silver, a ton and a half of pepper, 4,000 silk robes, and 3,000 fleeces (dyed red, just because).

Note that Alaric had come down from his initial demands. He was a barbarian, but not uncivilized. Even this amount, however, was more than held by the Roman public. It would be necessary for the senators and aristocrats to dip into their own pockets.

The results were predictable. Each aristocrat was assessed according to his wealth, but of course many came up short, hiding their riches, pleading poverty. Likewise, the taxations inflicted by Honorius (in part to support the barbarians in his army, most of whom were now encamped outside the walls with Alaric) and the graft in the upper levels of society meant there was little more of value to be confiscated from the people. As a result, and in a complete turnabout from the recent flirtation with paganism, it was decided to rob the gods.

In a vile replay of the original crime for which, it was said, Serena had been fatally punished, the various statues and idols around the city were stripped of their jewelry and ornaments. As pagan Zosimus noted, this rendered them into nothing more than powerless, inanimate objects. And when even that wasn't enough, some of those cast in gold and silver were melted down into ingots, including the statue of Virtus – virtue – deity of bravery and military strength. "On its destruction," sniffed Zosimus, "all that was left of Roman valor and daring was totally finished."

The agreed amount being readied for delivery to Alaric, he permitted a delegation to be sent to Ravenna to request Honorius' approval, as Sozomen admitted: "While he was laying siege to the city, the Romans gave him many presents, and when they agreed to convince the emperor to sign a peace treaty he eased the siege."

The delegation was headed up by one Priscus Attalus, a Greek who had managed to become a senator of some importance. Alaric assured them, and urged them to assure Honorius, that the king of the Goths desired nothing more than to enter into alliance with Rome and serve the Empire against all its enemies.

"When a delegation was sent with this goal," wrote Olympiodorus, "Alaric's enemies at court tried to thwart the peace process." As a result, no military command was awarded to Alaric, but Honorius and Olympius did permit the ransom to be paid to him. After all, it was not coming out of their pockets, but those of the senators and the citizens. It was their loss.

Though denied the command he wanted, Alaric upheld his end of the bargain, and lifted the siege. Boat traffic was permitted upriver. Hidden monies reappeared, deals were done in trade, and the famine was ended.

As the Goths prepared to depart, the barbarian slaves in Rome decided they would adhere to Alaric's original bargain, for their freedom. Almost all of them also packed their things and departed the city *en masse*, with the Romans undoubtedly glad to be rid of them. Some of the ex-slaves vented their bitterness on old masters, pausing to loot the boats bringing provisions up from the coast. "When Alaric learned of this, which was done without his knowledge or sanction," wrote Zosimus, "he did his best to stop it."

According to Zosimus, the additional people – probably the survivors of Radagaisus' band from a few years earlier – brought the Goths' warrior strength to 40,000. They withdrew a respectful distance north into Etruria, the homeland of the ancient Etruscans, to await developments.

Honorius and Olympius, secure in Ravenna, could look upon the lifting of the siege of Rome as a victory, having come out of it intact and at small cost to themselves. The Eternal City had survived. The Western Empire had survived. The matter of a few tens of thousands of unruly barbarians loose in its midst could be addressed in good time. After all, Alaric had declared his wish to be part of the Empire again. Whatever he did to Rome, he was a long way from forcing his wishes on Ravenna. The world had not stopped turning while the Goths occupied themselves with a victory of merely symbolic import.

In the constantly churning and flowing hierarchy of the slowly crumbling Empire, no one held total power, and therefore everyone held power. Honorius and Olympius, so recently pinned between enemies, suddenly found themselves surrounded by potential allies from whom to pick and choose. About the same time the Roman delegation had arrived with Alaric's terms, another delegation arrived from Gaul. Like Alaric, the self-proclaimed emperor Constantine wished to be more than self-proclaimed. He desired an alliance between himself and Honorius, in order that they should rule together over a united Western Empire. Constantine's army, composed as it was largely of barbarians, had proven capable of vanquishing other barbarians, and would prove useful if – when – it became necessary to crush the upstart Alaric.

And just in case none of that worked out, word came that five fresh Roman legions had arrived just across the Adriatic, in Dalmatia. "These regiments consisted of six thousand men," wrote Zosimus, "who for strength and discipline were the flower of the whole Roman army."

It seems likely these legions had been sent into Illyricum by Honorius' co-emperor, his nephew Theodosius II in Constantinople, or at least by his praetorian prefect Anthemius, to meet Alaric's proposed invasion of the province, or fill the void left when he vacated it. The death of Stilicho had at least resulted in a warming of relations between the Eastern and Western Empires. Having put down its own barbarian threat, the East stood ready to assist the West in doing the same. The legionaries in Dalmatia were ready to come to Ravenna's assistance and do Honorius' bidding.

Even if that meant betraying his newfound friends.

XXVI

Poena Cullei

AD 409

*The emperor Honorius was now entering on the consulship,
having enjoyed that honor eight times, and the emperor
Theodosius in the east three times.*

Zosimus

Stilicho and Serena, as Roman citizens, had been given the blessing
of relatively quick deaths. Romans could be fiendishly imaginative in
their methods of punishment. In the case of parricide, the murder of
a parent, a penalty called *poena cullei* (punishment of the sack) was
employed. The offender was sewn into a leather bag with a rooster,
a dog, a snake, and a monkey, then thrown into deep water. In terror
of drowning, the animals would of course tear each other, and the
victim, to shreds.

Trapped together with no way out, unable to work together to save
themselves…the *poena cullei* might also serve as a description of the
players in the Western Empire in 409.

That was young Emperor Honorius' banner year. Having divested
himself of his overbearing father-in-law Stilicho, successfully
out-bluffed the barbarian Alaric and broken the siege of Rome,
he was – again – declared Western consul by a grateful people.
Furthermore, he was confirmed by the Eastern court, relations between
the dominions having thawed with the removal of Stilicho. Honorius

was senior emperor, ruling in precedence to his young nephew and co-consul Theodosius II (whom, admittedly, he had never met). Even the aspirations of Constantine, the usurper in Gaul, could be turned to advantage by Honorius' scheming master of offices, Olympius.

"When the emperor heard his request," wrote Zosimus of Constantine's offer to co-rule, "seeing as it was difficult for him to mount wars with Alaric and his barbarians close by, and in concern for the safety of his cousins Verenianus and Didymus who were in the rebel's hands, he not only granted his petition, but even sent him an imperial toga."

Constantine, of course, was running his own deception. By this time he had already executed both Verenianus and Didymus. To bring that up in the midst of his plea for official recognition, obviously, would not have been helpful. By the time Honorius learned of his perfidy, Constantine was already wearing the purple robe of state. Like Maximus and Valentinian II before him, he had become the legitimate ruler of a third of the empire.

Problem was, his third was on no steadier ground than Honorius'. Constantine's general in Hispania, Gerontius, resented taking orders from Constantine's son, the ex-monk turned *Caesar* Constans II, and threatened to take that province for himself. He had struck an alliance with the Vandals, who had crossed the Rhine, broken through Constantine's rear in Gaul, and were poised to unite with Gerontius in Hispania. As co-emperor, Constantine's promise was to support Honorius, but in turn Honorius was to support him.

First, however, Honorius had to get his own house in order. The peace with Alaric was uneasy at best. With Olympius still obsessed with rooting out the remaining adherents of Stilicho, it was decided to send a few lower dignitaries of the court to Rome to look after imperial interests. Chief among these delegates was the senator Attalus, now appointed as *comes sacrarum largitionum*, count of the sacred largesses, in charge of customs collections, mines, mints, and state-run manufacturing, not to mention income taxes on merchants, moneylenders, craftsmen, prostitutes and senators – in effect, city treasurer and controller. For protection on his mission, and to serve as a garrison in Rome in case of future trouble, a military escort was cobbled together from the Roman soldiery who had followed Honorius to Ravenna. Zosimus recorded, "Their commander, Valens, was a man eager for the greatest and most dangerous endeavors. He declined, therefore, to march by a road unguarded by the enemy, lest he appear cowardly."

This Valens proved just as inept as his namesake emperor when it came to dealing with barbarians. Alaric, having been relatively polite in his dealings with Ravenna so far, wasn't about to let Rome be garrisoned with troops. He blocked Valens's road and attacked. Zosimus claims only a hundred or so of the Romans (among them Valens and Attalus) escaped to Rome.

If Alaric thought the Romans had learned their lesson, he was mistaken. With winter over and the high alpine passes cleared, his brother-in-law Athaulf marched over the mountains with his mixed force of Goths and Huns to meet him. Along the way he took the opportunity, according to Zosimus, to strike at an old family enemy:

> Sarus was stationed with a small barbarian force in Picenum, allied with neither the emperor nor with Alaric. Athaulf, who nursed a grudge against him from the old days, brought his whole army to Sarus's location. As soon as Sarus heard of his approach, and unable to fight since he had only three hundred men, he decided to flee to Honorius, and join him in the war against Alaric.

Despite his ongoing difficulties with Goths, Honorius could use fresh troops, particularly those like the Amali clan, with a hatred for Alaric. He accepted Sarus and his brother Sigeric into his service. They informed him of Athaulf's advance.

"When the emperor heard he was coming and that he had only a small force with him," wrote Zosimus, "he ordered all his soldiers, both horse and foot, from the different towns under their own officers, to attack him."

As commander of the court guards, Olympius personally led the attack. He intercepted Athaulf near Pisa, on the Ligurian coast. According to Zosimus, the Romans killed 1,100 of his warriors, losing only seventeen of their own. This would seem to be imperial propaganda, though, since it was Olympius who retreated to Ravenna, and Athaulf continued down the coast to join up with Alaric.

However it went, the two sides had lost more soldiers during the peace than they had during the siege. Alaric, still controlling the roads between Ravenna and Rome, permitted a second delegation under Pope Innocent to go to Ravenna, this time providing a military escort of his own.

They found a new administration in power. Olympius' failure to prevent Athaulf from linking up with Alaric had created an opening for his enemies. Jovius, the would-be *praefectus praetorio Illyrici*, knew Alaric from their days in Epirus and felt the Master of Offices had become an impediment to peace. Just as Olympius had stirred up a mutiny in Ticinum, Jovius raised one in Classis, Ravenna's military port. The rebellious soldiers and sailors demanded the removal of Olympius' generals Turpilio and Vigilantius. Honorius, as usual at the mercy of his own troops, ordered them exiled. "They were therefore put on board a ship, but those appointed to carry them to the place of exile murdered them," confided Zosimus. "Jovius indeed had commanded them to do so, fearing that if they ever returned and discovered the plot he had staged against them, they might incite the emperor to punish him for it."

With his generals went Olympius' power. Before he met the same fate as Stilicho, he boarded his own ship and fled into self-imposed exile in Dalmatia. In his stead, in March or April, ever-pliable Honorius named Jovius a patrician and *praefectus praetorio Italiae*. "Jovius," wrote Zosimus, "having now shifted all control of the emperor to himself, resolved to send envoys to Alaric, to ask him to come to Ravenna and to assure him that they would conclude the peace treaty there."

Alaric wasn't fool enough to put himself in Honorius' grasp, but couldn't pass up the opportunity to deal more directly with the imperial court. He agreed to meet with Jovius at Ariminum, about thirty miles down the coast. "Alaric demanded a certain amount of gold per year, and a supply of grain, and that he and his barbarians could live in Venetia, Noricum, and Dalmatia." Food, a stipend, and a homeland; basically the same request Alaric had made, and been refused, before he invaded Italy – in fact, basically the same request the Goths had been making of the Romans since before the battle at Adrianople.

Zosimus recorded, "Jovius, having written down these demands in Alaric's presence, sent them to the emperor, along with other letters in which he privately advised him to appoint Alaric commander of both his armies, for in return he might be willing to relax his demands further, and agree to peace on bearable middling conditions."

In Ravenna, Honorius was at last making his own imperial decisions. With Stilicho dead, Olympius in exile, and Jovius in Ariminum, the emperor's puppet masters had lost control of his strings. He was finally free to handle the Empire as he saw fit. Matters of mere gold and food were almost beneath his consideration. As for Alaric, with Stilicho gone, the king of the Goths was perhaps the best military commander still available, not to mention also in command of the largest army in the Empire. Naming him *magister utriusque militiae* – supreme military commander, the same rank held by Stilicho before his demise – would make him a friend and ally, or at the very least no longer an enemy.

Honorius took Alaric's request, and Jovius' recommendations, into consideration, rendered thoughtful judgment, dictated his reply and had it couriered back down the coast to his envoy. According to Sozomen, "Jovius unwisely awaited the imperial messenger in Alaric's camp, and commanded the emperor's response to be read in front of all the barbarians."

Imagine the dismay of all present to hear Jovius censured for daring to suggest imperial decisions. The envoy must have been terrified to continue, but it was too late to back out. "It was proper for Jovius, as court prefect with knowledge of what the public revenues could sustain, to assign quantities of grain and gold," Honorius had decreed, "but no honor or command would ever be awarded to Alaric or any of his family."

In retrospect Honorius may have recalled previous emperors held captive to the mercy of barbarian generals – Valentinian II with Arbogastes, Arcadius with Gainas – and decided not to put himself in that position, in which case his response seems less insensible. And the concessions of food and land were generous, just as Alaric requested. That last part might be put down to Honorius' temporary lack of diplomatic advisors, or for that matter anyone left who would dare to disagree with him. It was as though the boy couldn't resist stamping his imperial foot – not so much what he said, as the way he said it.

No barbarian king, though, could suffer such a personal insult in front of his warriors without having his authority undermined, perhaps fatally. Immediate retribution was required. Sozomen wrote,

"On finding that honor was denied him, Alaric, enraged at the insult, ordered the war trumpets to be blown, and marched on Rome."

Jovius, doubtless happy to have escaped the conference with his life, hurried back to Ravenna, though he probably felt himself under no less threat from an angry emperor. His bridge to Alaric having been well and truly burned, he now sided completely with Honorius, not only backing the imperial decision but advising the emperor to follow through. "Wanting to absolve himself of all blame," wrote Zosimus, "he convinced Honorius to swear several oaths never to make peace with Alaric, and to wage continual war against him, which he himself also swore by touching the emperor's head, and had all others who held office do the same."

Swearing on the head of an emperor, the representative of God on earth, was an irrevocable oath. There could be no turning back.

"The barbarian chief, however, soon had second thoughts," wrote Sozomen of Alaric, who had not even reached Rome before his temper cooled and he showed himself to be a more level-headed politician than those in Ravenna. He enlisted bishops from the various cities along the road to Rome into another peace delegation, "sending word he no longer desired any post of honor, but was still willing to ally with the Romans, if they would simply grant him some grain, and some territory of minor importance to them, where he might establish his people."

Zosimus added, "He only requested as much grain per year as the emperor was willing to grant, and would forget about the gold, if the Goths and the Romans lived together in friendship and allied against anyone who should rise against the empire."

Surely the emperor could not be so obstinate as to risk losing the Eternal City over a mere matter of procurements for the Goths.

Too late. The imperial administrators, Zosimus admitted, might have been able to go back on an oath sworn to God, from whom they might have expected understanding and forgiveness. From the emperor they could expect none. There would be no concession to the Goths' demands, no matter how far Alaric changed his position.

Besides, Honorius surely felt his own position to be ever more secure. Time was now working in his favor. In Jovius' absence, he had advertised himself as in need of troops.

As many as 10,000 Huns had answered the call.

On last report the Huns were in Castra Martis, in Moesia, where their chieftain Uldin had been loftily dictating terms to the generals of Thrace, and therefore Constantinople. He had, however, overestimated his control over his own people. The Huns had been dealing with Romans now for a few years, and some of them had become enamored of Roman ways. According to Sozomen:

> When things were hopeless, God gave undeniable proof of favor toward the emperor, for not long afterward Uldin's chieftains and their retainers were discussing the Roman manner of government, the emperor's kindness, and his promptness and generosity in seeing the best and good men received proper reward. It was God's work that from the love of these points they deserted to the Romans, whose camp they joined, together with their warriors.

It was not only the Roman Empire that suffered constant rebellions and usurpations. The larger part of Uldin's forces, ever mercenary, decided to fight for Roman gold. The Hunnish chieftain barely escaped back over the Danube with his life. Many of his loyal warriors were slain, and others taken captive. Constantinople by now having considerable experience with large numbers of barbarians within its borders, it was thought that having all these Huns on hand risked an uprising. The captives were therefore sold into slavery overseas, where they could never make further trouble for the Empire. Mercenaries, on the other hand, needed to go where the fighting was. What better gift could young Theodosius II make to his uncle Honorius, than a gift of Goth-hating troops, when and where they were most needed?

Things were all going Honorius' way. At the same time a new envoy, Jovius (not the same Jovius as the one who had been switching sides in Italy), arrived from Gaul. The new emperor Constantine asked forgiveness for slaying the rebellious Theodosians, Verenianus and Didymus, the deed having not been done on his orders. Further, he offered now to march to his fellow emperor's aid in Italy.

Constantine, as usual, was being disingenuous. The more accurate interpretation is, he was pleading to come over the Alps and under Honorius' protection. The new emperor's third of the Empire was falling apart. With hostile Vandals occupying western Gaul, Britannia was completely cut off from Rome. "So the Britons armed themselves," recorded Zosimus, "and undertook many dangerous campaigns in their own defense, until they freed their cities from the barbarians [i.e., Scots and Picts] who assaulted them."

The once tight-knit fabric of the Empire was tearing at the seams. Rome was no longer to be obeyed out of respect, or even fear. Its legions could not even defend the Eternal City, much less the outer provinces, as Zosimus conceded: "Not just the Britons, but some of the Celtic tribes also seceded from the empire, no longer living under Roman law but as they saw fit... In the same way, all of Armorica and other provinces of Gaul freed themselves, banishing Roman governors and officials, and raising governments of their own."

Not least of these was Gerontius. At his capital of Terraco (modern Tarragona on the Catalonian coast of Spain) he finally took his rebellion in Hispania to the next level. Just as Arbogastes had elevated Eugenius in 392, Gerontius – a Briton, a barbarian, ineligible for the post – nominated his own emperor, Maximus of Hispania. One of Gerontius' retainers (and possibly his son, which would seem to indicate he had a Roman mother), this Maximus was nothing like Magnus Maximus who had come roaring out of Britannia in 383. There was nothing "magnus" about this Maximus, whom the ancient sources describe as humble and reticent. He was more like Eugenius had been for Arbogastes – malleable, compliant, easily ordered about.

Gerontius and Arbogastes and Constantine had proven it. Amid the anarchy of the declining Empire, any man with enough warriors backing him could name his own emperor – or proclaim himself one – and any man with enough men backing him could make it so.

And Alaric had many, many warriors.

XXVII

SECOND SIEGE

AD 409

*A victorious leader, who united the daring spirit of a barbarian
with the art and discipline of a Roman general, was at the head
of an hundred thousand fighting men; and Italy pronounced with
terror and respect the formidable name of Alaric.*

Gibbon[1]

Upon the return of Alaric and the Goths to Rome, sentries and civic
leaders atop the walls could see the sinuous march of barbarian
warriors wind around the city like the coils of a python, gradually
constricting. This in itself was nothing they had not seen the previous
year, when the Goths had proven incapable of breaching the city walls.
They were known to be low on provisions themselves. This time the
city would likely outlast them, at least until Emperor Honorius sent
his Eastern auxiliaries to its relief, or Emperor Constantine arrived
with his own barbarian army.

Any Romans feeling secure in their defenses, however, would have
been dismayed to see a contingent of barbarians head off along the
banks of the Tiber, toward the coast.

Fifteen miles downstream, where the river lets out into the
Tyrrhenian Sea, the twin cities of Ostia and Portus served as Rome's
gateway to the world. On the south side of the river's mouth, Ostia

[1]*History*, Vol. III, p. 225

was the original port town, but had long since proven insufficient to Rome's needs. By Alaric's day its population of perhaps 100,000 worked, or served the workers and sailors, in Portus, the newer complex of artificial harbors and canals carved out of the north side. Vessels of up to 500 tons would home on the island lighthouse marking the entrance to the seaside basin built by the emperor Claudian, with two breakwaters enclosing some 500 acres, twenty feet deep, capable of handling 300 ships. Another 200 could pass through a narrow channel to the inland harbor dug by the emperor Trajan, a 600-acre hexagon with each side 1,200 feet long. Today the inner harbor is a private lake and the outer harbor, like Classis at Ravenna, is filled with silt and inland from the coast, but even in the 2nd century the Greek orator and author Aelius Aristides marveled of Portus:

> Here all the crops of the seasons and the produce of each province is brought from every land and sea. The ships never stop arriving and departing, so that one would admire not only the harbor, but even the sea. Everything comes here that is produced or grown… whatever is not found here, is not something which ever existed or exists.

At any given moment there were probably a thousand or so ships plying the Mediterranean with spices, olive oil, wine, slaves, and the all-important tons of grains and cereals that kept Rome fed. They all put in at Portus, and their goods passed through the town or were stored in its warehouses.

On landing in late AD 409 sailors, knowing nothing of recent developments upriver, would have been startled to see long-haired barbarians monitoring the docksides, and to be told that the Goths had taken over the town. The only supplies moving upriver to Rome were those necessary to feed the barbarians laying siege to it. Alaric's army could now sit outside the city walls indefinitely, or at least until Honorius either made a fight of it, or gave in.

But why should Alaric wait for Honorius to decide?

There were now, depending on how they were counted, four or five sitting Roman emperors. Honorius in Ravenna, Theodosius II in Constantinople, Constantine III and his son *Caesar* Constans II in Vienne, and Maximus of Hispania.

The more of anything there is, the cheaper and less important each becomes. With such a plethora of Roman emperors, why should there not be one more – one more amenable to Alaric?

Zosimus recorded, "Alaric, seeing that he could not secure a peace on his conditions, nor held any hostages to force one, attacked Rome again, threatening to storm it if the citizens did not join him against the emperor Honorius."

This was a novel strategy: if the emperor refused to govern the Empire, then the Empire would have a new emperor. The memory of the previous year's famine being still fresh in the minds of the senators, and wishing to avoid another siege and more privation, they agreed to the Goth's demands. Elderly Priscus Attalus, who was only there on behalf of Honorius, was the nearest thing to leader of the city. He was a pagan, but that was of small import, and even some advantage, as Sozomen reported:

> The pagans, knowing the religious leanings and prior education of Attalus, believed he would openly support their religion and restore their old temples, their feasts, and altars. On the other hand the Arians believed that, as soon as he was in power, Attalus would make their creed supreme over the others, as they had reigned during the reigns of Constantius and Valens.

Given entry to the city, Alaric proclaimed Attalus *Augustus*, emperor. The old man was immediately baptized – by a Gothic bishop, Sigesarius, in the Arian faith, naturally – and awarded a diadem and purple toga. Galla Placidia probably attended, or was made to attend, the ceremony in which her half-brother was usurped; at this point the imperial princess amounted to nothing more than a hostage, another tool to be used against Honorius.

On Attalus' accession, rank and privilege trickled down to various senators and aristocrats, who adapted remarkably well to the new way of things. Lampadius, who had railed against Stilicho's "pact of servitude" with Alaric, now accepted the post of praetorian prefect, and the general Valens who had only barely escaped Alaric's wrath with his life was named *magister equitum*. Alaric's brother-in-law Athaulf became *comes domesticorum equitum*, commander of the elite guard cavalry. And Alaric himself was awarded the rank once

Stilicho's: *magister utriusque militiae*. The king of the Goths had finally achieved his dream…even if he had to create an emperor of the Romans to do it.

Yet whatever Alaric expected of him, Attalus saw himself as no puppet of the Goths. He had grand designs for the Empire that was now his. "Attalus convened the senators," wrote Sozomen, "and gave a long and very elaborate speech, in which he promised to restore the senate's ancient customs, and also to bring Egypt and the other provinces of the East back under Italian control."

"He made an arrogant speech," concurred Zosimus, the pagan, "in which he pompously assured them that he would subdue the whole world to Rome, and even achieve greater doings than that. This perhaps angered the gods, who soon afterwards removed him."

Alaric himself had more modest goals. He had seen the riches and plenty of Africa as it was offloaded from the ships at Portus, and being no fool, knew that the key to Rome was the grain from Africa. As soon as the ships returned to Carthage with news of the usurpation, the likelihood was that Heraclianus, Stilicho's executioner, who owed his position as *comes Africae* to Honorius, would declare for him and, as Gildo had, cut off the grain shipments. Alaric came to the same conclusion that Stilicho had. "Alaric wisely suggested that Attalus send a sufficient force to Africa, to Carthage, to depose Heraclianus from his throne," wrote Zosimus, "before he, being loyal to Honorius, interfered with their plans."

Attalus, on the other hand, expected that a diplomatic envoy with a small military escort would be sufficient to encourage Heraclianus to submit, and he was not so Christianized that he would not take the advice of pagan soothsayers over his own general. "He was deceived by the predictions of some diviners," admitted Sozomen, "who convinced him that he would conquer Africa without a battle."

Attalus was more concerned with securing his own power than his people's food supply. "Disregarding the advice of Alaric, he gave command of the African expedition to Constantine, yet assigned him no soldiers of worth," sniffed Zosimus.* It matters little, as the imperial ambassador was not destined to enjoy a long career, nor to

---

*This envoy was not Constantine III, who was still in Gaul, but yet another Constantine. Just to make it more confusing, Sozomen refers to him as Constans.

have much effect on events. His was a mere sideshow for Attalus, who had his eye on Honorius. "In the meantime, while the outcome in Africa was still uncertain, he undertook a campaign against the emperor, at Ravenna."

Alaric, now a good Roman general, obeyed his emperor, at least for the time being. With him and Attalus at its head, the barbarian army departed Rome and marched back toward Ravenna.

It took Honorius no time at all to panic. "When he heard that Attalus had reached Ariminum, with an army of both Roman and barbarian troops," wrote Sozomen, "Honorius wrote to acknowledge him as emperor, and sent the highest officials of his court to serve him, and offer him a part of the empire."

Jovius, having by now switched sides often enough so that nobody should have trusted him, took the missive to Attalus. According to Zosimus, the new emperor replied that he "would not leave Honorius as much as the title of emperor, nor even a whole body, for he intended to banish him to an island, and to cut a few pieces off him as well."

At this point Honorius was in such a state of terror that he had ships readied in Classis for his immediate escape to Constantinople and the court of his nephew. Theodosius II, or more properly his advisor Anthemius, was way ahead of the situation. Honorius was relieved of the predicament, according to Zosimus, by the timely arrival that night, by boat, of 6,000 of those Eastern troops from across the Adriatic, many of them undoubtedly Huns who had deserted Uldin. Sozomen says it was 4,000, but whatever the number, it was enough: "Honorius manned the walls of the city with these reinforcements, for he thought the native troops too inclined to mutiny."

Honorius decided to hold out in Ravenna until he found out which way Heraclianus, in Africa, was going to go. Whoever held Africa and its food held the Empire.

When Attalus' envoy Constantine, or Constans, arrived with his paltry force and word that he was to be deposed, Heraclianus simply arrested him, executed him, and declared for Honorius. And like any loyal African commander, his first step was to cut off further grain shipments to Rome and send them to Ravenna instead.

Alaric held the power once wielded by Stilicho. Now he got a taste of the troubles that came with it. This was the same problem Stilicho had faced against Gildo, and Alaric did not have the luxury of being able to import provisions from other provinces. This resistance in Africa was not unexpected – in fact, it was just as Alaric had predicted – and he and his new emperor had a falling out over it. "Alaric advised that five hundred barbarians be sent to Africa against Heraclianus," wrote Sozomen, "but the senators and Attalus objected that Africa ought not to be entrusted to barbarians."

Just as Gainas and Fravitta had found, Alaric was learning that a barbarian could ascend to the very pinnacle of Roman power, and still be regarded as nothing more than a barbarian.

With troops from the East and provisions from Africa arriving in Ravenna, continuing the siege was pointless. Attalus elected to return to Rome to oversee management of the famine that was sure to ensue. To keep his barbarian army from becoming overtaken by it, or frustrated from the lack of plunder, Alaric took a roundabout route across the north of Italy, through Aemilia and Liguria, forcing the cities there to declare for him and against Honorius. His success was mixed. Bononia, where Sarus had mutinied against Stilicho, refused to submit. As spring turned into summer Alaric returned south to Rome to see how his new emperor fared.

Things couldn't get much worse.

"The famine was so severe," recorded Sozomen, "that people ate chestnuts instead of grain, and some were suspected of having eaten human flesh."

Yet among these civilized Romans avarice was still stronger than hunger. The city merchants were no better than Heraclianus. "The food sellers concealed all their stocks, hoping to make huge profits by pricing their goods as they liked," wrote Zosimus. "By these means the people were reduced to such difficulty, that some, as if they wished that it might be made available, cried out in the Hippodrome, 'Set a price on human flesh.'"

"During the siege of Rome," conceded Olympiodorus, "the citizens turned to cannibalism."

The Senate was ready to admit that Alaric had been right all along, to put his Goths aboard ships in Portus and turn them loose in Carthage to do away with Heraclianus and forcibly free up the food supply. Emperor Attalus, with an increasingly imperious hand, had overruled them. He had seen what a Roman army composed of barbarians – commanded by barbarians – meant for Rome, and would not trust the city's food supply to such, even against a treacherous Roman like Heraclianus. His distrust of barbarians was plain to see; his distrust of fellow Romans was becoming more pronounced. The general Valens had been arrested on charges of treason. Jovius, playing all sides again, came to whisper in Alaric's ear that as soon as Attalus gained enough power he would turn on him as well, and the Goth would end up like Stilicho, with an emperor who owed everything to him, betraying and murdering him.

Stilicho had been half-Roman, and his loyal Roman half had been his undoing. Alaric was a full-blooded barbarian who owed these Roman emperors nothing, and had had his fill of them. "It then became plain to Alaric that God disapproved of Attalus as emperor," wrote Sozomen, "and thinking it futile to belabor a matter so beyond his reach – and after receiving certain pledges from Honorius – he deprived Attalus of his title."

The would-be emperor was reminded of the limits of his power when armed Goths collected him and marched him up the Via Flaminia to Alaric's headquarters in Ariminum. Sozomen took up the story:

All the parties concerned convened outside the city walls. Attalus cast aside the symbols of imperial power. His officers also threw down their weapons, and Honorius granted pardon to everyone for everything, commanding that each was to hold the honor and office which he had previously held. But Attalus and his son returned to Alaric, for he thought his life would still be in danger if he continued to live among the Romans.

Attalus was made a guest in Alaric's home, his safety guaranteed by the pardon from Honorius. After all, Alaric still had another bargaining chip in his pocket. "He also held Placidia, the emperor's sister, as a hostage," wrote Zosimus, "though she was given all the honor and comfort due a princess."

Soon after this entry in Zosimus' *Historia Nova*, New History, the account abruptly cuts off. This is attributed to the death of the author, which occurred about a hundred years after the last events he covered. Some historians believe, however, there was reason for Christian monks to do away with the latter parts of his work, for

310

pagan Zosimus never hesitated to blame Christians where he thought blame due. And, as events at Rome reached their inevitable conclusion, there was plenty of blame to go around.

After this display of contrition, Alaric can be excused for thinking Honorius would surely be in a benevolent mood, and willing to bargain for Rome's survival. And indeed the emperor agreed to a face-to-face meeting. In July Alaric, with Attalus in tow, ventured forward under truce from Ariminum to meet Honorius some seven miles outside Ravenna. With his reign no longer threatened – at least, not until Constantine III arrived from Gaul – Honorius should have been more inclined to bargain with the barbarians. Perhaps he was. Not all of his courtiers and generals, however, were eager for a deal to be struck between Romans and Goths. Of all Honorius' commanders, there was one even better acquainted than Jovius with Alaric.

Sarus.

Since his battle with Athaulf, the Amali leader and his brother Sigeric had been sheltering within Ravenna's walls under Honorius' protection. With his archenemy this close, though, they took the opportunity to emerge at the head of their troops. According to Sozomen:

> Sarus, barbarian-born and highly experienced in war, had only about three hundred men with him, but all well armed and highly skilled. He distrusted Alaric on account of their former hatred, and reasoned that a treaty between the Romans and Goths would do him no good. Suddenly attacking with his men, he killed some of the barbarians.

Casualties were light – neither Alaric nor Athaulf were hurt – but this violation of truce was not something a civilized people should have condoned. Rightly or wrongly, Alaric held Honorius responsible. He realized now there could never be peace between them, that the emperor and his minions cared little for what befell any lesser beings, including the hundreds of thousands in the Eternal City.

So be it.

Alaric returned to Ariminum, roused his troops, and for the last time put them back on the road to Rome.

XXVIII

Third Siege

AD 410

Alaric, having named, unnamed, renamed, and again unnamed
his own emperor in practically less time than it takes to tell,
could only laugh at it all, realizing
the empire was a farce.

Orosius

Rome had now been under siege, on and off, for over a year. Now it was doubly besieged, by the Goths outside its walls and the Africans withholding grain from its ports. Roman citizens, who had prided themselves as the pinnacle of civilization, had been reduced to barbarism – worse than barbarism, animalism. "In their desperation the starving people resorted to repellent food," heard Jerome, "and tore each other apart just to have flesh to eat. Not even the mother spared the baby at her breast."

The difference was, the famine was now hitting the Goths as hard as the citizenry. For a year and a half they had camped outside the walls, just north of the city in the *Horti Lucullani*, the 500-year-old gardens of 1st-century BC general and politician Lucius Licinius Lucullus. Alaric would not be able to remain there much longer. The previous winter he had brought a fully supplied army to Rome, and been able to pick off supply ships coming up the Tiber from Portus. This year he was as much under siege as the Romans. Soon he would have to move his army off in search of winter quarters. If the Goths were to take the Eternal City, it would have to be done quickly.

A little over 125 years later the 6th-century historian Procopius of Caesarea lived through another year-long, unsuccessful siege of Rome, then held by the Byzantine general Belisarius against the Ostrogothic king, Vitiges. A few years later Procopius compiled his *Historia de Bella* (*History of the Wars*), which included an account of the events of 410. He reported two different versions of Alaric's third siege. In one, the city was betrayed by a Roman matron, Anicia Faltonia Proba. She was a daughter of the Anicii, an old and powerful family; her husband, Sextus Claudius Petronius Probus, had served as Roman consul for the year 371, and her twin sons Anicius Hermogenianus Olybrius and Anicius Probinus had shared that honor in 395, the last year before the emperor Theodosius divided the Empire into East and West. (On that occasion, before he became associated with Stilicho, Claudian wrote his first panegyric in their honor.) Her husband had died in 390, and both her sons in 397. Without a man of the house, Proba – now a powerful woman in her own right, whom Claudian even fifteen years earlier had called "the world's glory, whose increased power increases the power of Rome" – was able to do as she wished. And she wished to spare the people of Rome any further suffering. Procopius revealed:

> Proba, a woman of very unusual distinction for her wealth and renown among the Roman upper class, pitied the Romans who were being devastated by hunger and their other privations, for they were already even tasting each other's flesh. Seeing that things were hopeless, since the enemy held both the river and the harbor, she commanded her servants, they say, to open the gates by night.

But Procopius also told another story, in which Alaric, unable to overcome the defenses by tactics alone, resolved to take the city by guile. He hatched a masterful Trojan Horse of a plan to take advantage of civilized Roman greed:

> From the boys in the army who had not yet grown beards but who had just come of age, he chose out 300 of good birth and brave beyond their years, and told them in secrecy that he intended

to present them to some of the Roman patricians, pretending they were slaves.

Alaric dispatched envoys into the city under truce. They addressed the senators, declaring that the king of the Goths admired them for their loyalty to Honorius, and had resolved to give up the siege. First, however, he wished to make a gift of slaves to each of them. Having recently lost so many of their servants to the Gothic forces, the senators gladly accepted the offering of these boys, though in the city's extremity one must wonder if they were intended to be slaves, sacrifices, or dinner.

Both stories have their flaws, but like any good yarn they have an element of truth. Would an aristocratic Roman woman take it upon herself to decide that her people would be better off being massacred by invading barbarians, than killing each other for food? Possibly. Would her servants be able to open a city gate without interference from the guards? Doubtful. On the other hand, would a handful of senators, deprived of slaves and unused to doing their own work – and having apparently never read Homer's *Iliad* – gratefully take several hundred of the enemy's young men within their walls? Conceivably; certainly to this point they had not shown themselves to be paragons of wisdom. Would those 300 fake slaves all be able to escape their duties on the appointed hour and arm themselves? Surely some could.

What all the sources agree on (Roman sources, at least), is that Rome was not conquered from without, but from within, either by Proba's servants or Alaric's Trojan slaves. Or perhaps, though history does not record it, simply by a few desperate, starving citizens finally resolved to throw themselves on barbarian mercy.

Outside, the Goths gathered to the north of the city, where the old Via Salaria, the Salt Road from Castrum Truentinum, modern Porto d'Ascoli on the Adriatic coast, arrived at the Aurelian Walls. As part of Honorius' renovations, the Porta Salaria, the Salarian Gate, had been reinforced with a pair of semi-circular defensive towers and three overhead windows or firing ports, and was shuttered by a portcullis, but these often had a built-in, man-sized door for convenience. That was all that stood between Rome and its conquerors.

Having been pushed to the precipice, Alaric stood on the cusp of history. By all accounts, though, he did not desire posterity to remember him as a merciless barbarian. According to Orosius, "He ordered that anyone who sought sanctuary on holy ground, especially in the basilicas of the holy apostles Peter and Paul, should be left alive and safe. He permitted his men to plunder as much as they desired, but gave orders that they should shed no blood."

"He allowed each of his men to seize as much of Roman wealth as he could, and to loot all the houses," agreed Sozomen, "but out of respect toward the apostle Peter, he decreed the large, capacious church built over his tomb to be an asylum."

We can imagine the Goths – this pack of wolves, Alaric's famished, threadbare, vengeful horde – agreeing to whatever their chieftain ordered, while they were outside the walls.

Once on the inside…well, that would be a different matter.

Inside the walls, the people who had started out as a motley collection of outcast Greeks and Trojans, Latins and Etruscans – colonists, fugitives, bandits, and ruffians, according to Plutarch "a mingled rabble of poor and unknown people" – in a few thatch-roofed huts on the banks of the Tiber, had over the course of 1,100 years risen to become marble-pillared masters of the world. Since that day when Camillus had driven Brennus beyond the walls, they had proven themselves superior to – more civilized than – any who came before them: the Greeks, Egyptians, Celts, Phoenicians. Romans prided themselves on being the most clever, most politic, most warlike, and, when necessary, most brutal people in history. Above all, they prided themselves on their Eternal City.

At noon on August 24, a Wednesday on the old Julian calendar, two years and two days after the death of Stilicho, somebody – Proba's servants, Alaric's fake slaves, or simply a few Roman citizens seeking just to survive the malfeasance of their betters; it doesn't really matter who – opened the Salarian Gate to the invaders.

The day had come.

Barbari ad portam.

XXIX

The Graveyard of the Romans

AD 410

> *So, after this great excess of sacrileges, without any*
> *sign of repentance, the final, long-awaited doom*
> *overtook the City.*

Orosius

No direct eyewitness accounts of the fall of Rome in AD 410 have survived. Its chroniclers – Socrates Scholasticus, Sozomen, Orosius, Augustine, and of course Gibbon – all wrote secondhand, repeating hearsay, years, decades, or even centuries after the fact. Those who lived through it, whether conquerors or conquered, left no accounts. Many would have been illiterate, their stories were lost or, of course, they never lived to tell the tale.

The closest we come to a survivor account reaches us by way of Demetrias, granddaughter of Proba, the wealthy matron whom Procopius accused of sending servants to open the city gates to Alaric. Only eleven or twelve at the time of the sack, Demetrias was apparently too young to interest the rapacious Goths, and escaped ravishment. Proof of this is in the letter she wrote three years later, after she, her mother Anicia Juliana, and grandmother Proba had departed Rome for Carthage. At age fourteen Demetrias had been pledged in marriage, but wished to preserve her virginity and become a nun instead. There's no word of whether her mother and grandmother came through the sack equally unscathed, or how the family trauma affected Demetrias' wish to abstain from men forever.

Nevertheless, her mother Anicia Juliana opposed her decision. Still rich and powerful herself – wealthy Romans only held a small fraction of their assets within the city, deriving most of their income from their estates in the countryside and abroad – she had written to the church fathers of the day for advice: Augustine in Hippo; Jerome in Bethlehem; and in Carthage, the lesser-known Pelagius. Her letters are lost to history. Augustine rejoiced in Demetrias' decision without referring to her travails. Pelagius, a Celt born in Britannia, might well have been called a barbarian himself, but he certainly lived in Rome in the years leading up to the sack, either getting out of the city just before Alaric closed the Portus or, arguably, living through the sack himself. He knew Demetrias' family personally, and in his reply to her dwelled only briefly on their mutual bitter experience, his point being that all the wealth and power civilization could bestow came to nothing at the point of a barbarian sword:

It happened not long ago, as you yourself have heard, the shrill wail of the war-horn and the cries of the Goths, and Rome, the mistress of the world, shivered under the weight of despairing terror. Where were our nobles then? Where were the holders of the high ranks of the aristocracy? Terror threw everything into confusion and chaos, every house mourned, and fear spread everywhere. Slave and aristocrat were as equals. All faced death the same, except that those with the gentler life feared it more.

Neither Pelagius nor Demetrias could have ever forgotten those war trumpets blaring outside the walls, heralding their eventual breach and the incipient downfall of the Eternal City. In light of that, Pelagius advised the girl to follow her heart and preserve her virginity if she wished. Many other Roman girls had not been given the choice.

In his reply, Jerome – perhaps in response to Demetrias' own description of the sack – rather indelicately reminded her why, in deciding her future, she should *carpe diem*, seize the day:

It has not been long since you shook in barbarian hands, clinging to your grandmother and your mother, hiding under their cloaks for safety. You have been a captive and your chastity was not yours to keep. You have trembled under enemies' lustful glare; you have hidden the pain of seeing God's virgins raped. Your city, so long the capital of the world, is become the grave of the Romans.

Rome in AD 410 was forty times the size it had been in Brennus's day. The Salarian Gate was near the Colline, where the Gauls had entered, but well outside it – in fact, the Salarian was just about the farthest gate from the heart of the city, a good two miles from the Forum. That was a long way to fight a battle street-to-street and house-to-house with sword and shield. Like Brennus, though, having sprung their surprise, the Goths apparently met little initial resistance, and some of the more contemplative among them surely halted a moment just inside the gate. The Salarian is at the top of Quirinal Hill, the highest point in old Rome. It's easy to imagine Alaric and his commanders, having finally achieved the barbarian dream of centuries, looking down on the splendors of the Eternal City spread below them, realizing the enormity of what they had done, and what they were about to do. Orosius, for one, alluded to lightning strikes during the Goth invasion, and it may be that the barbarians took advantage of a thunderstorm to cover their final assault, or as a signal from above of holy vengeance about to descend on the city. "Everyone with common sense," admitted Sozomen, "knew that the disasters this siege brought upon the Romans were indications of holy anger sent to punish them for their lavish living, their depravity, and their many acts of injustice to each other and to strangers."

As the flickering bolts lit up marble columns, gold statuary and age-old shrines and temples, the Goths would have realized the dream was real. It was all theirs for the taking. They stood literally astride history. And they were about to make their own mark on it, with fire and sword.

As Socrates wrote, "After this the barbarians with Alaric, ravaging everything in their path, finally took Rome itself, which they laid waste, burning the tremendous number of the monumental buildings and other historic artwork it contained. The money and valuables they looted and split up among themselves."

From the Salarian Gate, the main street forked left and right. To the right, the Alta Semita, the High Path, ran along the crest of Quirinal Hill past the Horti Sallustiani, the Gardens of Sallust. The 1st-century politician and historian Gaius Sallustius Crispus had risen from a plebeian family to back Julius Caesar, who appointed him governor of Africa Nova (not Egypt, but Numidia – modern-day Tunisia, Libya, and part of Morocco). After skimming a great part of the province's wealth into his own pocket, Sallust had returned to Rome and, like Lucullus, built his own *horti*, a landscaped pleasure garden complete with topiary, shaded pavilions and arcades, statues and fountains, even a temple to Venus. It was so magnificent that after Sallust's death Emperor Tiberius turned it into a public park.

This figures in our story because Sallust, no saint himself but already disappointed with Rome's moral and political decline, was well acquainted with Brennus's *vae victis*: woe to the vanquished. In a way, he had predicted the fate of Rome when he wrote that during any sack, in accordance with the rules of war "...maidens would be raped, and youths beaten, children would be torn from their parents' arms, matrons would serve at the whim of the conquerors, temples and homes would be looted, massacres and fires would ensue, and everywhere would be killing, bodies, blood and mourning."

Predicted, because Procopius, writing over a century after Alaric and the Goths took Rome, still bore witness to the initial destruction they wrought: "They fired the houses near the [Salarian] gate, including the house of Sallust, who in olden times wrote the history of the Romans, and much of this house has stood half-burned to this day."

That he wrote this over a hundred years after Sallust's house fell attests to the destruction that Rome was about to undergo, and from which it never really recovered.

Sallust was right. And the Goths were just getting started.

To the left from the Salarian Gate, the street led through the remains of the Porta Collina, the old Colline Gate, and along the *agger*, the sloped rampart of the old Servian Wall. This neighborhood was called the Castra Praetoria, after the *castra*, the fortress of the old Praetorian Guard which had been incorporated into Aurelian's city wall.

The Goths had nothing to fear from Praetorians, who had been disbanded by Constantine I almost a hundred years earlier.*

Facing the Castra Praetoria, and by far the largest, most imposing structures in the neighborhood, were the Baths of Diocletian: an immense complex taking up some thirty-two acres amid the densely populated hilltop neighborhoods. In happier times the baths served as much more than public swimming pools. There were gymnasiums, gardens and exercise yards, saunas and steam rooms, a library, reading rooms and auditoriums. These together could accommodate up to 3,000 bathers, food and wine vendors, masseurs, annointers, and attendants to serve them. For citizens of Rome, to laze about the baths doing business, enjoying conversation, partaking of food, libation, friendship, and even a little sex, was the very height of civilized life.

There is no account of events in the Baths of Diocletian that August day. Yet the facility was open to the public, and bathing was one of the last pleasures available to citizens of the time. The pools were probably a lot less crowded than usual, but emaciated and haggard Roman men, women, and children surely came seeking respite from the stress of the siege and the stifling August heat.

But the Goths took the city by surprise, and being so close to the Salarian Gate the baths would have been one of their first stops. At some point, in the entrance to the *natatorium*, the swimming pool nearest the courtyard, dripping bathers would have confronted the first of the leering, long-haired barbarians – leather-clad and filthy, reeking of sweat, their drawn swords already stained with blood.

Pickings could not be made any easier. Allowing for just a modicum of cutting and hacking, it can safely be assumed that the bath waters ran red.

Beyond the baths, the city heights branched into two ridges, the Quirinal and Esquiline Hills, with the smaller Viminal Hill between them. The invading Goths poured along the crests of these ridges and down into the valleys between, their progress marked by the fires of

---

*Some of the more superstitious among the barbarians might have trod lightly, however, as just outside the Colline was where any Vestal Virgin who had broken her vows over the centuries had been buried alive.

torches and burning houses like the pyroclastic flows of volcanic ash of which the ridges had originally been formed. And, as they flowed out into the greater city, by the screams of citified Romans suddenly face to face with barbarism.

In the valley between the Virinal and Esquiline Hills lay a slum, the Suburra, wall-to-wall with squalid tenements, notorious for its whorehouses. It was likely spared large-scale destruction. It had little to offer in the way of wealth, and when women are free for the taking, whores become worthless. No barbarian would bother with a low-born woman when he could take one high-born.

In the upper-class neighborhoods atop the hills, the Goths stood before rich Roman homes, the likes of which they had rarely seen, into which they would never have been invited. Certainly they were not invited now, but a barred door would not have stopped them. The roof of a typical Roman *domus* was low and square, sloped and tiled, but wide open in the middle to let in light and rainwater, unfortunately also allowing easy access for any halfway athletic and determined intruder. While distracting the occupants with barbarians at the door – *barbari ad ianuam!* – it would be nothing for a handful of men to boost a few more up onto the eaves, from where they could scale the roof to the central opening, the *compluvium*, and let themselves down into the *atrium* below. A few swings of the sword to clear any recalcitrant male servants or men of the house, unbar the door, and the time had come to make up for years of maltreatment, servitude, and massacres. Any occupants, whether slaves or masters, who had not made it in time to the *posticum*, the servant's entrance at the side or back, had run out of luck. Pleas and sobbing would avail them nothing. They had had their laugh while the Goths' wives and children were being murdered.

In February 1793 a team of workmen applied themselves to digging a well a few hundred yards north of the Colosseum, behind the monastery of San Francesco di Paola, at the foot of the Esquiline Hill. The largest of all the Seven Hills of Rome, in the old days the Esquiline had been a dump yard and cemetery for the poor and for criminals, whose bodies were left to rot or be eaten by vultures and dogs. As the city expanded, however, the breezy heights of the Esquiline above the fever-infested lowlands of the Forum became the domain of consuls, senators, and even emperors. Excavation frequently yielded surprises.

The work was slow, and not until two months into it did the diggers penetrate the remains of a Roman *domus*. Furthermore, in a corner of it, they hit on a treasure trove: a silver dinner service including spoons and forks, eight plates, a fluted dish, a ewer (pitcher or jug), saucers, and candelabras, plus gilded statuettes, lamps of rock crystal, and mosaics. The most impressive pieces are a sixteen-sided round silver casket with a domed lid, designed to hold four identical silver canisters and a silver flask (included), and a silver wedding casket full of toiletries and jewelry, with bas-reliefs depicting and an inscription naming a bride, Projecta, and her groom Secundus, all of pure silver with heavy gilding. In total the trove weighed almost one hundred pounds.

The dating of the objects is to this day a subject of contention among historians. In her portrait, the bride's hairstyle of coiled braids is reminiscent of sculptures of Empress Flavia Julia Helena, mother of Constantine I, which might date it to her time as *Augusta*, about AD 325–330. On the other hand, the groom's square-cut beard fits more with the era of Emperor Julian, the Apostate (r. AD 355–363) or even Eugenius.

Fashions go in and out of style, of course. What's more interesting is the combination of pagan imagery and Christian inscription. The domed casket is decorated with eight of the nine inspirational Muses.* (Missing is Erato, the muse of love poetry, which might indicate the Muse Casket was not a wedding gift.) Projecta's wedding casket is inscribed *SECVNDE ET PROIECTA VIVATIS IN CHRI* – Secundus and Projecta may you live in Christ – but at the same time adorned with a naked Venus at her toilette, attended by erotes and nereids, and Projecta at hers, attended by torchbearers and handmaidens. The box may have been commissioned by a pagan buyer and had the Christian inscription applied later, but the combination of pagan imagery and Christian inscription is not incongruous. It would instead have been intended to draw a flattering analogy between a Christian bride and Venus, the personification of love.

*Urania (muse of astronomy), Melpomene (tragedy), Clio (history), Polyhymnia (sacred poetry), Terpsichore (dance), Euterpe (flutes and lyric poetry), Thalia (comedy and pastoral poetry), and Calliope (epic poetry).

On little more basis (it must be said) than having the same name, Projecta has been tenuously identified with a contemporary young Roman woman eulogized by Pope Damasus in AD 383. She married around the same time as Stilicho and Serena, but died at the age of just sixteen. Damasus named her father as one Florus, just as tenuously linked to the *magister officiorum* and praetorian prefect of the East by that name, who served under and was distantly related to Theodosius the Great. Her husband is presumed to have been Turcius Secundus, son of a long line of urban prefects. (In his epitaph Damasus names her widowed husband as "Primus," but the pope was fond of wordplay and might have been implying that Secundus was first in her heart.) The silver ewer is inscribed with the feminine name Pelegrina, and the plates are inscribed with her monogram in gold: *Pelegrina filia Turcii*, Pelegrina daughter of the family of the Turcians, making Pelegrina probably the mother, sister, or daughter of Turcius. Though the style and craftsmanship of the caskets seem to be the work of a single, presumably Roman silversmith or smithy, this all seems to add up to the cache being handed down, and added to, through several generations, probably from AD 330–380 or even later, as family heirlooms.

The Italian workers initially attempted to cover up the find and sell the items on the black market. The plot was discovered, the pieces recovered, and sold abroad to collectors for about 1,450 Roman *scudi*,* about $8.4 million today. (Most of them are now on display in the British Museum.) Currencies fluctuate but worth stays the same; this trove is as huge a treasure today as it was in 1793, and in the late 4th century as well. It was the collected wealth of an entire family.

The Turcii persisted almost to the 6th century – Turcius Rufius Apronianus Asterius was a *praefectus urbi* before becoming Western consul in 494 – but whichever branch of the family lived in the villa at the foot of the Esquiline Hill evidently did not. Generations of them having spent the better part of a century amassing their treasure, they buried it well. The Goths never found it.

But not a single member of the entire family ever came back for it.

---

*The silver coinage of the Papal States at the time, worth about 3.3–3.35 grams of gold each.

On the Campus Martius, the Field of Mars north of the Capitoline Hill, the Goths broke into the Mausoleum of Augustus, who was said to have ordered a basket of soil from every province of the Empire to be poured on his tomb, so that the entire world would be his grave. Inside, the barbarians stood in the very shadow of emperors – Augustus, Tiberius, Caligula, Claudius – whose ashes for four centuries had rested there in golden urns. Then, according to legend (without actual evidence, but very believably), the Goths dumped the ashes on the floor and made off with the urns.

On the Caelian Hill, they broke into the Lateran Palace, the palace of popes, and carried off the one-ton *ciborium*, the silver canopy that stood on columns over the altar in the sanctuary, a gift from Constantine I a hundred years earlier. Luckily the pope was not in residence. "Another demonstration that the razing of the City was due to God's wrath rather than to the daring of the enemy," wrote Orosius, "is the fact that the blessed Innocent, the bishop of Rome, was through the hidden hand of God in Ravenna at the time, even as Lot the Just was withheld from the Sodomites, and did not bear witness to the destruction of the sinful city." A great relief, it can be imagined, to the vast majority of Romans.

For three centuries the *Templum Pacis*, the Temple of Peace, built in AD 71 by Emperor Vespasian just off the main Forum, had housed trophies of war, including the treasures of Herod's Temple in Jerusalem, looted by Vespasian's son, the future emperor Titus in AD 70. Just as depicted on the Arch of Titus, the great menorah, silver trumpets, the mortar and pestle used for preparing the incense, and the gold-leafed table of God's bread had been stolen from the Jews, and now, according to Procopius, they were stolen from the Romans, with both temples so badly damaged that neither was ever fully repaired.

The Curia Julia, the nondescript meeting house of the Senate – those craven cowards who had supported Honorius, then Attalus, then Honorius again – was also damaged and would require renovation. The Basilica Julia, a massive office building on the south side of the Forum, was set alight and partially destroyed. Across from it, the wooden-roofed Basilica Aemilia, a kind of great indoor shopping mall, was looted and set afire, burning so hot that remaining fragments of the marble floor still show greenish-brown stains, said to be bronze coins that melted into it.

Demetrias was not the only Roman virgin to have survived the sack. Jerome also wrote to console another upper-class Roman maiden, Principia, on the loss of their mutual friend, Marcella. About 85 in 410, Marcella was a colleague and correspondent of Jerome who became an informal religious teacher in a time when women were forbidden that vocation. In her youth she had been widowed after less than a year, leaving her independently wealthy, but she had given away most of her riches to the poor. Marcella and Principia had lived together with others of a similar religious bent. Asceticism being then all the rage, they renounced worldly pleasures like rich dining, fine clothing, and sexual pleasure in favor of spiritual attainment, though a cynic might note that their asceticism did not extend to leaving the comfort of Marcella's palatial home on the Aventine Hill.

This was Rome's most exclusive neighborhood, with well over a hundred palaces of senators and aristocrats, where the emperors Vitellius, Trajan, and Hadrian lived before assuming their thrones. As a result, in 410 it was almost totally ransacked and destroyed. Socrates put it succinctly: "Many of the principal senators they slew for a variety of excuses."

Italian archaeologist Rodolfo Lanciani recalled his work of uncovering the Aventine in the 19th century:

> The signs of destruction are everywhere the same: traces of flames which blackened the red ground of the frescoes, and caused the roofs to fall on the mosaic or marble pavements of the ground floor; coins scattered among the ruins, belonging, with rare exceptions, to the fourth century; statues that had been restored over and over again; marbles stolen from pagan buildings, mostly from sepulchral monuments, and utilized for hurried restorations; and Christian symbols on lamps and domestic utensils... The Aventine paid dearly for the partiality shown for it by the noble and the wealthy. The treasures accumulated in its palaces roused the cupidity of the invaders, and led them to excesses of plunder and destruction such as were spared to more humble districts of the City.

"As was to be expected in such an anarchy, one of the bloody-handed conquerors found his way into Marcella's house," recounted Jerome in his letter, as though it was necessary to walk Principia through the horror again. "…When the soldiers entered she is said to have greeted them without any fear, and when they demanded gold she showed them her coarse dress to prove she had no hidden treasure."

The barbarians refused to believe anyone living in such a mansion did not have gold hidden away, and to encourage Marcella to talk, set to beating its whereabouts out of her with whips and cudgels.

"They said she felt no pain," Jerome comforted Principia, "but threw herself at their feet and pleaded with tears for you, that you might not be killed, or because of your youth have to endure what she, as an old woman, did not fear."

One can well imagine Marcella's tearful pleading, and Principia's as well. The Goths tore the house apart before believing the old woman might be speaking the truth. As Jerome told it, they had a change of heart and took pity on their victims. To keep them safe, they bore the women out through one of the southern gates to the Basilica of St. Paul, which Theodosius the Great had laid down in 386 and Pope Innocent consecrated in 402. Too late. A few days later Marcella, giving thanks that Principia was unharmed, and leaving her worldly goods to her, died in her arms. Their once stately mansion was never repaired. Considered a founder of the Christian monastic system, Marcella, like Jerome, was later named a saint by the church.

The sack went on for three days. After their initial lust and greed were sated, more of the barbarians remembered their Christianity, or had attacks of conscience. According to Sozomen, "One of Alaric's young warriors spotted a lovely woman and, captivated by her beauty, tried to rape her, but she fought hard for her virtue."

The Goth drew his sword and gave her a bloody cut on the neck, but still the girl refused to give in, preferring death to dishonor. Here was the highest example of civilization, and rather than take her by force, the barbarian not only escorted her to the sanctuary of St. Peter's Basilica, he gave her six gold pieces to pay the warriors guarding it, and warned them to keep her safe for her husband.

Augustine marveled over such tales:

All the injury, then, which Rome suffered in the recent disaster – all the killing, looting, burning, and pain – was the customary outcome of war. What was unusual, however, was that wild barbarians showed a gentle side, that the largest churches were selected and set aside as sanctuaries for those given quarter. In them no one was slain, no one was dragged out by force, many were sent in by their relentless enemies to preserve their freedom, and none were led into slavery.

By now St. Peter's had become, as Alaric had decreed, a safe harbor for the refugees of the city. Simply invoking the apostle's name may have become something of a safe word. According to Orosius, one of the Goths broke into a church and confronted the prioress, demanding gold and silver. She put up no resistance, but revealed a trove of dishes, bowls, and cups that astonished the barbarian. It did not come without a warning. "This is the sacred service of the Apostle Peter," she told him. "Take it, if you dare! You will have to answer for their theft. As for me, since I cannot save them, I am not worthy of keeping them."

What St. Peter's dinner service was doing anywhere other than in his own church goes unexplained, but the Goth sent word of the find to Alaric. He ordered that the trove should immediately be taken to the apostle's basilica, with the prioress and any others with her given safe escort there as well. This was a bit of a march; the Old St. Peter's Basilica that Constantine I had raised on the historical site of the Circus of Nero was on the same grounds as the current Vatican, halfway across the city on the far side of the Tiber. So the pieces were handed out one to each person and, holding them overhead, they all got underway. Calling a truce, a mixed force of Goths and Romans with drawn swords were enlisted to march on either side, but proved unnecessary. The very sight of this procession stunned and astounded everyone who saw it, and many fell in on the march. Somebody began to sing a hymn, and for a moment Goth and Roman, pagan and Christian, Arian and Nicene, barbarian and citizen, all put aside their differences, crossed over the water in reverence, and conveyed the saint's treasure and his followers safely to their rightful home.

"It was a matter of whether the situation or the rightness stirred them," wrote Orosius in amazement. "…Who can consider such things without wonder? Who can describe them with sufficient praise?"

Perhaps, as the procession wound through the streets below, the singing rose to the heights of the Palatine Hill and echoed in the empty halls of the Palace of Domitian that dominated the crest. After having their way with the palace and its treasures the Goths abandoned it. It had not been a permanent imperial residence in decades, and would never be one again, destined over the centuries to fall into ruins which remain today. The most recent occupant was probably Galla Placidia, and though nothing is known of her whereabouts during the sack, it stands to reason that as an honored guest of the Goths she would be given one last chance to fetch any of her things that remained, and perhaps give an impromptu tour to Athaulf, Alaric's brother-in-law. She needed to stay on his good side. It seems Athaulf, though already married to his lord's sister, had taken somewhat of a fancy to a Roman woman who not so long ago would have been deemed above him. Galla the Roman princess was destined to become a barbarian queen.

And at some point in those three days in Rome, Alaric himself surely paused in the blackened remains of the Forum, where the burned-out basilicas of Aemilia and Julia still smoldered on either side, the Temple of Peace was a gutted ruin, and wreaths of smoke still rose through marble pillars and pediments on the surrounding hilltops. Here, eight centuries past, Brennus had first stood in awe at the achievements of Rome. Just a few steps away in the Curia Julia, the Roman Senate had decided history. Illustrious Caesars had made lofty speeches from the Rostrum at the northwestern end of the Forum. And near it, beside the Arch of Septimius Severus, anyone might look up at a chunk of marble, tipped on end and set on a block of travertine.

To the honor and virtue
of the most loyal soldiers
our lords Arcadius, Honorius and Theodosius,
lifelong Augusti,
after the end of the Gothic War
through the good providence of the perpetual ruler,
our lord Honorius
and the strategy and bravery

...

...

...

[signed]

328

The Senate and People of Rome.
This monument's preparation
accomplished by Psidius Romulus, v.c,
Prefect of the City, and deputy
in charge of judging imperial considerations.

Alaric could have run his hand over the rough space where several lines of the inscription in the marble had been erased with hammer and chisel: the lines with the name and rank of Flavius Stilicho, onetime master of cavalry and infantry in attendance on the emperor, guardian of the imperial dynasty, protector of empire…and son of a barbarian.

Damnatio memoriae.

The Romans had cut and carved and obliterated Stilicho's name off his own monument. If the Senate and People of Rome had their way, his name would be erased from all history. The marble block, though cracked and stained, stands in the Forum to this day.

No matter.

For better or worse, if not for Stilicho, Alaric would not have been standing in the flaming ruin of the Forum of Rome, the Eternal City, eternal no more. But Stilicho was dead, and Alaric had carved and chiseled the name of his old enemy, his old friend, into the heart of Rome in fire and blood, for all time.

XXX

FINIS

AD 410

> *In truth, Rome, which was founded and grew through the deeds*
> *of ancient heroes, was more disgracefully brought down by their*
> *descendants while its walls still stood, than it is now*
> *by the destruction of them.*

Augustine

In Ravenna, Honorius, informed by one of his eunuchs that Rome had fallen, cried out, "But it has just eaten out of my hands!" The servant had to explain that he had not meant Honorius' prize fowl, but the city, on which the emperor let out a sigh of relief that his bird still lived. Procopius, who recorded the story, sniffed, "So great, they say, was the foolishness of this emperor."

"The third day after entering the City," wrote Orosius, "the barbarians took their leave of their own accord."* Compared to the sack by Brennus and his Gauls in 387 BC, who had spent months destroying the city, the 410 sack of Rome might appear to be child's play. In truth, however, Rome had nothing left to offer Alaric and the Goths. They still had to eat, and the now-ruined city had been practically picked clean even before they entered.

---

*According to Gibbon the Goths remained in the city six days, which may be when the last of them pulled out.

Furthermore, August and September are malaria season in Rome, and as northerners the Goths, like Brennus's Gauls before them, were especially susceptible. The decision was not whether to go, but whither.

All of the recent fighting in Italy had taken place in the north of the country, in the Po Valley and the foothills of the Alps. The locals there were accustomed to barbarians on their doorstep, the pickings would be tough and scant, and the idea had the added disadvantage of placing the Goths between two Roman emperors – Honorius in Ravenna and Constantine in Gaul – and their armies. Either one, on his own, would have given Alaric a fight. To get caught between them was to court disaster.

The south of Italy, on the other hand, was a different story – a land of huge estates, ranches, and orchards that, although traditionally poorer than the north, had been spared the recent hardships of war. The Goths marched down the coast into what the Romans called Campania Felix, the Fertile Country, around Capua and Neapolis (modern Naples), a land of olive orchards and grain fields. It had not, however, been rich enough to feed Rome in place of Africa, and could not keep Alaric's Gothic horde from hunger for long.

Farther south, in Lucania, the mountainous arch of the Italian foot, the land wasn't so lush. Over the ages, people there had often sided with Rome's enemies – Pyrrhus, the Carthaginians, the Samnites – with the result that armies had marched back and forth over it, the few important cities had been crushed, and the area had slid into economic decline. It was not going to make much of a long-term home for the Goths.

Way down in Bruttium, modern Calabria, the toe of the boot, things were even worse. The people there had also been victimized by both sides in the Roman civil wars, and were still under frequent raids by pirates, to which Rome had paid little attention. They might even have welcomed a new set of overlords. To become cornered in Bruttium, however, was a mistake that Rome's foes Hannibal and Spartacus had made to their regret.

Alaric was under no illusions. He had conquered Rome the city, which was more than Hannibal or Spartacus or anyone since Brennus had done, but that in no way meant he had conquered Rome the

Empire. Those earlier opponents had learned the bitter lesson: Romans could always generate more armies, more manpower, and keep coming back to fight again. Like Hannibal and Spartacus, Alaric was a long way from home, and he knew the Romans would not permit him to make a home in Italy.

Also like Hannibal and Spartacus, however, he did not intend to remain in Italy. As the Goths had proven, not even Romans could survive in Rome, if not for the grain fields of Africa.

Africa was the key.

In their days Hannibal and Spartacus had to contend with the imperial navy, which had made the Mediterranean a Roman lake, *Mare Nostrum*, "Our Sea." As we have seen, the navy's glory days were past. The armada Stilicho had assembled thirteen years earlier to take him to Greece had been the last great naval fling of the Western Empire. The Eastern navy, which had delivered the extra troops to Honorius' garrison of Ravenna just in time to thwart Alaric's siege, remained a threat, but only if they caught the Goths on the water. The Goths, as Gainas had demonstrated, were no ocean voyagers, and Alaric did not intend them to become a naval power, nor even to fight a naval battle. They would remain at sea no longer than it took to cross over to Africa. A voyage from Italy to Cape Bon in Libya could take as little as two days, but more often twice that long, around the north side of triangular Sicily, and even a day longer around the eastern and southern sides.

After the Goths abandoned the harbors at Portus and Ostia, word would immediately have spread across the western Mediterranean of Rome's fall, and any loyal Roman captains might be expected to avoid putting in anywhere along Italy's southern coasts lest they fall into Gothic hands. On the other hand, Alaric needed sailors as much as ships, and with his newfound wealth could afford to pay them. He may have found any number of ship captains from the far-flung reaches of the Empire, with more loyalty to coin than to Rome.

The port at Rhegium, modern Reggio on the Calabrian coast, offered a natural harbor just a few miles across the Strait of Messina from the city of that name. Since its founding by Greeks in the 8th century BC, Rhegium had been a center of fishing, shipping, and commerce. If vessels were to be found, or built, they would be there. Not wishing to undergo the fate of Rome, the city put up no fight. Late in 410 the Goths moved in. "There came Alaric, king of the Visigoths," wrote Jordanes, using the later name for the tribe, "with the riches of all Italia which he had taken in spoils, and from there, as we have said, he intended to sail via Sicily to peaceful Africa."

Given that it's unknown exactly how many men, women, and children were following Alaric, he may not have required a huge armada to carry them all. Roman cargo ships of the late Empire were the largest seen in Europe until the 16th century. Even smaller transport vessels routinely carried seventy tons of cargo. The shipwreck discovered in 1967 off La Madrague de Giens, east of Toulon on the south coast of France, dated to the 1st century BC, measured 130 feet long and thirty feet across, would have displaced over 500 tons, and carried 400 tons of goods. The 2nd-century Syrian writer Lucian of Samosata famously described a Roman ship, the *Isis*, which he saw in the Athenian port of Piraeus, as 180 feet long, about fifty feet across the beam, and over forty feet deep, said to be capable of carrying enough grain to feed the city for a year. It would have displaced on the order of 1,200 tons. And this was several hundred years before Alaric's time. Admittedly, these were cargo ships, not passenger vessels, but people like the Goths, used to hardship, might have tolerated a short voyage packed tight as Roman *amphorae*, storage bottles, if it meant escaping imperial retribution to a new and better homeland. A little armchair math using modern airlines' "standard person" of about 185 pounds and two bags of twenty-five pounds each gives about eight people per ton of cargo weight, meaning even the smaller Roman ships might carry a hundred passengers, and the big ones perhaps over 1,000, though probably fewer given requirements of personal space. Again depending on the Goth head count and the capacity of the ships, a task force of a hundred or so might have got the job done in one voyage. To make numerous trips back and forth increased the risk exponentially. By the time the Goths arrived in Rhegium, word of the sack had almost certainly reached Carthage. Whether Heraclianus, having sided with Ravenna, expected the Goths to invade Africa is doubtful, but the longer Alaric waited, the more surely word would spread that he was gathering ships. Heraclianus' war galleys would be patrolling the North African coast, ready to observe and report any strange fleet or landing. The Goth crossing would have to be made all at once, putting their entire manpower ashore before Heraclianus' army could intervene.

October through March is the wettest time of year in the Strait of Messina. The *scirocco*, the strong southeast wind typical of the winter months, comes swirling up from North Africa, often blowing at forty-five knots and kicking up ten-foot whitecaps. In storm conditions gusts can reach seventy knots, and if blowing in opposition to the tidal currents through the Strait, raise twenty-foot waves. Over southern Italy, red sand picked up in North Africa mixes with water drawn off the Mediterranean to fall as unnerving "blood rain" that stains everything it touches. The *scirocco* is understandably said to cause bad moods and even disease. It often peaks in November – just around the time Alaric sought to make his crossing. He had little choice. Even then an old Greek saying, "caught between Scylla and Charybdis," referred to the notorious rock and whirlpool which historically menaced shipping in the Strait, but meant choosing the lesser of two evils. To stay in Italy meant starvation and war. To go to Africa also meant war, but hopefully on a full stomach.

The day before the onset of a *scirocco* is usually calm, clear, ideal sailing weather. Alaric would have leaped on the opportunity. Astute local captains, though, would not have had to consult calf livers to know the future. They would have noticed low clouds to the southeast over the mainland and cumulus piling up atop Mount Etna, the 11,000-foot Sicilian volcano visible forty miles to the southwest, foretelling an impending storm. If for nothing more than their own safety, they would have warned Alaric, but would he have listened? Obstinate, devious Romans had been impeding and delaying him for years. Alaric was the conqueror of Rome. Would God have permitted him that, only to inflict disaster on him afterward?

So the Goths embarked and raised sail for Africa. Barely had they set out into the channel than catastrophe ensued. The *scirocco* came down hard, and as the Goths would have timed their launch to coincide with a southward tide, the conflict between wind and water caught the ships between them. Alaric must have rued the day he thought God on his side. As Jordanes put it, "Since man is not free to do whatever he likes without God's approval, that terrible strait sank a number of his ships and threw the rest into chaos."

Orosius tells of Goths "shipwrecked and drowned in sight of their comrades." The fleet, full of drenched, seasick, and terrified survivors, struggled back into port to assess the disaster. The remaining ships, battered and waterlogged, would need repairs before any attempt could be made to sail again – that is, if any of their captains still obeyed Alaric's command.

In the event, they never had to make that choice. God wasn't through punishing Alaric. As the Goths pushed back up the toe of the Italian boot along the Via Popilia seeking a home for the winter, they came to Consentia, modern Cosenza, in a mountain valley where the Busento and Crati Rivers converge. The town garrison had once stood off Alexander the Great's uncle, Alexander of Epirus, and thereafter remained a bulwark of Rome. The Goths had resorted to their old tactics of siege – meaning, attempting to bully tribute out of the city – when Alaric suddenly fell ill.

Besides farms, the lowlands of southern Italy are pocked with swamps and bogs. On their way down the coast along the Appian Way, forty miles from Rome, the Goths would have crossed the Pontine Marshes, a great mosquito-infested fen covering 180 square miles that was not drained until the early 20th century. As late as the 1920s it was estimated that eighty percent of people spending just one night in the Pontine Marshes came down with malaria.

August and September are the peak season for the disease, which was so endemic in the capital that it was called "Roman fever." At the time it was thought to be caused by *miasma*, bad air, later called by the medieval Italians *mal aria*. No one at the time suspected the cause to be the Anopheles mosquito or the parasite it transmitted, *Plasmodium falciparum*, which causes the deadliest form of the disease.

Though the exact cause of Alaric's illness is to this day unknown, malaria is the best guess. If not in the Pontine Marshes, he could well have become infected in Rome. As Brennus and his Gauls had learned to their despair, the Forum, where Alaric might have stood looking up at Stilicho's poor monument, was originally a lowland marsh.

The Romans had drained it but, shielded from the cleansing wind by the surrounding hills, it was ever notorious for mosquitos.

Death by malaria is one of the most inglorious that can befall a warrior. In the early stages of their life cycle, the parasites enter the liver to mature, and symptoms don't appear until a week to a month, sometimes up to a year, after infection, when they come out to replicate in red blood cells. When those dying cells begin to clog the veins, the victim shivers through sudden chills and then sweaty fevers, nausea, vomiting, diarrhea, and bloody urine. If the infection becomes severe, the major organs, including the brain, kidneys, and lungs, become starved for blood and shut down, resulting in confusion, seizures, coma, kidney failure, and death.

One of the few ancient writers to mention any specifics of Alaric's demise, Jordanes, noted only that after losing many of his ships in the Strait of Messina, "Alaric was downcast by his setback and, while still pondering what to do next, was suddenly overwhelmed by an unexpected death, and left behind human worries."

That's a polite way to put it. It's surprising that contemporary Christian writers like St. Augustine, Jerome, and Orosius did not make more of a moral tale from Alaric's story. The image of the conqueror of the Eternal City – the king of barbarians who altered the course of Western civilization – still only about forty years old, laid low by disease and dying in bed, shivering and sweating, delirious, comatose, soiling himself, offers a lesson for the high and mighty.

"His people grieved for him with the utmost devotion," Jordanes continued. "Then, diverting the river Busentus from its course near Consentia – for this stream's pure waters flow from the foot of a mountain near that town – they forced a band of captives into the middle of the dry bed to dig his grave."

This as not as farfetched as it sounds, even for barbarians without the advantage of Roman engineering. The *fiumare* (small rivers) of Calabria often run dry; even today the Busento and Crati are neither very wide nor deep. Sufficient manpower could have forced them around the chosen gravesite. Hundreds, perhaps thousands of workers would have remembered the location, but the Goths saw to it that none of them would tell of it. Jordanes added, "So none would ever identify the place, they put all the diggers to death." Since the site was presumably visible from the hillside village of Consentia, this begs the question of what the Goths did with the townspeople.

Today the confluence of the rivers at the southern end of town is marked with a statue of the king of the Goths, rather incongruously standing atop his horse's head, looking down on the spot. For centuries the site has been the destination of treasure seekers from Alexander Dumas to Heinrich Himmler, in search of the riches of Rome said to have been interred with the dead king. Jordanes described the trove simply as "profuse treasures," and as with most such stories, over the centuries rumor and speculation have only enlarged the hoard. Today locals insist that, besides Alaric's horse and personal belongings, it includes ten wagonloads of gold and silver, and perhaps even the sacred Jewish menorah from the Temple of Peace. Drones, ground-penetrating radar, infrared, and electromagnetic sensors have all been employed to locate the tomb, without success.

So passed Alaric, the king of the Goths, the conqueror of Rome, into legend. There he has remained for all the centuries since, and long may he so remain. The manner of his entombment offers another abject lesson for the high and mighty, those pharaohs and kings and emperors who in their Ozymandian pretensions seek to secure their place in history with magnificent shrines to themselves. The pyramids of Egypt, the mausoleums of the Caesars, the burial mounds of Mycenae and Scandinavia, even the Church of the Holy Sepulcher in Jerusalem, all in their time became the property and trophies of conquerors: ransacked, defiled, emptied.

Times change. Majesty and reverence are forgotten, grandeur is only for looting. Permanence is fleeting; impermanence is forever. By rendering his remains ethereal, the Goths preserved the legend of their king, Alaric, sacrosanct for eternity.

Epilogue

The Triumph of Barbarism

AD 1787

*The decline of Rome was the natural and inevitable effect
of immoderate greatness. Prosperity ripened the principle
of decay; the causes of destruction multiplied with the
extent of conquest; and as soon as time or accident had
removed the artificial supports, the stupendous fabric
yielded to the pressure of its own weight.
The story of its ruin is simple and obvious;
and instead of inquiring why the Roman empire was destroyed,
we should rather be surprised that it had subsisted so long.*

Gibbon[1]

Near midnight on June 27, 1787, over 2,500 years after Rome's
founding and almost 1,377 years after its fall, Edward Gibbon
finally set down his quill pen upon completion of the sixth volume
of his magnum opus, *The History of the Decline and Fall of the
Roman Empire*. By this time he was no longer living in London. The
year after publication of his third volume the British government
of Lord Frederick North had fallen, largely due to its loss of the
colonial war, and as a minister of parliament and one of North's

[1] *History*, Vol. III, p. 631

supporters Gibbon was out on his ear. He had left his home on Bentinck Street and repaired to the estate of an old friend at Lausanne in Switzerland, where he finished his work in the garden summer house.

That was not the only change in the world since Gibbon had first set pen to paper. In 1781, just before publication of his second and third volumes, the Iron Bridge opened for travel over the Severn River in Shropshire: the world's first cast-iron arch, a harbinger of things to come. In 1783, in France, the Montgolfier brothers had made the first human flights in hot-air balloons. By 1785 the water-powered loom and cotton mill were revolutionizing the textile industry. Steam power, machine tools, and the mechanized factory system were all on the cusp of changing humanity.

These great advances in science and industry, though, had not been matched by politics and government. The Americans had united their states and, with French help, thrown off the English monarchy and re-invented republican democracy, but nobody yet knew whether it would prove successful. Inspired by their anti-English allies and the corruption of their own monarchy, bowed under big-city social and economic inequality perhaps unseen since the height of Rome, the French were boiling toward their own revolution. Of Paris's population of 600,000, 200,000 were out of work. The vast majority of that nation's taxes were bled from the urban and rural poor while the rich aristocracy, cloistered in Versailles, let them eat cake. In just a few years they would learn the lessons of Rome all over again.

"In the preceding volumes of this History, I have described the triumph of barbarism and religion," wrote Gibbon, "and I can only resume, in a few words, their real or imaginary connection with the ruin of ancient Rome."[1]

"Although memory of it is still fresh," wrote Orosius in the years after the sack, "anyone seeing the numbers of Romans themselves and hearing them talk would think 'nothing had happened,' as even they admit, unless perhaps he noticed some charred remains still standing." He wrote his *Historiarum Adversum Paganos Libri VII* (*Seven Books*

---

[1] *History*, Vol. VI, p. 626

of History Against the Pagans), in Hispania during 416–417 at the urging of St. Augustine of Hippo, to back up the church's position that Christianity had nothing to do with the fall of Rome. He therefore downplayed its horrors, maintaining that compared to catastrophes of the past – the sack by Brennus, the fire under Nero – through God's mercy the city had escaped lightly.

Writing from Hippo Regina in North Africa, to which many Roman refugees like Demetrias and her family had fled, St. Augustine had to take a more personal view. We know many, many women of Rome suffered rape during the sack of 410 because Augustine devoted no fewer than six chapters of Book I of his masterwork, *De Civitate Dei Contra Paganos* (*On the City of God Against the Pagans*), to them. Prior to that, no fathers of the church had given much thought to comforting rape victims, who were viewed as embarrassments to their male kin – soiled, shamed, unfit for marriage, for whom suicide was not only condoned, but encouraged. After August of 410, however, there must have been so many such women of Rome that even the church could not ignore them. In Ravenna, Pope Innocent I does not seem to have been up to the task, but Augustine could not ignore their plight. Employing *consolatio*, a rhetorical technique generally used for comforting exiles or parents who had lost a child, he admitted that during the sack "not just wives and unwed maids, but consecrated virgins were violated as well," but insisted, "...nothing another person does with the body, or to the body, is in any way the fault of the person to whom it is done, so long as that person cannot escape it without sin."* When asked why God allowed such evil to be perpetrated – indeed, why God permitted the destruction of the new capital of Christianity in the first place – he fell back on the technique of priests and prophets from time immemorial: "If you ask why this event was permitted, it is truly a deep circumstance of the Creator and Governor of the world, for 'unsearchable are His judgments, and His ways past finding out.'"[2]

---

*Though in a passage that today sounds coldhearted and outdated, Augustine also insisted to Roman virgins who had been raped during the sack that God had not misjudged them or let them down, but that they might have brought rape upon themselves for having been excessively proud of their virginity.

[2]Romans 11:33

It's doubtful that 5th-century women, much less the rape victims of Rome, took much consolation from *The City of God*, or ever even read it. Augustine, however, is revered as one of the earliest, most important fathers of the Latin church, whose writings influenced the development of Western philosophy and Western Christianity, and *The City of God*, written to console Christians and assure them their religion was not at fault for the sack of Rome, is regarded as one of his most important works. It might be said that through him the sack of Rome was not only a turning point in the political history of the West, but in the history of Christianity as well.

For his part St. Jerome famously wrote from Bethlehem, "As I dictate, my voice breaks and sobs choke my words. The City which had conquered the whole world was itself conquered." But he too absolved God of blame for the sack, putting it squarely on the shoulders of Stilicho: "This humiliation has been inflicted on her not through any fault of her emperors, who are both most pious men, but by the misdeeds of a semi-barbarian traitor [*semibarbari proditoris*] who used our own money to arm our foes against us."

Gibbon felt exactly the opposite. He was later excoriated by Catholics and Protestants alike for putting the fall of the Empire on Christianity, to the extent that he felt it necessary to pen a peevish rebuttal the year after the publication of his last volume. As he saw it, neither Stilicho nor Alaric were to blame. "The deepest wounds were inflicted on the empire during the minorities of the sons and grandsons of Theodosius," he opined, "and, after those incapable princes seemed to attain the age of manhood, they abandoned the church to the bishops, the state to the eunuchs, and the provinces to the barbarians."[1]

"And so the Eastern Empire was saved from the travails of war," wrote Sozomen, "and governed with great organization, despite all predictions, for its emperor was still young. Meanwhile, the Western Empire fell into confusion, because many tyrants rose up."

With the Goths having done their worst to Rome and still in the south mourning their king, the court of Honorius decided the

[1] *History*, Vol. III, p. 636

more pressing situation was in Gaul. There, the upstart emperor Constantine III was under siege in his capital at Arelate (modern Arles) by his own rebel general, Gerontius, and his puppet emperor, Maximus of Hispania. They had already taken Vienne and slain Constantine's son, the *Caesar* Constans II.

As always, Honorius needed a strongman to do his military work. With Stilicho dead, Olympius in exile, and Jovius untrustworthy, the next man up was the general Flavius Constantius, in whom Honorius finally found someone worthy and capable of inheriting the legacy of Stilicho.

First of all, Constantius eliminated his rivals, seeing to it that Olympius was arrested and clubbed to death for his crimes. In 411 he bore the imperial standards over the Alps, and on his arrival Gerontius' troops, being rebels against a rebel, decided they had been fighting for Honorius all along and flocked to his banner. Gerontius and Maximus abandoned the siege and fled for Hispania, where their remaining soldiers turned on them. Gerontius committed suicide. Maximus went into exile among barbarians.*

Far from relieving Constantine, Constantius laid his own siege to Arles. The would-be emperor held out in hopes that his barbarian general Edobichus, who had been holding down northern Gaul for him, would come to his rescue. On arrival, however, Edobichus was swiftly betrayed by friends, ambushed, defeated, and had his head delivered to Constantius. In the power vacuum left behind him along the Rhine, the Burgundians under their king Gundahar, and the Alans under theirs, Goar, raised up yet another usurper, the Gallo-Roman ex-senator Jovinus. His generals dead, his dream of empire lost, Emperor Constantine surrendered to Constantius, though not before taking vows as a priest. It didn't save him. Constantius promised him safe passage, but Honorius still held the deaths of his Spanish cousins against the usurper. Constantine was executed.

In 412 Heraclianus, Stilicho's killer and ruler of North Africa in Honorius' name, having once employed starvation against Alaric's

---

*Some historians believe he is the same Maximus who staged yet another revolt about ten years later, was captured, put on display in Rome and executed on the occasion of Honorius' tricennalia celebration, in January 422.

Rome, decided to use the same strategy against Honorius'. Cutting off the city's grain supply was not as effective as in 410, though, because by then its population had dropped by half. And having now experienced Rome's loss, Ravenna was more inclined to send troops to its defense, probably including the Eastern reinforcements and the Hunnish ex-followers of Uldin. When Heraclianus arrived from Carthage with a fleet said by Orosius to number 3,700 ships to take the city for his own and proclaim himself *Augustus*, he found resistance too stiff for his liking and fled back to Carthage, where for his failure he was taken prisoner by his own men and executed.

This failure of leadership, this constant uproar of rebels and usurpers, would render the Western Empire divided, weakened, and vulnerable to the barbarian hordes swirling around it. As Gibbon put it,

> The victorious legions, who, in distant wars, acquired the vices of strangers and mercenaries, first oppressed the freedom of the republic, and afterwards violated the majesty of the purple. The emperors, anxious for their personal safety and the public peace, were reduced to the base expedient of corrupting the discipline which rendered them alike formidable to their sovereign and to the enemy; the vigor of the military government was relaxed and finally dissolved by the partial institutions of Constantine; and the Roman world was overwhelmed by a deluge of barbarians.[1]

When the Goths recovered from the loss of Alaric, Jordanes wrote, "They bequeathed the kingdom of the Visigoths to his kinsman Athaulf, a man of impressive appearance and great charisma; for though not tall, he was known for his handsome visage and body."

Rather than pursue Alaric's strategy of escaping Italy by sea, and as advised by the ex-emperor Pricus Attalus, Athaulf took advantage of the opportunity created by the Empire's abandonment of Gaul. Pressured by Constantius, who wanted the Goths out of Italy any way they would go, he marched them up the peninsula and over the Alps, intending to strike a bargain with Jovinus and join his barbarian empire of Burgundians and Alans. (Besides Attalus, Athaulf's entourage still

[1] *History*, Vol. III, p. 631

included the imperial half-sister Galla Placidia, who would have lent an air of legitimacy to the new empire.) The union was spoiled, however, by Athaulf's old foe Sarus. After wrecking the peace conference between Honorius and Alaric, he had departed the imperial court under a cloud, reached Gaul first and entered into Jovinus' service. On Athaulf's arrival, the two of them resumed their old blood feud.

Athaulf finally captured Sarus and put him to death. Jovinus took this as an affront to his authority, and when choosing his co-emperor passed Athaulf over in favor of his own brother, Sebastianus. Athaulf, taking offense in turn, sent word to Ravenna offering to overthrow them both in exchange for a peace treaty. Honorius agreed, and Athaulf made good on his offer. Sebastianus' head was sent to Ravenna. Jovinus was besieged in Valentia (modern Valence, France), captured, and executed.

Upon this expression of goodwill, and with Athaulf remaining as last man standing in Gaul, relations between Goths and Romans thawed. In January 414 Athaulf, attired in a Roman toga in a Roman ceremony, with the treasures of Rome as bridal gifts, took Galla Placidia as his wife. She bore him a son, Theodosius, the foundation of a new Romano-Gothic dynasty. As ruler of Gaul in the name of Rome, Athaulf became, almost in spite of himself, what Alaric had always longed to be. In the style of Claudian giving Alaric voice, Orosius put words in Athaulf's mouth:

> At first I wanted to blot out the name of Rome and make all Roman territory part of a Gothic empire. I desired Romania to become Gothia, and for Athaulf to be what Caesar Augustus had been. But bitter experience has taught me that the untamed savagery of the Goths will never obey laws, and that without laws there is no state. So I have more wisely chosen a different destiny, of infusing the Roman name with Gothic vigor, and I hope to be remembered by posterity as undertaking the restoration of Rome, since I found it impossible to change this Empire into another.

It was not to be. The Romans could not be satisfied to have barbarians as their equals. Constantius, feeling that Gaul was rightfully his, coaxed permission from Honorius to blockade its Mediterranean ports, cutting the province off behind the wall of the Alps. In response, Athaulf renamed Priscus Attalus as his emperor, but was forced to withdraw into northern Hispania. Attalus was captured by Constantius and banished. The infant Theodosius died and was buried in a silver-plated coffin (later exhumed and reinterred in Rome).

And Athaulf could not escape the curse of barbarism. Five years after the fall of Rome, the king of the Goths was stabbed to death by a follower of Sarus, whose brother Sigeric was proclaimed by the Amali faction as his successor. Sigeric ruled for one week, in which he killed every one of Athaulf's six children by his first wife and forced his queen Galla into a twelve-mile march of shame before his horse, along with the rest of his captives. At the end of the week, however, Sigeric was himself assassinated and replaced by Wallia, a relative of Athaulf's, who as a peace overture sent Galla back to Honorius. The grateful but vacillating emperor granted the Goths' wish for a homeland: Aquitaine, where they would reside for the rest of the century just as Alaric always wished – as Roman *foederati*, battling the Vandals and Alans in Spain and even joining the Roman general Flavius Aetius to finally defeat Attila's Huns at the Battle of the Catalaunian Plains in 451. For many years their kingdom, comprising southern France and most of Spain, would be the strongest in Western Europe.

Yet however much the Goths aspired to be Roman, they were still regarded as barbarians, even by conquered Romans, whose utter overturn in fortunes was lamented by the Christian monk Salvianus, writing from Gaul in the mid-6th century:

> Where now are the ancient wealth and valor of Rome? In old days the Romans were the mightiest of men, now they are weak. Then they were feared, but now live in fear. Barbarous nations paid them tribute, but these same nations now demand their tribute... The barbarians use us like masters who hire out extra slaves for pay. In this way, we are never free of having to pay. We pay tribute constantly, for the privilege of constantly paying.

No one in Rome or Ravenna gave any further thought to the provinces. They didn't have time. The utter fecklessness and duplicity among the Roman aristocracy that led up to the sack of 410 only accelerated in its aftermath, in a dizzying succession of usurpations and betrayals. To start, in 417, as a reward for services rendered, Honorius married

Constantius to Galla, against her wishes. She bore him a daughter, Justa Grata Honoria, and a son, Placidus Valentinianus. Constantius' star was on the rise. He had been named consul in 414, again in 417 and 420, and in 421 became co-emperor alongside Honorius, but reigned for just seven months before dying in Ravenna. Two years later Honorius, the feeblest of all the many emperors to rise and fall during his reign and the one most responsible for the fall of Rome, also died. The Roman Empire devolved to Galla, who now reaped the reward for years of serving husbands not of her choice. She ruled as regent for her son, Emperor Valentinian III, through the turbulent years of the dying Empire until finally passing away, still empress, in 450.

Meanwhile, under Gothic pressure, the Vandals, Stilicho's father's people, departed Hispania in 429 and set up their own kingdom in North Africa. While Rome and Constantinople were preoccupied with the Huns, the Vandals proceeded to dominate the western Mediterranean, taking Sicily, Corsica, Sardinia, and the Balearics. (St. Augustine died in AD 430 during a Vandal siege of Hippo Regius.)

In 442 the Vandal king Genseric and Valentinian III struck a peace treaty, betrothing Genseric's son Huneric to Valentinian's daughter Eudocia. As she was only five years old, marriage had to wait, and it was during this fateful interim that a wealthy senator and aristocrat, Petronius Maximus, rose to power. After Valentinian seduced, or raped, Maximus' wife, Maximus – grandson of Anicia Faltonia Proba, cousin of Demetrias – laid his own path to power. He convinced Valentinian that his general Aetius planned to assassinate him, on which Valentinian struck first, personally killing Aetius. Maximus then incited two of Valentinian's, formerly Aetius', *bucellari*, barbarian bodyguards, to avenge their commander by assassinating their emperor. When the dust settled Maximus had bribed his fellow senators and palace officials to accept him as emperor, and forced Valentinian's widow, Empress Licinia Eudoxia, to marry him.* Furthermore, he broke off the betrothal of Eudoxia's daughter to Huneric in favor of his own son, Palladius.

Empress Eudoxia, however, was a daughter of Theodosius II, first cousin once removed of her husband Valentinian, and an old hand at palace games. She took the family's frequent disregard for imperial

---

* Maximus' first wife, if seduced, was cast aside; if raped – and presumably having never read Augustine – also presumably took her own life. Either way, she made no further role in history.

duty to a whole new level. Maximus having broken the old treaty with Ginseric, the empress took advantage of the Vandal's ire by actually *inviting him and his barbarians to come conquer Rome*.

The resulting Vandal sack in AD 455 lasted two weeks and left, if nothing else, the tribe's name as a synonym for acts of wanton destruction, and if it did not totally destroy the city, it did what Alaric's sack had not: it finished off the Western Empire. After the Vandals left, the rest of the barbarians moved in. Goths, Gauls, and Burgundians either picked or backed a succession of battling puppet rulers, until finally in 476 the barbarian Flavius Odoacer deposed the child emperor Romulus Augustulus and named himself King of Italy, making his capital at Ravenna.

As for Rome, by this time its population had fallen to under 100,000 – a tenth of its heyday – the denizens wandering deserted temples and baths and tearing down its monuments and stone buildings to build their own shabby homes, shops, and churches. Eventually the city would dwindle to the *abitato*, a village not much larger or better than its tribal origins under Romulus, tucked in the bend of the Tiber amid the ancient ruins. Cattle, sheep, and goats would graze the grass growing up through the cracked and desolate cobblestone streets, and the Forum of Rome would be renamed the Campo Vaccino, the Cow Pasture.

Zosimus, reporting on these events from Constantinople, wrote, "In this way, the Roman Empire, having been devastated bit by bit, has become the abode of barbarians, or rather having lost all its people, is reduced to such a state that no person can tell where its cities once stood."

In the centuries since the fall of Rome, and particularly after Gibbon, historians have assigned a myriad of causes for the catastrophe, everything from its slave economy and constant civil wars to epidemic plagues, general corruption, and immorality, right down to lead in the pipes. Some of this is overwrought thinking, when the direct cause of the fall of Rome is, of course, obvious: the invasion of the city by a barbarian horde. For those seeking a comparison to modern times, it might be more productive to simply examine how and why the Goths succeeded when the barbarians who came before them failed.

In part this can surely be put down to the sheer ineptitude of the Roman elite, from the rubber-stamp Senate and selfish, power-grabbing aristocracy to Emperor Honorius, none of whom particularly served or cared for the common people...but also to the man who did more than anyone to ward off Rome's fall: Stilicho himself.

After Theodosius' death Stilicho became the father that Honorius had lost. He and Serena raised the boy as their own, but crucially did not raise him to rule. They raised him in order for Stilicho to rule *through* him – malleable, suggestible. Incompetent. And the moment Stilicho's back was turned, that suggestibility and incompetency was used against him, to his fatal detriment and that of the Western Empire. With little choice, Stilicho carried on Theodosius' policy of filling the ranks of the Roman army with barbarian soldiers. In the end it was not a Roman army, but a barbarian army. Most *foederati* had little actual loyalty to the Empire. When provoked, and with their general removed, they easily turned against it.

As for Alaric, he can hardly be blamed for the sack. As has been seen, he went out of his way to avoid it. He had always aspired to be civilized, to be Roman. What he perhaps didn't realize, however, was that the Romans were just another breed of barbarian, a people we today would hardly call civilized. Yes, they were technically advanced – great engineers, and their arts and architecture still inspire – but socially still savage, as evidenced by too many facets of their culture. Slavery. Ill treatment of women. Gladiatorial death games. Imaginative, bloody public tortures and executions of prisoners. Religious prosecutions and sectarian violence, unabated under Christianity, even between various sects of the same faith. And above all, the lawless, chaotic, often violent transfer of power from one ruler to another. Look at the number of emperors or would-be emperors the Romans went through just in Alaric's day: Valens, Gratian, Magnus Maximus and his son Flavius Victor; Eugenius; Theodosius, Honorius, Arcadius and Theodosius II; Marcus and the second Gratian; Constantine and his son Constans; Maximus of Hispania and Jovinus. And that's not counting powers behind the throne like Rufinus, Eutropius, Arbogastes, Gainas, Anthemius, Olympius, Gerontius, and, yes, Stilicho. All of them struggling as much against each other as against the Goths, who played the factions to their advantage.

Most of this time Alaric, and Alaric alone, led the Goths, who within their own boundaries were by comparison a peaceful people, seeking no wars that were not forced on them. Who then, the Romans or Goths, were as a people less barbaric, more civilized? It's not hard to see why, under Valens, Theodosius, and Honorius, the barbarians were practically invited in, and later, under Licinia Eudoxia, *literally* invited in. The Romans – East and West, Christian and pagan – were a people divided against themselves, no more civilized than the barbarians outside the walls.

Rome had been dealing with foreigners for centuries, either fending them off or admitting and integrating them: Italians, Gauls, Celts, Britons, even many of the Germanic tribes. Rome's failure to either conquer or integrate the Goths – to make them Roman, even though that was their most ardent wish – and instead alienating them, left the Empire with what amounted to a hostile nation within its own borders. Immigration wasn't the issue then, and though much noise is made about it, immigration is not the issue today, another era of great migrations. The crux of the matter is *assimilation*. Assimilation of outsiders – even homegrown outsiders – benefits a host culture, just as it did Rome in the golden age of the *Pax Romana*. Without assimilation, though, as with the Goths after Adrianople, newcomers are simply invaders.

Odd that in attempting to explain, or excuse, the fall of Rome, neither Augustine, Jerome, Orosius, nor Pelagius thought to quote their messiah, as in the gospel of Luke: "Every kingdom divided against itself is brought to desolation; and a house divided against a house falls." Gibbon, the enlightened anti-religionist, might be excused for not quoting the Bible, but his contemporaries knew the sentiment well enough. In March 1799, only a few years after Gibbon's death, the American Patrick Henry – one of the revolutionary firebrands who caused the sundering of the British Empire – knew it from personal experience, as a fact applicable not only to his newly united states but to all societies down through history. He said as much, in his last public words before his own passing, speaking of his America but in terms equally applicable to all humanity: "United we stand, divided we fall. Let us not split into factions which must destroy that union upon which our existence hangs."

Not even Gibbon – or for that matter, Claudian – could have said it any better.

SOURCES

Ammianus Marcellinus, Roman soldier and historian, wrote one of the last major surviving histories of Rome, the *Rerum Gestarum Libri XXXI* (*Thirty-One Books of Achievements*), usually called the *Res Gestae*. The first thirteen books, chronicling the history of Rome from the accession of the emperor Nerva in AD 96, have been lost. The surviving eighteen books cover the period from AD 353 to the death of Valens at the Battle of Adrianople in 378.

St. **Augustine** was named bishop of Hippo Regius in Numidia, Roman North Africa in AD 395 until 430. His book, *De Civitate Dei Contra Paganos* (*The City of God Against the Pagans*), was written just after the sack of Rome, not so much as a declaration against the Goths but to assure Christians that their faith was not the cause of the catastrophe.

The 18th-century English Roman Catholic priest and hagiographer Alban **Butler** spent thirty years compiling *The Lives of the Fathers, Martyrs and Other Principal Saints*, four volumes first published in London, 1756–1759.

Claudius Claudianus, called simply **Claudian**, was an Alexandrian poet who composed for the court of Honorius and particularly for the general Stilicho, for whom he served almost as a propagandist and press agent.

Athenian teacher and rhetorician **Eunapius** was born around AD 350 and seems to have lived into the reign of Theodosius II. His *Universal History* cuts off at the year 404 and is in large part lost, but Zosimus (see below) relied heavily on it and recounts much of it almost verbatim.

Renatus Profuturus **Frigeridus** was a 5th-century historian of whom little is known, and whose work survives only in fragments, mostly as transcribed by Gregory, the 6th-century Gallo-Roman bishop of Tours.

The *Gallic Chronicle of 452* (*Chronica Gallica A. CCCCLII*) is the oldest preserved historical work from Gaul. A series of annals in Latin, it covers the years from 379 when Theodosius I was named as co-emperor, to Attila's invasion of Italy in 452. Its focus is on Gaul, the Western emperors and popes, with little remark on events in the East.

The 6th-century British monk **Gildas** Sapiens, Gildas the Wise, was best known for his *De Excidio et Conquestu Britanniae* (*On the Ruin and Conquest of Britain*), which is the only contemporary account of the Britons from the Roman conquest to that of the Anglo-Saxons.

Eusebius Sophronius Hieronymus, better known as St. **Jerome** of Stridon, was born about the mid-340s and was a late convert to Christianity. In his youth he was quite the ladies' man, and even in later years got on better with women than with men, supported as he was by a number of Roman matrons. He left Rome in 385 and commented on its fall from Bethlehem, in the very cave where Christ was said to have been born. He viewed the sack as God's punishment for the Romans' libertine ways.

Jordanes, sometimes called Jordanis or Jornandes, was a 6th-century Byzantine bureaucrat and historian, thought to be of Gothic ancestry. His *De origine actibusque Getarum* (*The Origin and Deeds of the Goths*), commonly abbreviated *Getica*, written around AD 551, is said to be an abridgment of the lost *Gothici Historia* by Magnus Aurelius Cassiodorus Senator, a Roman statesman, scholar, and writer in the court of Theodoric the Great, king of the Ostrogoths. As Cassiodorus' work is lost, the *Getica* remains the only contemporaneous account of the origin and history of the Goths, even though some historians regard it as fanciful or Gothic propaganda.

Titus Livius, known as **Livy**, was a Roman historian of the 1st centuries BC and AD. His monumental history of Rome and the Romans, *Ab Urbe Condita* (*From the Founding of the City*), comprised the earliest legends of the foundation of Rome to the reign of *Caesar* Augustus, to whom he was a personal friend.

Olympiodorus of Thebes was an early 5th-century Roman diplomat, poet, and historian. His twenty-two-volume history of the Western Roman Empire 407–425, since lost but quoted by other writers of the day, was written in Greek for Emperor Theodosius II.

Paulus **Orosius**, probably born in what is now Portugal around AD 380, was a theologian, priest, and historian, a student of and collaborator with Augustine of Hippo. His *Seven Books of History Against the Pagans* was of great influence on later historians, both for its coverage and for Orosius' methodology.

Philostorgius was a church historian in Constantinople during the 4th and 5th centuries, of whom little else is known. His twelve-volume account of the Arian controversy, *Ekklisiastikí Istoría* (*Church History*) appeared in the late 420s and was subsequently lost. The 9th-century historian Photius found a library copy and wrote an epitome of it, which survived.

Procopius of Caesarea, a 6th-century Byzantine historian, often considered the last major historian of Western antiquity, had personal experience with latter-day Goths. He was a lawyer for Belisarius, the Byzantine general who attempted to reclaim the Roman West from the Ostrogothic Kingdom, endured the year-long Gothic siege of Rome in 537–538, and in 540 rode with Belisarius' army into Ravenna, then the Gothic capital.

Prosper of Aquitaine was a refugee of the Gothic invasion of that province, a disciple and defender of St. Augustine. He was a layman, and his *Epitoma chronicon* (*Chronological Summary*) cribbed from Jerome and others, but also drew from Prosper's own experience.

352

Socrates Scholasticus, also called Socrates of Constantinople, lived in that city circa 380–440. His *Historia Ecclesiastica* is, as the name implies, primarily a history of the church, but covers political and military subjects when relevant. He was a Christian, tolerant of all creeds including Arianism.

Sozomen (full name Salminius Hermias Sozomenus) was a lawyer and historian born in Palestine around AD 400. He based his *Ecclesiastical History* largely on that of Socrates Scholasticus and Olympiodorus of Thebes.

Synesius of Cyrene, born in modern-day Libya, was an envoy to the imperial court in Constantinople around the turn of the 5th century. To Emperor Arcadius he composed and read a speech, *De regno* (*The Kingdom*) on the essentials of wise rule, but also warning that the first priority must be against corruption and the assimilation of barbarians into the Roman army.

Publius (perhaps Gaius) Cornelius **Tacitus** was a Roman senator and historian at the turn of the first millennium. Among his many other works, *De Origine et Situ Germanorum* (*On the Origin and Situation of the Germanics*), written around AD 98, describes the lands and customs of the Germanic peoples, from those nearest the Roman frontier to those on the far shores of the Baltic.

Themistius, called *Euphrades*, The Eloquent, was a senator and prefect of Constantinople. He wrote thirty-six orations, thirty-three of which survive, although some are not totally intact. He was known for supporting the policies of Theodosius the Great toward the Goths and helping to sell it to his fellow politicians.

Bishop **Theodoret** of Cyrus in Syria wrote *The Ecclesiastical History* about 449–450 as a polemic against Arianism, which he considered heretical and the cause of the Roman defeat at Adrianople.

Publius Flavius Vegetius Renatus, usually called **Vegetius,** was a late 4th-century writer of whom almost nothing is known, other than that he was a Christian. His treatise *Epitoma rei militaris* or *De re militari* (*Concerning Military Matters*), served as a military manual through the Middle Ages right into the 19th century.

Greek historian **Zosimus** Historicus, "Zosimus the Historian," lived in Constantinople around the turn of the 6th century and was said be an officer of the imperial treasury. His *New History* draws almost totally on Eunapius up to the year 404, and after 407 on Olympiodorus, even adopting their differing views of Stilicho.

BIBLIOGRAPHY

Atanasov, Georgi. "The Portrait of Flavius Aetius (390–454) from Durostorum (Silistra) Inscribed on a Consular Diptych From Monza. In Studia Academia Šumenensis, 1, 2014." Academia.edu, University of Shumen Press, 2014. www.academia.edu/8782362.

Atkinson, Kenneth. *Empress Galla Placidia and the Fall of the Roman Empire.* Jefferson, North Carolina: McFarland & Company, Inc., Publishers, 2020.

Barnes, T. D. "The Victims of Rufinus." *Classical Quarterly* 34, no. 1 (1984): 227–230. www.jstor.org/stable/638352.

Blockley, Roger C. "The Division of Armenia between the Romans and the Persians at the End of the Fourth Century A.D." *Historia: Zeitschrift Für Alte Geschichte* 36, no. 2 (1987): 222–234. www.jstor.org/stable/4436006.

Blockley, Roger C. *The Fragmentary Classicising Historians of the Later Roman Empire. Eunapius, Olympiodorus, Priscus and Malchus.* Cambridge: Cairns, 2007.

Boin, Douglas. *Alaric the Goth: An Outsider's History of the Fall of Rome.* United States: W. W. Norton, 2020.

Boin, Douglas. "An Ancient Roman Lesson in the Power of Welcoming Immigrants." *Time*, June 9, 2020. https://time.com/5850622/rome-immigrants/.

Bradley, Henry. *The Goths: From the Earliest Times to the End of the Gothic Dominion in Spain.* United Kingdom: T. Fisher Unwin, 1890.

Brooks, Deanna. "Prosper's Chronicle: A Critical Edition and Translation of the Edition of 445." University of Ottawa, 2014. https://boudicca.de/blog/wp-content/uploads/2020/06/Deanna.pdf.

Brown, Michael. "Prudentius' *Contra Symmachum*, Book II: Introduction, Translation and Commentary." Newcastle University, 2003. https://theses.ncl.ac.uk/jspui/bitstream/10443/1010/1/Brown%2003.pdf.

Burns, Thomas. *Barbarians Within the Gates of Rome: A Study of Roman Military Policy and the Barbarians, Ca. 375–425 A.D.* Bloomington, IN: Indiana University Press, 1994.

Cameron, Alan. "Theodosius the Great and the Regency of Stilico." *Harvard Studies in Classical Philology* 73 (1969): 247. www.academia.edu/25506845/Theodosius_the_Great_and_the_Regency_of_Stilic.

Cameron, Alan. "A Note on Ivory Carving in Fourth Century Constantinople." *American Journal of Archaeology* 86, no. 1 (1982): 126–129. doi:10.2307/504301.

Cameron, Alan. "The Date and the Owners of the Esquiline Treasure." *American Journal of Archaeology* 89, no. 1, Centennial Issue (Jan., 1985): 135–145. https://www.jstor.org/stable/504776.

Cameron, Alan. *The Last Pagans of Rome*. United States: Oxford University Press, USA, 2010.

Cameron, Alan, and Jacqueline Long. *Barbarians and Politics at the Court of Arcadius*. Berkeley: University of California Press, 1993. http://ark.cdlib.org/ark:/13030/ft729007zj/.

Cancella, Michael. "Meet the New Boss: Stilicho, the Rise of the Magister Utriusque Militiae and the Path to Irrelevancy of the Position of Western Emperor." Columbia University, 2010. https://academiccommons.columbia.edu/doi/10.7916/D8HD82MR.

Claudianus, Claudius. *Claudian. Vol. I*. United States: Harvard University Press, 1922. http://penelope.uchicago.edu/Thayer/E/Roman/Texts/Claudian/home.html.

Collins, Derek. "Mapping the Entrails: The Practice of Greek Hepatoscopy." *American Journal of Philology* 129, no. 3 (2008): 319–345. https://www.jstor.org/stable/27566714.

Crawford, Peter. "The Battle of Frigidus River." The Ancient World. Academia.edu, 2012. www.academia.edu/6458613/_The_Battle_of_Frigidus_River.

Diodorus Siculus. "The Historical Library of Diodorus the Sicilian/Book XIV/Chapter XIII." Wikisource. https://en.wikisource.org/w/index.php?title=The_Historical_Library_of_Diodorus_the_Sicilian/Book_XIV/Chapter_XIII.

Doležal, Stanislav. "Rethinking a Massacre: What Really Happened in Thessalonica and Milan in 390?" *Eirene: Studia Graeca et Latina* 50. (2014): 89–107. www.researchgate.net/publication/291928066_Rethinking_a_massacre_What_really_happened_in_Thessalonica_and_Milan_in_390.

Elsner, Jas. "Visualising Women in Late Antique Rome: The Projecta Casket." In C. Entwhistle (ed.), *Through a Glass Brightly: Studies in Byzantine and Medieval Art and Archaeology*, Presented to David Buckton. Oxford: Oxbow, 2003, 22–36. www.academia.edu/6686976/_Visualising_Women_in_Late_Antique_Rome_The_Projecta_Casket_in_C_Entwhistle_ed_Through_a_Glass_Brightly_Festschrift_for_David_Buckton_Oxford_Oxbow_2003_22_36

Elton, Hugh. "Fravitta and Barbarian Career Opportunities in Constantinople." *Medieval Prosopography* 17, no. 1 (1996): 95–106. www.jstor.org/stable/44946209.

Fields, Nic. *Hadrian's Wall AD 122–410*. Oxford: Osprey Publishing, 2003.

Forsman, Deanna. "Becoming Barbarian: An Examination of Stilicho in Fifth-Century Latin Sources." Academia.edu, 2020. www.academia.edu/22442248 /Becoming_Barbarian_An_Examination_of_Stilicho_in_Fifth-Century_Latin _Sources.

Gibbon, Edward. *The Autobiography and Correspondence of Edward Gibbon, the Historian*. London: Alex Murray & Son, 1869.

Gibbon, Edward. *The History of the Decline and Fall of the Roman Empire*. Vol. I. London: W. Strahan, 1776. https://archive.org/details/historyofdeclin e01gibb_0.

Gibbon, Edward. *The History of the Decline and Fall of the Roman Empire*. Vol. II. London: W. Strahan, 1781. https://archive.org/details/historyofdeclin e02gibb_0.

Gibbon, Edward. *The History of the Decline and Fall of the Roman Empire*. Vol. III. London: W. Strahan, 1781. https://archive.org/details/historyofdeclin e03gibb_0.

Gibbon, Edward. *The History of the Decline and Fall of the Roman Empire*. Vol. IV. London: W. Strahan, 1788. https://archive.org/details/historyofdeclin e04gibb_0.

Gibbon, Edward. *The History of the Decline and Fall of the Roman Empire*. Vol. V. London: W. Strahan, 1788. https://archive.org/details/historyofdeclin e05gibb_0.

Gibbon, Edward. *The History of the Decline and Fall of the Roman Empire*. Vol. VI. London: W. Strahan, 1788. https://archive.org/details/historyofdeclin e06gibb_0.

Gordon, Arthur Ernest. *Illustrated Introduction to Latin Epigraphy*. Berkeley: University of California Press, 1983.

Greatrex, Geoffrey B. "The Background and Aftermath of the Partition of Armenia in A.D. 387." *Ancient History Bulletin* 14, 2000. Partition of Armenia 387, Dalhousie University, 2020. aix1.uottawa.ca/~greatrex/arme nia.html#b49.

Greatrex, G., and M. Greatrex. "The Hunnic Invasion of the East of 395 and the Fortress of Ziatha." Byzantion 69, no. 1 (1999): 65–75. www.jstor.org/ stable/44172154.

Heather, Peter. "The Huns and the End of the Roman Empire in Western Europe." *Oxford Academic Journals*, English Historical Review, Feb. 1995.

Heather, Peter J. *The Fall of the Roman Empire: A New History of Rome and Barbarians*. New York: Oxford University Press, 2006.

Hodgkin, Thomas. *Italy and Her Invaders, Vol. 1: The Visigothic Invasions*. Kiribati: Clarendon Press, 1880. http://penelope.uchicago.edu/ Thayer/E/Gazetteer/Places/Europe/Italy/_Texts/HODIHI/2d_edition/1/.

Kalas, Gregor. "Writing and Restoration in Rome: Inscriptions, Statues and the Late Antique Preservation of Buildings." In Goodson, C., Lester, A. E., and

Symes, C. (eds). *Cities, Texts, and Social Networks 400–1500*. Burlington: Ashgate, 2010, pp. 21–43.

Karlsson, Jonas. "The First Chapter of the Historia Monachorum in Ægypto." Uppsala University Publications, 2013. www.uu.diva-portal.org/smash/get/ diva2:929186/FULLTEXT01.pdf.

Kulikowski, Michael. *Rome's Gothic Wars: From the Third Century to Alaric (Key Conflicts of Classical Antiquity)*. Cambridge, United Kingdom: Cambridge University Press, 2006. https://erenow.net/ww/romes-gothic-wars -from-the-third-century-to-alaric/.

Lawrence, Thomas Christopher. "Crisis of Legitimacy: Honorius, Galla Placidia, and the Struggles for Control of the Western Roman Empire, 405– 425 C.E." University of Tennessee, Knoxville, 2013. https://trace.tennessee .edu/cgi/viewcontent.cgi?referer=https://www.google.com/&httpsredir =1&article=2780&context=utk_graddiss.

Livius, Titus. *The History of Rome, Vol. 1*. Edited by Ernest Rhys. Translated by Rev. Canon Roberts, *Livy's History of Rome*. London: J. M. Dent & Sons, Ltd., 1905. http://mcadams.posc.mu.edu/txt/ah/Livy/Livy05.html.

MacDowall, Simon. *Late Roman Infantrymen 236–565 A.D*. Oxford: Osprey Publishing, 1994.

MacDowall, Simon. *Adrianople* AD *378: the Goths Crush Rome's Legions*. Oxford: Osprey Military, 2007.

Marcellinus, Ammianus. *The Roman History of Ammianus Marcellinus: During the Reigns of the Emperors Constantius, Julian, Jovianus, Valentinian, and Valens*. London: G. Bell & Sons, 1911. www.gutenberg.org /files/28587/28587-h/28587-h.htm.

Martin, Gunther and Jana Grusková. "'Scythica Vindobonensia' by Dexippus(?): New Fragments on Decius' Gothic Wars." Greek, Roman, and Byzantine Studies. https://grbs.library.duke.edu/article/view/15071/6581.

Mathisen, Ralph. "Peregrini, Barbari, and Cives Romani: Concepts of Citizenship and the Legal Identity of Barbarians in the Later Roman Empire." *American Historical Review* 111, (2006): 1011–1040. www .researchgate.net/publication/249218257_Peregrini_Barbari_and_Cives _Romani_Concepts_of_Citizenship_and_the_Legal_Identity_of_Barbarians _in_the_Later_Roman_Empire.

Maurice, Emperor. *Maurice's Strategikon: Handbook of Byzantine Military Strategy*. Philadelphia: University of Pennsylvania Press, Incorporated, 2001.

McLynn, Neil B. *Ambrose of Milan: Church and Court in a Christian Capital*. Berkeley, CA: University of California Press, 1994.

Mierow, Charles Christopher, and Jordanes. *The Origin and Deeds of the Goths*. United States: Princeton University Press, 1908.

Miller, M. "Stilicho's Pictish War." *Britannia* 6 (1975): 141–145. JSTOR. www.jstor.org/stable/525995.

357

Nguyen, Nghiem L. "Roman Rape: An Overview of Roman Rape Laws from the Republican Period to Justinian's Reign." *Michigan Journal of Gender & Law* 13, 1 (2006). https://repository.law.umich.edu/mjgl/vol13/iss1/3

Orosius. *The Seven Books of History Against the Pagans*. Translated by Roy DeFerrari, Internet Archive, The Catholic University of America Press, Inc., 1964. https://archive.org/details/thesevenbooksofhistoryagainstthepagans.

Paulinus (Deacon). "On the Life of St. Ambrose, Bishop of Milan." http://www.stseraphimstjohnsandiego.org/St._Seraphim_of_Sarov_and_St._John_of_Kronstadt_Orthodox_Church/LIVES_OF_SAINTS/Entries/2017/7/15_Paulinus_(Deacon)__On_the_Life_of_St._Ambrose%2C_Bishop_of_Milan.html.

Philostorgius. *Epitome of the Ecclesiastical History of Philostorgius, compiled by Photius, Patriarch of Constantinople*. Translated by Edward Walford. London: Henry G. Bohn, York Street, Covent Garden, 1855. http://www.tertullian.org/fathers/philostorgius.htm.

Plutarch. "The Life of Camillus." *The Parallel Lives. Vol. II*. Loeb Classical Library, 1914. http://penelope.uchicago.edu/Thayer/E/Roman/Texts/Plutarch/Lives/Camillus*.html.

Polybius. *The Histories. Book II*. Loeb Classical Library, Vol. I, 1922–1927. http://penelope.uchicago.edu/Thayer/E/Roman/Texts/Polybius/2*.html.

Procopius. "History of the Wars/Book III." Wikisource, the Free Online Library. en.m.wikisource.org/wiki/History_of_the_Wars/Book_III.

Procopius. *History of the Wars, Books V And VI: The Gothic War*. Translated by H. B. Dewing. London: William Heinemann Ltd., 1919. https://www.gutenberg.org/files/20298/20298-h/20298-h.htm.

Ridley, Ronald T. "The Finding of the Esquiline Silver Treasure: An Unpublished Letter." *The Antiquaries Journal* 76 (1996): 215–222. doi:10.1017/S000358150004748X. www.cambridge.org/core/journals/antiquaries-journal/article/finding-of-the-esquiline-silver-treasure-an-unpublished-letter/C8F738F14A87BB279DBC80E325DDBAC4.

Roberts, Mike. *Rome's Third Samnite War, 298–290 bc: The Last Stand of the Linen Legion*. United Kingdom: Pen and Sword Military, 2020.

Shelton, Kathleen J. "The Esquiline Treasure: The Nature of the Evidence." *American Journal of Archaeology* 89, no. 1, Centennial Issue (Jan., 1985): 147–155. https://www.jstor.org/stable/504777.

Sideris, Georges. "The Rise and Fall of the High Chamberlain Eutropius: Eunuch Identity, the Third Sex and Power in Fourth-Century Byzantium." In Fletcher, C., Bradt, S., Moss, R. E., and Riall, L. (eds). *The Palgrave Handbook of Masculinity and Political Culture in Europe*. London: Palgrave Macmillan, 2018, pp. 63–84. https://23021200.blogspot.com/2019/04/georges-sideris.html

St. Gregory of Nazianzen. "Funeral Orations by St. Gregory Nazianzen and St. Ambrose." *The Fathers of the Church: A New Translation.* Volume 22: Translated by Leo McCauley et al., Internet Archive, Fathers of the Church, Inc., Jan. 1, 1970. archive.org/details/fathersofthechur012812mbp.

St. Jerome. *Church Fathers: Letters of St. Jerome.* New Advent, 2020. www .newadvent.org/fathers/3001.htm.

Szekely, Melinda. "Theodosius and the Goths." Semanticscholar.org. Semantic Scholar, 2020, https://pdfs.semanticscholar.org/d667/1eeb505be299c9222cd 54a5cf161ec150b90.pdf.

"The Stanford Geospatial Network Model of the Roman World." ORBIS. http://orbis.stanford.edu/.

Theodoret of Cyrus. *Ecclesiastical History.* Edited by D. P. Curtin. Translated by Blomfield Jackson. Amazon Digital Services LLC, 2019.

Vegetius. *The Military Institutions of the Romans (De Re Militari).* Digital Attic, 2001. http://www.digitalattic.org/home/war/vegetius/.

"The Visigothic Code." Edited by S. P. Scott, Documenta Catholica Omnia, The Library of Iberian Resources Online, July 202 AD, http://www.documentaca tholicaomnia.eu/03d/0506-0506,_AA_VV,_Leges_Romanae_Visigotorum_ %5bScott_JP_Curatore%5d,_EN.pdf.

Vasiliev, A. A. "Imperial Porphyry Sarcophagi in Constantinople." Dumbarton Oaks Papers 4 (1948): 1–26. Accessed October 8, 2020. doi:10.2307/1291047.

Ward, Roy Bowen. "Women in Roman Baths." *Harvard Theological Review* 85, no. 2 (1992): 125–147. http://www.jstor.org/stable/1509900.

Ward-Perkins, Bryan. *The Fall of Rome and the End of Civilization.* New York: Oxford University Press, 2006.

Wasdin, Katherine. "Honorius Triumphant: Poetry and Politics in Claudian's Wedding Poems." *Classical Philology* 109, no. 1 (2014): 48–65. www.jstor .org/stable/10.1086/673850.

Wijnendaele, Jeroen W. P. "The Career and 'Revolt' of Gildo." Ghent University Academic Bibliography, Ghent University, 2020. biblio.ugent.be/publication /8511675/file/8551049.pdf.

Wijnendaele, Jeroen W. P. "Stilicho, Radagaisus, and the So-Called 'Battle of Faesulae' (406 CE)." *Journal of Late Antiquity* 9.1 (Spring): Johns Hopkins University Press. core.ac.uk/download/pdf/91281213.pdf.

Wyeth, William. "Tribigild in Phrygia: Reconsidering the Revolt and the Settlement of Barbarians in the 4th Century Roman Empire." Academia.edu. www.academia.edu/1907235/Tribigild_in_Phrygia_Reconsidering_the_revolt _and_the_settlement_of_barbarians_in_the_4th_century_Roman_Empire.

Zosimus the Historian. *The History of Count Zosimus … Translated from the Original Greek, with the Notes of the Oxford Edition.* (A Comparative View of Ancient and of Modern Geography.) United Kingdom: J. Davis, 1814. www.livius.org/sources/content/zosimus.

INDEX

assimilation 40–41, 43, 68, 350
Asterius, Turcius Rufius Apronianus 323
Athanaric 67
Athaulf 196, 285, 286, 298–99, 306
 and Galla Placidia 328
 and Gaul 344–46
Athens 151–52
Attalus, Priscus 297–98, 306–11, 346
Attila 130, 170
Augusta Treverorum 79
Augustine of Hippo, St. 33, 85, 107–8, 112, 231, 317
 De Civitate Dei Contra Paganos (On the City of God Against the Pagans) 341–42
 and Rome 292, 326–27
Augustulus, Romulus 348
Aurelian Walls 214, 290
Aurelianus 182
Aurora 179–80
Ausonius, Decimius 116
auxiliaries 44, 45, 48, 50–53, 54
Aventine Hill 325

bacaudae (freebooters) 244
Bacurius Hiberus 46, 52, 56, 61, 100–1
 and Frigidus 104, 105
banditry 89, 90–93
barbarians 22, 23, 25, 279–80, 340, 349–50
 and decimation 257
 and Jerome 238–39
 see also Alemanni; Franks; Gauls; Goths; Huns; Vandals
Basilica of St. Peter (Rome) 247, 326–27
Bathanarius 175, 276
Baths of Diocletian 320
Bauto, Flavius 66, 74, 82
Belgians 72
Belisarius 313
Bellona 178
Berbers 160; see also Mascezel

Berengar I of Italy, King 144–45
Boeotia 150–51
Bononia 241, 256–57, 259–60, 265–66
Brennus 25, 28, 29, 32, 33–34
Britannia 39, 40, 61, 175–76, 277–78, 302–3
 and mutiny 237–38, 240–41
 and Stilicho 147–48
 see also Wales
Burgundians 343
Butheric 86–87, 88
Butler, Alban 110
Byzantine Empire 144, 226

Caesar (co-emperors) 60–61
Caesar, Julius 39–40, 41, 206, 233–34
Caledonia 175
Camillus, Marcus Furius 27, 31–32, 33, 34, 35
Cannae 56, 289
Capitoline Hill 30–32, 269, 271, 288, 293, 324
Caracalla, Emperor 41
Carolingian Empire 144–45
Carthage 159, 160, 203, 276
Cassiodorus, Magnus Aurelius 49
Cassius Dio, Lucius 153
Catherine the Great, Empress 17
cavalry 44, 48, 49, 50, 52–53, 54–55
 and training 75
Celts 26, 29, 40, 65, 230, 238
Chapel of St. Petronilla (Rome) 248
charioteers 86, 87
Charlemagne, Holy Roman Emperor 144
Charles III of Spain, King 17–18
Charles V, Holy Roman Emperor 247
Christian VII of Denmark-Norway, King 17

Christianity 62–63, 66, 72, 79–80, 87
 and Antioch 188
 and Eutropius 166–67
 and Frigidus 109–10
 and games 216–17
 and Lycopolis 98–99
 and Rome 340–42
 and sanctuary 268–69, 278–79
 and sects 178–79
 and Theodosius 112–13
 see also John Chrysostom; Origenists; paganism
Chronicle of Edessa 128
Citadel 30, 31, 32, 33
Classis 153–54, 299
Claudian (Claudius Claudianus) 21, 44, 65–66, 85, 178, 218–19
 and Africa 160, 162–63
 and Alaric 131, 287
 and Britannia 175
 and Eutropius 98, 119, 149
 and Frigidus 108, 109
 and Gainas 179–80
 and Goth invasion 205–7, 210–11, 212
 and Greece 155, 156–57
 and Honorius 166, 167–68, 204
 and Huns 78, 127, 129–30, 170
 and northern revolt 200, 201
 and Rufinus 87–88, 137, 138, 141, 143
 and Saulus 208, 209
 and Serena 75, 76
 and Stilicho 71, 93, 183–84
Clemens, Aurelius Prudentius 69, 209
Clusium 26–27
coins 65, 96, 183, 237, 243
comets 185, 189
Cominius, Pontius 32
Commodus, Emperor 22
conscription 64
Consentia 336–37
Constans 251–52, 284
Constans II 297

INDEX

ACKNOWLEDGMENTS

I've dedicated this book to my small but growing audience of readers, specifically those who enjoyed my previous effort, *The Last Viking*. However, once more the folks at Osprey Publishing and Bloomsbury Publishing get credit for polishing *At the Gates of Rome* and presenting it to the public.

In New York, Krynn Hanold, Publicity Assistant at Bloomsbury, and in England, Elle Chilvers, Osprey Marketing Executive, without whom nobody would ever hear of my books. Copyeditor Anne Halliday, and proofreader Margaret Haynes, who I don't doubt strained her Oxford degree correcting my Latin translations. Ian Hughes, MA, author of *Stilicho: The Vandal Who Saved Rome*, whose peer review proved him much more than my peer. Gemma Gardner, Osprey Senior Desk Editor, for her remarkable patience with my nitpicking changes. And above all, Osprey Commissioning Editor Kate Moore, whose sharp reader's-eye view and knowledge of history were essential to wringing the wrongs out of my initial draft. For decades Osprey books have been my first choice when researching any military history topic. To have my work included in the Osprey catalog – again – is a great honor.

And, of course, thanks most of all to my agent, Scott Mendel, Managing Partner of Mendel Media Group LLC, who handles the business and leaves me to handle the writing. It's an ideal relationship.